THE ROUGH GUIDE TO

TOKYO

Forthcoming titles include

The Algarve • The Bahamas • Cambodia
Caribbean Islands • Costa Brava
New York Restaurants • South America • Zanzibar

Forthcoming reference guides include

Children's Books • Online Travel • Videogaming
Weather

Rough Guides online

www.roughguides.com

Rough Guide Credits

Text editor: Clifton Wilkinson
Series editor: Mark Ellingham
Production: Mike Hancock
Cartography: Maxine Repath
Proofreading: Ken Bell

Publishing Information

This second edition published September 2001
by Rough Guides Ltd,
62–70 Shorts Gardens, London, WC2H 9AH

Distributed by the Penguin Group:
Penguin Books Ltd, 27 Wrights Lane, London W8 5TZ
Penguin Putnam, Inc. 375 Hudson Street, New York 10014, USA
Penguin Books Australia Ltd, 487 Maroondah Highway,
PO Box 257, Ringwood, Victoria 3134, Australia
Penguin Books Canada Ltd, 10 Alcorn Avenue,
Toronto, Ontario, Canada M4V 1E4
Penguin Books (NZ) Ltd,
182–190 Wairau Road, Auckland 10, New Zealand

Typeset in Bembo and Helvetica to an original design by Henry Iles.
Printed in Spain by Graphy Cems.

400pp, includes index
A catalogue record for this book is available from the British Library.

ISBN 1-85828-712-X

THE ROUGH GUIDE TO

TOKYO

by Jan Dodd and
Simon Richmond

ROUGH GUIDES

We set out to do something different when the first Rough Guide was published in 1982. Mark Ellingham, just out of university, was travelling in Greece. He brought along the popular guides of the day, but found they were all lacking in some way. They were either strong on ruins and museums but went on for pages without mentioning a beach or taverna. Or they were so conscious of the need to save money that they lost sight of Greece's cultural and historical significance. Also, none of the books told him anything about Greece's contemporary life – its politics, its culture, its people and how they lived.

So with no job in prospect, Mark decided to write his own guidebook, one which aimed to provide practical information that was second to none, detailing the best beaches and the hottest clubs and restaurants, while also giving hard-hitting accounts of every sight, both famous and obscure, and providing up-to-the-minute information on contemporary culture. It was a guide that encouraged independent travellers to find the best of Greece, and was a great success, getting shortlisted for the Thomas Cook travel guide award, and encouraging Mark, along with three friends, to expand the series.

The Rough Guide list grew rapidly and the letters flooded in, indicating a much broader readership than had been anticipated, but one which uniformly appreciated the Rough Guide mix of practical detail and humour, irreverence and enthusiasm. Things haven't changed. The same four friends who began the series are still the caretakers of the Rough Guide mission today: to provide the most reliable, up-to-date and entertaining information to independent-minded travellers of all ages, on all budgets.

We now publish more than 150 titles and have offices in London and New York. The travel guides are written and researched by a dedicated team of more than 100 authors, based in Britain, Europe, the USA and Australia. We have also created a unique series of phrasebooks to accompany the travel series, along with an acclaimed series of music guides, and a best-selling pocket guide to the Internet and World Wide Web. We also publish comprehensive travel information on our Web site: **www.roughguides.com**

Help us update

We've gone to a lot of trouble to ensure that this Rough Guide is as up to date and accurate as possible. However, things do change. All suggestions, comments and corrections are much appreciated, and we'll send a copy of the next edition (or any other Rough Guide if you prefer) for the best letters.

Please mark letters "**Rough Guide Tokyo Update**" and send to:

Rough Guides, 62–70 Shorts Gardens, London, WC2H 9AH, or
Rough Guides, 4th Floor, 345 Hudson St, New York NY 10014.

Or send email to: mail@roughguides.co.uk
Online updates about this book can be found on
Rough Guides' Web site ⓦ www.roughguides.com

The authors

Simon Richmond has written guidebooks for many parts of the world for several different publishers, and regularly contributes to magazines and newspapers in the UK and Australia. Few places have captured his heart as much as Japan, where he lived for two and a half years in the early 1990s working as an editor and journalist in Tokyo.

Since the early 1990s, when she lived in Tokyo and discovered *onsen*, **Jan Dodd** (ⓦ www.jandodd.com) has been searching for the ultimate *rotemburo*. She has written several guidebooks and provides Asian and European coverage for books, magazines, newspapers and Web sites. As well as contributing regularly to *The Rough Guide to France*, Jan is co-author of *The Rough Guide to Vietnam* and *The Rough Guide to Japan*, and author of the forthcoming *Rough Guide to the Dordogne and Lot*.

Acknowledgements

The authors would like to thank the staff of JNTO in Tokyo, Australia and London, Tetsuo Sanada and colleagues at Japan Youth Hostels, Tobita Katsuo of the Japanese Inn Group, Herb Donovan and Kaya Laterman. Many thanks also to Clifton Wilkinson and Jo Mead at Rough Guides.

Jan would like to give a big thanks to Sekiwa Tomioka and Sawa Isao and family for their generous hospitality and to Taguchi Kazunari and Tanaka Yoko at the JNTO in Tokyo for all their assistance. Many thanks are also due to Tada Taku, Andreas Reissland, Neil & Cathy Richards in Yokohama, Ian ("Chippendale") Cronin and Sean McGoldrisk and friends in Shimoda.

Simon would like to thank the staff at the JNTO Sydney for all their assistance. In Tokyo, many thanks to Kenichi at Taito Ryokan, Laura Holland, Prue Moodie, Matt Wilce, Kaya Laterman, Herb & Keiko, Miya Kawaguchi at the Park Hyatt, members of the Maple Club on the trip to Kawagoe, and Yumiko for helping me track down that London bus.

Readers' Letters

Janet Armstrong, Bente, Pierre Berthe, Martin Crane, Andy Lareau, Tim Letheren & Denise Deaton, Anna-Elisa Liinamo, Geoff McCall, James McMahon, Robert Morton, Margaret in Toronto, Paul in Tokyo, Mark Peters, Benoit d'Udekem, Wengseng.

CONTENTS

MAP LIST

Colour Map Section

Introduction

Nothing quite prepares you for Tokyo; love it or hate it, the restless capital of Japan, home to twelve million people, packs a powerful punch. Initial impressions can be off-putting: ugly buildings are tarted up with eyeball-searing neon and messy overhead cables, pavements teem with crowds and roads are clogged with bumper-to-bumper traffic. Yet behind the barely ordered chaos lie remnants of a very different past. Step back from the frenetic main roads, and chances are you'll find yourself in a world of tranquil backstreets, where wooden houses are fronted by neatly clipped bonsai trees; wander beyond the high-tech department stores, and you'll find ancient temples and shrines. In this city of 24-hour shops and vending machines a festival is held virtually every day of the year, people regularly visit their local shrine or temple and scrupulously observe the passing seasons. And at the centre of it all is the mysterious green void of the Imperial Palace – home to the emperor and a tangible link to the past.

It's almost impossible to be bored in Tokyo and first-time visitors should be prepared for a massive assault on the senses – just walking the streets of this hyperactive city can be an energizing experience. With money to spend, you can pick up the coolest fashions, eat in fabulous restaurants and dance in the hippest clubs. But you'll also be surprised how affordable many things are. Cheap and cheerful *izakaya* (bars that serve food) and noodle shacks far outnumber the big-ticket French restaurants and high-class *ryōtei*, where geisha serve minimalist Japanese cuisine, while day tickets for a sumo tournament or a Kabuki play can be bought for the price of a few drinks. Many of the city's highlights are even free: a stroll through the evocative **Shitamachi** area around Asakusa and the major Buddhist temple **Sensō-ji**; a visit to the tranquil wooded grounds of **Meiji-jingū**, the city's most venerable Shinto shrine, and the nearby teenage shopping mecca of Harajuku; the frenetic fish market at **Tsukiji**; the crackling, neon-saturated atmosphere of the mini-city **Shinjuku** – you don't need to part with lots of cash to explore this city.

High-speed limited-express and Shinkansen trains put several important sights within day-trip range of Tokyo, including the ancient temple and shrine towns of **Kamakura** to the south and **Nikkō** to the north. **Mount Fuji**, 100km southwest of the capital, can be climbed between June and September, while the adjoining national park area of **Hakone** offers relaxed hiking amid beautiful lakeland scenery, and the chance to take a dip in an *onsen* – a Japanese mineral bath. **Kawagoe**, to the north, offers a glimpse of traditional Japanese houses and some great eating experiences.

Financial scandals, economic doldrums and the Sarin gas attack by terrorists on the subway in 1995 have left Tokyo less ebullient than it was in the "bubble years" of the mid-1980s, but, this precocious 21st-century city can afford to take a breather and let the rest of the world catch up.

Legend says that a giant catfish sleeps beneath Tokyo Bay, and its wriggling can be felt in the hundreds of small tremors that rumble beneath the capital each year. Around every seventy years the catfish awakes, resulting in the kind of major earthquake seen in 1995 in Kobe. There is a long-running, half-hearted debate about moving the Diet and main government offices out of Tokyo, away from danger. Yet, despite the fact that the city is well overdue for the Big One, talk of relocating the capital always comes to nothing. Now, more than ever before, Tokyo is the centre of Japan, and nobody wants to leave and miss any of the action.

When to visit

One of the best times to visit Tokyo is in the spring, usually from April to early May, when flurries of falling cherry blossom give the city a soft pink hue. October and November are also good months to come; this is when you'll catch the fireburst of autumn leaves in Tokyo's parks and gardens.

Avoid visiting during the steamy height of summer in August and early September, when soaring humidity has Tokyoites scurrying from one air-conditioned haven to another. From January through to March temperatures can dip to freezing, but the crisp blue skies are rarely disturbed by rain or snow showers. Carrying an umbrella in any season is a good idea, especially during *tsuyu*, the rainy season of June, and in September, when typhoons occasionally strike the coast. Note that many attractions shut for several days around New Year, when Tokyo becomes a ghost town. In mid-February cheap accommodation can be near impossible to secure as high school seniors from around Japan descend on the capital to sit college entrance exams.

Before deciding when to visit, check the city's calendar of festivals and special events, which range from grand sumo tournaments to the Sannō and Kanda *matsuri* (festivals) held alternate years (see Festivals, p.259 and Sports and Martial Arts, p.265).

Tokyo's climate

	F°		C°		RAINFALL	
	AVERAGE DAILY		AVERAGE DAILY		AVERAGE MONTHLY	
	MAX	MIN	MAX	MIN	IN	MM
Jan	49	33	10	1	4.3	110
Feb	50	34	10	1	6.1	155
March	55	40	13	4	9	228
April	65	50	18	10	10	254
May	73	58	23	15	9.6	244
June	78	65	25	18	12	305
July	84	72	29	22	10	254
Aug	87	75	31	24	8	203
Sept	80	68	27	20	11	279
Oct	70	57	21	14	9	228
Nov	62	47	17	8	6.4	162
Dec	58	38	12	3	3.8	96

BASICS

Getting there from Britain and Ireland

Tokyo is Japan's main international air gateway from Britain with four airlines (All Nippon Airways, British Airways, Japan Airlines and Virgin) flying non-stop from London into New Tokyo International Airport (better known as Narita). Direct flights from London take around twelve hours. There are also plenty of European and Asian airlines with indirect flights to Tokyo via their hub cities.

There are no direct flights **from Ireland** – you'll need to stop over in Europe en route, with the cheapest deals usually being via London (Ryan Air flies daily from Dublin to London for IR£50).

AIRLINES AND FLIGHT AGENTS

Airlines

Aeroflot ⓣ 020/7355 2233; ⓦ *www.aeroflot.com*
Air France ⓣ 0845/084 5111; ⓦ *www.airfrance.co.uk*
All Nippon Airways (ANA) ⓣ 020/7478 1911; ⓦ *www.ana.co.jp*
Alitalia ⓣ 0870/544 8259; ⓦ *www.alitalia.co.uk*
British Airways ⓣ 0345/222111; ⓦ *www.britishairways.co.uk*
Cathay Pacific ⓣ 020/7747 8888; ⓦ *www.cathaypacific.com*

Finnair ⓣ020/7408 1222; ⓦ*www.finnair.com*

Japan Airlines (JAL) ⓣ0845/774 7700; ⓦ*www.jal-europe.com*

KLM Royal Dutch Airlines ⓣ0870/507 4074; ⓦ*www.klm.com*

Korean Air ⓣ020/7916 3010; ⓦ*www.koreanair.com*

Lufthansa ⓣ0345/737747; ⓦ*www.lufthansa.com*

Malaysia Airlines ⓣ0870/607 9090; ⓦ*www.malaysianairlines.com*

Ryan Air ⓣ01/609 7800; ⓦ*www.ryanair.ie*

SAS Scandinavian Airlines ⓣ0845/607 2772; ⓦ*www.scandinavian.net*

Singapore Airlines ⓣ0870/608 8886; ⓦ*www.singaporeair.co.uk*

Swissair ⓣ020/7434 7300; ⓦ*www.swissair.com*

Thai International ⓣ0870/606 0911; ⓦ*www.thaiair.com*

Virgin Atlantic Airways ⓣ01293/747747; ⓦ*www.virginatlantic.com*

Flight agents

Aran Travel ⓣ091/562 595; ⓦ*www.granary-suites.ie*

AWL Travel ⓣ020/7222 1144; ⓦ*www.awlt.com*

Bridge the World ⓣ020/7911 0900; ⓦ*www.bridgetheworld.com*

Dial-a-Flight ⓣ0870/333 4488; ⓦ*www.dialaflight.com*

Emerald Travel ⓣ020/7312 1700; ⓦ*www.emerald.co.uk*

North-South Travel ⓣ01245/608291; ⓦ*www.northsouthtravel.co.uk*

Quest Worldwide ⓣ020/8547 3322.

STA Travel ⓣ020/7361 6145; ⓦ*www.statravel.co.uk*

Trailfinders UK ⓣ020/7628 7628, Ireland ⓣ01/677 7888; ⓦ*www.trailfinders.co.uk*

Travel Cuts ⓣ020/7255 1944; ⓦ*www.travelcuts.co.uk*

usit Campus UK ⓣ0870/240 1010, Ireland ⓣ01/602 1600; ⓦ*www.usitcampus.co.uk*

usit Now UK ⓣ01232/324 073, Ireland ⓣ01/602 1777 or 677 8117.

FARES AND BUYING TICKETS

To find out the best deals to Japan, contact a flight agent – see the box above for a list of dependable ones. You should also check the ads in the travel pages of the weekend newspapers, regional listings magazines, Teletext and Ceefax and **Web sites** such as *www.ebookers.com*, *www.travelocity.co.uk*, *www.expedia.co.uk* and *www.deckchair.com* for special deals and the latest prices. **Students** and people **under 26** can often get discounts through specialist agents such as STA (see opposite).

Seasons differ from airline to airline, but generally July, August and December are the most expensive months to travel. If you're not tied to particular dates, check the changeover dates between seasons; you might make a substantial saving by travelling a few days sooner or later. **Return fares** to Tokyo from London start from around £500. However, you can find occasional special deals from as low as £300, so it pays to shop around.

OPEN-JAW, ROUND-THE-WORLD AND COURIER FLIGHTS

If you want to see more of Japan you could consider an **open-jaw ticket**, allowing you to fly into Tokyo and out of another city, say Ōsaka, or vice-versa. Both JAL and ANA offer open-jaw tickets for the same price as a simple return. A further option is a **round-the-world** (RTW) ticket; hunt around for agents who include Tokyo on their global itineraries. Prices start at around £800 for a one-year open ticket.

Another way to cut the cost of a flight – although you'll be limited on your luggage – is to apply for a **courier flight**, where in exchange for a lower fare you carry documents or parcels from airport to airport. Courier flights start at around £200 return. For details, contact the International Association of Air Travel Couriers (01305/264 564, *www.aircourier.co.uk*); they are agents for numerous courier companies.

PACKAGES AND TOURS

Japan isn't a difficult country for the independent traveller to negotiate, nor need it be horrendously expensive. However, if you're worried about the cost or the potential language problems, a **package tour** is worth considering. Packages tend to come into their own if you want to stay in upmarket hotels – these usually offer cheaper rates for group bookings. All tours use scheduled airline flights, so it's usually no problem extending your stay beyond the basic package. If you want to venture off the traditional tourist-beaten track, however, package tours will not be for you.

For a return flight, five nights' accommodation at a three- to four-star hotel, airport transfers and a sightseeing tour, prices begin around £800, based on double occupancy. You'll pay more if you're on a package that combines Tokyo with other areas of Japan or on a specialized tour.

SPECIALIST TOUR OPERATORS

Carrick Travel Ltd ⓣ 01926/311 415; ⓦ *www.carricktravel.com*

Explore Worldwide UK ⓣ 01252/760 000; Ireland ⓣ 01/679 3948; ⓦ *www.exploreworldwide.com*

Far East Gateways ⓣ 0161/437 4371; ⓦ *www.gateways.co.uk*

Jaltour ⓣ 020/7495 1775; ⓦ *www.jaltour.co.uk*

Japan Travel Centre ⓣ 020/7287 1388; ⓦ *www.japantravel.co.uk*

The Imaginative Traveller ⓣ 020/8742 8612; ⓦ *www.adventurebound.co.uk*

KR Tours ⓣ 020/7499 7611; ⓦ *www.krtours.co.uk*

Getting there from the USA and Canada

A number of airlines serve Tokyo International Airport (Narita) non-stop from North America including All Nippon, American, Delta, Korean, Northwest and United, with connections from virtually everywhere in Canada and the United States. The recent Asian financial turmoil has led to a sharp decline in inter-Asian tourism, and the airlines are trying to make up the slack by increasing volume from North America. As a result, many flights are offered at up to half-price, so keep a sharp eye out for special offers. It's also possible to reach Japan via Europe, though this can be a lot more expensive.

Flying time across the Pacific is fifteen hours from New York, thirteen hours from Chicago and ten hours from Los Angeles and Seattle.

FARES AND BUYING TICKETS

The cheapest of the airlines' published fares is usually an **Apex** ticket, although this will carry certain restrictions:

you have to book – and pay – at least 21 days before departure, spend at least seven days abroad (maximum stay three months), and you tend to get penalized if you change your schedule. Some airlines also issue **Special Apex** tickets to under–24s, often extending the maximum stay to a year. Many airlines offer youth or student fares to **under-26s**; a passport or driving licence is sufficient proof of age, though these tickets are subject to availability and can have eccentric booking conditions. It's worth remembering that most cheap return fares involve spending at least one Saturday night away and that many will only give a percentage refund if you need to cancel or alter your journey, so make sure you check the restrictions carefully before buying a ticket.

You can normally cut costs further by going through a **specialist flight agent** – though once you get a quote, check with the airlines and you may turn up an even better deal. If you travel a lot, **discount travel clubs** are another option – the annual membership fee may be worth it for benefits such as cut-price air tickets and car rental. The Internet is a useful resource; check out the **Web sites** Ⓦ *www.cheaptickets.com*, Ⓦ *www.travelocity.com* and Ⓦ *www.lastminute.com* to compare prices.

High season is July and August and at Christmas and New Year when seats are at a premium; prices drop during the shoulder seasons – April through June and September through October – and you'll get the best deals in the low season, January through March and November through December (excluding Christmas and New Year). Note also that flying on weekends ordinarily adds $200–250 to the round-trip fare.

The **fares** quoted below give a rough idea of what you can expect to pay for a round-trip ticket to Tokyo bought direct from the airlines (midweek low season to weekend high season); they are exclusive of airport tax, which is an extra $20. From Chicago tickets cost $930–1600; from Los Angeles $675–1600; from Vancouver CAN$900–1400; from New York $960–1800; from San Francisco $675–1450; from Seattle $830–1400; and from Toronto CAN$1215–1650. However, unless you need to travel at very short notice, you are likely to get a much better deal through a specialist flight agent or consolidator (see overleaf).

AIRLINES AND FLIGHT AGENTS

Airlines

All Nippon Airways (ANA) ⓣ1-800/235-9262; ⓦ*www.allnipponairways.com*

Air Canada US ⓣ1-800/776-3000; ⓦ*www.aircanada.ca*

Air France US ⓣ1-800/237-2747, Canada ⓣ1-800/667-2747; ⓦ*www.airfrance.com*

Air New Zealand US ⓣ1-800/262-1234, Canada ⓣ1-800/563-5494; ⓦ*www.airnewzealand.com*

American Airlines ⓣ1-800/433-7300; ⓦ*www.americanairlines.com*

Asiana Airlines ⓣ1-800/227-4262; ⓦ*www.flyasiana.com*

British Airways US ⓣ1-800/247-9297, Canada ⓣ1-800/668-1059; ⓦ*www.britishairways.com*

Cathay Pacific ⓣ1-800/233-2742; ⓦ*www.cathaypacific.com*

Continental Airlines ⓣ1-800/231-0856; ⓦ*www.continental.com*

Delta Airlines ⓣ1-800/241-4141; ⓦ*www.delta.com*

Japan Airlines (JAL) ⓣ1-800/525-3663; ⓦ*www.japanairlines.com*

Korean Airlines ⓣ1-800/438-5000; ⓦ*www.koreanair.com*

Malaysia Airlines ⓣ1-800/552-9264; ⓦ*www.malaysiaaurkubes.com*

Northwest Airlines ⓣ1-800/447-4747; ⓦ*www.nwa.com*

Singapore Airlines ⓣ1-800/742-3333; ⓦ*www.singaporeair.com*

Swissair ⓣ1-800/221-4750; ⓦ*www.swissair.com*

United Airlines ⓣ1-800/241-6522; ⓦ*www.united.com*

Flight agents

Air Brokers International ⓣ 1-800/883-3273 or 415/397-1383.

Air Couriers Association ⓣ 1-800/282-1202; ⓦ *www.aircourier.org*

Cheap Tickets Inc. ⓣ 1-800/377-1000; ⓦ *www.cheaptickets.com*

Council Travel ⓣ 1-800/226-8624; ⓦ *www.counciltravel.com*

Discount Airfares Worldwide On-Line ⓦ *www.etn.nl/discount.htm*

Education Travel Center ⓣ 1-800/747-5551; ⓦ *www.edtravel.com*

High Adventure Travel ⓣ 1-800/350-0612; ⓦ *www.highadv.com*

International Association of Air Travel Couriers ⓣ 561/582-8320; ⓦ *www.courier.org*

Mr Cheaps ⓣ 1-800/672-4327; ⓦ *www.mrcheaps.com*

Now Voyager ⓣ 212/431-1616; ⓦ *www.nowvoyagertravel.com*

Skylink ⓣ 1-800/AIR-ONLY.

STA Travel ⓣ 1-800/781-4040; ⓦ *www.statravel.com*

Student Flights ⓣ 1-800/255-8000; ⓦ *www.isecard.com*

Travel Avenue ⓣ 1-800/333-3335 or 312/876-6866; ⓦ *www.travelavenue.com*

Travel Cuts ⓣ 1-800/667-2887; ⓦ *www.travelavenue.com*

Travelocity ⓦ *www.travelocity.com*

ROUND-THE-WORLD, CIRCLE PACIFIC AND COURIER FLIGHTS

If Tokyo is only one stop on a longer journey, you might want to consider buying a **round-the-world** (RTW) ticket. Some travel agents can sell you an "off-the-shelf" RTW ticket that will have you touching down in about half a dozen cities (Tokyo is on many itineraries); others will have to assemble one for you, which can be tailored to your needs but is apt to be more expensive. Figure on $3000 to $5000 for a RTW ticket including Japan. It may also be worth checking out the **Circle Pacific** deals offered by many of the major airlines; these allow four stopovers at no extra charge, if tickets are bought fourteen to thirty days in advance.

A further possibility is to see if you can arrange a **courier flight**. In return for shepherding a parcel through customs and possibly giving up your baggage allowance, you can expect to get a deeply discounted ticket. You'll probably also be restricted in the duration of your stay. Details of courier-flight brokers – the Air Couriers Association, International Association of Air Travel Couriers and Now Voyager – are listed opposite.

PACKAGES AND TOURS

A number of **tour operators** in the US and Canada offer tours in Japan, with most focusing on Tokyo. Before booking, confirm exactly what expenses are included, what class of hotel you'll be offered and how large a group you'll be joining.

SPECIALIST TOUR OPERATORS

Abercrombie & Kent Ⓣ 1-800/323-7308; Ⓦ *www.abercrombiekent.com*

Adventure Center Ⓣ 1-800/227-8747; Ⓦ *www.adventure-center.com*

Asia Transpacific Journeys Ⓣ 1-800/642-2742; Ⓦ *www.southeastasia.com*

Cross-Culture Ⓣ 1-800/491-1148; Ⓦ *www.crosscultureinc.com*

Geographic Expeditions Ⓣ 1-800/777-8183; Ⓦ *www.geoex.com*

Guides for All Seasons Ⓣ 1-800/457-4574.

Japan & Orient Tours Ⓣ 1-800/377-1080; Ⓦ *www.jot.com*

Japan Travel Bureau Ⓣ 1-800/223-6104; Ⓦ *www.jtbusa.com*

Journeys East Ⓣ 1-800/527-2612; Ⓦ *www.journeyseast.com*

Kintetsu International Express Ⓣ 1-800/422-3481; Ⓦ *www.kintetsu.com*

Northwest World Vacation Ⓣ 1-800/800-1504; Ⓦ *www.nwaworldvacations.com*

Orient Flexi-Pax Tours ⓣ1-800/545-5540; ⓦ*www.orientflexipax.com*
Pacific Holidays ⓣ1-800/355-8025; ⓦ*www.pacificholidaysinc.com*
TBI Tours ⓣ1-800/221-2216; ⓦ*www.tbitours.com*
Tour East ⓣ416/929-0888; ⓦ*www.toureast.com*
Vantage Travel ⓣ1-800/322-6677; ⓦ*www.vantagetravel.com*
Worldwide Adventures ⓣ1-800/387-1483; ⓦ*www.worldwidequest.com*

Getting there from Australia and New Zealand

There's plenty of choice of **flights** to Japan from Australia and New Zealand, with both Australian, Japanese and other regional airlines regularly serving Tokyo (Narita Airport).

Increased competition, particularly on services from Eastern Australia (Sydney, Brisbane and Cairns) to Tokyo, means that fares on these routes are generally the cheapest.

FARES AND BUYING TICKETS

Whatever kind of ticket you're after, your first call should be one of the **specialist travel agents** listed overleaf. All Nippon Airways, Ansett, Asiana, Cathay Pacific, Garuda Indonesia, JAL, Korean Air, Malaysia Airlines, Philippine Airlines, Qantas and Singapore Airlines all offer regular non-stop services: prices for a return flight (with a maximum stay of six months) **to Tokyo** from Sydney, Cairns or Brisbane are around A$1399; fares from Melbourne or Adelaide range from A$1499 to A$1699. Return fares with Garuda, Malaysia Airlines or Korean can be as low as A$1100, but these generally restrict stays to ninety days or less and tend to involve longer flight times and stops en route.

Tickets valid for stays of up to a year are around A$2000, though special fares are sometimes available to holders of working holiday visas, which can bring prices down to nearer the A$1400 mark.

From Western Australia, only Qantas flies direct from Perth to Japan, with fares starting at A$1650, but other regional carriers, including Cathay Pacific, Malaysia and Singapore Airlines, offer cheaper fares for flights via Hong Kong, Kuala Lumpur and Singapore respectively.

From New Zealand, Air New Zealand, Ansett New Zealand, Garuda, Qantas and Singapore Airlines, among others, operate regular or code-share services to Japan, with fares starting at NZ$1399, though the most direct routings will cost at least NZ$1595. Air New Zealand has services to Nagoya and Ōsaka as well as Tokyo via a code share with JAL.

AIRLINES AND FLIGHT AGENTS

Airlines

Air New Zealand Australia ⓣ13 2476, New Zealand ⓣ09/357 3000; ⓦ*www.airnewzealand.com*

ANA (All Nippon Airways) ⓣ02/9367 6700; ⓦ*www.ana.co.jp*

Ansett Australia ⓣ13 1414, New Zealand ⓣ09/379 6404; ⓦ*www.ansett.com.au*

Garuda Australia ⓣ02/9334 9944 or 1300/365 330, New Zealand ⓣ09/366 1855; ⓦ*www.garuda-indonesia.com*

JAL (Japan Airlines) Australia ⓣ02/9272 1111, New Zealand ⓣ09/379 9906; ⓦ*www.japanairlines.com*

Korean Air Australia ⓣ02/9262 6000, New Zealand ⓣ09/307 3687; ⓦ*www.koreanair.com*

Malaysian Airlines Australia ⓣ13 2627, New Zealand ⓣ09/373 2741; ⓦ*www.malaysianairlines.com*

Philippine Airlines ⓣ02/9279 2020; ⓦ*www.philippineair.com*

Qantas Australia ⓣ13 1211, New Zealand ⓣ09/357 8900 or 0800/808 767; ⓦ*www.qantas.com.au*

Singapore Airlines Australia ⓣ13 1011, New Zealand ⓣ09/379 3209; ⓦ*www.singaporeair.com*

Flight agents

Anywhere Travel Sydney ⓣ02/9663 0411.

Budget Travel Auckland ⓣ09/366 0061 or 0800/808 040.

Destinations Unlimited Auckland ⓣ09/373 4033.

Flight Centres Australia ⓣ13 1600; ⓦ*www.flightcentre.com*; New Zealand ⓣ09/3358 4310.

Northern Gateway Australia ⓣ08/8941 1394.

STA Travel Australia ⓣ1300/360 960; ⓦ*www.statravel.com.au*; New Zealand ⓣ09/366 6673.

Thomas Cook Australia ⓣ1800/801 002, New Zealand ⓣ09/379 3920.

Trailfinders Australia ⓣ02/9247 7666; ⓦ*www.trailfinders.com.au*

Travel.Com.Au Australia ⓣ02/9249 5444; ⓦ*www.travel.com.au*

Tymtro Travel Australia ⓣ02/9223 2211 or 1300 652 969.

FLIGHTS

An **open-jaw ticket**, which enables you to fly into one Japanese city and out of another, saves on backtracking and doesn't add hugely to the cost – count on around A$1900 out of Sydney, flying with JAL or Qantas.

Given enough time to make the most of them, **round-the-world** tickets offer greater flexibility and represent good value compared to straightforward return flights. Virtually any combination of stops is possible, as more and more airlines enter into partnerships to increase their global coverage. A sample itinerary from Melbourne to Tokyo, followed by New York, Montréal, Paris, London, Prague, and back to Melbourne costs from A$2680, but ultimately your choice will depend on where you want to travel before or after Japan – again, a good travel agent is your best ally in planning a route to suit your preferences.

PACKAGES AND TOURS

Package deals can be an economical and hassle-free way of getting a taste of Tokyo. Five-night **packages** in Tokyo from eastern Australia start at A$1399 (NZ$1700 from Auckland) with Air New Zealand, Ansett Australia or Qantas (book through travel agents), including return airfare, transfers, twin-share accommodation and breakfast.

A few specialist agents and operators, such as Jalpak and Japan Experience (and others listed overleaf), offer more comprehensive **tours**; most can also arrange Japan Rail passes and book accommodation in regional Japan – either in business-style hotels or at more traditional minshuku and *ryokan* through consortia, such as the Japanese Inn Group. Prices start at A$1449 for three nights' accommodation, including international flights and transfers. More comprehensive tours involve planned itineraries and tours around particular destinations in Japan, eg a tour taking in the highlights of both Tokyo and Kyoto.

Tours catering for **special interests** tend to be expensive. Japan Experience Tours, for example, offers fifteen-night **language programmes**, including airfares, accommodation in Tokyo and tuition, for A$3200–3500. Active Travel's Japantrek company offers specialist itineraries, including fifteen-day craft tours in Kyūshū, Kyoto, Nara and Tokyo, for A$5690, including airfares.

SPECIALIST PACKAGE TOUR OPERATORS

Adventure World Australia ⓣ02/9956 7766 or 1800/221 931, New Zealand ⓣ09/524 5118.

Active Travel Australia ⓣ1800 634 157; ⓦ*www.activetravel.com.au*

Asia and World Travel Australia ⓣ07/3229 3511.

Jalpak Travel Australia ⓣ02/9285 6602.

Japan Travel Bureau Australia ⓣ02/9510 0100.

Japan Experience Tours Australia ⓣ02/9247 3086.

Nippon Travel Agency Australia ⓣ02/9338 2333, New Zealand ⓣ09/309 5750.

Visas and red tape

All visitors must have a valid **passport** to enter Japan, but not everyone needs a visa. Citizens of Austria, Germany, Ireland, Liechtenstein, Mexico, Switzerland and the UK can stay in Japan for up to ninety days without a visa provided they are visiting for tourism or business purposes. This stay can be extended for another three months (see below).

Citizens of Argentina, Australia, the Bahamas, Barbados, Belgium, Canada, Chile, Colombia, Costa Rica, Croatia, Cyprus, Denmark, Dominica, El Salvador, Finland, France, Greece, Guatemala, Honduras, Iceland, Israel, Italy, Lesotho, Luxembourg, Malta, Mauritius, the Netherlands, New Zealand, Norway, Portugal, San Marino, Singapore, Slovenia, Spain, Surinam, Sweden, Tunisia, Turkey, Uruguay and the USA can also stay for up to ninety days without a visa, though this is unextendable. Anyone wishing to stay longer will have to leave the country, then re-enter.

All other nationalities must apply for a visa in advance from the Japanese embassy or consulate in their own country. These are usually free, though in certain circumstances you may be charged a fee of around ¥3000 for a single-entry visa. The rules on visas do change from time to time, so check first with your embassy or consulate, or on the

JAPAN NATIONAL TOURIST ORGANIZATION (JNTO) OFFICES

Australia Level 33, The Chifley Tower, 2 Chifley Square, Sydney, NSW 2000 (Ⓣ02/9232-4522, Ⓔ*jntosyd@tokyonet.com.au*).

Canada 165 University Ave, Toronto, Ontario, M5H 3B8 (Ⓣ416/366-7140, Ⓔ*jnto@interlog.com*).

UK Heathcoat House, 20 Savile Row, London W1X 1AE (Ⓣ020/7734 9638, Ⓦ*www.jnto.go.jp*).

USA One Rockefeller Plaza, Suite 1250, New York, NY 10020 (Ⓣ212/757-5640, Ⓔ*info@jntonyc.org*); 401 North Michigan Ave, Suite 770, Chicago, IL 60611 (Ⓣ312/222-0874, Ⓔ*jntochi@mcs.net*); 360 Post St, Suite 601, San Francisco, CA 94108 (Ⓣ415/989-7140, Ⓔ*sfjnto@webjapan.com*); 515 Figueroa St, Suite 1470, Los Angeles, CA 90071 (Ⓣ213/623-1952, Ⓔ*info@jnto-lax.org*).

New Zealand
See Australia, above.

Japanese Foreign Ministry Web site (Ⓦ*www.mofa.go.jp/jp_info/visi/index.html*), for the current situation.

VISA EXTENSIONS

To get a **visa extension** you'll need to fill in two copies of an Application for Extension of Stay, available from Tokyo's Immigration Bureau (see "Directory", p.296). These must then be returned along with passport photos, a letter explaining your reasons for wanting to extend your stay, and a processing fee of ¥4000. In addition, you may be asked to show proof of sufficient funds, and a valid onward ticket out of the country. If you're not a national of one of the few countries with six-month reciprocal visa exemptions, expect a thorough grilling from the immigration officials. An easier option – and the only alternative available to nationals of those countries who are not eligible for an extension – is a short trip out of the country, say to South Korea or Hong Kong, but you'll still have to run the gauntlet of immigration officials on your return.

WORKING HOLIDAY AND RE-ENTRY VISAS

Citizens of Australia, Britain, Canada, France, New Zealand and South Korea, aged between 18 and 30, can apply for a **working holiday visa**, which grants a six-month stay and one possible six-month extension. This entitles the holder to work for a maximum of twenty hours a week, and is intended primarily to subsidize bona fide travellers. You need to apply at least three weeks before leaving your home country, and must be able to show evidence of sufficient funds, which effectively means a return ticket (or money to buy one) plus around US$2000, or the equivalent, to live on while you look for work. Contact your local embassy or consulate to check the current details of the scheme.

If you enter Japan on a working holiday visa or plan to stay longer than three months, you must apply for an **Alien Registration card** from the nearest local government office within 90 days of arrival. Also if you leave Japan temporarily and you're working in the country, you must get a **re-entry visa** before you leave if you wish to return and continue working. Re-entry visas are available from local immigration bureaux.

JAPANESE EMBASSIES AND CONSULATES

Australia 112 Empire Circuit, Yarralumla, Canberra ACT 2600 ⓣ02/6273 3244; Level 34, Colonial Centre, 52 Martin

Place, Sydney, NSW 2000
☎ 02/9231-3455;
Ⓦ *www.japan.org.au*

Canada 255 Sussex Drive, Ottawa, Ontario KIN 9E6 ☎ 613/241-8541; Suite 2702, Toronto Dominion Bank Tower, Toronto, Ontario, M5K 1A1 ☎ 416/363-7038; Ⓦ *www.embassyjapancanada.org*

Ireland Nutley Bldg, Merrion Centre, Nutley Lane, Dublin 4 ☎ 01/269-4244; Ⓦ *www.mofa.go.jp/embjapan/ireland/index.html*

New Zealand Level 18, Majestic Centre, 100 Willis Street, Wellington 1 ☎ 04/473 1540; Level 12, ASB Bank Centre, 135 Albert Street, Auckland 1 ☎ 09/303-4106; Level 5 Forsyth Barr House, 764 Colombo St, Christchurch 1 ☎ 03/366-5680; Ⓦ *www.japan.org.nz*

UK 101–104, Piccadilly, London, W1V 9FN ☎ 020/7465 6500; 2 Melville Crescent, Edinburgh EH3 7HW ☎ 0131/225 4777; Ⓦ *www.embjapan.org.uk*

USA 2520 Massachusetts Ave NW, Washington DC, 20008-2869 ☎ 202/238-6700; 299 Park Ave, New York, NY 10171 ☎ 212/371-8222; 50 Fremont St, Suite 2300, San Francisco, California 94105 ☎ 415/777-3533; Ⓦ *www.embjapan.org*

You'll find addresses for other embassies and consulates on the Ministry of Foreign Affairs Web site (Ⓦ *www.mofa.go.jp/j_info/visit/visa/index.html*) and links to many of them from the UK Embassy site (Ⓦ *www.embjapan.org.uk/links_emb.html*).

CUSTOMS

The **duty free allowance** for bringing goods into Japan is 400 cigarettes or 100 cigars or 500 grammes of tobacco; three 760cc bottles of alcohol; 57 grammes of perfume; and gifts and souvenirs up to a value of ¥200,000. As well as firearms and drugs, Japanese customs officials are particularly strict about the import of pornographic material, which will be confiscated if found.

Money and costs

Despite its reputation as an outrageously expensive city, with a little careful planning Tokyo is a manageable destination even for those on a fairly modest budget. The key is to do what the majority of Japanese do: eat in local restaurants, stay in Japanese-style inns and take advantage of any available discounts. That said, if you make the wrong choice of bar or take a longish taxi ride, it can blow your budget sky high.

CURRENCY

The **Japanese currency** is the **yen** (¥), of which there are no subdivisions. Notes are available in denominations of ¥1000, ¥2000, ¥5000 and ¥10,000, while coins come in values of ¥1, ¥5, ¥10, ¥50, ¥100 and ¥500. Apart from the ¥5 piece, a copper-coloured coin with a hole in the centre, all other notes and coins indicate their value in Western numerals. Note that, at the time of writing, ticket, change and vending machines have not yet been upgraded to accept the new ¥2000 notes and ¥500 coins (older, more silver-coloured ¥500 coins are OK). The **exchange rate** at time of writing was ¥175 to £1, ¥120 to US$1 and ¥60 to A$1.

For current exchange rates, see *www.xe.net/currency*

COSTS

The absolute **minimum daily budget** for food and accommodation alone is ¥5000 (£29/US$42/A$83) if you stay in a youth hostel and eat in the cheapest local restaurants. By the time you've added in transport costs, entry tickets, meals in decent restaurants and a few nights in a *ryokan* or business hotel, you'll be reaching a more realistic expenditure of at least ¥8000–¥10,000 (approximately £46–57/US$67–83/A$133–167) per day.

Note that a five percent **consumption tax** is levied on virtually all goods and services in Japan, including restaurant meals and accommodation. There is no hard-and-fast rule as to whether this tax is included in the advertised price or added at the time of payment.

TRAVELLERS' CHEQUES AND PLASTIC

Japan is still very much a cash society and you'll be settling most bills in yen. Though crime isn't a serious problem, it's always safest to carry the bulk of your money in **travellers' cheques**. The most widely accepted brands are American Express, Visa and Thomas Cook, in dollars, sterling or, of course, yen.

Credit and debit cards are becoming more widely accepted, especially in hotels, restaurants and shops geared-up to serving foreigners; the most useful cards are Visa and American Express, followed closely by Mastercard and Diners Club. However, many places still don't accept cards issued abroad, so check beforehand if it's important.

For **cash withdrawals**, nearly all post offices now have **ATMs** accepting foreign-issued cards, identified with a sticker saying "International ATM Service"; you can opt for instructions in English. Bear in mind that the system is still relatively new and it's best not to rely on cards completely.

In addition, Visa (Ⓣ 0120-133173, Ⓦ *www.visa.com*), Mastercard (Ⓣ 00531-11-3886, Ⓦ *www.mastercard.com*) and Citibank (Ⓣ 0120-504189, Ⓦ *www.citibank.co.jp*) have a good spread of ATMs; call their 24hr toll-free English-language helplines to find the machine nearest you, or consult the relevant website. JNTO (see p.18) can also provide lists of locations. Most of these machines are accessible outside normal banking hours and some are open 24hrs. If you're having problems, pick up the phone beside the ATM and ask to speak to someone in English.

Finally, Visa and Mastercard holders can make over-the-counter cash withdrawals from Tokyo Mitsubishi Bank's head office (2-7-1 Marunouchi), while major branches of Mitsui Sumitomo Bank handle Visa card withdrawals only.

BANKS AND EXCHANGE

To exchange cash or travellers' cheques, look for banks announcing "Foreign Exchange Bank" in English outside the front door; Tokyo Mitsubishi Bank generally handles the broadest range of currencies. Banking hours are Monday to Friday 9am to 3pm; all Japanese banks close on Saturdays, Sundays and public holidays. Most larger post offices (see Directory, p.298) also exchange cash or travellers' cheques. Their rates are usually similar to the rates at banks, and they have slightly longer opening hours (Mon–Fri 9am–4pm). If you need to change money outside normal banking hours try your hotel, or the big department stores, most of which have an exchange desk. Note, however, that they usually only handle US dollars.

EMERGENCY CASH

In an emergency, **wiring money** is the quickest option. You'll need to contact one of the major Japanese banks to check exactly how they handle these transfers and the charges they levy, then call on a reliable friend to make the arrangements at the other end. The whole process can take several days and hefty charges are made at both ends (in Japan, typically around ¥2500 for yen transfers, while charges for other currencies are generally built into the exchange rate employed). Alternatively, you can use MoneyGram (Ⓦ *www.moneygram.com*), whereby you receive the transfer via a MoneyGram agent; charges vary according to the amount, but can be up to ten percent.

Opening hours and national holidays

Business hours are generally from Monday to Friday, 9am to 5pm, though private companies often open on Saturday mornings as well. Most **shops** are open from 10am to 7pm or 8pm, with one day off a week, while **restaurant** hours are usually 11.30am to 2pm and 5pm to 9.30pm; again, many restaurants close one day per week. **Banks** are generally open Monday to Friday, 9am to 3pm. For post offices, see p.298.

Museums usually close on Monday, except when Monday is a national holiday, in which case they close on Tuesday instead. Unless otherwise stated, last entry is thirty minutes before closing.

Banks, offices and many smaller shops close on **national holidays**, while department stores, public museums and most restaurants stay open – though they may take the

NATIONAL HOLIDAYS

If one of the holidays listed below falls on a Sunday, then the Monday is also a holiday.

Jan 1	New Year's Day
Second Mon in Jan	Adults' Day
Feb 11	National Foundation Day
March 20/21	Spring Equinox
April 29	Greenery Day
May 3	Constitution Memorial Day
May 4	Kokumin no Shukujitsu (a "bridge" day between the two holidays)
May 5	Children's Day
July 20	Marine Day
Sept 15	Respect-for-the-Aged Day
Sept 23/24	Autumn Equinox
Second Mon in Oct	Sports Day
Nov 3	Culture Day
Nov 23	Labour Thanksgiving Day
Dec 23	Emperor's Birthday

following day off instead. Over New Year (Dec 28–Jan 3), "Golden Week" (April 28–May 5) and Obon (the week around August 15), virtually the whole of Tokyo shuts down.

Customs and etiquette

Japan is famous for its complex web of social conventions and rules of behaviour. Fortunately, allowances are made for befuddled foreigners, but you'll get a good response – and even draw gasps of astonishment – if you show an understanding of the basics. The main danger areas are shoes and bathing, which, if you get them wrong, can definitely cause offence. See also p.178 and p.218.

SHOES AND SLIPPERS

It's customary to change into **slippers** when entering a Japanese home or a *ryokan*, traditional restaurant, temple and, occasionally, a museum or art gallery. As a rule, if you come across a slightly raised floor and a row of slippers, then use them; either leave your shoes on the lower floor, on the shelves, or in the lockers provided. Once inside, remove your slippers before stepping onto **tatami**, the rice-straw flooring, and remember to change into the special **toilet slippers** lying by the bathroom door when you go to the toilet.

BATHING ETIQUETTE

Taking a traditional Japanese bath is a ritual that's definitely worth mastering. Key points to remember are that the tub is only for soaking, and that everyone uses the same water. Before stepping in, soap down thoroughly – showers and bowls are provided, as well as soap and shampoo in many cases – and rinse well. If the temperature in the bath is too hot, it's OK to add a little cold water, but the trick is to get in slowly and then keep as still as possible; some people say putting a cold towel on your head helps. *Ryokan* and the more upmarket public bathhouses provide small towels which can be draped to good effect – though no one minds full nudity. Lastly, the bath in a *ryokan* or family home is filled once each evening, so, whatever you do, don't pull the plug out. For more on bathing, see Directory, p.298.

THE GUIDE

Introducing the city

The best way to think of Tokyo is not as one city, but as several mini-cities, linked by the railway and subway systems. The capital is vast, spreading from the mountains in the north and west to tropical islands some 1300km to the south. As a visitor, however, you're unlikely to stray beyond the eleven most central of Tokyo's 23 wards (*ku*): Bunkyō-ku, Chiyoda-ku, Chūō-ku, Meguro-ku, Minato-ku, Shibuya-ku, Shinagawa-ku, Shinjuku-ku, Sumida-ku, Taitō-ku and Toshima-ku.

Details on studying and working in Tokyo can be found in the *Directory*, pp.297 and 300, while information on long-term accommodation in the city is in *Accommodation*, p.171.

A useful reference point is the **Yamanote line**, an overland train loop which connects and encloses virtually everything of interest to visitors. Sightseeing destinations outside of the loop are mainly within what was once called **Shitamachi**, or "low city", east of the Imperial Palace, including Asakusa and Ryōgoku, and on Tokyo Bay to the south, including the futuristic man-made island of Ōdaiba.

Get your bearings by tracing the Yamanote route on our Greater Tokyo map (see colour map 2), starting at the mini-city of **Shinjuku**, in the west, where a cluster of skyscrapers provides a permanent directional marker wherever you are. From Shinjuku, the line heads north towards department-store-dominated **Ikebukuro**, where the sixty-floor Sunshine Building, east of the station, is another landmark. The train line then veers east towards **Ueno**, jumping-off point for a park and some major museums. Further east, at **Asakusa**, is Sensō-ji, Tokyo's most important Buddhist temple.

From Ueno the Yamanote runs south to **Akihabara**, the electronic discount shop district. Bisecting Akihabara station is the Sōbu line which, together with the Chūō line from Tokyo station, heads directly west, providing the shortest rail route back to Shinjuku. Handy stations along these two lines include **Suidōbashi** for the baseball and concert venue Tokyo Dome and Kōrakuen garden, **Iidabashi** for the Tokyo International Youth Hostel, and **Sendagaya** for the Metropolitan Gymnasium and the gardens of Shinjuku Gyoen. East of Akihabara, on the other hand, the Sōbu line runs across the Sumida-gawa to the sumo centre of **Ryūgoku**.

We've divided this guide into Tokyo's most popular areas, starting with the central districts around the Imperial Palace, then heading east, north and west of the centre before ending with the southern Tokyo Bay districts.

From Akihabara the Yamanote continues south through **Tokyo Station**, with the Imperial Palace and business districts of Ōtemachi and Marunouchi immediately to the west. Further south lie the entertainment districts of **Ginza** (closest stop Yūrakuchō) and **Shimbashi**, the next station south on the Yamanote. East of Ginza is Tokyo Bay, around which are the gardens of Hama Rikyū and the mammoth fish market at **Tsukiji**.

After Shimbashi, the Yamanote stops at **Hamamatsuchō** (connected by monorail to Haneda Airport), on the west side of which is Tokyo Tower and the nightlife district of **Roppongi**. The Rainbow Bridge across to the island of Ōdaiba in Tokyo Bay is clearly visible as the Yamanote veers down to **Shinagawa**, a hub of upmarket hotels, with rail connections through to Kawasaki and Yokohama.

Just before Shinagawa the line turns sharply north and heads towards Meguro, a mainly residential suburb and **Ebisu**, one of the city's most up-and-coming entertainment areas. Next along the line is trendy **Shibuya**, where the shops, restaurants and clubs constitute teen-fashion central for Japan. On the western flank of equally hip **Harajuku**, the next stop after Shibuya, are the wooded grounds of **Meiji-jingū**, the city's most important shrine, and Yoyogi Park. Yoyogi, the station after Harajuku, is also on the Sōbu line, and is just one stop from the start of your journey at Shinjuku.

The telephone code for central Tokyo is 03. To call Tokyo from abroad, dial 81-3 followed by the subscriber's number.

Arrival

Arriving in Tokyo from abroad, you'll almost certainly touch down at New Tokyo International Airport. Otherwise, if you're coming to the capital from elsewhere in Japan, your arrival points will be one of the main train stations (Tokyo, Ueno or Shinjuku), the ferry port at Ariake on Tokyo Bay, or the long-distance bus terminals, mainly at Tokyo and Shinjuku stations.

BY AIR

Some 66km east of the city centre, **New Tokyo International Airport**, better known as Narita, has two terminals (flight information ☎0476/34-5000); which one you arrive at depends on the airline you fly.

There are **cash machines** that accept foreign credit and cash cards and **bureau de change** outlets at both terminals (Terminal 1: 6.30am–11pm; Terminal 2: 7am–10pm) which offer the same rates as city banks. The main **tourist information centre** (daily 9am–8pm; ☎0476/34-6251) is at the newer Terminal Two; staff here can provide maps and leaflets. The Welcome Inn counter next door can make hotel bookings, free of charge, for their member inns. Terminal One has a smaller information centre (daily 9am–8pm), providing much the same service. If you have a JR rail pass exchange order, you can arrange your pass for use immediately or at a later date at the JR travel agencies (not the ticket offices) in the basements of both terminals; English signs indicate where these are. There are direct bus and train connections from Narita to Haneda Airport for transfers to domestic flights; the bus (1hr 20min; ¥3000) is more frequent than the train (1hr 10min; ¥1580).

Most domestic flights touch down at **Haneda Airport** (flight information ☎5757-8111), located on a spit of land jutting into Tokyo Bay, 20km south of the Imperial Palace. The only international connection at Haneda is provided by Taiwan's China Airlines. There is no tourist office here, but the airport information desk can provide you with an English-language map of Tokyo.

Getting into the city from the airports

The fastest way into Tokyo **from Narita** is on one of the frequent JR or Keisei **trains** which leave from the basements

TOKYO: ARRIVAL

Airports		
New Tokyo International Airport (Narita)	Shin-Tokyo Kokusai Kuko	新東京国際空港
Haneda Airport	Haneda Kuko	羽田空港
Bus, ferry and train stations		
Ikebukuro	Ikebukuro-eki	池袋駅
Shibuya	Shibuya-eki	渋谷駅
Shinagawa	Shinagawa-eki	品川駅
Shinjuku	Shinjuku-eki	新宿駅
Tokyo	Tokyo-eki	東京駅
Ueno	Ueno-eki	上野駅

of both terminals. Keisei offers the cheapest connection into town: the no-frills **tokkyū** (limited express) service, which costs ¥1000 to Ueno (every 30min; 1hr 10min). This service stops at Nippori, a few minutes north of Ueno, where an easy transfer can be made to the Yamanote or the Keihin Tōhoku lines, which continue through Tokyo to Yokohama. If you're staying around Ueno, or not carrying much luggage, this – or the slightly faster and fancier Skyliner (¥1920) – is the best option.

JR runs the more luxurious red and silver **Narita Express** (N'EX) to several city stations. The cheapest fare is ¥2940 to Tokyo Station (every 30min; 1hr), and there are frequent direct N'EX services to Shinjuku (hourly; 1hr 20min) for ¥3110. The N'EX services to Ikebukuro (¥3110) and Yokohama (¥4180) are much less frequent; you're better off going to Shinjuku and changing onto the Yamanote line for Ikebukuro, while there are plenty of trains to Yokohama from Tokyo Station. A lot less expensive than the N'EX are JR's *kaisoku* (rapid) trains, which,

LEAVING TOKYO BY AIR

If you're **leaving** Tokyo from Narita Airport, it's important to set off around four hours before your flight, though you can skip the queues to some extent by checking in and completing immigration formalities at the **Tokyo City Air Terminal** (TCAT; daily 8am-6pm; ☎3665-7111), located above Suitengumae Station on the Hibiya line. Not all airlines have desks at TCAT, so check first. The onward journey is then by limousine bus – allow at least one hour – with departures every ten minutes (¥2900). Having been through immigration at TCAT, a special card allows you to scoot through the "crew line" at passport control in Narita. Nevertheless, during peak holiday periods queues at the baggage check-in and immigration desks at both Narita and TCAT can be lengthy. **International departure tax** from Narita is no longer levied as a separate payment, but is included in the price of your ticket.

despite their name, chug slowly into Tokyo Station (hourly; 1hr 20min) for ¥1280.

Limousine buses are useful if you're weighed down by luggage, but they are pricey and prone to delays in traffic. Buy tickets from the limousine bus counters in each of the arrival lobbies; the buses depart from directly outside (check which platform you need) and stop at a variety of places around the city, including all the major hotels and train stations. The journey to hotels in Shinjuku and Ikebukuro costs around ¥3000 and takes a minimum of one hour thirty minutes. For a staggering ¥20,000 you can take a **taxi** to the city centre, but the journey is no faster than by bus. Taxis line up at stand 9 outside the arrivals hall of Terminal One and stand 30 outside the arrival hall of Terminal Two.

From Haneda Airport you can take a twenty-minute monorail journey to Hamamatsuchō Station on the

Yamanote line (every 5–10min; daily 5.20am–11.15pm) for ¥460. There are also less frequent **rail** services stopping at Shinagawa and Shimbashi en route to Narita. A **taxi** from Haneda to central Tokyo costs ¥6000, while a **limousine bus** to Tokyo Station is ¥900.

BY TRAIN

High-speed Shinkansen trains on the Tōkaidō line from Ōsaka, Kyoto and other points south pull in at **Tokyo Station**, just east of the Imperial Palace. All Shinkansen services from the north (the Hokuriku line from Nagano, the Jōetsu line from Niigata and the Tōhoku lines from Yamagata and Morioka) also arrive at Tokyo Station, with the majority stopping first at **Ueno**. Both Tokyo and Ueno stations are on the Yamanote line and are connected to several subway lines, putting them within reach of most of the capital. Long-distance JR train services from the west stop at Tokyo and Ueno stations, Shinjuku Station on Tokyo's west side and Ikebukuro Station in the city's northwest corner.

Arriving in Tokyo on a non-JR rail line, you'll terminate at different stations: the Tōkyū Tōyoko line from Yokohama terminates at Shibuya Station, southwest of the Imperial Palace; the Tōbu Nikkō line runs from Nikkō to Asakusa Station, east of Ueno; and the Odakyū line from Hakone finishes at Shinjuku Station, the terminus also for the Seibu Shinjuku line from Kawagoe – all these stations have subway connections, and only Asakusa is not on the Yamanote line.

BY BUS

Long-distance **buses** terminate at several major stations around the city, making transport connections straightforward. The main overnight services from Kyoto and Ōsaka terminate at the bus station beside the eastern Yaesu exit of Tokyo Station – other arrival stations for buses are Ikebukuro, Shibuya, Shinagawa and Shinjuku.

BY BOAT

The most memorable way to arrive in Tokyo is by long-distance **ferry**, sailing past the suspended roads and monorail on the Rainbow Bridge and the harbour wharfs to dock at **Tokyo Ferry Port** at Ariake on the man-made island of Odaiba (see p.135) in Tokyo Bay. There are ferry connections to Tokyo from Kita-Kyūshū in Kyūshū, Kōchi and Tokushima on Shikoku, and Naha on Okinawa-Hontō. Buses run from the port to Shin-Kiba Station on both the subway and the JR Keiyō line and a ten-minute ride from Tokyo Station. A taxi from the port to central Tokyo shouldn't cost more than ¥2000.

Information

The central **Tourist Information Centre**, or TIC (Mon–Fri 9am–5pm, Sat 9am–noon; ☎3201-3331), is in the basement of Tokyo International Forum, close to Yūrakuchō Station (Map 7, C5). Staff here speak English and can provide excellent city **maps** and a broad spread of tourist literature. If you're in Tokyo for more than just a few days or plan to wander off the normal routes, it's well worth investing in Kodansha's bilingual *Tokyo City Atlas* (¥2100), which gives more detail and, importantly, includes the *chōme* and block numbers to help pin down addresses (see box, p.42).

TOKYO ON THE INTERNET

Narita Airport

Ⓦ*www.narita-airport.or.jp/airport_e/index_e.html*

Complete with flight information, floor plans and the lowdown on local access.

PriceCheck Tokyo

Ⓦ*www.pricechecktokyo.com*

Lists prices for a whole range of items, from caffè latte to a tube of toothpaste. If it's not there, they'll find the price for you.

Tokyo Classified

Ⓦ*www.tokyoclassified.com*

Digital version of the weekly freebie magazine with property rentals, employment, personal ads, events listings, restaurant and bar reviews, and much, much more. Now rivalling Tokyo Q (see below) as the city's best site.

Tokyo Meltdown

Ⓦ*www.bento.com/tleisure.html*

Get the lowdown on the arts and entertainment scene, covering bars, clubs, museums, galleries and architecture. Has links to the Tokyo Food Page (Ⓦ*www.bento.com/tf-rest.html*) and the Tokyo Subway Platform (Ⓦ*www.bento.com/platform.html*), with helpful information plus plenty of weird stuff for avid trainspotters.

Tokyo Q

Ⓦ*www.nokia.co.jp/tokyoq*

One of Tokyo's top Web sites, containing a weekly roundup of current news and upcoming arts events, as well as the latest restaurant listings and links to some of the city's more quirky sites.

To find out **what's on** in the city, pick up the weekly freesheet *Tokyo Classified* (Ⓦ*www.tokyoclassified.com*), packed with ads and reviews, features and listings for film and music events. For traditional and performance arts, however, *Tokyo Journal* (¥600; Ⓦ*www.tokyo.to*) is still better. The two main English-language dailies are the *Japan Times* and *Daily Yomiuri* – both publish sporadic listings and Thursday's *Daily Yomiuri* is especially good for cinema listings. The TIC also posts details of selected events on its noticeboard and hands out more comprehensive monthly lists of festivals and the like on request. Alternatively, Teletourist (Ⓣ3201-2911) provides 24-hour pre-recorded information in English on events in and around Tokyo.

City transport

The easiest way to get around Tokyo is by **train** and **subway**. Both systems are colour-coded, have station signs in English and Japanese and directional arrows on the platform signs so you know which station is coming next. Where subway and train lines interconnect, English signs guide you along the tunnels to the right platform. The trains are clean, safe and efficient and, though they can get packed to the gunnels during rush hour (particularly 7.30–9am), only rarely do the infamous white-gloved platform attendants shove commuters into carriages.

Once you've got to the area you wish to explore, **walking** is the best way to get yourself from one sight to another, and you're almost guaranteed to see something interesting on the way. **Cycling**, if you stick to the quiet backstreets, can also be a good way of zipping around (see *Directory*, p.294 for rental places).

SIGHTSEEING TOURS

For a quick overview of Tokyo, there are several **bus tours**, ranging from half-day jaunts around the central sights to visits out to Kamakura, Nikkō and Hakone. The tours are not cheap, but are a hassle-free way of covering a lot of ground with English-speaking guides, though all the places they visit are easy enough to get to independently.

Sunrise Tours (Ⓣ5620-9500, Ⓦ*www.jtb.co.jp*), run by Japan Travel Bureau (JTB), offers six basic options, from the cheapest, half-day Cityrama Tokyo Morning (¥3300), covering Meiji-jingū, the Imperial Palace East Garden and Asakusa, to Dynamic Tokyo (¥12,000 including lunch), a full-day tour taking in Tokyo Tower, Asakusa, a tea ceremony, a river cruise and a drive through Ginza, or you can splurge on a Geisha Night tour (¥18,000). Other options are Sukiyaki Night (¥7500), with a *sukiyaki* dinner and monorail ride over Tokyo Bay, and Kabuki Night (¥10,800). One- and two-day excursions start at ¥11,000 for a day in Kamakura, ¥9,500 by bus round Fuji and Hakone, and ¥11,500 for a trip to Nikkō. **Japan Gray Line** (Ⓣ3436-6881, Ⓦ*www3.tky.3web.ne.jp/~easy5*) runs one full-day and two half-day city tours and a one-day Fuji–Hakone excursion, with roughly the same itinerary and prices as Sunrise Tours. Tours with either company can be booked at the TIC in Yūrakuchō and at all major hotels.

In addition, **Odakyū Q Tours** (Ⓣ5321-7887, Ⓦ*www.odakyu-group.co.jp/english*), located in Tokyo's Shinjuku Station (see p.98), offers unaccompanied excursions including your train fare, lunch and an explanatory English-language guidebook. The most interesting options are their one-day Kamakura (¥5000), Hakone Panorama (¥9500) and Hakone History and Hot Springs (¥9500) "courses".

UNRAVELLING TOKYO ADDRESSES

Tokyo is divided into 23 wards (*ku*), which are subdivided into districts (*chō*), then local areas (*chōme*), blocks and, finally, individual buildings. For example, the address 1-12-33 Akasaka, Minato-ku, identifies building number 33, somewhere on block 12 in area number 1 of Akasaka district, Minato ward.

Most buildings bear a small metal tag with their number (for example, 1-12-33, or just 12-33), while lamp posts often have a bigger plaque with the district name in *kanji* and the block reference (such as 1-12). Note that the same address can also be written 12-33 Akasaka 1-chōme, Minato-ku.

Often a bar, restaurant or other establishment has an indication of the floor it's on preceding the address: 2F, Ebisu AM Bldg means that what you're looking for is on the second floor of the Ebisu AM building; B1, Bunkamura means it's in basement one of the Bunkamura building and so on. Note that in Japan ground-level is classed as the first floor.

THE SUBWAY

Its colourful map may look like a messy plate of *yakisoba* (fried noodles), but Tokyo's **subway** is relatively easy to negotiate. There are two systems, the eight-line TRTA (which stands for Teito Rapid Transit Authority, but is also referred to as the Eidan) and the four-line Toei, run by the city authority, which also manages the buses and the tram line. The systems share some of the same stations, but unless you buy a special ticket from the vending machines that specifies your route from one system to the other, you cannot switch mid-journey between the two sets of lines. Subways have connecting passageways to overland train lines, such as the Yamanote.

Tokyo's subway is laid out on map 3

Leaving a station can be complicated by the number of exits (sixty in Shinjuku, for example), though maps near the ticket barriers and on the platforms indicate where the exits emerge, and strips of yellow tiles on the floor mark the routes to the ticket barriers. Subway trains run daily from around 5am to just after midnight.

Tickets

Pay for your **ticket** at the vending machines beside the electronic ticket gates – apart from major stations (marked with a triangle on the subway map), there are no ticket sales windows. If fazed by the wide range of buttons, buy the cheapest ticket and sort out the difference with the gatekeeper at the other end. You must always buy separate tickets for subways and overland trains, unless you're using an SF Metro or Pasunetto card (see below).

The cheapest subway ticket is ¥160 and, since most journeys across central Tokyo cost no more than ¥190, few of the **travel passes** on offer are good value for short-stay visitors. However, if you're going to be travelling around a lot, it makes sense to buy *kaisuken,* carnet-type tickets where you get eleven tickets for the price of ten – look for the special buttons on the automated ticket machines at the stations. Off-peak tickets give you twelve tickets for the price of ten, but can only be used 10am–4pm weekdays; Sat/Hol tickets, fourteen for the price of ten, but can only be used on Saturday, Sunday and public holidays. Handiest of all is the **SF Metro Card**, or **Pasunetto Card**, which saves you no money but can be used on both Eidan and Toei subways and all the private railways (but not JR) in the Tokyo area. As you go through a ticket barrier, the fare is deducted from the card's stored value; these cards can be bought from ticket offices and machines, and also used in machines to pay for tickets if the amount left on your card isn't enough to cover your journey. If you're here for a month or more and will be travelling the same route most days, you might buy a *teiki* season ticket, which runs for one, three or six months and covers your specified route and stations in between.

TRAINS AND TRAMS

Spend any length of time in Tokyo and you'll become very familiar with the JR **Yamanote train line** that loops around the city centre (see p.31 for a summary of its route). Other useful JR train routes include the **Chūō line** (orange), which starts at Tokyo Station and runs west to Shinjuku and beyond; the yellow **Sōbu line** from Chiba in the east to Mitaka in the west, running parallel to the Chūō line in the centre of Tokyo and doubling as a local service, stopping at all stations; and the **Keihin Tōhoku line**, with blue trains, running from the north, through Tokyo Station, to Yokohama and beyond. It's fine to transfer between JR lines on the same ticket, but you must buy a new ticket if you transfer to a subway line. Trains run daily from around 5am to just after midnight.

As on the subway, **tickets** are bought from vending machines. The lowest fare on JR lines is ¥130. Like the subways, JR offers prepaid cards and *kaisuken* (carnet) deals on tickets. The pre-paid Orange Card (not always orange, just to confuse things) comes in denominations of ¥1000, ¥3000, ¥5000 (worth ¥5300) and ¥10,000 (worth ¥10,700), and is available from station vending machines. The card must be re-inserted into the vending machines to pay for individual tickets (the price is deducted from the value of the card), and can be used on the JR system anywhere in Japan.

Central Tokyo's last remaining **tram** service, the Toden Arakawa line, loops round from Waseda in the northwest to Minowa, above Asakusa, on the northeast. Though not a particularly useful route for visitors, it passes through some interesting backstreets, especially between Higashi-Ikebukuro and Kōshinzuka. There's a flat-fare of ¥160, paid on entry, and stations are announced in English. Trams run from around 6am to 10pm.

BUSES

Although Tokyo's **buses** are handy for crossing the few areas without subway and train stations, all the signposts are in Japanese, so you'll need to recognize the *kanji* names of places, or memorize the numbers of useful bus routes on the map available from tourist information centres. The final destination is displayed on the front of the bus, along with the route number. You pay on entry, dropping the flat rate of ¥200 into the fare box by the driver. There is a machine in the box for changing ¥1000 notes. A recorded voice announces the next stop in advance, as well as issuing constant warnings about not forgetting your belongings when you get off the bus. If you're not sure when your stop is, ask your fellow passengers. Buses run from around 5.30am to midnight.

FERRIES

Double-decker **ferries**, known as *suijō basu* (water buses), ply the 35-minute route between the Sumida-gawa River Cruise stations at Asakusa, northeast of the city centre, and Hinode Sanbashi, on Tokyo Bay (daily to 6.15pm; every 40min; ¥660). The large picture windows, which give a completely different view of the city from the one you'll get from the streets, are reason enough for hopping aboard one, especially if you want to visit both Asakusa and the gardens at Hama Rikyū, then stroll into Ginza. The ferries stop at the gardens en route, and you can buy a combination ticket for the ferry and park entrance for ¥960.

TAXIS

For short hops around the centre of Tokyo, **taxis** are often the best option, though heavy traffic can slow them down. The basic rate is ¥660 for the first 2km, after which the meter racks up ¥80 every 274m, plus a time charge when the taxi is moving at less than 10km per hour. Between 11pm and 5am rates are about twenty percent higher.

You can flag down a taxi on most roads – a red light next to the driver means the cab is free; green means occupied – and there are designated stands in the busiest parts of town. When the taxi stops, the driver will press an automatic door-opening button. Try to have your destination written down (preferably in Japanese) and don't be surprised if the driver looks blank; finding addresses in Tokyo is a skill that even cabbies are not expert in, and a stop at a *kōban* (local police box) may be necessary to locate your destination. Tipping the driver is not expected.

After the trains stop at night, be prepared for long queues at taxi stands, especially in areas such as Roppongi and Shinjuku. Taxis can be **booked** in advance, though it's best to get a Japanese-speaker to do it for you. The contact details of several firms are listed in the *Directory* on p.299.

Imperial Palace and around

Concealed in a green swathe of central Tokyo, wrapped round with moats and broad avenues, the enigmatic **Imperial Palace** lies at the city's geographical and spiritual heart. Home to the emperor and his family, the palace hides behind a wall of trees and is closed to the public, but the nearby parks make a natural start to any exploration of Tokyo. The most attractive is **Higashi Gyoen**, the East Garden, where remnants of old Edo Castle still stand amid formal gardens, while to its north **Kitanomaru-kōen** is a more natural park containing a motley collection of museums. Just outside the park's northern perimeter, the nation's war dead are remembered at a highly controversial shrine, **Yasukuni-jinja**, while life in Japan during World War II is portrayed at the equally contentious new **Shōwa-kan**.

East of the Imperial Palace you'll find an area of banks and corporate headquarters, as well as **Tokyo Station** and the Tokyo Information Centre, housed in the spectacular new **Tokyo International Forum**. Built at either end of the twentieth century, these two very distinctive buildings, together with the excellent **Idemitsu Museum of Art**, constitute the district's major sights. This area is also known for its theatres and cinemas, as well as some wonderfully atmospheric drinking and eating places tucked under the railway tracks. Finally, on the palace's western flank stands Japan's seat of power, the **National Diet Building**, more attractive inside than out.

THE IMPERIAL PALACE 皇居

Map 2, E7. Hibiya Station.

An austere expanse of spruce lawns and manicured pine trees, the **Imperial Plaza** forms a protective island in front of the east gate of the modern **Imperial Palace**. Since the palace is generally off limits, the main reason to venture across the windswept avenues towards the massive, stone ramparts – a legacy of the former castle – is to view one of its most photogenic corners, **Nijūbashi**. Here, two bridges span the moat and a jaunty little watchtower perches on its grey stone pedestal beyond; with any luck, you'll catch it framed in a fringe of fresh green willow while swans glide by. Though the bridges are a late-nineteenth-century embellishment, the tower dates back to the seventeenth century and represents one of the castle's few original structures still standing.

Until this century, emperors were regarded as living deities, but on August 15, 1945 a stunned nation listened to Emperor Hirohito's quavering voice announcing Japan's surrender to the Allied forces, and a few months later he renounced his divine status. Today, the emperor is a head of state with no governmental power, though he is still held in respect by the general public, helped by the extremely deferential media. However, polls reveal a growing indifference to the imperial institution, particularly among the young, while more radical papers are

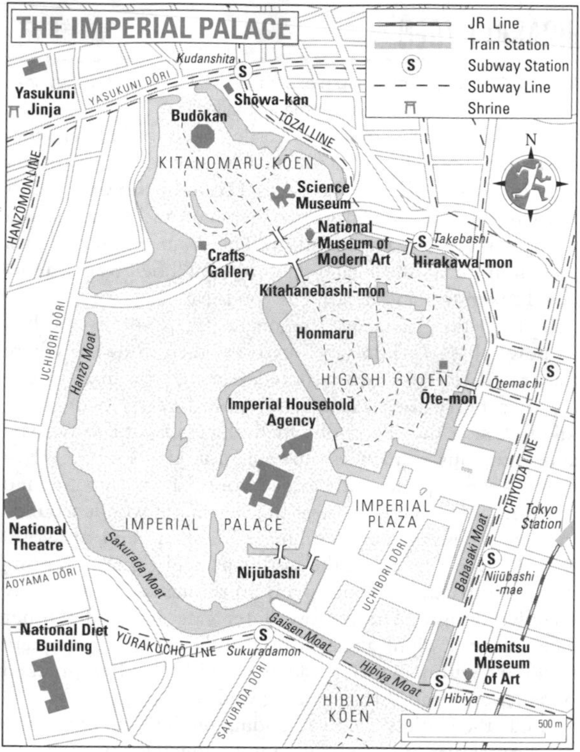

growing bolder in their publication of allegations and critical commentary.

Twice a year – on December 23, the emperor's birthday, and on January 2 – thousands of well-wishers file across Nijūbashi to greet the Imperial Family with a rousing cheer of *banzai*.

HIGASHI GYOEN 東御苑

Map 2, F7. Daily 9am–4.30pm except Mon & Fri, closed occasionally for court functions; free. Ōtemachi Station.

There's little evidence of Edo Castle's once magnificent fortifications beyond several formidable gates and the towering, granite walls, but today's **Higashi Gyoen** (East Garden), an ornamental garden hemmed in by moats, is a pleasant place for a quiet stroll. The main entrance is via Ōte-mon, the eastern gate; on entry you'll be given a numbered token to hand in again as you leave.

In 1603 the Tokugawa shogunate (see p.349) established its power base in Edo (as Tokyo was then known), where they ruled for over two hundred years. By the mid-seventeenth century their castle encompassed nearly two square kilometres, at the centre of which offices of state, armouries and luxurious residences clustered round a soaring, five-tiered keep topped with gilded roofs. The keep burned down in 1657, while most of the remaining wooden buildings were destroyed in bombing raids at the end of World War II. Even Ōte-mon, the castle's principal gate, is a postwar reconstruction – but as you go through note its highly effective design. The narrow outer gate and wider inner gate are set at right angles to each other, creating a square enclosure within which invaders could be held and picked off at leisure from the containing walls.

Inside the garden, the first building on the right contains a small **museum** (free) exhibiting just a tiny fraction of the six thousand artworks in the imperial collection. It's worth a quick look to see what's currently on display, while the shop just beyond stocks informative maps of the garden (¥150). From here a path winds gently up, beneath the beautifully engineered walls of the main citadel, and then climbs more steeply towards Shiomizaka, the "Tide-Viewing Slope", from where it was once possible to gaze across Edo Bay, rather than, as now, across the concrete blocks of Ōtemachi. You emerge on a flat grassy area, empty apart from the stone foundations of the inner keep and a scattering of modern edifices, among them the bizarre, mosaic-clad **Imperial Music Hall**. Built to commemorate the sixtieth birthday of the then empress in 1963, the hall is now used for occasional performances of court music.

KITANOMARU-KŌEN 北の丸公園

Map 2, E6. Kudanshita Station.

The northern citadel of Edo Castle is now occupied by **Kitanomaru-kōen**, an extensive park with a couple of worthwhile museums. To the left of the park entrance, the **Crafts Gallery** (Tues–Sun 10am–5pm; ¥420; Ⓦ*www3.momat.go.jp/e_crafts/index.html*) is the most interesting. Housed in a Neo-Gothic red-brick pile, the gallery exhibits top-quality traditional Japanese crafts, many of them by modern masters. The gallery is part of the **National Museum of Modern Art**, five minutes' walk east down the main road, which specializes in twentieth-century Japanese art but is closed for reconstruction until the summer of 2002 at the earliest.

Just inside the entrance to Kitanomaru-kōen stands the white concrete **Science Museum** (daily 9.30am–4.50pm; ¥600; Ⓦ*www.jsf.or.jp*). Aimed at the early teens or younger, it's often inundated with school parties, but some of the interactive displays are great fun and worth exploring, in spite of the hefty entrance fee. Start on the fifth floor and work your way down, stopping to step inside an Escher room, "listen" to the earth's magnetic field or get a bug's-eye view of life.

The park's last major building is the **Budōkan** martial arts hall, built in 1964 to host Olympic judo events. The design, with its graceful, curving roof and gold top-knot,

SHRINES AND TEMPLES

Japan's main religions are the indigenous **Shinto**, incorporating ancient animism with ancestor-worship, and **Buddhism**, which was imported from Korea in the sixth century. They co-exist happily, fulfilling distinct roles in society. Most Japanese will visit a Shinto shrine to pray for exam success or to get married, but will eventually be interred or cremated according to Buddhist rites.

Although Shinto's myriad gods (*kami*) inhabit all natural things, the focus of daily worship is the shrine (*-jinja* or *-jingū*). It stands in an area of sacred ground entered via one or more *torii*, symbolic gates made of two gently inclined uprights, topped with one or two crosspieces. Near the shrine itself, you'll find a large basin of water where worshippers purify themselves by rinsing their hands and mouth. Standing in front of the sanctuary, they then throw some coins into the large wooden box, shake the bell-rope to inform the deities of their presence, and pray: the standard practice is to bow deeply twice, clap twice, pray with eyes closed and finish with another low bow.

Buddhist temples (*-tera*, *-dera* or *-ji*) are usually much grander affairs, where worshippers enter the compound via an imposing entrance gate flanked by two guardian gods. Again, people often purify themselves with water before entering the main hall to pray before a statue of the Buddha. Of the several Buddhist sects in Japan, **Zen** is probably the most famous, a meditative form of the religion with a rigid moral code, which flourished in Kamakura (see p.327) during the thirteenth century.

pays homage to a famous octagonal hall in Nara's Hōryū-ji temple, though supposedly there's a strong hint of Mount Fuji as well. It was here that the Beatles played in 1966, and today the huge arena is still used for big-name concerts.

YASUKUNI-JINJA AND AROUND 靖国神社

Map 10, B5. Kudanshita Station.

Across the road from Kitanomaru-kōen, a grey steel *torii*, apparently the tallest in Japan, marks the entrance to **Yasukuni-jinja**. This shrine, whose name means "for the repose of the country", was founded in 1869 to worship those supporters of the emperor killed in the run-up to the Meiji Restoration. Since then the names of military personnel who died in subsequent wars have been added, including some two million from World War II, amounting to nearly 2.5 million souls.

For more on Tokyo's history see pp.349-355.

All sorts of tensions revolve around this shrine. It was a focus for the aggressive nationalism that ultimately took Japan to war in 1941 and later, in 1979, a number of Class A war criminals (hanged in 1948) were enshrined here. Equally controversial are the visits made by cabinet ministers on the anniversary of Japan's defeat in World War II (August 15); ministers usually maintain they attend as private individuals but in 1985 Prime Minister Nakasone caused an uproar when he signed the visitors' book under his official title.

For most ordinary Japanese, however, Yasukuni is simply a place to mourn family and friends, and for the most part it's a peaceful spot. At the end of a long tree-lined avenue, its surprisingly unassuming Worship Hall is built in classic Shinto style, solid and unadorned except for two gold imperial chrysanthemums embossed on the main doors. Immediately north of the hall, the shrine's **military museum** (daily: March–Oct 9am–5pm; Nov–Feb 9am–4.30pm; ¥500; Ⓦ*www.yasukuni.or.jp*) contains a sad collection of personal possessions, including blood-stained uniforms, letters and faded photographs. The most disturbing displays concern the Kamikaze pilots and other suicide squads active during World War II. It's hard to miss them: the museum's central hall is dominated by a replica glider, its nose elongated to carry a 1200-kilo bomb, while a spine-chilling, black *kaiten* (a manned torpedo) lours to one side.

SHŌWA-KAN

Map 10, D5. Tues–Sun 10am–5.30pm; ¥300. Kudanshita Station.

There's scarcely a mention of bombs or destruction at the **Shōwa-kan**, a corrugated windowless building east along Yasukuni-dōri from Yasukuni-jinja, which is odd because the new museum is devoted to life in Japan during and after World War II. To be fair, the government originally wanted it to document the war's origins, but ran into bitter opposition from pacifists, insistent on tackling the hot-potato issue of responsibility, and a right-wing lobby opposed to any hint of Japan being the aggressor. After twenty years of argument, they eventually decided on a compromise that pleases almost no one by sticking to a safe, sanitized portrayal of the hardships suffered by wives and children left behind. Nevertheless, there's some interesting material, most notably that concerning life during the Occupation: film-clips of the soup-kitchens and black markets, a film-poster advertising *Mrs Miniver* and a clutch of American sweet-wrappers, all carefully preserved since the war. For Japanese readers, they have also amassed a vast archive of war-related documents.

TOKYO INTERNATIONAL FORUM 東京国際フォーラム

Five minutes' walk east of the Imperial Palace, across Babasaki moat, lies the old red-brick frontage of **Tokyo**

Station (Map 2, G7). Erected in 1914, the station was a much grander affair before an air raid removed its domes and top two stories in 1945, but it's still an attractive building. Behind lies a confusing mess of multi-level tracks and underground passages, which can also be accessed from the eastern, "Yaesu" entrance.

Walking south from Tokyo Station's west entrance, past the central post office, you'll reach the gleaming blocks of **Tokyo International Forum** (Map 7, C5) with the Tokyo Tourist Information Centre (see p.38) in the basement. Designed by architect Raphael Viñoly, this is a remarkable building, with a stunning, boat-shaped main hall, a sixty-metre-high atrium sheathed in 2600 sheets of "earthquake-resistant" glass and a ceiling ribbed like a ship's hull; it's best viewed from the seventh-floor walkways and looks magical at night. The complex is Tokyo's premier art and convention centre, with four main event halls, a vast exhibition space and all the latest in technological wizardry.

IDEMITSU MUSEUM OF ARTS 出光美術館

Map 7, C6. Tues–Sun 10am–5pm; ¥500. Yūrakuchō or Hibiya Station.

From the south exit of the International Forum, head west two blocks to find the Imperial Theatre, showing big-budget Western musicals, and above it, on the ninth floor, the **Idemitsu Museum of Arts**. This magnificent collection of mostly Japanese art includes many historically important pieces, ranging from fine examples of early Jōmon (10,000 BC–300 BC) pottery to Zen Buddhist calligraphy, hand-painted scrolls, richly gilded folding screens and elegant *ukiyo-e* paintings of the late seventeenth century. The museum also houses valuable collections of Chinese and Korean ceramics, as well as slightly incongruous works by French painter Georges Rouault and American artist Sam Francis.

NATIONAL DIET BUILDING 国会議事堂

Map 2, E8. Mon–Fri, 9.30am–4pm, except when the House of Councillors is in session; call ⓣ3581-3100 to check; admission free. Kokkai Gijidomae Station.

Kasumigaseki, to the west of the Imperial Palace, is the political heart of Tokyo, with all the major ministries occupying six blocks along Sakurada-dōri. Appropriately enough, given the inscrutable nature of Japanese bureaucracy, Kasumigaseki translates as "Barrier of the Mists". The main point of interest is the squat, three-storey **National Diet Building**, dominated by a central tower block decorated with pillars and a pyramid-shaped roof. The Diet is supposedly based on the Senate Building in Washington DC, though Japan's style of government has more in common with the British parliamentary system. On the left stands the House of Representatives, the main body of government, while on the right, the House of Councillors, which is similar to Britain's House of Lords, is open for forty-minute **tours**. Some of the guides speak English and in the actual chamber a taped English commentary is played explaining what you can see.

There's an Edwardian-style grandeur to the Diet's interior, especially in the carved-wood debating chamber and the central reception hall, decorated with paintings reflecting the seasons and bronze statues of significant statesmen. You'll have to observe the room the emperor waits in when he visits the Diet through a glass panel: it's decorated in real gold. The tour finishes at the Diet's front garden, planted with native trees and plants from all of Japan's 47 prefectures.

Ginza and Nihombashi

A compact grid of streets southeast of the Imperial Palace, **Ginza** is home to the city's greatest concentration of upmarket shops and restaurants. This is a district that repays idle wandering, best when dusk transforms its streets into neon-lit canyons. The shops spill north along Chūō-dōri, past the fine **Bridgestone Museum of Art**, as far as the venerable **Mitsukoshi** department store in the high-finance district of **Nihombashi**, named after its famous historical bridge.

GINZA 銀座

GINZA, the "place where silver is minted", took its name after Shōgun Tokugawa Ieyasu started making coins here in the early 1600s. It was a happy association – Ginza's Chūō-dōri grew to become Tokyo's most fashionable shopping street, the epitome of style and sophistication and *the* place to be seen. Though some of its shine has faded in the recent recession, and cutting-edge fashion has moved elsewhere, Ginza still retains much of its elegance and its snob appeal.

For more information on shopping in Tokyo see pp.274-292.

On its western edge Ginza starts at the Sukiyabashi crossing where Sotobori-dōri and Harumi-dōri intersect. The **Sony Building** (Map 7, D7; daily 11am–7pm), on the crossing's southeast corner, is one of several Ginza landmarks and a popular meeting place. It's also a must for techno-freaks, with six floors of the latest Sony gadgets to try out. Continuing east on Harumi-dōri you quickly reach the heart of Ginza, an intersection known as the **Ginza Yon-chōme crossing**. Among a number of famous emporia clustered round this junction, Wakō department store started life roughly a century ago as the stall of a young, enterprising watchmaker who developed a line called Seiko (meaning precision); Wakō's clock tower, built in 1894, is one of Ginza's most enduring landmarks. Immediately to its north, Kimuraya bakery was founded in 1874, while Mikimoto Pearl opened next door a couple of decades later. South of the crossing, just beyond the cylindrical, glass San'ai Building, the Kyūkyodō shop is filled with the smell of *sumi-e* ink; it's been selling traditional paper, calligraphy brushes and inkstones since 1800.

Heading on east down Harumi-dōri, you can't miss the colourful **Kabuki-za** (Map 7, F7), the city's principal Kabuki theatre. The original European-style building, inaugurated in 1889, was replaced in 1925 with more traditional heavy roofs and an elaborately decorated porch – today's building is a 1950s replica. Performances take place twice daily during the first three weeks of the month, and a visit is highly recommended (see p.251).

BRIDGESTONE MUSEUM OF ART ブリヂストン美術館

Map 7, F4. Tues–Sun 10am–6pm; ¥700. Kyōbashi Station.

Heading north from Ginza along Chūō-dōri, there's little to hold your interest until you reach the **Bridgestone**

GINZA'S MODERN ART GALLERIES

Ginza and its northern neighbours Kyōbashi and Nihombashi contain over two hundred **contemporary art galleries**, often just a single room rented out to amateur groups or aspiring individuals. It's therefore a bit of a lucky-dip, but visiting these galleries should yield one or two exhibitions that appeal and, as they're all free, it's worth popping in on the off-chance. Selected exhibitions are listed in *Tokyo Journal* and *Tokyo Classified*, or try one of the more accessible galleries below, where you can pick up fliers for other galleries around town.

Inax 3–6–18 Kyōbashi (map 7, F5). This design plaza boasts two galleries on its 2nd floor, showing contemporary art and art and design works. Located on Chūō-dōri, just under the northern Shuto expressway. Closed Sun. Kyōbashi Station.

Gallery Kobayashi B1, Yamato Bldg, 3-8-12 Ginza (map 7, F7). Profiles a wide range of up-and-coming local artists. Closed Sun. Ginza Station.

Leica Gallery 3F, 3-5-6 Ginza (map 7, E6). Great photo gallery with changing exhibitions. It's above the Matshushima Gallery on Chūō-dōri opposite Matsuya department store. Open daily. Ginza Station.

Gallery Natsuka & b.p 8F, Ginza Plaza 58, 5–8–17 Ginza (map 7, E7). Well-respected gallery showcasing young artists. Just down from the Ginza Yon-chōme crossing. Closed Sun. Ginza Station.

Tsubaki B1, 3–2–11 Kyōbashi (map 7, E5). Smart place in the basement opposite Inax. Upstairs on the corner, tiny Kyōbashi gallery is easier to spot. Closed Sun. Ginza Station.

Yoseido 5–5–15 Ginza (map 7, D7). Mainly exhibits contemporary Japanese paintings. Closed Sun. Ginza Station.

Museum of Art. This superb collection, established in 1952 by the founder of a tyre company, focuses on the Impressionists and continues through all the great names of early-twentieth-century European art, plus a highly rated sampler of Meiji-era Japanese paintings in Western style. It's not an extensive display, but a rare opportunity to view works by artists such as Renoir, Picasso and Van Gogh with, often, hardly anyone else around.

In front of the Bridgestone Museum, Yaesu-dōri heads west towards the "back" entrance of Tokyo Station, while Chūō-dōri continues north. On the right-hand side, a row of cheerful red awnings announces another of Tokyo's grand old stores, **Takashimaya** (Map 7, F3), which dates back to a seventeenth-century kimono shop and is worth popping into for its glorious set of old-fashioned lifts. Across the street, **Maruzen** is a relative upstart, a bookstore founded in 1869 to import Western texts as part of Japan's drive to modernize; the store still rates as one of Tokyo's best for foreign-language books.

For details of foreign-language bookstores, see p.279.

While you're in the neighbourhood, it's worth tracking down the lively little **Kite Museum** (Map 7, F2; Mon–Sat 11am–5pm; ¥200) on a backstreet between Takashimaya and the river; there's no English sign, but it's on the fifth floor above *Taimeiken* restaurant (see p.188). Since 1977 the restaurant's former owner has amassed over four hundred kites of every conceivable shape and size, from no bigger than a postage stamp to a monster 8m square.

Back on the main drag, Chūō-dōri finally rumbles across **Nihombashi** (the "Bridge of Japan"; Map 7, F1), from which this district takes its name. The original arch of red lacquer, built in the early seventeenth century and a favourite scene for *ukiyo-e* artists, marked the start of the

Tōkaidō, the great road south to Kyoto. Since then all road distances have been measured from the bridge's mid-point and, though the wooden bridge has long gone, a bronze marker still indicates kilometre zero. The present double-span of stone, erected in 1911, should be an attractive sight with its wrought-iron lamps and bronze statues. However, prior to the 1964 Olympics the government, needing a quick solution to Tokyo's traffic problems, routed the new Shuto Expressway over the city's waterways – in the process they smothered the historic bridge under flyovers.

MITSUKOSHI 三越

Map 7, E1. Daily 10am–7pm. Mitsukoshi-mae Station.

For many people, the foremost attraction of Nihombashi lies just north of the bridge, among the glittering display cases of Tokyo's most impressive department store, **Mitsukoshi**. The shop traces its ancestry back to a dry goods store opened in 1673 by Mitsui Takatoshi, founder of the Mitsui trading empire. The secret of his success was simple: he introduced fixed prices, put all goods on display, gave no credit and insisted on continuous innovation. His was the first store in Japan to offer a delivery service, the first to sell imported goods, the first with an escalator and so on, though until 1923 customers were still required to take off their shoes and don Mitsukoshi slippers. The oldest and most interesting part of today's store is the north building, dating from 1914, whose main atrium is dominated by a weird and wonderful statue, carved from 500-year-old Japanese cypress, of Magokoro, the Goddess of Sincerity.

Akasaka and Roppongi

Nightlife is what **Akasaka** and **Roppongi**, southwest of the Imperial Palace, are all about. After a hard day's work, the bureaucrats and politicians from nearby Kasumigaseki and Nagatachō head for glitzy Akasaka, a major entertainment district which is also home to many of Tokyo's luxury hotels and best restaurants. Meanwhile, a younger generation of Japanese and *gaijin* party down in Roppongi, roughly 1km south.

A handful of sights in these areas will keep you occupied if you find yourself here during the day. Akasaka's premier shrine, **Hie-jinja**, with its attractive avenue of red *torii*, has a long and fascinating history, as does **Zōjō-ji,** near Roppongi – once the temple of the Tokugawa clan. **Tokyo Tower**, Roppongi's most famous sight, has long since been outdone in the height stakes, but on a clear day it still commands an impressive view of the bay area.

AKASAKA 赤坂

To the southwest of the Imperial Palace, beside the government area of Kasumigaseki, is **AKASAKA**. Once an agricultural area (*akane*, plants that produce a red dye, were farmed here, hence the name, which means "red slope"), Akasaka developed into an entertainment district in the late nineteenth century, when *ryōtei* restaurants, complete with performing geisha, started opening to cater for the modern breed of politicians and bureaucrats. Akasaka still has its fair share of exclusive establishments, shielded from the hoi polloi by high walls and even higher prices. Their presence, along with the headquarters of the TBS TV station and some of Tokyo's top hotels, lends the area a degree more glamour than perhaps it deserves. Don't let this put you off; the prices at many of the restaurants and bars here are no worse than anywhere else in Tokyo.

Hie-jinja 日枝神社

Map 4, G4. Akasaka-mitsuke Station.

At the southern end of Akasaka's main thoroughfare, Sotobori-dōri, stands a huge stone *torii* gate, beyond which is a picturesque avenue of red *torii* leading up the hill to tranquil **Hie-jinja**, a Shinto **shrine** dedicated to the god Oyamakui-no-kami, protector against evil.

Although the ferroconcrete buildings date from 1967, Hie-jinja's history stretches back to 830, when it was first established on the outskirts of what would become Edo. The shrine's location shifted a couple more times before Shogun Tokugawa Ietsuna placed it here in the seventeenth century as a source of protection for his castle (now the site of the Imperial Palace). These days the temple hosts the **Sannō Matsuri**, one of Tokyo's most important **festivals**, every June 10–16. Every other year, the festival includes a spectacular parade on June 15 involving four hundred participants dressed in period costume and carrying fifty sacred *mikoshi* (portable shrines).

THE HIE-JINJA INSURRECTION

In February 1936, the Hie-jinja became the command centre for an attempted coup by a renegade group of 1400 soldiers, intent on restoring power to the emperor, who was being increasingly marginalized by the military-controlled government. Government buildings were seized and two former premiers and the inspector general of military training were killed before the insurrection crumbled after just four days. The soldiers surrendered and nineteen of their leaders were executed near where the NHK Broadcasting Centre in Shibuya (see p.120) stands today.

The front entrance to Hie-jinja is actually through the large stone *torii* on the east side of the hill, beside the *Capitol Tōkyū Hotel*. Some 51 steps lead up to a spacious enclosed courtyard in which roosters roam freely and salarymen bunk off work to idle on benches. To the left of the main shrine, look for the carving of a female monkey cradling its baby, a symbol that has come to signify protection for pregnant women.

New Ōtani Hotel and around ニューオータニホテル

Map 4, D1. Akasaka-mitsuke Station.

Heading north from the shrine along Sotobori-dōri and across Benkei-bashi, the bridge that spans what was once the outer moat of the Shogun's castle, will take you to the **New Ōtani** hotel. Within the hotel's grounds is a beautiful traditional Japanese garden, originally designed over four hundred years ago for the *daimyō* Katō Kiyomasa, lord of Kumamoto in Kyūshū. You can stroll freely through the garden or admire it while sipping tea in the hotel lounge. Also worth a browse is the hotel's small **art gallery** (Tues–Sun

10am–6pm; ¥500, free to guests), with works from Japanese and European artists, including Chagall and Modigliani, and a tea ceremony room, where tea (¥1050) is served in the traditional way from Thursday to Saturday between 11am and 4pm. The top-floor bars and restaurants of the hotel provide spectacular views of the city, especially at night, when the twisting ribbon of the Shuto Expressway flows below like a yellow river through an explosion of neon.

Suntory Museum of Art サントリー美術館

Map 4, C2. Tues–Sun 10am–5pm, Fri till 7pm; ¥500 or more depending on exhibition. Akasaka-mitsuke Station.

Returning across the Benkei-bashi, pop into the elegant **Suntory Museum of Art**, on the eleventh floor of the Suntory Building, near the Akasaka-mitsuke Station. The changing exhibitions of Japanese ceramics, lacquerware, paintings and textiles are worth checking out – and there's a traditional tea ceremony room, where tea and sweets are served for around ¥300.

From the museum, walking up Aoyama-dōri will bring you to the colourful **Toyokawa Inari** (also known as Myōgon-ji), a rare example of a combined temple and shrine, something that was much more common across Japan before the Meiji government forcibly separated Shintō and Buddhist places of worship. The temple's compact precincts are decked with red lanterns and banners and the main hall is guarded by statues of pointy-eared foxes – the messengers of the Shinto god Inari – wearing red bibs.

Akasaka Detached Palace 迎賓館

Map 2, C8. Yotsuya Station.

Toyokawa Inari borders the extensive grounds of the grand,

European-style **Akasaka Detached Palace** (Geihinkan), which serves as the official state guest house. When it was completed in 1909, this vast building, modelled on Buckingham Palace on the outside and Versailles on the inside, only had one bathroom in the basement and the empress's apartments were in a separate wing from her husband's; this was fine by the emperor since he was in the habit of taking his nightly pick from the ladies-in-waiting. Some members of the imperial family, including the crown prince, still live within the grounds of the palace, which, unfortunately, puts it off limits to humble visitors.

ROPPONGI 六本木

Roughly 1km south of the hushed grounds of the Akasaka Detached Palace is the distinctly livelier area of **ROPPONGI**, meaning "six trees", though there's hardly a twig in sight today. The area was once reputed to be home to six *daimyō*, all of whom coincidentally had the Chinese character for "tree" in their names. From the Meiji era onwards, Roppongi was a military stamping ground, first for the imperial troops and then, during the American Occupation, for the US forces. When the US army moved out in 1958, TV Asahi moved in, the *gaijin* community started hanging out here and today's entertainment district was born.

Bars and nightclubs – including those in Roppongi – are listed on p.226 and p.234.

Once the almost exclusive domain of upmarket bars, clubs and restaurants, Roppongi is now peppered with discount shops, pachinko parlours and karaoke clubs, and on the corners of Roppongi crossing, bouncers hand out leaflets for strip joints and sleazy hostess clubs. But, if you're up for a night of partying, Roppongi remains one of the best places in Tokyo to head for.

Nogi-jinja 乃木神社

Map 11, C2. Nogizaka Station.

Around 500m northwest of the main crossing, along Gaien-Higashi-dōri, is **Nogi-jinja**, a small **shrine** honouring the Meiji-era, General Nogi Maresuke, a hero in both the Sino-Japanese and Russo-Japanese wars. When the Emperor Meiji died, Nogi and his wife followed the samurai tradition and committed suicide in his house within the shrine grounds. The house is still here and is open just two days annually (12 & 13 Sept, 9.30am–4.30pm; free); on other days you'll have to squint through the windows to catch sight of the general's blood-soaked shirt. On the second Sunday of every month, there's a good antique flea market in the shrine grounds.

Close to Nogi-jinja is Tokyo's top cemetery, Ayoma Reien. See p.115

Tokyo Tower and around 東京タワー

Map 11, H6. Daily: March–Nov 9am–8pm, Aug until 9pm; Jan, Feb & Dec 9am–7pm; main observatory ¥820; top observatory ¥1420. Kamiyachō Station.

Although you can reach **Tokyo Tower** by walking east from Roppongi crossing along Gaien-Higashi-dōri, the closest subway station is Kamiyachō. From here, walk uphill and you can't miss the 333-metre vermilion tower, which opened in 1958 and topped its Parisian role model by several metres. Today the place feels more like an amusement arcade than the Eiffel Tower, with souvenir shops, an aquarium, waxworks and even a holographic "Mystery Zone" aimed at luring visitors in. The top observation deck is 250 metres high but, unless it's an exceptionally clear day, you're better off saving your cash. At pavement level, look out for the sculpture commemorating the dogs who accompanied a Japanese expedition to the South Pole in 1959.

On the way back towards Roppongi, a couple more architectural oddities you'll not fail to miss are *Volga* (see Eating, p.200), a kitsch, miniature copy of Moscow's St Basil's, and the monumental **Reiyūkai**, the main **temple** of a new Buddhist sect. It's possible to look around this vast, glossy black pyramid that looks like an alien spaceship (Thurs–Tues 6am–5pm).

Nearby is the **Ōkura Shūkokan** (daily except Weds 10am–4.30pm; ¥500, free to hotel guests), an art museum established in 1917 by the self-styled Baron Ōkura Tsuruhiko next to the elegant *Ōkura* hotel. This Chinese-style building is looking a little worse for wear, but inside, its two floors display intriguing oriental ceramics, paintings, prints and sculptures from a collection of over 1700 traditional works of art. The museum is on the hill above Kamiyachō subway station.

Zōjō-ji 増上寺

Map 11, I6. Daimon Station.

Tokyo Tower stands on the northwestern flank of **Shiba Kōen**, a park whose main point of interest is **Zōjō-ji**, the family temple of the Tokugawa clan. Zōjō-ji dates from 1393 and was moved to this site in 1598 by Tokugawa Ieyasu, the first Tokugawa shogun, in order to protect southeast Edo from evil spirits and provide a way-station for pilgrims approaching the capital from the Tōkaidō road. This was once the city's largest holy site, with 48 sub-temples and over a hundred other buildings. Since the fall of the Tokugawas in 1868, however, the temple has been razed to the ground by fire three times, and virtually all of the current buildings date from the mid-1970s.

The main remnant of the past is the imposing **Sangadestsu-mon**, a 21-metre-high gateway dating from 1612 and the oldest wooden structure in Tokyo. The name translates as "Three Deliverances Gate" (Buddhism is supposed to save believers from the evils of anger, greed and stupidity) and the gate is one of Japan's Important Cultural Properties (see below). As you pass through, keep an eye out for the tower with a large bell, said to have been made from melted metal hairpins donated by the ladies of the shogun's court. Look out too for the pair of Himalayan Cedar trees, one planted by US President General Grant when he visited the temple in 1879 and the other planted by President George Bush in 1982. Ahead lies the Taiden (Great Main Hall), the temple building often starring in the foreground of many publicity photographs of Tokyo Tower. To the right are ranks of **jizō** statues, capped with red bonnets and decorated with plastic flowers and colourful windmills that twirl in the breeze. Amid this army of mini-guardians lie the remains of six shoguns, behind a wrought-iron gate decorated with dragons.

Important cultural properties are protected buildings, recognized by the government as being of cultural and historical importance.

Kanda and across the Sumida-gawa

Kanda, the region immediately north and west of Nihombashi, straddles Tokyo's crowded eastern lowlands – the former Shitamachi (see History, p.350) – and the more expansive western hills. The area's scattered sights kick off at **Ochanomizu** with historic Kanda Myōjin, a lively Shinto shrine, and an austere monument to Confucius, Yushima Seidō. Below these lie the frenetic, neon-seared streets of **Akihabara**, the "Electric City" dedicated to technological wizardry. Heading west on the JR Sōbu Line, **Suidōbashi** has a couple of minor attractions in Tokyo's foremost baseball stadium and a classic seventeenth-century garden, while a studious hush prevails among the secondhand bookshops of **Jimbōchō,** just to the south.

East from Akihabara, the Sōbu Line crosses the Sumida-gawa to **Ryōgoku**, the heartland of Sumō and home to the absorbing, ultra-modern Edo–Tokyo Museum. Further south, the delightful **Fukagawa-Edo Museum** is an atmospheric re-creation of a mid-nineteenth-century Shitamachi neighbourhood, while the nearby **Museum of Contemporary Art** gathers together the best of post-1945 Japanese art in one spacious, top-class venue.

OCHANOMIZU お茶の水

Map 10, F3. Ochanomizu Station.

A lively student area with some fine modern architecture (see box on p.100), **OCHANOMIZU** is home to an eclectic group of religious buildings. A few minutes' walk south of the Kanda-gawa, the Byzantine flourishes of the Russian Orthodox **Nikolai Cathedral** (Map 10, G4; Tues–Fri 1–3pm; free) stand out from the characterless blocks around. Completed in 1891 using plans sent from Russia, its copper domes were down-sized following the 1923 earthquake, but, inside, the recently refurbished iconostasis positively glows in the soft light.

On the Kanda-gawa's north bank, one of Tokyo's more distinctive shrines, **Yushima Seidō** (Map 10, G3; Sat, Sun & hols 10am–5pm, closed 4pm in winter; free), hides among trees. Dedicated to the Chinese sage, Confucius, the Seidō (Sacred Hall) was founded in 1632 as an academy for the study of the ancient classics. Several decades later it developed into an elite school for the sons of samurai and high-ranking officials of the Tokugawa shogunate, for whom Confucianism provided the State's ethical foundation. Today, the quiet compound's main feature is the Taisen-den, or "Hall of Accomplishments", where a statue of Confucius is enshrined. An imposing, black-lacquered building, rebuilt in 1935, its only adornment is four tiger-like guardians poised on the roof tiles.

Immediately north of Yushima Seidō, a *torii* and the area's last remaining traditional wooden shop, Amanoya, famous for its sweet, ginger-laced sake (*amazake*), mark the entrance to **Kanda Myōjin** (Map 10, G3; 9am–4.30pm; free). This is one of Tokyo's oldest shrines, founded in 730 AD, and also hosts one of its top three **festivals**, the Kanda Matsuri (see p.262). It originally stood in front of Edo Castle, where it was dedicated to the gods of farming and fishing. Later, the tenth-century rebel Taira Masakado – who was beheaded after declaring himself emperor – was also enshrined here; according to legend, his head "flew" to Edo where it was honoured as something of a local hero. When Shogun Tokugawa Ieyasu was strengthening the castle's fortifications in 1616, he took the opportunity to move the shrine but mollified Masakado's supporters by declaring him a guardian deity of the city.

AKIHABARA 秋葉原

Map 10, I4. Akihabara Station.

Southeast of Kanda Myōjin, a blaze of adverts and a cacophony of competing audio-systems announce **AKIHABARA**, Tokyo's most famous discount shopping area for electrical and electronic goods of all kinds. Today's high-tech stores (see p.289 for more) are direct descendants of a postwar blackmarket in radios and radio parts held beneath the train tracks around Akihabara Station. Eventually the trade was legitimized, but you can recapture some of the atmosphere in the narrow passages under the tracks just west of the station, or among the tiny, specialist stalls of **Tokyo Radio Depāto** (Map 10, H4), four floors stuffed with plugs, wires and tools for making or repairing radios; follow the Sōbu Line tracks west from Akihabara Station to find the store just off Chūō-dōri.

Cutting-edge technology of an earlier age is celebrated on the opposite bank of the Kanda-gawa in the **Transportation Museum** (Map 10, H5; Tues–Sun 9.30am–5pm; ¥310). The highlight is the train section, where you'll find Japan's first steam locomotive, built in Britain in 1871, and a wooden passenger carriage used by Emperor Meiji in 1877, complete with carpets and silk padding. Best of all are the simulators with their levers, buttons and screens, where you can drive a suburban JR train or put a Shinkansen through its paces.

SUIDŌBASHI 水道橋

Map 10, E3. Suidōbashi Station.

Two stops west of Akihabara, the JR Sōbu Line rumbles into **Suidōbashi**, where the slides and rides of "Big Egg City" punctuate the skyline. It's named after its centrepiece, the plump, white-roofed **Tokyo Dome** (Map 10, D2), which is Tokyo's major baseball venue and home ground for both the Yomiuri Giants and Nippon Ham Fighters; if you're here during the season (April–Oct), it's well worth trying to get tickets for the atmosphere alone (see p.299 for details). The Dome's **Baseball Museum** (Tues–Sun 10am–6pm; Oct–March closes 5pm; ¥400; Ⓦ*www.baseball-museum.or.jp*), on the other hand, is only for diehard fans who'll appreciate the footage of early games and baseball memorabilia.

For more on baseball and other sports in Tokyo, see p.265.

On the west side of Big Egg City, **Koishikawa-Kōrakuen** (Map 10, C2; daily 9am–5pm; ¥300) is a fine example of an early-seventeenth-century stroll **garden**. Winding paths take you past waterfalls and stone lanterns over daintily humped bridges and down to the shores of a small lake draped with gnarled pines. The design incorporates miniaturized Chinese and Japanese beauty spots, the most obvious being Small Lushan, represented by rounded hills of bamboo grass. The entrance gate lies in the garden's southwest corner, midway between Suidōbashi and Iidabashi stations.

JIMBŌCHŌ 神保町

Map 10, E5. Jimbōchō Station.

From Suidōbashi hop on the Toei Mita subway one stop, or walk 1km south down Hakusan-dōri to **Jimbōchō**, a lively student centre which is also home to dozens of secondhand **bookshops**. You'll find the more interesting shops along the south side of Yasukuni-dōri, in the two main blocks either side of Jimbōchō subway station, where racks of dog-eared novels and textbooks sit outside shops stacked high with dusty tomes. Most are in Japanese, but some dealers specialize in English-language books – both new and old – while a bit of rooting around might turn up a volume of old photographs or cartoons in one of the more upmarket dealers. Note that many shops close on either Sunday or Monday.

See p.279 for more on buying books in Tokyo.

ACROSS THE SUMIDA-GAWA 隅田川

Three times a year **RYŌGOKU**, east of central Tokyo on the JR Sōbu Line, bursts into life when the grand sumo tournaments fill the **National Sumo Stadium** (Map 10, Ryōguku inset) with a two-week pageant of thigh slapping, foot stamping and arcane ritual. If you're in Tokyo at the right time – they take place over a fortnight in January, May and September – try to see a few bouts. Seats are usually available during the opening rounds, when you can also get closer to the action.

At other times of year, you can get a taster at the one-room historical **museum** (Mon–Fri 10am–4.30pm; closed during tournaments; free) beside the stadium, or simply wander the streets immediately south of the train tracks. Here you'll find a sumo-town where shops sell outsize clothes and wrestlers live in what are called **stables** (*heya*) – with a bit of organizing it's possible to visit their early-morning training sessions (ask at the TIC). There's a good chance of bumping into junior wrestlers in their *yukata*, wooden *geta* and slicked-back hair, popping out to a neighbourhood store or for a quick snack of *chanko-nabe*. If you're feeling peckish yourself, *Tomoegata* restaurant (see p.196) is one of the best places to sample this body-building hot-pot.

See p.270 for more on sumo and buying tickets.

Ryōgoku's other draw is the colossal **Edo–Tokyo Museum** (Map 10, Ryōgoku inset; Tues–Sun 10am–6pm, Thurs & Fri till 8pm; ¥600; Ⓦ*www.edo-tokyo-museum.or.jp*) behind the sumo stadium, covering Tokyo's history from the days of the Tokugawa shogunate to postwar reconstruction. The exhibition starts with a bang on the sixth floor, as you cross a soaring Nihombashi, the "Bridge of Japan" (see p.60), over the roofs of famous Edo-period landmarks – a Kabuki theatre, a lord's residence and a Western-style office – on the main floor below. Tickets last a whole day and allow re-entry, and there are a couple of restaurants and a decent museum shop in the complex.

Fukagawa Edo Museum 深川江戸資料館

Map 2, I7. Daily 9.30am–5pm, closed 2nd & 4th Mon; ¥300.
Morishita or Monzen-nakachō Station.

Though it's a bit of a trek to get to (fifteen minutes' walk from the nearest station), anyone interested in Tokyo history shouldn't miss the captivating **Fukagawa Edo Museum** which re-creates a Shitamachi neighbourhood. The museum's one-room exhibition hall could be a film set for nineteenth-century Edo, and contains seven complete buildings – the homes of various artisans and labourers, a watchtower and storehouses. As you walk through the rooms furnished with the clutter of daily life, you're accompanied by the cries of street-vendors and birdsong, while the lighting shifts from dawn through to a soft dusk. It's worth investing in their English-language guidebook (¥500) before going in.

Museum of Contemporary Art 東京都現代美術館

Map 2, I8. Tues–Sun 10am–6pm, Fri till 9pm; ¥500; more for special exhibitions. Ⓣ5245-4111; Ⓦ*www.tef.or.jp/mot* Kiba Station.

Fifteen minutes' walk north from Kiba Station (on the Tōzai subway line), a severe glass and grey-steel building houses Tokyo's premier modern art venue, the **Museum of Contemporary Art**. Inside, vast chambers of white space provide the perfect setting for this choice collection of works by Japanese and Western artists, most notably Roy Lichtenstein, from post-1945 avant-garde, through the 1950s' abstract revolution to pop art, minimalism and beyond. Only 150 pieces are displayed at a time but you can view the rest of the collection (some 3500 items) in the audio-visual library. There are also bookshops, cafés, a well-stocked art library and an information centre. Note that the museum closes twice yearly for two weeks while the permanent exhibits are changed, so it's a good idea to phone before setting off.

Asakusa

Last stop on the Ginza line heading north, **ASAKUSA** is the site of Tokyo's most venerable Buddhist temple, **Sensō-ji**, whose towering worship hall attracts a continual throng of petitioners and tourists. Stalls outside peddle trinkets and keepsakes as they have done for centuries, while in the surrounding streets old-fashioned **craftshops** displaying exquisite hair combs or paper fans compete for attention with an array of restaurants, drinking holes and fast-food stands. There's an infectious, carnival atmosphere to Asakusa, which explodes each May when the Sanja Matsuri, one of Tokyo's biggest **festivals**, fills the streets with crowds. The area also hosts numerous smaller events – ask at the **information centre** (Map 5, G6; daily 10am–8pm), in front of Sensō-ji's main gate, if there's anything in the offing; they also offer Sunday afternoon walking tours of the area in English (1.30pm & 3pm; free).

SENSŌ-JI 浅草寺

Map 5, G3. Asakusa subway Station.

The magnificent temple of **Sensō-ji** (also known as Asakusa Kannon) was founded in the mid-seventh century to enshrine a tiny golden image of Kannon, the Goddess of Mercy, caught in the nets of two local fishermen. Most of the present buildings are postwar reconstructions, but

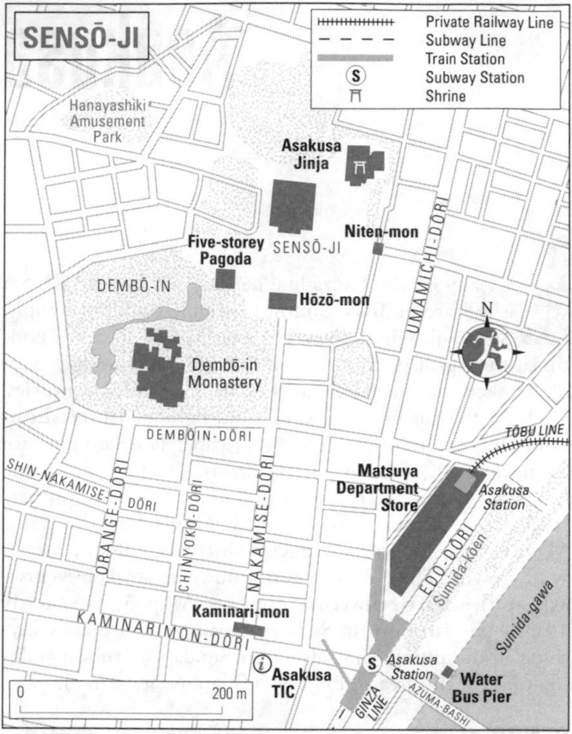

there's a great atmosphere as you draw near the main hall, with its sweeping, tiled roofs.

For more on religion in Japan see p.52.

The main approach starts under the great **Kaminari-mon**, or "Thunder Gate", named for its two vigorous

GETTING TO ASAKUSA BY RIVER

One of the best ways of getting to Asakusa is **by river**. Sightseeing ferries (known as *suijō*, "water buses") follow the Sumida-gawa north from Hama Rikyū Teien via Hinode Pier (see p.45 for details) to dock under Azuma-bashi, opposite Philippe Starck's eye-catching Flamme d'Or Building. Heading back down-river, departures are roughly every forty minutes (daily 9.50am–6.15pm, Sat & Sun last boat 6.55pm; ¥620 to Hama Rikyū Teien, ¥660 to Hinode Pier), though note that 3.25pm is the last departure stopping at Hama Rikyū Teien.

guardian gods of Thunder and Wind, and proceeds along **Nakamise-dōri**, a colourful parade of small shops packed with gaudy souvenirs, tiny traditional dolls, kimono accessories and *sembei* rice crackers in sweet-scented piles. Finally, a double-storied treasure gate, **Hōzō-mon**, sheltering even more imposing guardians, stands astride the entrance to the temple grounds.

Inside the compound, people cluster round a large, bronze incense bowl to waft pungent "breath of the gods" over themselves before approaching the stone-flagged prayer floor of Sensō-ji's **main hall**. Though there's nothing much to see inside – the little Kannon, said to be just 6cm tall, is hidden from view – the place is full of life, with coins rattling in the wooden coffers, swirling plumes of incense smoke and a constant bustle of people coming to pray or buy charms. Three times a day (6am, 10am & 2pm) drums echo through the hall as priests chant sutras beneath the altar's gilded canopy.

To the right of the main hall stands **Asakusa-jinja**, a seventeenth-century Shinto shrine dedicated to the two fishermen brothers who netted the Kannon image, and their overlord. In mid-May this is the focus of the tumultuous **Sanja Matsuri** (festival of the three guardians), when the shrine's three *mikoshi* (portable shrines), each weighing around 1000 kilos, join a seething procession through the streets of Asakusa. Nearby stands **Niten-mon**, an attractively aged gate spattered with pilgrims' votive papers. From here a road heads east to the Sumida-gawa and a narrow strip of park. A pleasant picnic-spot at any time of year, **Sumida-kōen** comes into its own during the cherry-blossom season and again in mid-summer, when the river provides a stage for one of Tokyo's great fireworks displays (last Sat of July).

WEST OF SENSŌ-JI

A reconstructed **five-storey pagoda** (Map 5, G3) lords it over the west side of Sensō-ji's courtyard. Walk west from here and you plunge into an area of cinemas, pachinko parlours and drinking dives known as **Rokku**, "Block 6". For a while in the mid-nineteenth and early twentieth centuries this was Tokyo's centre of popular culture, where movies, cabaret and striptease played to enthusiastic crowds. Today a handful of the old venues survive, most famously Rokku-za with its nightly strip show, and it's worth taking a wander through the district – if only to get a feel for the less sophisticated side of city life.

One block east of the Rox department store, look out for a giant baseball glove pinned to the front of a building – or listen for the crack of wood on leather. In a nation besotted with baseball but short on space, the answer is indoor batting cages, such as this **Rox Dome Sugo Batting Stadium** (Map 5, F4; daily 10am–2am; from ¥300 for 16 balls). The idea is to try and hit balls hurtling towards you at up to 130km per hour. It's tremendous fun, especially on weekdays when it's quieter, and a great way to work up a thirst.

From behind Rox the rather grandly named Rokku Broadway leads past betting shops and strip joints north into **Hisago-dōri**, a covered shopping street with a few interesting traditional stores. At the top end is **Gallery**

Takumi, a crafts gallery (Map 5, F1; daily 10am–8pm; free) where on weekends you can see different artisans at work, or on weekdays watch the video presentations; various items are on sale at their annex a couple of doors further up the same street (daily except Tues 10am–6pm).

Drum Museum and Kitchenware Town

Kokusai-dōri parallels Rokku Broadway to the west, and across from Rox, **Miyamoto Unosuke Shōten** (Map 5, D5; Wed–Mon 9am–6pm; ⓦ*www.miyamoto-unosuke.co.jp*) is easily identifiable from the elaborate *mikoshi* in the window. The shop is an Aladdin's cave of traditional Japanese percussion instruments and festival gear. Since 1861, however, the family passion has been drums, resulting in an impressive collection which now fills the fourth-floor **Drum Museum** (Map 5, E5; Wed–Sun 10am–5pm; ¥300). There's every type of percussion material here and, best of all, you are allowed to have a go on some: a red dot on the name card indicates those not to be touched; blue dots you can tap lightly, just with your hands; and the rest have the appropriate drumsticks ready waiting.

Continuing westwards from this corner, after a few blocks you hit another main road, Kappabashi-dōgu-gai. This is **Kitchenware Town** (Map 5, C5), a wholesale district where you can kit out a restaurant in approximately five hundred metres. You don't have to be a bulk-buyer, though, and this is a great place to pick up unusual souvenirs, such as the plastic food displayed outside restaurants to tempt customers. This practice dates from the nineteenth century, originally using wax, but came into its own about thirty years ago when foreign foods were being introduced to a puzzled Japanese market. The best examples are completely realistic; try Maizuru or Tokyo Biken for a particularly mouth-watering show.

ASAKUSA'S TRADITIONAL CRAFT SHOPS

Wander the arcades and backstreets of Asakusa and you'll come across all sorts of traditional **craft shops** which haven't changed much over the last hundred years. Below is just a selection of what's on offer.

Adachiya Nakamise-dōri (Map 5 inset, A4). Not traditional but in the spirit of Asakusa, this shop sells clothes for dogs.

Bengara 2-35-11 Asakusa (Map 5, H3). The best place to look for *noren*, the split curtain hanging outside every traditional shop or restaurant. Closed Thurs.

Bunsendō Nakamise-dōri (Map 5 inset, A4). A specialist in high-quality paper fans. Closed one Mon per month.

Fujiya 2-2-15 Asakusa (Map 5 inset, B2). Hand-printed cotton towels or *tenugui* designed by octogenarian Kawakami Keiji. Some Fujiya towels are now collectors' items. Closed Thurs.

Hyakusuke 2-2-14 Asakusa (Map 5 inset, B1). Geisha and Kabuki actors have been coming here for over a century to buy their cosmetics, including a skin cleanser made from powdered nightingales' droppings. Closed Tues.

Kurodaya 1-2-5 Asakusa (Map 5 inset, B6). Kurodaya has been selling items made of traditional *washi* paper, and woodblock prints, since 1856. Closed Mon.

Sukeroku Nakamise-dōri (Map 5 inset, B1). Pint-sized shop famous for its miniature, handmade plaster dolls in Edo-period costume.

Takahisa Ningyō Shin-Nakamise-dōri (Map 5, F5). Rows of richly decorated battledores (*hagoita*), traditionally used by young girls playing shuttlecock at New Year.

Tokiwadō 1-3 Asakusa (Map 5 inset, A6). Various types of *Kaminari okoshi* "thunder crackers" on sale beside Kaminarimon gate.

Yonoya 1-37-10 Asakusa (Map 5 inset, A3). Tokyo's finest hand-crafted boxwood combs and hair decorations. Closed Wed.

Ueno

Most people visit **UENO** for its **park** (kōen), which is one of Tokyo's largest open spaces and contains a host of good **museums**, as well as a few relics from a vast temple complex that once occupied this hilltop. After a stroll through the park, your first stop should be the prestigious **Tokyo National Museum**, which alone could easily fill a day, though there's also a very worthy **Science Museum** and the more lively **Museum of Western Art**. Save an hour for the endearing **Shitamachi Museum**, which harks back to Ueno's proletarian past.

Much of downtown Ueno has a rough-and-ready feel, especially round the station and the bustling **Ameyoko-chō market**, extending south under the train tracks. Further west, there's a more sedate atmosphere among the worshippers at **Yushima Tenjin** and at **Tokyo University**'s ivory towers.

UENO KŌEN 上野公園

Map 14, D7–F2. Ueno Station.

Ueno Kōen is cut through with wide avenues where families come to feed the pigeons at weekends, and where all Tokyo seems to flock during the cherry-blossom season in spring.

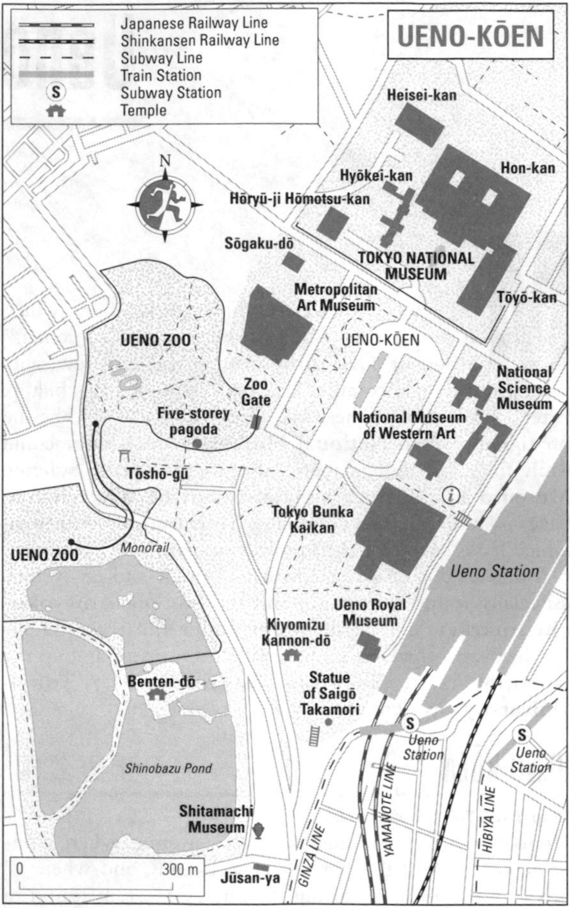
UENO-KŌEN
Japanese Railway Line
Shinkansen Railway Line
Subway Line
Train Station
Subway Station
Temple
N
Heisei-kan
Hon-kan
Hyōkei-kan
Hōryū-ji Hōmotsu-kan
Sōgaku-dō
TOKYO NATIONAL MUSEUM
Metropolitan Art Museum
Tōyō-kan
UENO ZOO
UENO-KŌEN
National Science Museum
Zoo Gate
Five-storey pagoda
National Museum of Western Art
Tōshō-gū
Tokyo Bunka Kaikan
UENO ZOO
Monorail
Ueno Station
Ueno Royal Museum
Kiyomizu Kannon-dō
Benten-dō
Statue of Saigō Takamori
Ueno Station
Ueno Station
Shinobazu Pond
YAMANOTE LINE
HIBIYA LINE
GINZA LINE
Shitamachi Museum
0
300 m
Jūsan-ya

THE BATTLE OF UENO

In 1624 the second shogun, Tokugawa Hidetada, chose Ueno hill for a magnificent temple, **Kan'ei-ji**, to protect his castle's northeast quarter. Eventually the temple incorporated the Tokugawa's mortuary temple, a shrine dedicated to the first shogun and the tombs of six of his successors. When the shogunate collapsed early in 1868, this was the natural place for Tokugawa loyalists to make their last stand, in what became the **Battle of Ueno**. Though the shogun had already resigned and Edo Castle surrendered peacefully, roughly two thousand rebel samurai occupied Kan'ei-ji until the Meiji army, superior in numbers and weaponry, attacked. Whether it was fires caused by the shelling or deliberate arson on either side, nearly all the temple buildings were destroyed.

From Ueno Station there are two routes into the park: "Park Exit" leads to the main, west gate beside the **information desk** (Map 14, F5; Tues–Sun 9am–5pm); while "Shinobazu Exit" brings you to the southern entrance. Taking the latter option, climb the steps up into the park, to find a bronze **statue** of **Saigō Takamori**, a thickset man in sandals and a summer kimono out walking his dog. Despite his casual appearance, this is the "Great Saigō", leader of the armies which helped bring Emperor Meiji to power. Though he later committed ritual suicide after an ill-fated rebellion, the popular general was soon rehabilitated – though without his military uniform.

Following the path northwards, the red-lacquered **Kiyomizu Kannon-dō** (Map 14, E6) comes into view on the left. Built in 1631, this temple is one of Kan'ei-ji's few remnants (see box above). It is dedicated to *Senju Kannon* (the 1000-armed Kannon), whose image is displayed only in February, but the second-rank *Kosodate Kannon* receives more visitors as the bodhisattva in charge of conception. Hopeful women leave dolls at her altar during the year, to be burnt at a rather sad ceremony held on September 25.

The temple faces west across a broad avenue lined with cherry trees towards **Shinobazu Pond**, once an inlet of Tokyo Bay, and now sheltering a permanent colony of wild black cormorants. A causeway leads across its reeds and lotus beds to an octagonal-roofed temple, **Benten-dō** (Map 14, D6). Inside the half-lit worship hall, Benzai-ten (the goddess of good fortune, water and music among other things) is just visible, her eight arms clutching holy weapons, while the ceiling sports a snarling dragon.

For more on Japanese shrines and temples, see p.52.

Heading back into the park on the tree-lined avenue, a tall grey *torii* and an avenue of 250 massive stone and copper lanterns mark the approach to **Tōshō-gū** (Map 14, C5; daily Jan, Feb & Oct 9am–5pm; March & Sept 9am–5.30pm; April–Aug 9am–6pm; Nov & Dec 9am–4.30pm; ¥200). This was the city's main shrine dedicated to the first shogun, Tokugawa Ieyasu, who died in 1616 and is buried in Nikkō (see p.307); the current building dates from 1651. For once it's possible to penetrate beyond the screened entrance. Inside, the worship hall's faded decorative work contrasts sharply with the gleaming black lacquer and gold of Ieyasu's shrine room behind. Before leaving, take a look at the Chinese-style front gate where two golden dragons carved in 1651 by Hidari Jingorō – he of Nikkō's sleeping cat (see p.308) – attract much attention; so realistic is the carving that, according to local legend, the pair sneak off at midnight to drink in Shinobazu Pond.

The seventeenth-century **five-storey pagoda** rising above the trees to the north of **Tōshō-gū** is now marooned inside **Ueno Zoo** (Tues–Sun 9.30am–5pm, last entry 4pm; ¥600). For a century-old zoo in the middle of a crowded city, this place is less depressing than might be feared, thanks mainly to its luxuriant vegetation. The prime attraction is the pandas, who snooze away on their concrete platform. As ever, weekends are the busiest time, and it's a good idea to bring a picnic since prices inside are expensive.

Tokyo National Museum 東京国立博物館

Map 14, F3. Tues–Sun 9am–5pm; April–Sept till 8pm on Friday; ¥420; ⓦ*www.tnm.go.jp* Ueno Station.

Dominating the northern reaches of Ueno Park, the **Tokyo National Museum** claims the world's largest collection of Japanese art, from ancient archeology to the modern day, as well as an extensive array of oriental antiquities. Displays are rotated every few months and, though the museum tends towards old-fashioned reverential dryness, there's always something worth going in for, particularly the special exhibitions.

It's best to start with the **Hon-kan**, the central building, built in monumental Japanese style. Here you'll find English-language booklets at the lobby information desk and a good museum shop in the basement. The Hon-kan presents the sweep of Japanese art, from Jōmon-period pots (pre-fourth century BC) to early-twentieth-century painting, via colourful Buddhist mandalas, exquisite lacquerware and even seventeenth-century Christian art from southern Japan.

In the building's northwest corner look out for a passage leading to the new **Heisei-kan** where the splendid Japanese Archeology Gallery contains important recent finds. Though it covers some of the same ground as the Hon-kan, modern presentation and lighting really bring the objects to life – the best are refreshingly simple and burst with energy. Highlights are the chunky, flame-shaped Jōmon pots and a collection of super-heated Sue stoneware, a technique introduced from Korea in the fifth century. Look out, too, for the bug-eyed, curvaceous clay *dogū* figures of the Jōmon period, and the funerary *haniwa* from the fourth to sixth centuries AD; these terra-cotta representations of houses, animals, musicians and stocky little warriors were placed on burial mounds to protect the deceased lord in the afterlife.

In the southwest corner of the compound, behind the copper-domed Hyōkei-kan, built in 1908 and now an Important Cultural Property in its own right, lurks the **Hōryū-ji Hōmotsu-kan**. This sleek new gallery contains a selection of priceless treasures donated over the centuries to Nara's famous Hōryū-ji temple. The most eye-catching display comprises 48 gilt-bronze Buddhist statues in various poses, each an island of light in the inky darkness.

The museum's final gallery is the **Tōyō-kan**, on the opposite side of the compound, housing a delightful hotch-potch of oriental antiquities where Javanese textiles and nineteenth-century Indian prints rub shoulders with Egyptian mummies and a wonderful collection of Southeast Asian bronze buddhas. The Chinese and, particularly, Korean collections are also interesting for their obvious parallels with the Japanese art seen earlier. If you've got the energy, it's well-worth taking a quick walk through, though there's frustratingly little English labelling.

National Science Museum 国立科学博物館

Map 14, F4. Tues–Sun 9am–4.30pm; ¥420; Ⓦ*www.kahaku.go.jp* Ueno Station.

A minute's walk from the National Museum, on the park's east side, the **National Science Museum** is easily identified by a life-size blue whale statue outside. Compared with Tokyo's other science museum (see p.51), this one has fewer interactive exhibits but a great deal more information, some of it in English, covering natural history as well as science and technology. Best is the Science Discovery Plaza, in the new building at the back, where pendulums, magnets, mirrors and hand-powered generators provide entertainment for the mainly school-age audience.

National Museum of Western Art 国立西洋美術館

Map 14, F5. Tues–Sun 9.30am–5pm; Friday till 8pm; ¥420; Ⓦ*www.nmwa.go.jp* Ueno Station.

Next stop south is the **National Museum of Western Art**, instantly recognizable from the Rodin statues populating the forecourt of Le Corbusier's gallery. It was erected in 1959 to house the mostly French Impressionist paintings left to the nation by Kawasaki shipping magnate Matsukata Kōjirō. Since then works by Rubens, Tintoretto, Max Ernst and Jackson Pollock have broadened the scope of this impressive collection.

Shitamachi Museum 下町風俗資料館

Map 14, D7. Tues–Sun 9.30am–4.30pm; ¥300. Ueno Station.

The last, but by no means the least, of Ueno's museums lies a few minutes' walk to the west in a distinctive, partly traditional-style building beside Shinobazu Pond. The **Shitamachi Museum** opened in 1980 to preserve something of the Shitamachi, the proletarian quarters of old Edo (see p.351) while the area was still within living memory. Downstairs, a reconstructed merchant's shop-house and a tenement row were familiar sights in early-1920s' Tokyo before the 1923 earthquake destroyed the greater part of

Shitamachi. Upstairs is devoted to rotating exhibitions focusing on articles of daily life, all of which have been donated by local residents. You can take your shoes off to explore the shop interiors, and handle most items. There's plenty of information in English, plus a well-produced museum booklet (¥400).

SOUTH OF UENO PARK

Map 14, E7–D9.

Ueno town centre lies to the south of the park and is a raw and lively mix of discount outlets, market streets, a sprinkling of upmarket stores and craft shops, and a warren of drinking clubs, "soaplands" (a euphemism for brothels) and restaurants.

The biggest draw for both bargain-hunters and sightseers is **Ameyoko** (Map 14, E7), a **market** area south of Ueno Station, which extends nearly half a kilometre along the elevated JR train lines, spilling down side-alleys and under the tracks. The name, an abbreviation of **Ameya Yoko chō** or "candy sellers' alley", refers to stalls peddling syrup-coated sweet potatoes here during the food shortages immediately after World War II. The district became famous for a black market which developed under the arches, reaching its peak in the early 1950s. These days the *yakuza* (professional criminal gangs) are less obvious, but Ameyoko-chō retains a flavour of its shady past: gruff men with sandpaper voices shout out their wares; stalls selling bulk foodstuffs, cheap shoes, clothes, jewellery and fish are all jumbled up, cheek by jowl, and under the arches a clutch of *yakitori* bars still tempt the market crowds.

Chūō-dōri, Ueno's main thoroughfare, runs parallel to the train tracks a couple of blocks further west. Its two major landmarks are **Matsuzakaya** (Map 14, D9), a 300-year-old department store, and a young fashion store called

AB-AB (pronounced *Abu-Abu*; Map 14, E7), up near Ueno Park. The blocks west of Chuō-dōri contain a seedy nightlife area, in the midst of which you'll find a number of traditional craftshops. **Jūsan-ya** (Map 14, D7), opposite the Shitamachi Museum, is probably the most famous; since 1736, successive generations have produced beautiful boxwood combs from this tiny workshop.

Yushima Tenjin 湯島神社

Map 14, B8. Yushima Station.

From the Matsuzakaya junction Kasuga-dōri heads west to **Yushima Tenjin** (also known as *Yushima-jinja*), a shrine dedicated to Tenjin, the god of scholarship. The best time to visit is in late February when the plum trees are in blossom and candidates for university entrance exams leave mountains of *ema* (wooden votive tablets) inscribed with their requirements.

Tokyo University 東京大学

Map 14, A7. Hongō-sanchōme Station.

The shrine stands a few minutes' walk south of the nation's top-ranking **Tokyo University**, whose graduates fill the corridors of power. Founded in 1869, Tōdai – as it's commonly known – occupies the former estate of the wealthy Maeda lords, though there's little sign of their mansion beyond a scummy pond and the one-storey, red-lacquer gate, **Aka-mon**, which forms the university's front, west entrance. The campus these days is a sleepy, decidedly unkempt place, but in 1968 it was the setting for student riots, partly in protest against the Vietnam War. The students' occupation of the main hall ended in January 1969, when over eight thousand police, four thousand canisters of tear gas and an array of water cannon finally prised them out after a two-day battle.

Ikebukuro and around

Northwest of central Tokyo, **IKEBUKURO** is dominated by two bewilderingly vast department stores glaring at each other from opposite sides of its equally confusing station. The western district, **Nishi-Ikebukuro**, is the more appealing for its bars and restaurants, as well as the attractive campus of **Rikkyō University**. East of the tracks, **Higashi-Ikebukuro** is the area's main shopping centre, with a reputation for discounted cameras and electronic goods to rival Akihabara (see p.289). Apart from a pretty tacky entertainment district, Higashi-Ikebukuro's only other draw is the monstrous Sunshine City, a sixty-storey building whose prime attraction is a museum of ancient oriental art. Ikebukuro has always been viewed as rather un-hip and downmarket, but there are signs among the trendy new fashion stores, clubs and restaurants that this is beginning to change.

East of Ikebukuro there are a couple of sights within easy reach of the Yamanote Line. **Rikugi-en** is one of the city's most attractive Edo-period gardens, while nearby **Sugamo** boasts the silver generation's very own shopping street and a temple with an interesting statue. From Sugamo it's a short walk to Kōshinzuka Station on the Toden Arakawa Line, where you can pick up a tram back to Higashi-Ikebukuro.

WEST TO RIKKYŌ UNIVERSITY 立教大学

Ikebukuro Station handles around one million passengers per day (second only to Shinjuku), and its warren of connecting passages, shopping arcades and countless exits are notoriously difficult to navigate. Things are even worse on the west side, where the helpfully colour-coded signs mutate to blue, indicating you are now in **Tōbu** territory. Tōbu is Japan's largest department store (Map 9, D4) and comprises three interconnected buildings, including the glass-fronted Metropolitan Plaza (Map 9, C5). There's an art museum and six floors of restaurants in the main building, plus five more in its Spice 2 annex.

The nearby **Metropolitan Art Space** (Map 9, C5) also belongs to the Tōbu empire. Though well known as a concert and theatre venue, the building's main claim to fame is its long escalator – best on the way down for a dizzying, ninety-second descent beneath the glass atrium.

Behind the Art Space, take any of the small roads heading west, through an area of lanes rich in restaurants and bars, and turn left along tree-lined Rikkyō-dōri to find a red-brick gateway on the left. This is the main entrance to **Rikkyō University** (Map 9, A4), which was founded in 1874 by an American Episcopalian missionary, Bishop Channing Moore Williams. Passing through the gateway will bring you to the old university courtyard, which has an Ivy League touch to its vine-covered halls and grassy quadrangle.

EAST IKEBUKURO 東池袋

Over on the **east side** of Ikebukuro Station, **Seibu** rules. This is the company's flagship store, the largest in the country until Tōbu outgrew it a few years back. Though the group has been retrenching in recent years, Seibu has a history of innovation and spotting new trends, being the first to target "office ladies" and other young women with money to burn. Apart from the main store, there's also Parco and Loft, Seibu offshoots specializing in fashion, household goods and music respectively.

You'll find restaurant listings for Ikebukuro on p.194.

Head east from Ikebukuro Station, and you can't miss the sixty-storey-high **Sunshine 60** (Map 9, H5). Just in front of it lurks the smaller but equally distinctive, metallic blue **Amlux** showroom (Map 9, G4; Tues–Sun 11am–8pm), Toyota's very own non-stop motor show. After taking in the high-tech architecture and moving wall of TV screens, you can try out the latest safety devices in the Safety Feeling Zone, visit the sensorama theatre and, last but not least, sit inside the latest models.

An underground passage leads from the Amlux basement into the Sunshine 60 tower, one of four buildings comprising the **Sunshine City** complex of shops, offices, exhibition space, hotel and cultural centres. The most interesting aspect of this much vaunted "city within a city" is that it stands on the site of old Tokyo Prison, where Japan's war criminals were incarcerated after 1945 and where the seven Class A criminals were hanged. The main reason for coming here is to visit the **Ancient Orient Museum** (Map 9, I5; daily 10am–5pm; ¥500), on the seventh floor of the Bunka Kaikan cultural centre, displaying archeological finds from the Middle East and Syria in particular. While there are the inevitable bits of old pot, the collection focuses on more accessible items such as statues, jewellery, icons and other works of art, including some superb Gandhara Buddhist statues from Pakistan and a charming, wide-eyed Mother Goddess made in Syria around 2000 BC.

RIKUGI-EN 六義園

Map 2, E2. Daily 9am–5pm; ¥300. Komagome Station.

Tokyo's best surviving example of a classical Edo period stroll-garden is **Rikugi-en**, with its entrance five minutes' walk south of Komagome Station on Hongō-dōri, taking a right turn one block before the next major junction.

In 1695 the fifth shogun granted one of his feudal lords, Yanagisawa Yoshiyasu, a tract of farmland to the north of Edo. Yanagisawa was both a perfectionist and a literary scholar: he took seven years to design his celebrated garden – with its 88 allusions to famous scenes, real and imaginary, from ancient Japanese poetry – and then named it Rikugi-en, "garden of the six principles of poetry", in reference to the rules for composing *waka* (poems of 31 syllables). In 1877, Iwasaki Yatarō, founder of Mitsubishi, bought the land and restored it as part of his luxury villa. The family donated the garden to Tokyo city authorities in 1938.

Few of the 88 landscapes have survived – the guide map issued at the entrance identifies a mere eighteen, but Rikugi-en still has a rhythm and beauty, kicking off with an ancient, spreading cherry tree, then slowly unfolding along paths that meander past secluded arbours and round the indented shoreline of an islet-speckled lake.

SUGAMO 巣鴨

Map 2, E2. Sugamo Station.

On the north side of **SUGAMO** JR Station a shopping street, Jizō-dōri, branches left off the main road, marked by an arch with orange characters. The street is nicknamed *obāchan no Harajuku* or "old ladies' Harajuku", in ironic reference to Tokyo's epicentre of young fashion. Jizō-dōri is, of course, anything but fashionable; shops here sell floral aprons, sensible shoes, long-johns and shopping trolleys, interspersed with speciality food stores, household products and pharmacies selling traditional and Western medicines.

This all arose because of a temple, **Kogan-ji**, 100m up on the right, dedicated to "thorn-removing" Togenuki Jizō, who provides relief from both physical pain and the metaphorical suffering of the soul. In case a prayer doesn't work, people also queue up in front of a small Kannon statue, known as the Migawari Kannon, tucked into a corner of the temple forecourt. Each person in turn pours water over the statue and wipes whatever part of its anatomy corresponds to their own ailment, thus transferring it to the Kannon – until recently people used brushes but now it's hand towels only as the poor goddess was being scrubbed away. Despite the sad undertones, there's a good atmosphere, enlivened by a number of quack doctors who set up stalls outside.

Jizō-dōri continues north as far as Kōshinzuka Station, less than ten minutes' walk from the temple, where you can pick up a **tram** on the **Toden Arakawa Line**. Early-twentieth-century Tokyo boasted a number of tram services, of which only this twelve-kilometre stretch remains, running north from Waseda to Asukayama and then looping south-east to the suburbs above Ueno. The most interesting section lies between Kōshinzuka and Higashi-Ikebukuro, rocking and rolling along narrow streets and through Tokyo backyards; tickets are ¥160 and it's pay as you enter, with station signs and announcements in English.

Shinjuku

The mini-city of **SHINJUKU**, with its skyscrapers, swanky department stores and seedy red-light district, is the modern heart of Tokyo and one area you can't afford to miss. From the love hotels and hostess bars of Kabukichō on the east side, together with the tiny, no-frills bars of the Golden Gai and Shomben Yokochō (piss alley), to the shop-till-you-drop department stores and high-tech towers, a day and evening spent in Shinjuku will show you Tokyo at its best and worst.

Shinjuku lies some 4km west of the Imperial Palace, and is split in two by a thick band of railway tracks. The western half, **Nishi-Shinjuku**, with its soaring skyscrapers, is a showcase for contemporary architecture; the raunchier eastern side, **Higashi-Shinjuku**, is a non-stop red-light and shopping district, and the inspiration for Ridley Scott's Bladerunner. Also on the east is one of Tokyo's most attractive parks, **Shinjuku Gyoen**, a spacious combination of Japanese, English and French landscape gardens.

NISHI SHINJUKU 西新宿

If there is one area of Tokyo in which you can fully appreciate Japan's monumental wealth and economic power it is

Nishi Shinjuku, a plantation of dizzying skyscrapers where there was once a water reservoir. In themselves, few of these towers of glass, concrete and steel are worth spending much time exploring, though most of them have free observation rooms on their upper floors, and a wide selection of restaurants and bars with a view. Collectively, however, their impact is striking, mainly because their scale, coupled with the spacious streets surrounding them, is so unusual for Tokyo.

To reach this area, head for the west exit at Shinjuku Station and take the pedestrian tunnel beyond the two fountains in the sunken plaza in front of the Odakyū department store. Alternatively, get off the subway Toei Line no 12 at Tochōmae Station, right beside the Tokyo Metropolitan Government Building.

It's easy to get hopelessly lost in Shinjuku Station, a messy combination of three terminals (the main JR station, the mini-city's apex, and the Keiō and Odakyū stations, beside their respective department stores on the station's west side), connecting subway lines and an incredible sixty exits. There's also the separate Seibu Shinjuku Station, northeast of the JR station. The best advice is to head for street level and get your bearings from the skyscrapers to the west.

Tokyo Metropolitan Government Building 東京都庁

Map 13, A6. Tochōmae Station.

At the end of Chūō-dōri, the main road running through Nishi Shinjuku, you can't miss the **Tokyo Metropolitan Government Building** (TMGB), a 400,000-square-metre complex designed by top Tokyo architect, **Tange Kenzō** (see box, p.100). Thirteen thousand city bureaucrats come here to work each day, and the entire complex – which includes twin 48-storey towers, an adjacent tower block, the Metropolitan Assembly Hall (where the city's councillors meet) and a sweeping, statue-lined and colonnaded plaza – feels a bit like Gotham City. Tange was actually aiming to evoke Notre Dame in Paris, and there's certainly something of that grand cathedral's design present in the shape of the twin towers. But the building's real triumph is that it is unmistakably Japanese; the dense criss-cross pattern of its glass and granite facade is reminiscent of both traditional architecture and the circuitry of an enormous computer chip.

Both twin towers have free observation rooms on their 45th floors (Mon–Fri 9.30am–5pm, Sat & Sun 9.30am–7pm). It's worth timing your visit for dusk, so you can see the multicoloured lights of Shinjuku spark and fizzle into action as the setting sun turns the sky a deep, photochemical orange. The TMGB also has some inexpensive cafés on its 32nd floor, and there are others on the ground floor of the Metropolitan Assembly Hall.

Shinjuku Park Tower and around 新宿パークタワー

Behind the TMGB, on the south side of a dusty park, is **Shinjuku Park Tower** (Map 13, B7), another building on which Tange's modernist style is confidently written. The chic credentials of this complex of three linked towers, all topped with glass pyramids, are vouched for by the presence of the luxurious *Park Hyatt Hotel* (which occupies the building's loftiest floors), the Conran Shop, and the excellent **Living Design Centre Ozae** (Mon, Tues & Thurs–Sun 10.30am–6.30pm; entrance fee varies with exhibition), a museum specializing in interior design, with regularly changing exhibitions by both Japanese and

MODERN ARCHITECTURE IN TOKYO

Though few locals would see the devastation wrought by earthquakes and World War II as a blessing, it has given Tokyo the opportunity to re-create itself architecturally. This opportunity has often been squandered through construction of claustrophobic masses of grey concrete, steel and glass, and yet the array of **modern architecture** is frequently dazzling, and constitutes the most enduring legacy of the bubble years of the late 1980s when Tokyo had the cash, technical know-how and gung-ho planning laws to give architects a blank canvas.

Japan's top post-war architect **Tange Kenzō** has done more than most to define Tokyo's eclectic style – his monumental Tokyo Metropolitan Government Building (see above) in Shinjuku has been described as the last great edifice of post modernism, though some would argue that he has gone one step further with the other-worldly Fuji TV building in Ōdaiba (see p.140). The 1964 Olympics' National Yoyogi Stadium and United Nations University are other structures in Tange's Tokyo canon.

Andō Tadao, former boxer, self-taught architect and recipient of the UK Royal Gold Medal for architecture in 1997, also has buildings in Tokyo; the Collezione building, close to Omotesandō in Harajuku, is a good example of his liking for rough concrete and bold structural forms. Andō's best work, however, such as Ōsaka's Church of Light, the Literature Museum in Himeji and the contemporary art museum Benesse House on Naoshima, can be seen around his hometown of Ōsaka.

Other notable Japanese architects who made their mark in the 1980s are **Maki Fumihiko**, whose work includes the futur-

Western designers. There's a regular free shuttle bus that runs from beside Sanwa Bank opposite the Odakyū department store to the south side of the Tower.

istic Tokyo Metropolitan Gymnasium in Sendagaya, the Spiral Building near Omotesandō, with its deliberately fragmented facade, and the ambitious Hillside Terrace in ritzy Daikenyama, a complex of homes, offices and shops developed over a 23 year period; **Arata Isozaki**'s Ochanomizu Square Building, just north of the Imperial Palace, is a good example of how old and new architecture can be successfully combined; and **Rokkaku Kijo**'s Tokyo Budōkan, the martial arts mecca, visibly takes its inspiration from traditional Japanese art – in this case, paintings of overlapping mountains fading into the mists.

Many top foreign architects have used Tokyo as a canvas on which to work out their most extravagant designs: in Asakusa, look for **Philippe Starck**'s Super Dry Hall, with its enigmatic "golden turd" on the roof; and **Sir Norman Foster**'s Century Tower at Ochanomizu, which incorporates the vernacular design of the *torii*, ten of which appear to be piled on top of each other on the building's facade. Light floods into the soaring glass hall of **Rafael Viñoly**'s Tokyo International Forum in Yūrakuchō, while **Sir Richard Rogers**' Kabukichō Building, swathed in a framework of stainless-steel rods, is hidden on a Shinjuku side street.

If you want to spend a day checking out some of these buildings, apart from Shinjuku, go out to Ōdaiba (p.135) or walk from Sendagaya Station along Gaien-nishi-dōri to Aoyama-dōri, turn right and continue to the crossing with Omotesandō, where you can either continue down to Shibuya or turn right and walk towards Harajuku. Either way, you'll pass many of the best examples of modern Tokyo architecture. Recommended to take with you is Noriyuki Tajima's *Tokyo: A Guide to Recent Architecture*, an illustrated pocket-sized guidebook.

A ten-minute walk west of the tower, and connected to Hatsudai Station on the Keiō Line, is **Tokyo Opera City** which, apart from its concert and recital halls (see p.244), has 54 floors of offices, shops and restaurants. On the fourth floor of this 234-metre-high tower is the **NTT Intercommunication Centre** (Tues–Sun 10am–6pm, Fri till 9pm; ¥800), the most far-out interactive exhibition space in Tokyo. Displays of high-tech art in the past have included a soundproof room where you can listen to your own heart beat, light-sensitive robots you control with your brain waves, and an installation of juggling wire figures, which look like 3D computer images. There's also an electronic library with Internet terminals, and an Internet café.

Behind Tokyo Opera City is the **New National Theatre**, an ambitious complex of three performing arts auditoria which opened in October 1997.

Shomben Yokochō しょんべん横丁

Returning to Shinjuku Station, in the blocks between the Keiō department store and the *Keiō Plaza Hotel*, you'll find the long-distance bus station, the main post office and branches of top camera retailers, Yodobashi and Sakuraya, selling the latest photographic gizmos at keen prices. Squashed up against the railway tracks running north from the Odakyū department store are the narrow alleyways of the **Shomben Yokochō** (Map 13, E3), a cramped, four-block neighbourhood of ramshackle mini-bars and restaurants. Although its name means "**piss alley**", don't be put off exploring this atmospheric quarter – you're less likely to get ripped off for a drink here than in the similar Golden Gai district of Kabukichō. A pedestrian tunnel at the southern end of the alleys, just to the right of the cheap clothes outlets, provides a short cut to the east side of Shinjuku Station and Studio Alta.

For places to eat in Shinjuku see p.165, for places to drink see p.202.

EAST SHINJUKU 東新宿

Some days it seems as if all of Tokyo is waiting at Shinjuku's favourite meeting spot, beneath the huge TV screen on the **Studio Alta** building (Map 13, F3). It's worth bearing this in mind if you arrange to meet anyone here – a better option is the plaza opposite Studio Alta, from where you can fully soak up the supercharged atmosphere, especially at night, when everything is ablaze with neon. To the southeast of here is **Shinjuku-dōri**, where the upmarket shops include **Isetan**, with its mouth-watering food halls in the basement, a wide range of restaurants on the top floor and an art gallery which frequently holds good exhibitions (check local English-language newspapers and magazines for details).

Kabukichō and around 歌舞伎町

Directly to the north of Studio Alta, across the wide boulevard of Yasukuni-dōri, lies the red-light district of **Kabukichō**. The heart of the area is the **Koma Theatre** (Map 13, G2), where modern Japanese musicals and samurai dramas are performed. In front is a tatty plaza lined with cinemas and radiating streets packed with bars and restaurants. Stray a block or so further north and you'll find yourself in the raunchier side of Kabukichō, where strip shows and hostess bars are crammed in the narrow streets. There's a good chance of spotting members of the *yakuza* crime syndicates here – the punch-perm hairdos and 1970s-style clobber are giveaway signs – but the overall atmosphere of Kabukichō is not unlike London's Soho, where the porn and crime underworld nestles unthreateningly beside less salacious entertainment.

Local shopkeepers come to pray for business success at the attractive local shrine, **Hanazono-jinja** (Map 13, H3), one block east of Kabukichō. The shrine predates the founding of Edo, but the current granite and vermilion buildings are modern re-creations. Come here at night, when spotlights give the shrine a magical ambience.

From here, you're well poised to take a stroll through the **Golden Gai**, the low-rent drinking quarter where intellectuals and artists have rubbed shoulders with Kabukichō's demimonde since the war. In this compact grid of streets there are around two hundred **bars**, many of them quirkily decorated, virtually all no larger than broom cupboards and universally presided over by no-nonsense mama-sans. You probably won't want to stop for a drink; at most only regulars are welcome, and many will fleece you rotten. In recent years, the cinderblock buildings have been under threat from both property redevelopers and their own fifty-year-old collapse-by date: catch it while it lasts, since it is among Tokyo's fast-disappearing links with its raffish past.

Takashimaya Times Square and around

Map 13, G7. Shinjuku Station.

A sharp contrast to the Golden Gai is provided by **Takashimaya Times Square**, a sleek new shopping and entertainment complex near the Shin-Minami ("new south") entrance to Shinjuku Station, and on the opposite side of the tracks, Odakyū's **Southern Tower** office, shopping, dining and hotel development. Inside Times Square, you'll find branches of the Takashimaya department store, interior design and handicrafts superstore Tōkyū Hands, and the vast, seven-floor Kinokuniya bookstore. There's also **Shinjuku Joypolis** (daily 10am–11.15pm; ¥300), a high-tech amusement park packed with Sega virtual-reality rides and such like, and **Tokyo IMAX Theatre** (¥1300) which screens 3D films on its six-storey-high cinema screen – both good places to keep kids occupied if you want to go shopping.

Shinjuku Gyoen and around 新宿御苑

Map 13, I7. **Gardens** Tues–Sun 9am–4.30pm, last entry 4pm; ¥200. **Greenhouse** 11am–3.30pm; free. **Tea house** 10am–4pm; ¥700. Shinjuku-Gyoen-mae Station.

Five minutes' walk southeast of Takashimaya Times Square, near the Shinjuku-Gyoen-mae subway station, is the main entrance to **Shinjuku Gyoen**, possibly Tokyo's most beautiful **garden**. The grounds, which once held the mansion of Lord Naito, the *daimyō* of Tsuruga, on the Edo coast, became the property of the imperial household in 1868, and the 150-acre park was opened to the public after World War II.

Apart from its sheer size, the park's main attraction is its imaginative design. The southern half is traditionally Japanese, with winding paths, stone lanterns, artificial hills and islands in ponds linked by zig-zag bridges. There's also the traditional **teahouse** *Rakūtei* where you can sample green tea and sweet cakes. At the northern end of the park are formal French-style gardens, with neat rows of tall birch trees and hedge-lined flowerbeds. The middle of the park is modelled on English landscape design, and on the eastern flank next to the large **greenhouse**, packed with sub-tropical vegetation and particularly cosy on a chilly winter's day, a nineteenth-century **Imperial wooden villa** is being reconstructed. In spring, the whole park bursts with pink and white cherry blossoms, while in early November, kaleidoscopic chrysanthemum displays and golden autumn leaves are the main attractions. There are several cafés within the gardens where you can grab a reasonable lunch for around ¥900, but it's much nicer to bring a picnic and relax in the tranquil surroundings. An alternative entrance to the gardens is through the western gate, a five-minute walk under and alongside the railway tracks from Sendagaya Station.

Walking back towards Shinjuku Station will take you past the **gay district** of Shinjuku Nichōme. During the day the area is inconspicuous, but come nightfall the bars spring into action, catering to every imaginable sexual orientation. Most bars are strictly Japanese only (or charge prices only the Japanese will pay) – but a few welcome *gaijin*. Close by is **Taisō-ji**, a temple founded in 1668, which has the city's largest wooden statue of Yama, the King of Hell. The statue is in the temple building next to a large copper Buddha dressed in a red bib and cap. You have to press a button to illuminate the 5.5-metre Yama, whose fiercesome expression is difficult to take seriously once you've spotted the offerings at his feet – a few tins of fruit are the norm.

See p.245 for gay listings in Tokyo.

Harajuku and Aoyama

South of Shinjuku are the super-chic residential, shopping and entertainment districts of **Harajuku** and **Aoyama**, a collective showcase for contemporary Tokyo fashion and style. Consumer culture reigns supreme in these streets packed with smart cafés, designer boutiques and hip young spenders in search of the latest labels. But the best reasons for coming here are to visit Aoyama's historic cemetery and the verdant grounds of the city's most venerable shrine, **Meiji-jingū**. Neighbouring **Yoyogi Kōen** was the focus of the 1964 Olympics and several of the stadia surrounding it are a legacy of that event, as is the cosmopolitan atmosphere that pervades the designer shops and cafés along elegant **Omotesandō**, a tree-lined boulevard often referred to as Tokyo's Champs Elysées.

MEIJI-JINGŪ 明治神宮

Map 8, A1. Meiji-Jingūmae and Harajuku stations.

The Emperor Meiji, during whose reign Japan began to modernize, was such an important figure that immediately

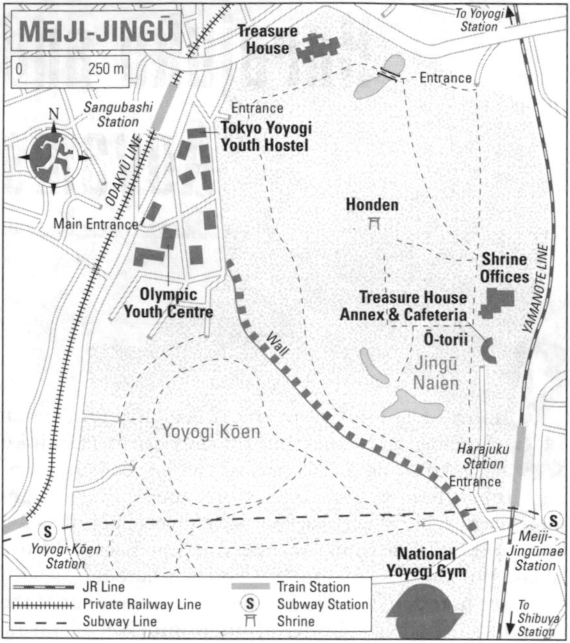

after his death in 1912 work began on his grand shrine, **Meiji-jingū**. Together with the neighbouring shrines to General Nogi and Admiral Togo (see p.113), Meiji-jingū was created as a symbol of imperial power and was rebuilt in 1958 after being destroyed during World War II. Not only is this Tokyo's most important Shinto holy place, it is also a precious oasis of calm and greenery and an escape from the dust and grime of the city streets.

The shrine is split into two sections: the **Outer Garden**, between Sendagaya and Shinanomachi stations, contains the

FESTIVALS AT MEIJI-JINGŪ

Meiji-jingū is the focus of several important **festivals** during the year, the most popular of which is **Hatsumode** (first visit of the year to a shrine), held on January 1 and attracting three million visitors – traffic lights have to be operated within the shrine grounds to control the crowds on the day.

More entertaining is **Seijin-no-hi** (Adults' Day) on January 15; on this day, 20-year-olds attend the shrine, the women often dressed in elaborate, long-sleeved kimono, with fur stoles wrapped around their necks. The gravel approach is lined with ice sculptures and there is a colourful display of traditional archery by costumed archers.

Between April 29 and May 3 and on November 1 and 3, **bugaku** (court music and dances) are performed on a stage erected in the shrine's main courtyard, while **Shichi-go-san-no-hi** (Seven-five-three Day) on November 15 provides an opportunity to see children of these ages dressed in delightful mini-kimonos.

Meiji Memorial Picture Gallery and several sporting arenas, including the National Stadium and Jingū Baseball Stadium; the more important **Inner Garden**, next to Harajuku Station, includes the emperor's shrine, his empress Shōken's iris gardens, the imperial couple's Treasure House and extensive wooded grounds. Apart from during the festivals (see box), Meiji-jingū is best visited mid-week, when its calm serenity can be appreciated without the crowds.

For more on Emperor Meiji, see p.352.

The Outer Garden and around 神宮外苑

Map 2, C8. Gaienmae Station.

The highlight of the Outer Garden is the **Meiji Memorial Picture Gallery** (daily 9am–5pm; ¥300), which stands at the northern end of the long, gingko-tree lined road running alongside the rugby and baseball stadiums. From the outside, the gallery resembles the National Diet building (see p.56), with its stern, European-style exterior. Inside, the entrance hall, liberally decorated with marble, soars up to a central dome, on either side of which are halls containing forty large paintings which tell the life story of the Emperor Meiji – more interesting for the depiction of Japan emerging from its feudal past than for their artistic merits.

To one side of the gallery looms the 75,000-seater **National Stadium**, Japan's largest sporting arena, built for the 1964 Olympics. Today it regularly plays host to J-League football games and other major sporting events.

West of the stadium, and best viewed from outside Sendagaya Station, is the **Tokyo Metropolitan Gymnasium**. At first glance the building looks like a giant alien spacecraft, but on closer examination it's clear that the inspiration is a traditional samurai helmet. The corrugated stainless-steel-roofed building houses the main sports arena, while in the block to the right are public swimming pools and a subterranean gym, the latter crowned with a glass pyramid roof (entrance to the swimming pool, which includes a heated deck, is ¥450).

The Inner Garden 神宮内苑

Map 8, A1. Jingū Naien daily 8.30am–5pm; ¥500. Treasure House daily Jan–March & Dec 9.30am–3.30pm, April–Nov 8.30am–4pm; ¥500 entry to both buildings. Harajuku or Meiji-jingūmae Station.

The most impressive approach to the Inner Garden is through the southern gate next to Harajuku's toy-town-style station building, complete with mock-Tudor clock tower. From here a wide gravel path runs through densely forested grounds to the twelve-metre-high **Ō-torii**, made from 1500-year-old cypress pine trees from Taiwan. Just before the gate, on the right, is the **Bunkakan**, a new complex housing a restaurant, café, gift shop and the generally uninteresting annex of the **Treasure House**; this is where you'll alight from your bus if you visit on an organised tour. To left of the Ō-torii is the entrance to the **Jingū Naien**, a traditional garden said to have been designed by the Emperor Meiji for his wife. The garden is at its most beautiful in June, when over one hundred varieties of irises, the Empress's favourite flowers, pepper the lush greenery with their purple and white blooms.

Returning to the garden's entrance, the gravel path turns right and passes through a second wooden *torii*, Kita-mon (north gate) leading to the impressive *honden* (central hall). With their Japanese cypress wood and green copper roofs, these buildings are a fine example of how Shinto architecture can blend seamlessly with nature. There are exits from the courtyard on its eastern and western flanks and following either of the paths northwards through the woods will eventually lead to the grassy slopes and pond before the main **Treasure House**. Don't bother entering; the contents of this museum are no more thrilling than the lumpen grey concrete building that houses them.

YOYOGI KŌEN AND AROUND 代々木公園

Map 8, A2. Harajuku or Meiji-jingūmae Station.

Apart from the wooded grounds of Meiji-jingū, **Harajuku** is also blessed with Tokyo's largest park, **Yoyogi Kōen**, a favourite spot for joggers and bonneted groups of kindergarten kids with their minders. The park was once an imperial army training ground and after World War II became known as "Washington Heights" as it was used to house US military personnel. In 1964, the land was used for the Olympic athletes' village, after which it became Yoyogi Kōen. Two of the stadia built for the Olympics remain the area's most famous architectural features. The main building of Tange Kenzō's **Yoyogi National Stadium**, which resembles Noah's ark, has a steel suspension roof that was a structural engineering marvel at the time. Inside are a swimming pool and skating rink (Mon–Sat noon–8pm, Sun 10am–6pm; ¥900). The smaller stadium, used for basketball, looks like the sharp end of a giant swirling seashell.

For more on the 1964 Olympic Games, see p.354.

The road that separates the stadia from the park, Inogashira-dōri, used to be closed every Sunday to allow bands to play and people to dance in the street. It became known as "**Din Alley**", and was one of Tokyo's highlights – a raucous and invigorating display of youth culture and general joie de vivre by a colourful cast of hippies, punks, rockabillies, grunge artists and plain weirdos. However, in 1996 the local authorities stopped the bands and re-opened the road to Sunday traffic (although connecting Omotesandō remains a pedestrian-only thoroughfare from 1pm to 5pm). Clusters of punky teenagers, dressed as their favourite pop idols, still hang out in groups beside the station, but the quiff-haired bikers jitterbugging around their Harley Davidsons at the entrance to Yoyogi Kōen, and a couple of guitarists on the bridge over the railway tracks, are the lone guardians of the anarchic flame.

OMOTESANDŌ 表参道

Harajuku's most elegant boulevard, the elm-lined **Omotesandō**, leads from the entrance to Meiji-jingū to the cluster of contemporary designer boutiques on the other side of Aoyama-dōri. Dense networks of streets stretch out on either side, packed with funky little shops, restaurants and bars. The most famous street is **Takeshita-dōri**, whose hungry mouth gobbles up teenage fashion victims as they swarm out of the north exit of Harajuku Station, and spits them out the other end on Meiji-dōri minus their cash. The shops sell every kind of tat imaginable, are hugely enjoyable to root around and provide a window on Japanese teen fashion. On Sundays the crush of bodies on the street is akin to that on the Yamanote line at rush hour.

Details on serious shopping in Tokyo are on pp.274-292.

Serious bargain-hunters shouldn't miss out on the outdoor antiques market held on the first and fourth Sundays of each month in the precincts of the neighbouring **Tōgō-jinja**. The market sells everything from fine *tansu* (traditional Japanese chests) to old kimono and crockery, but you need to get there early in the morning if you hope to snag any bargains. The **shrine** itself is dedicated to Admiral Tōgō Heihachiro, who led the victorious Japanese fleet against the Russians in the Russo-Japanese War of 1904–5.

Ōta Memorial Museum of Art 太田記念美術館

Map 8, B2. Tues–Sun 10.30am–5pm; ¥500. Meiji-jingūmae Station.
Walking back towards the crossing with Omotesandō, keep

an eye out for Laforet, a trendy boutique complex, behind which is the excellent **Ōta Memorial Museum of Art**. You'll have to leave your shoes in the lockers and put on a pair of slippers to wander the small galleries on two levels featuring *ukiyo-e* prints and paintings, which belonged to the late Ota Seizo, former chairman of the Toho Life Insurance Company. The art displayed comes from a collection of 12,000 pieces, which includes masterpieces by Utamaro, Hokusai and Hiroshige.

Returning to Omotesandō and heading east, you'll pass Kiddy Land, Harajuku's premier toy store where kids line up well before the opening hours to purchase the latest gimmick, and the Oriental Bazaar, a Chinese-style building packed with souvenirs. Opposite stand the ivy-covered **Aoyama Apartments**, built in 1925 as an experiment in modern living. Although many have been taken over by young fashion designers and artists, adding a bohemian flavour to the road, it's likely that this key area of real estate will soon fall to the developers' wrecking ball.

Nezu Museum of Art 根津美術館

Map 8, H6. Tues–Sun 9.30am–4.30pm; ¥1000. Omotesandō Station.

As it crosses Aoyama-dōri, Omotesandō narrows and develops into a street of swanky designer-label boutiques such as Comme des Garçons, Issey Miyake, Yohji Yamamoto and Calvin Klein. At the T-junction, just beyond the Andō Tadao-designed Collezione building (see box, p.100), turn right for the entrances to the **Nezu Museum of Art.** The rather steep entrance charge makes this small museum a bit of a luxury, but it does have a classy collection of oriental art, including many national treasures. The best time to visit is the ten-day period at the end of April and beginning of May, when two exquisite screen paintings of irises are displayed. Otherwise, the museum's nicest feature is its garden, which slopes gently away around an ornamental pond and features several traditional teahouses.

AOYAMA REIEN AND AROUND 青山霊園

Turning left at the end of Omotesandō, the road leads around into Tokyo's most important **cemetery**, officially entitled Aoyama Reien, but generally known as **Aoyama Botchi** (Map 8, I3). Everyone who was anyone, even Hachikō the faithful dog (see p.119), is buried here, and the graves, many decorated with elaborate calligraphy, are fascinating in their own right. Look out for the section where foreigners are buried; their tombstones provide a history of early *gaijin* involvement in Japan. That such an extensive slice of prime central Tokyo real estate, graveyard or not, has survived the developers' clutches for so long is nothing short of a miracle – perhaps it's because of Aoyama Botchi's splendid avenues of cherry trees, which many locals enjoy partying under during the *hanami* season.

Returning to Aoyama-dōri from the main entrance to the graveyard, the nearest subway station is Gaienmae. Five minutes' walk west, on the second floor of the Plaza 246 Building, diagonally opposite from Aoyama Bell Commons shopping centre, is the **Japan Traditional Crafts Centre** (daily except Thurs 10am–6pm; free; Map 8, G2), a display of arts and crafts from all over the country, including lacquerware, ceramics, dolls and handmade paper. Many of the items are for sale, there's an information desk where the attendants speak English, and a small library with English-language books on the traditional arts.

Continuing west along Aoyama-dōri, past the crossing with Omotesandō, you'll pass on your left the **Spiral Building** (Map 8, E5), which includes a gallery, a couple of restaurants and a trendy cards shop. The interior, with its sweeping, seemingly free-standing ramp walkway, is worth a look. On the opposite side of the street is Kinokuniya, supermarket to the smart set, and, closer to Shibuya, the funky **National Children's Castle** (Tues–Fri 12.30–5.30pm; Sat, Sun & hols 10am–5pm; ¥500), a large children's playground featuring a pool, roof-top cycle track, jungle gym, video and computer games room, and a small hotel. If you're looking for more distractions for the kids there are other options in nearby Shibuya (see opposite).

Shibuya

Immediately south of Harajuku, is **SHIBUYA**, birthplace of a million and one consumer crazes, where teens and twentysomethings throng **Centre Gai**, the shopping precinct that splits the district's rival department store groups: Tōkyū and Seibu. These companies took advantage of the real estate opportunities here in the wake of the 1923 earthquake to build their empires. Today, Tōkyū own the prime station site, the Mark City complex and the Bunkamura arts hall, while Seibu's outlets include the fashionable, youth-orientated Loft and Parco stores.

Frenetic as it is during the day, Shibuya is primarily an after-dark destination, when the neon signs of scores of restaurants, bars and cinemas fight it out with five-storey-tall TV screens for your attention.

In the plaza on the west side of Shibuya Station is the famous waiting spot of **Hachikō the dog** (see box, p.119), and the best place from which to take in the evening buzz. Head into the adjacent **Shibuya Mark City**, a new restaurant and hotel complex, for a bird's eye view of events below. Opposite, to the west, the 109 Building stands at the apex of **Dōgenzaka** and Bunkamura-dōri, the former leading up to one of Tokyo's most famous love hotel districts. This area is named after Owada Dōgen, a thirteenth-century highwayman who robbed travellers on their way through the then isolated valley.

BUNKAMURA AND AROUND

If you walk through Dōgenzaka, over the crest of the hill and past the On Air live music venues, you'll end up beside the main entrance to the **Bunkamura** (Map 12, A4), a complex with an excellent art gallery (displaying mainly Western art), a couple of cinemas, the two-thousand-seater Orchard Hall (home of the Tokyo Philharmonic Orchestra) and the Theatre Cocoon, which hosts some of the city's more avant-garde productions.

Walk a few minutes uphill behind the Bunkamura to reach the **Toguri Museum of Art** (Map 12, A4. Tues–Sun 9.30am–5.30pm; ¥1030), which displays Edo-era and Chinese Ming-dynasty (1368–1644) ceramics. Not to everyone's tastes, and on the pricey side, this small but exquisitely displayed collection, amassing some 6000 pieces, is worth the effort if you're interested in pottery. Carefully positioned mirrors enable you to inspect the fine detail of work on the underside of displayed plates and bowls, and there's a pretty garden beside the lobby which you can gaze out on while sipping tea or coffee.

Back down the hill, the knot of streets to the east of the **Tōkyū** department are a favourite stamping ground of Tokyo's hip young things. Emerging from the area's axis, Centre Gai, you're well poised to explore the **Seibu** stronghold (Map 12, D4). The main branch of the department store is at the base of Kōen-dori, close to the station, with the interior design specialist Loft and the clothes-dominated Parco complexes further up the hill. Behind Parco are the steps of Spain-zaka, with its emporiums of ephemera, and at the top of this narrow street are **Cinema Rise**, an imaginatively designed movie theatre which shows mainly

HACHIKŌ – THE TRUE STORY

The true story of **Hachikō** the dog proves that fame in Japan comes to those who wait. Every morning, the Akita pup faithfully accompanied his master Ueda Eisaburō, a professor in the department of agriculture at the Imperial University, to Shibuya Station, and would be back at the station in the evening to greet him.

In May 1925, Professor Ueda died while at work, but Hachikō continued to turn up every day at the station. By 1934, Hachikō had waited patiently for nine years and locals were so touched by the dog's devotion that a bronze statue was cast of him. In 1935, death finally reunited Hachikō with his master when he was buried with Ueda in Aoyama cemetery. The stuffed skin of the dog created a doppleganger Hachikō, which can be viewed at the National Science Museum (see p.88). During World War II, the original Hachikō statue was melted down for weapons, but was quickly reinstated beside the station in 1948. Today, this is the most famous rendezvous in all of Tokyo, though the throngs of people around the small statue and the rats that rummage through the rubbish in the surrounding bushes do not make it a particularly convivial place to hang out in.

foreign art-house films (see p.255) and **Tōkyū Hands**, a giant handicrafts store, good for unusual souvenirs.

TOBACCO AND SALT MUSEUM AND AROUND たばこと塩の博物館

Map 12, D1. Tues–Sun 10am–5.30pm; ¥100. Shibuya Station.

Walking back towards the upper slope of Kōen-dōri will bring you to the quirky **Tobacco and Salt Museum**. Take the lift at the side of the entrance desk to the fourth floor, which has temporary exhibitions, and work your way down past displays on the third, which focus on the harvesting of salt from the sea and other sources of sodium. The second floor has the tobacco exhibits, including two thousand packets from around the world, and dioramas showing how the leaves were prepared for smoking in the past. It's all in Japanese, and only on the ground floor are you allowed to light up your cigarettes.

If you've got kids in tow, there are a couple of places worth searching out close to the museum. Immediately east on Fire Street is **TEPCO Electric Energy Museum** (Thurs–Tues 10am–6pm; free), seven floors of exhibits relating to electricity. The English brochure says "Let's make friends with electricity" and TEPCO, Tokyo's power company, goes out of its way to convince you that this is possible. Look out for the laser that can etch your profile and name (in Japanese characters) on to a credit-card-sized piece of card. Nip under the railway tracks and across Meiji-dōri to reach **Tokyo Metropolitan Children's Hall** (daily 9am–5pm; free), an excellent government sponsored facility for kids, including a rooftop playground, library, music room and craft-making activities. In the evening, anyone can drop by here for the open air dance classes that take place in the courtyard outside.

NHK STUDIO PARK　ＮＨＫスタジオパーク

Map 2, A9. Daily 10am–6pm; closed third Mon of the month; ¥200. Shibuya Station.

At the top of Kōen-dōri, opposite the Shibuya Ward Office and Public Hall, is the NHK Broadcasting Centre, housing Japan's equivalent of the BBC. You can take an entertaining tour around part of the complex by visiting the NHK Studio Park. Although it's all in Japanese, much of the exhibition is interactive; you get to become a news reader and weather presenter and mess around on multi-media products. Try out the 3-D screen TV, but read the English instructions first on how to contort your body to get the desired effect.

JAPAN FOLK CRAFTS MUSEUM 日本民芸館

Map 2, A10. Tues–Sun 10am–5pm; ¥1000. Komaba-Tōdaimae Station.

A twenty-minute walk west of Dōgenzaka to Komaba-kōen, or two briefs stops from Shibuya on the Keiō Inokashira line to Komaba-Tōdaimae Station, brings you to the very impressive **Japan Folk Crafts Museum** (or Mingeikan). The visual pleasures of a visit to this excellent collection of textiles and ceramics begin even before you set foot in the handsome two-storey stone and stucco building; opposite is a nineteenth-century *nagayamon* (long gate house), transferred intact from Tochigi-ken. Inside, special exhibitions are mounted of these functional but beautiful objects, made by highly talented craftsmen; turn up Nov 23–Dec 3 for the annual new work competition and sale. There's a gift shop attached, which is a fine source of souvenirs.

Ebisu, Daikanyama, Meguro and Shinagawa

Up-and-coming **Ebisu**, just south of Shibuya, is currently bubbling with promise, as new shops, bars and clubs open their doors to a crowd hungry for somewhere different to go. Ebisu is also home to the excellent **Tokyo Metropolitan Photography Museum**. Neighbouring **Daikanyama**, a pleasant stroll uphill to the west, is one of Tokyo's classiest districts and a great place to chill out at a side-walk café or do a spot of window-shopping. Further south, **Meguro** has a couple of interesting museums, a splendid wedding hall, as well as the tranquil **National Park for Nature Study** and the serene gardens of **Happōen**. Heading east from here, towards the transport and hotel hub of **Shinagawa**, will bring you to the temple **Sengaku-ji**, a key location in Tokyo's bloodiest true-life samurai saga.

EBISU 恵比寿

There's a hip street vibe to **EBISU**, where new **bars and clubs** are opening up and pulling in party-goers bored with the Roppongi scene. The area is also making a bid to capture the daytime shopping crowd with the new **Atre** shopping centre, which towers above the station. To the south, and connected to the station by a long moving walkway, is **Yebisu Garden Place** (Map 6, E4), a huge shopping, office and entertainment complex on the site of the nineteenth-century brewery that once was the source of the area's fortunes and is still owned by Sapporo, one of the country's top four breweries.

Although Yebisu Garden Place, which includes the glitzy *Westin Hotel*, a 39-storey tower, cinema, performance hall and mock French chateau, was slated by professionals as an architectural disaster, it's worth visiting for two museums. On the eastern side of the complex, behind the Mitsukoshi department store, is the entertaining **Yebisu Beer Museum** (Tues–Sun 10am–6pm; free), which explains the history of beer in Japan and of the brewery that used to be on this site. Look out for the touch-screen video displays and a computer simulation, where one of the participants is chosen to be the leader of a virtual-reality tour around different aspects of the brewing process. There's also an opportunity to sample some of Sapporo's beers, at ¥200 for a small glass.

See p.219 for more information on drinking options in Ebisu.

Tokyo Metropolitan Museum of Photography 東京都写真美術館

Map 6, E4. Tues–Sun 10am-6pm; Thurs & Fri 10am–8pm; ¥500–1000 depending on the exhibition. Ebisu Station.

On the southwest side of Yebisu Garden Place is a second museum, the excellent **Tokyo Metropolitan Museum of Photography**. Here you'll find absorbing exhibits of major Japanese and Western photographers, along with study rooms and an experimental photography and imaging room. The museum has a policy of concentrating on one photographer at a time in its exhibitions, which allows you to see the artist's work develop and gain an understanding of the motivations behind it.

If you have time, head for the restaurants on the 38th and 39th floors of the **Yebisu Tower** next to the photography museum; you don't need to eat or drink here to enjoy the spectacular free views of the city.

DAIKANYAMA 代官山

A ten minute stroll west along Komazawa-dōri from Ebisu Station, or one stop from Shibuya on the Tōkyū Toyoko line, is **DAIKANYAMA**, home to some of the city's classiest homes, shops and watering holes. Hang out here a while and the village-like laid-back vibe becomes a refreshing break from the frenzy of nearby Shibuya. Daikanyama's contemporary style has been defined by the smart **Hillside Terrace** complex (map 6, A2), designed by Maki Fumihiko (see Modern Architecture box, p.100). Strung along leafy Kyū-yamate-dōri, the various stages of Hillside Terrace were developed over nearly a quarter century; head for the **Hillside Gallery** (Tues–Sun, 10am–5pm; free), opposite the Danish Embassy, to view interesting modern art exhibitions. Closer to the station is the smart new **Daikanyama Address** development (map 6, B2) where you'll find more groovy boutiques and ritzy restaurants and cafés beneath a couple of apartment towerblocks.

MEGURO 目黒

South of Ebisu, stylish **MEGURO** is mainly a residential area, but there are some sightseeing surprises to be found here, including a couple of good museums, a palace to nuptial bliss and a traditional garden with perhaps Tokyo's most adorable teahouse.

Meguro Gajōen 目黒牙城苑

Map 6, E7. Gallery Tues–Sun 10.30am–5.30pm; ¥500. Meguro Station.

A five-minute walk downhill west of the station, the towering complex of **Meguro Gajōen** replaces the original wedding hall built at the turn of the century and known as Ryugu-jō (fairytale dragon palace). Something of its fantastic nature remains in the many restored painted wooden carvings (huge *ukiyo-e*-style panoramas of kimonoed ladies and samurai warriors) and lacquer and mother-of-pearl inlaid scenes of flowers and birds, culled from the old building, which now decorate the enormous interior – big enough to host some twenty-odd weddings simultaneously. Visit on a weekend and the place buzzes with bridal parties. There's an expensive hotel, equally pricey restaurants (including a thatched farmhouse surrounded by a lush garden) and a good **gallery** with more prime examples of the art from the old wedding hall, plus special exhibitions.

Meguro Parasitological Museum 目黒寄生虫館

Map 6, C7. Tues–Sun 10am–5pm; free. Meguro Station.

Return to Meguro-dōri and walk west a few blocks across the Meguro-gawa and up the hill just beyond Yamate-dōri, to reach the quirky **Meguro Parasitological Museum**, founded in 1953 and the only museum in the world specializing in parasites. Two floors of exhibits display the dangers of creepy-crawlies in uncooked food, record-breaking tapeworms (one 8.8m long) pickled in jars, and some gruesome photographs of past victims, including one of a poor man whose swollen testicles scrape the ground. You can also pick up souvenir T-shirts, books and jewellery to amuse friends back home.

Tokyo Metropolitan Teien Art Museum 東京都庭園美術館

Map 6, F5. Daily 10am–6pm; closed 2nd and 4th Wed of the month; entrance fee depends on the exhibition. Shirokanedai Station.

Returning to the station and continuing east for five minutes down Meguro-dōri, past the raised Shuto Expressway, you'll come to the attractive **Tokyo Metropolitan Teien Art Museum**. This Art Deco building is the former home of Prince Asaka Yasuhiko, Emperor Hirohito's uncle, who lived in Paris for three years during the 1920s, where he developed a taste for the European style. Asaka commissioned Henri Rapin, a colleague of René Lalique, to design this villa, which was opened in 1933. It became a public museum with a regularly changing programme of art exhibitions in 1983 and is worth popping into for its gorgeous interior decoration and landscaped grounds which feature Japanese gardens, a pond and a tea ceremony house (entry to the gardens only is ¥200).

National Park for Nature Study 国立自然教育園

Map 6, F5. Tues–Sun 9am–4pm; May–Aug until 5pm; ¥200. Shirokanedai Station.

Next to the museum's grounds is the **National Park for Nature Study**. Covering about 200,000 square metres, the park is an attempt to preserve the original natural features of the Musashino Plain, before Edo was settled and developed into Tokyo. It partially succeeds – among the eight thousand trees in the park there are some that have been growing for five hundred years, frogs can be heard croaking amid the grass beside the marshy ponds, and the whole place is a bird-spotter's paradise. The best thing about the park is that entry at any one time is limited to three hundred people. You'll be given a ribbon to wear, which you have to return on leaving, making this one of the few public areas in Tokyo where you really can escape the crowds.

Happōen 八芳園

Map 2, D12. Daily 10am–5pm; free. Shirokanedai Station.

Five minutes' walk east of the National Park for Nature Study, turn off Meguro-dōri to reach the lovely **Happōen**. The garden's name means "beautiful from every angle" and, despite the addition of a modern wedding hall on one side, this is still true. A renowned adviser to the shoguns, Hikozaemon Okubo, lived here during the early seventeenth century, although most of the garden's design dates from the early twentieth century when a business tycoon bought up the land, built a classical Japanese villa (still standing by the garden's entrance) and gave it the name Happōen. Take a turn through its twisting pathways and you'll pass two-hundred-year-old bonsai trees, a stone lantern said to have been carved eight hundred years ago by the Heike warrior Taira-no Munekiyo, and a central pond. Nestling amid the trees is the delightful **teahouse** (daily 11am–5pm; ¥800), where ladies in kimono will serve you *matcha* and *okashi*. At weekends, especially, the whole scene is enlivened by many smartly dressed wedding parties, lining up for group photos against the verdant backdrop.

Sengaku-ji 泉岳寺

Map 2, D12. Sengaku Station.

From Happōen it's a ten-minute walk further east to **Sengaku-ji**, the temple where the graves of Asano Takumi (see box, below) and his 47 *rōnin* (masterless samurai) can be found. Most of the temple was destroyed during the war and has since been rebuilt, but a very striking gate, decorated with a metalwork dragon, remains, dating from 1836. In the temple grounds you'll see the statue and grave of Oishi Kuranosuke, the avenging leader of the 47 *rōnin*. A museum (daily 9am–4pm; ¥200) to the left of the main building contains the personal belongings of the *rōnin* and their master Asano, as well as a receipt for the severed head of Kira.

SHINAGAWA 品川

Immediately south of the temple is the transport and hotel hub of **SHINAGAWA**, the location of one of the original checkpoints on the Tōkaidō, the major highway into Edo during the reign of the shoguns. The volume of traffic passing through the Tōkaidō gate and the strictness of the guards in carrying out searches meant that Shinagawa developed, like Shinjuku, into a licensed district of lodgings and other services for travellers. Today the area has many good hotels, including several luxury complexes belonging to the Prince group (see Accommodation, p.163). In between the *Takanawa Prince* and the *New Takanawa Prince* hotels lie the

THE 47 *RŌNIN*

Celebrated in Kabuki and Bunraku plays, as well as on film, *Chushingura* is a true story of honour, revenge and loyalty which still retains its appeal for modern Japan.

In 1701, a young *daimyō*, Asano Takumi, became embroiled in an ultimately fatal argument at the shogun's court with his teacher and fellow lord Kira Yoshinaka. Asano had lost face in his performance of court rituals, and, blaming his mentor for his lax tuition, drew his sword within the castle walls and attacked Kira. Although Kira survived, the shogun, on hearing of this breach of etiquette, ordered Asano to commit *seppuku*, the traditional form of suicide, which he did.

Their lord having been disgraced, Asano's loyal retainers – the **rōnin**, or masterless samurai – vowed revenge. On December 14, 1702, the 47 *rōnin*, lead by Oishi Kuranosuke, Asano's faithful samurai, stormed Kira's villa, cut off his head and paraded it through Edo in triumph before placing it on Asano's grave in **Sengaku-ji**. Although their actions were in line with the samurai creed, the shogun had no option but to order the *rōnin's* deaths. All 47 committed *seppuku* on February 14, 1703, including Oishi's 15-year-old son. They were buried with Asano in Sengaku-ji and, today, their graves are still wreathed in the smoke from the bundles of incense placed by their gravestones.

former grounds and mansion of a member of the imperial family; the lovely traditional garden is still intact and can be viewed from either hotel.

Bayside Tokyo

It comes as something of a shock to many visitors (and some residents) that Tokyo is actually beside the sea. Yet many of the *ukiyo-e* masterpieces of Hokusai and Hiroshige depict waterside scenes of **Tokyo Bay**, and several of the city's prime attractions are to be found here. The teeming fish market of **Tsukiji**, to the east of Ginza, provides a rowdy, early-morning antidote to the serenity of the nearby traditional gardens at **Hama Rikyū** and Shiba (see p.68). Further east is **Tsukudashima**, a pocket of traditional wooden homes and shops dating back to the Edo period, while, to the south, across the Rainbow Bridge, lie the futuristic waterfront city and pleasure parks of **Odaiba**, built on vast islands of reclaimed land.

Beyond Odaiba on the north side of Tokyo Bay, older blocks of reclaimed land are given over to **Kasai Rinkai-kōen**, a seaside **park** boasting one of Tokyo's biggest aquariums and a birdwatching centre. Further east, the Cinderella spires of **Tokyo Disneyland** break the suburban skyline, and, though not everyone's cup of tea, this little bit of America can make a hugely enjoyable day out.

TSUKIJI 築地

Map 2, G9. Tsukiji Station.

A dawn visit to the vast **Tokyo Central Wholesale Market**, on the edge of Tokyo Bay, some 2km southeast of the Imperial Palace, is one of the highlights of any trip to Tokyo and is a must for raw-fish fans, who can breakfast afterwards on the freshest slices of sashimi and sushi.

Covering 56 acres of reclaimed land south of Ginza, the market is popularly known as **Tsukiji** (reclaimed land), and has been here since 1923. The area it stands on was created in the wake of the disastrous Furisode (Long Sleeves) Fire of 1657 (see p.351). Tokugawa Ieyasu had the debris shovelled into the marshes at the edge of Ginza, thus providing his lords with space for their mansions and gardens. In the early years of the Meiji Era, after the daimyō had been kicked out of the city, the authorities built a special residential area for Western ex-pats here. The market relocated to this area from Nihombashi after the 1923 earthquake, and there's talk of another move sometime around 2015 with various locations under debate.

Emerging from Tsukiji subway, you'll first notice the **Tsukiji Hongan-ji**, one of the largest and most Indian-looking of Tokyo's Buddhist temples. Pop inside to see the intricately carved golden altar and cavernous interior with room for one thousand worshippers. From the temple, the most direct route to the **market** is to continue along Shin-ōhashi-dōri, crossing Harumi-dōri (the route from Ginza), and past the row of grocers and noodle bars. On the next block lies the sprawling bulk of the market. Every day, bar Sundays and public holidays, over two million kilos of fish are delivered here from far-flung corners of the earth. Over four hundred different types of seafood come under the hammer, including eels from Taiwan, salmon from Santiago and tuna from Tasmania, but fish is not the only item on sale at Tsukiji, which also deals in meat, fruit and vegetables.

The auctions, held at the back of the market, aren't officially open to the public, but no one will stop you slipping in quietly to watch the buyers and sellers gesticulating wildly over polystyrene crates of squid, sea urchins, crab and the like. The highlight is the sale of rock-solid frozen tuna, looking like steel torpedoes, all labelled with yellow stickers indicating their weight and country of origin. Depending on their quality, each tuna sells for between ¥600,000 to ¥1 million. At around 7am, Tokyo's restaurateurs and food retailers pick their way through the day's catch on sale at 1600 different wholesalers' stalls under the crescent-shaped hangar's roof.

If you want to witness the frantic market auctions which start at 5am, you'll either have to walk or catch a taxi (the subway doesn't run that early), though if you can't make it for then, it's still worth coming along – the action in the outer markets continues through to midday.

Sloshing through water-cleansed pathways, dodging the produce-carrying trucks, and being surrounded by piled crates of seafood – some of it still alive – is what a visit to Tsukiji is all about. If all this makes you peckish, head for the outer market area (Jogai Ichiba), which is crammed with sushi stalls and noodle bars servicing the 60,000 people who pass through here each day. Good choices include *Daiwa Zushi*, open from 5.30am, which is actually within the market, while *Tatsuzushi* and the more expensive *Sushisei* are in the block of shops between the market and Tsukiji Hongan-ji. Expect to pay around ¥2000.

HAMA RIKYŪ TEIEN AND AROUND 浜離宮庭園

Map 2, F10. Tues–Sun 9am–4.30pm; ¥300. Tsukiji Station.
The entrance to **Hama Rikyū Teien** is less than a ten-

minute walk west of Tsukiji, but the contrast between the bustling market and this serene, traditional garden couldn't be more acute. The beautifully designed park once belonged to the shoguns, who hunted ducks here. Today the ducks are protected inside the garden's nature reserve and only have to watch out for the large number of cats that wander the idly twisting pathways.

Next to the entrance is a sprawling, 300-year-old pine tree and a manicured lawn dotted with sculpted, stunted trees. There are three ponds in the gardens – the largest is spanned by a trellis-covered bridge that leads to a floating teahouse, *Nakajima-no-Chaya* (¥500 for tea). One of the best times of year to come here is in early spring, when lilac wisteria hangs in fluffy bunches from the trellises around the central pond. From the Tokyo Bay side of the garden, you'll get a view across to the Rainbow Bridge, and can see the floodgate which regulates how much sea water flows in and out with the tides. By far the nicest way of approaching the gardens is to take a ferry from Asakusa, down the Sumida-gawa.

For further information on the ferry service see p.45.

Walking from Hama Rikyū towards Shimbashi Station, you'll notice a building that looks like a pile of cubes stacked by a child. The **Nakagin Capsule Mansion**, now offices, was once the world's first capsule hotel and on the ground floor you can look into one of the self-contained cubes still kept in its original 1971 state. Apart from it being so large (it's a room, rather than a capsule), what is really striking is how dated the cutting-edge technology of the time has become; the reel-to-reel tape player, dial phone and solid-state Trinitron colour television all look positively antiquated.

TSUKUDASHIMA 佃島

Map 2, H9. Tsukishima Station.

A rewarding diversion from Tsukiji, across the Sumida-gawa, is **TSUKUDASHIMA**, a tiny enclave of Edo-period houses and shops, clustered around a backwater spanned by a dinky red bridge. Sheltering in the shadow of the modern River City 21 tower blocks, the area has a history stretching back to 1613, when a group of Ōsaka fishermen were settled on the island by the shogun. In addition to providing food for the castle, the fishermen were expected to report on any suspicious comings and goings in the bay. For their spiritual protection, they built themselves the delightful **Sumiyoshi-jinja**, a shrine dedicated to the god of the sea. Every three years, on the first weekend in August, the shrine hosts the Sumiyoshi Matsuri festival, during which a special *mikoshi* (portable shrine) is dowsed in water as it is paraded through the streets – this is symbolic of the real dunking it would once have had in the river. The water well beside the shrine's *torii* has a roof with eaves decorated with exquisite carvings of scenes from the fishermen's lives.

The Tsukudashima community is also famous for **tsukudani**, delicious morsels of seaweed and fish preserved in a mixture of soy sauce, salt or sugar. You'll find eighteen different types of *tsukudani* served up at **Tenyasu Honten** (daily 9am–6pm), a weather-worn wooden shop typical of the area, outside of which hangs a tattered *noren* (cloth shop sign). Ask nicely and the white-aproned ladies, who sit cross-legged on a *tatami* platform, will allow you to take a peep behind the scenes to see how this delicacy is made. A wooden box set of six types of *tsukudani* costs around ¥2000.

To reach Tsukudashima on foot, head for the Tsukuda-Ōhashi Bridge, a ten-minute walk from Tsukiji subway station, past St Luke's Hospital. The area is easily spotted on the left side of the island as you leave the bridge, and shouldn't take you more than thirty minutes to explore. Beside the exit of Tsukishima subway station you'll see an open arcade of shops, along which are restaurants serving the area's other food speciality, **monjya**, a thinner type of *okonomiyaki* pancake that's worth trying.

ODAIBA お台場

Map 2, G13.

From Shimbashi Station the Yurikamome monorail line runs out to an **island** of reclaimed land in Tokyo Bay, officially called Rinkai Fukutoshin, but popularly known as **ODAIBA**. Despite its shaky start (see box, p.139), the island now boasts futuristic buildings linked by the monorail, a man-made beach, architectural wonders and sunny shopping plazas, all of which have turned it into such a local hit that on weekends the monorail is often swamped with day-trippers. In the evenings, the illuminated Rainbow Bridge, giant technicolour Ferris wheel and twinkling towers of the Tokyo skyline make Odaiba a romantic spot – you'll see plenty of canoodling couples staring dreamily at the glittering panorama.

The following description starts at the far south side of Odaiba and ends with a walk back across the Rainbow Bridge – easily the highlight of any trip out to this modern world.

Tokyo Big Sight and Palette Town 東京ビッグサイトとパレットトウン

Kokusai Tenjijo-Seimon and Aomi stations.

One stop from the monorail terminus at Ariake is the enormous Tokyo International Exhibition Centre, better known

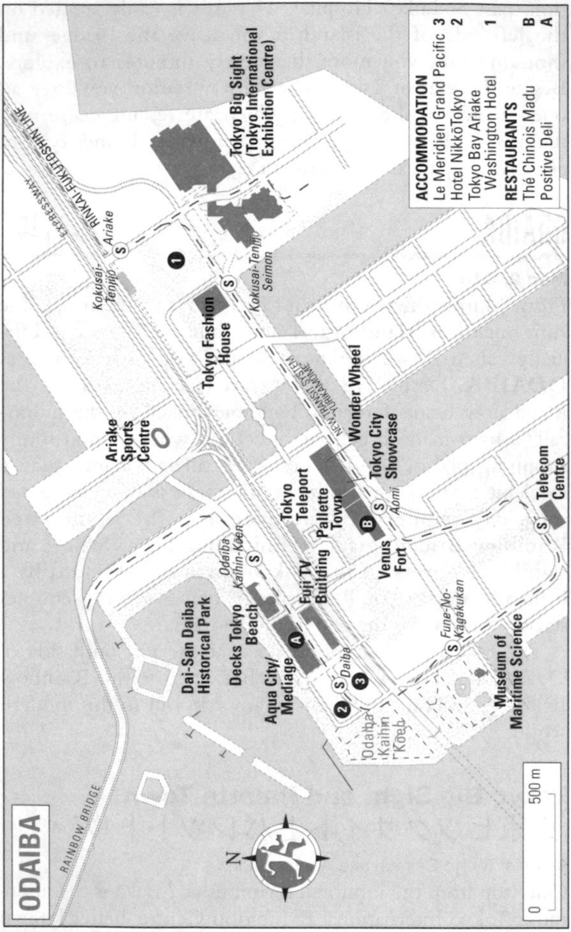
ODAIBA
ACCOMMODATION
Le Meridien Grand Pacific 3
Hotel NikkōTokyo 2
Tokyo Bay Ariake Washington Hotel 1
RESTAURANTS
Thé Chinois Madu B
Positive Deli A
Tokyo Big Sight (Tokyo International Exhibition Centre)
RINKAI-FUKUTOSHIN LINE
EXPRESSWAY
Ariake
Kokusai-Tenjijo
Kokusai-Tenjijo Seimon
Tokyo Fashion House
NEW TRANSIT SYSTEM YURIKAMOME
Wonder Wheel
Tokyo City Showcase
Ariake Sports Centre
Tokyo Teleport
Pallette Town
Aomi
Telecom Centre
Venus Fort
Odaiba Kaihin-Koen
Fuji TV Building
Dai-San Daiba Historical Park
Decks Tokyo Beach
Aqua City/ Mediage
Daiba
Fune-No-Kagakukan
Museum of Maritime Science
Odaiba Kaihin Koen
RAINBOW BRIDGE
N
0
500 m

GETTING TO ODAIBA

The most convenient way of reaching Odaiba is on the **Yurikamome monorail**, which arcs up to the Rainbow Bridge on a splendid circular line and stops at all of the area's major sites, including the Maritime Museum and the Tokyo Big Site exhibition centre, terminating at Ariake Station. A ¥800 one-day ticket is best if you intend to see all of the island – walking across Odaiba is a long slog. Buses from Shinagawa Station, southwest of the bay, cross the Rainbow Bridge and run as far as the Maritime Museum, stopping at Odaiba Kaihin Kōen on the way. Alternatively, you can hop on a ferry from Hinode Sanbashi to either Ariake (¥350) or the Maritime Museum (¥520) via Harumi and Odaiba Kaihin Kōen (¥400) – a journey which doubles as a quick, cheap cruise of Tokyo Bay.

Tokyo Teleport, a heliport in the centre of the island, is linked by train with Shin-Kiba subway and train station, on the east side of the bay. A line is also being constructed to connect the heliport with JR Osaki Station on the bay's west side.

as **Tokyo Big Sight**. The building, with its long moving walkways and cavernous interiors, looks like a sleek airport terminal, and its entrance is made up of four huge inverted pyramids. In front of it is a 15.5-metre sculpture of a red-handled saw, sticking out of the ground as if left behind by an absent-minded giant.

Beside Aomi Station, the next stop west, is the vast **Palette Town** shopping and entertainment complex. On the east side is potentially the most interesting piece of the package, **Toyota City Showcase** (daily 11am–9pm; free), displaying all of Toyota's range of cars. Enthusiasts will enjoy just strolling around this huge showroom, while even those with only a faint interest in cars will also want to take part in the fuel-injected fun by signing up for the various activities, such as designing your own car on computer, taking a ride in an electric vehicle (¥200) or a virtual reality drive (¥500), or even selecting any of Toyota's models and taking it for a test drive (¥300). Just behind the showroom are some more high-tech diversions, the best of which is the 115-metre-diameter **Wonder Wheel** (daily 10am–10pm; ¥900), a candy-coloured Ferris wheel that takes sixteen minutes to make a full circuit.

To make advance bookings for Toyota City Showcase (a good idea, given the size of the crowds) call ⓣ0070-800-849-000, or visit them on the Internet at ⓦ*www.megaweb.gr.jp*.

The upper floor on the west side of Palette Town is dominated by **Venus Fort**, described as a "theme park for ladies", but basically a shopping mall, designed as a mock Italian city, complete with piazza, fountains and Roman-style statues – even the ceiling is painted and lit to resemble a perfect Mediterranean sky through dawn to dusk. Most of the theme-style restaurants and shops here are totally bland, but the complex is worth passing through if only to gawp at the sheer lunacy of it all. Downstairs is Sun Walk, a more restrained shopping mall, at the back of which you'll find the **History Garage** (daily 11am–10pm; free), displaying a good range of classic cars and including a gallery with around 3000 miniature vehicles and an extensive range of car-related books.

Museum of Maritime Science and around 船の科学館

Mon–Fri 10am–5pm, Sat & Sun 10am–6pm. Fune-no-Kagakukan Station.

West of Palette Town is a fat finger of reclaimed land partly covered by Tokyo's container port and overlooked by the

ODAIBA: A BRIEF HISTORY

Odaiba takes its name from the cannon emplacements set up by the shogun in 1853 in the bay to protect the city from Commodore Perry's threatening Black Ships (see "History", p.351). However, the island is better known as the site of an ill-fated construction project of the late 1980s, which proved the downfall of the city's former governor, Suzuki Shunichi. The remains of the two cannon emplacements are now dwarfed by the huge landfill site – Rinkai Fukutoshin, of which Odaiba is a part – on which the Metropolitan Government set about constructing a 21st-century city in 1988. The economic slump and spiralling development costs slowed the project down, and, when the Rainbow Bridge linking Odaiba to the city opened in 1993, the area was still a series of empty lots. Suzuki's plan to spend more public money on an International City Exposition on the island in 1996 was the last straw for Tokyo's citizens: both the governor and his expo plan were kicked out in the 1995 elections. It wasn't long, though, before the area's fortunes took off again. Fuji TV's decision to relocate here in 1997 has encouraged many others to follow, including Sony, who are in the process of building a huge waterfront complex. Demand for Odaiba's apartment blocks, with their views and proximity to the beach, was also so high that allocation had to be decided by a lottery.

Telecom Centre, a wanna-be clone of Paris's Grande Arche at La Défense. The centre has a viewing platform on its twenty-first floor (¥600), which can be safely skipped in favour of the observatory at the top of the nearby Fune-no-Kagakukan, or **Museum of Maritime Science**. While you're here, check out the museum itself, housed in a concrete reproduction of a 60,000-ton, white cruise ship, with several floors of fascinating exhibitions, including detailed model boats and the engines of a giant ship. Docked outside are a couple of real ships: the *Soya*, which undertook scientific missions to the South Pole, and the *Yotei Marine*, a liner refitted as an exhibition space, which includes an evocative re-creation of the 1920s' Tokyo waterfront. Admission to the two ships only is ¥600; for the museum and the *Yotei Marine* ¥700 and for everything ¥1000. Within the museum grounds are a couple of lighthouses, submarines, a flying boat and two open-air swimming pools (daily July 18–Aug 31; ¥2800 including admission to the museum).

Heading around the waterfront from the museum, past the curious triangular tower (an air vent for the road tunnel that goes under Tokyo Bay), will lead you to the seaside park of **Odaiba Kaihin Kōen**.

The beach and around

Odaiba-kaihin-kōen Station.

To get to Odaiba's man-made **beach**, turn the corner of the island, and when the Rainbow Bridge comes into view you're there. As Japanese beaches go, it's not bad, but you'd be wise to avoid it on sunny weekends, when there's more raw flesh than sand on display. Fronting on to the beach are the Aqua City and Decks Tokyo Beach shopping malls. Apart from trendy shops and restaurants, the former includes the Mediage multiplex cinema, while the latter has its own brewery and **Joypolis** (daily 10am–11.30pm; ¥500 admission only), a multi-storey arcade filled with Sega's interactive entertainment technology.

Next to the mall, a surreal aura hangs over Tange Kenzō's **Fuji TV Building**, a futuristic block with a huge metal sphere suspended in its middle, that looks as if it's made from a giant Meccano set. Again you can pay to head up to the twenty-fifth floor viewing platform (Tues–Sun

10am–8pm; ¥500), or you can do the sensible thing and put the cash towards a cocktail in the Sky Lounge at the top of the neighbouring *Meridien Grand Pacific Hotel*, and have the view thrown in for free.

Rainbow Bridge レインボーブリッジ

Daily April–Oct 10am–9pm; Nov–March 10am–6pm; ¥300.

From the Sunset Beach row of restaurants beside the Decks mall you can walk across onto one of the shogun's gun emplacement islands, now a public park, or continue on for an exhilarating walk along the **Rainbow Bridge**. This 918-metre-long single-span suspension bridge has two levels, the lower for the waterfront road and the monorail, and the upper for the Metropolitan Expressway. On both sides stretches a pedestrian promenade linking the observation rooms in the anchorages at either end of the bridge. The walk along the bridge takes about forty minutes and provides magnificent views across the bay – even as far as Mount Fuji, if the sky is clear. One minute's walk from the shore-side observation room is the station for the monorail back to Shimbashi.

KASAI RINKAI-KŌEN 葛西臨海公園

Map 2, I10. Open 24hr; free. Kasai-Rinkai-kōen Station.

The flat expanse of **KASAI RINKAI-KŌEN** isn't the most attractive of landscapes, but there's more to it than first appears. For many Tokyo families this is a favourite weekend spot – for picnicking, cycling or summer-swimming on its small beach – while bird enthusiasts ogle water-birds and waders in the bird sanctuary. The park's biggest draw, however, is its large aquarium, **Tokyo Sea Life Park** (Tues–Sun 9.30am–5pm, last entry 4pm; ¥700), under a glass-and-steel dome overlooking the sea. The first thing you meet coming down the escalators are two vast tanks of tuna and sharks, the aquarium's highlight; go down again and you stand in the middle of this fishy world, surrounded by 2200 tons of water. Smaller tanks showcase sea life from around the world, from flashy tropical butterfly fish and paper-thin seahorses to the lumpy mudskippers of Tokyo Bay. Not everyone is here to admire the beauty of the fish – as you walk round, listen out for murmurs of *oishii* (the Japanese equivalent of "delicious!").

If you're heading back into central Tokyo from here, one of the nicest ways is to hop on a ferry for the 55-minute ride (¥800) via Ariake to Hinode Sanbashi near Hamamatsuchō. Boats leave hourly from the park's western pier, with the last departure at 5pm.

TOKYO DISNEYLAND 東京ディズニーランド

Map 1, E4. Daily 8am–9/10pm; Ⓦ*www.tokyodisneyland.co.jp/index_e.html* Hours may vary and it's occasionally closed for special events, so phone first on the information hot line (Ⓣ047/354-0001); ¥4500 for a one-day "passport" covering all attractions except the Shootin' Gallery; on certain evenings a ¥4500 "starlight passport" is available for entry after 5pm. Maihama Station.

The big daddy of Tokyo's theme parks, **Tokyo Disneyland** is a pretty close copy of the Californian original, plonked in commuter land, fifteen minutes' train ride east of the city centre. Its theme-lands, parades and zany extravaganzas follow the well-honed Disney formula but, whatever your preconceptions, it's hard not to have a good time. To get your money's worth, you should aim to spend a whole day here. Note that you can't bring your own food, but there are around fifty restaurants, cafés and fast-food joints.

Disneyland sits in front of Maihama Station on the JR Keiyō line from Tokyo Station. From Odaiba, pick up the Keiyō line at Shin-Kiba Station.

Inside, World Bazaar offers shops and general services (stroller rentals, bank, lockers and information). Of the six theme-lands, Tomorrowland's Star Tours and Space Mountain offer the most heart-stopping rides. However, there's more fun and excitement in store with the opening in late 2001 of a whole new resort, the neighbouring **Disney Sea Park**. A monorail encircles the two sites, stopping near Maihama Station at a new shopping and hotel complex, where real addicts can enjoy their complimentary Mickey toiletries before breakfasting with the mouse himself in the Art Deco *Disney Ambassador Hotel*.

The new park may relieve some of the pressure, but at present Disneyland attracts over 30,000 visitors per day on average, which means that queues are inevitable – from thirty minutes up to one hour for the more popular attractions and at peak times such as weekends and holidays.

If you're still here after dark, watch as the illuminations take over and hundreds of dancers and Disney characters parade by, twinkling with fairy lights like a walking fireworks display. As Walt said, "the magic never ends".

It's possible to buy tickets before you set out at the Tokyo Disney Resort Ticket Centre (Map 7, C7; daily 10am–7pm; ☎3595-1777) in the Hibiya Mitsui Building near Hibiya subway station.

LISTINGS

Accommodation

Tokyo offers the full range of **accommodation**, from first-class hotels that are as luxurious as any in the world, to bottom-end dormitory bunks. The main difficulty is finding somewhere at an affordable **price**, particularly if you're on a limited budget or travelling alone. Room **availability** is another problem, particularly over national holidays (see p.25) and in late February, when thousands of students descend on Tokyo for the university entrance exams. Note also, that budget and mid-range accommodation will be in short supply during the soccer World Cup in June 2002 (see p.268 for more).

If you arrive without a reservation, head for the Welcome Inn counter in Terminal 2 of Narita Airport (see p.34) which provides a free **booking service** at their member inns. In central Tokyo, the main Welcome Inn Reservation Centre is next to the Tokyo TIC in the basement of Tokyo International Forum (Mon–Fri 9.15–11.30am & 1–4.45pm; Ⓣ3211-4201, Ⓕ3211-9009, Ⓦ *www.jnto.go.jp*). It's also possible to telephone the hotel or *ryokan* direct as most places can handle straightforward requests in English.

What kind of place you stay in will depend on your budget. Basically you've got a choice between a standard, Western-style **hotel**, which can be expensive, a traditional,

ACCOMMODATION PRICES

All accommodation in this book has been graded according to the following price codes, which represent the **cheapest double or twin room available**, including tax; note that rates may increase during peak holiday periods. In the case of hostels providing dormitory accommodation and capsule hotels, the code represents the charge per bed.

❶ under ¥3000	❷ ¥3000–5000	❸ ¥5000–7000
❹ ¥7000–10,000	❺ ¥10,000–15,000	❻ ¥15,000–20,000
❼ ¥20,000–30,000	❽ ¥30,000–40,000	❾ over ¥40,000

family-run **ryokan** (see box, p.150), which is slightly cheaper, a **capsule hotel** (see p.168) and a **youth hostel** (see p.170).For tips on finding **long-term accommodation**, see p.171.

When choosing your **area**, bear in mind that central Tokyo, comprising Ginza, Nihombashi, Hibiya and Akasaka, belongs to expensive, world-class establishments and upmarket business hotels, plus a sprinkling of middle-range places. For cheaper rooms, there's a greater choice in Shinagawa, Shibuya and Shinjuku to the south and east, and especially in Ueno and Ikebukuro in the north. Also in the north, Asakusa is set slightly apart from Tokyo's main thrust, but offers a few well-priced rooms in an appealing area. In the last few years, several top-class establishments have sprung up in Tokyo's new suburban satellites, notably the Odaiba development in Tokyo Bay.

While most places listed below are within easy access of either a **subway** or **train station**, remember that trains stop running around midnight; if you're a night owl, aim to stay near one of the entertainment districts to avoid taxi fares. Our listings below show the nearest station for each hotel.

The telephone code for Tokyo is 03. To call Tokyo from abroad, dial 81-3, followed by the subscriber's number.

HOTELS AND RYOKAN

Whether in the de luxe or business categories, **hotels** generally provide Western-style rooms with en-suite bathrooms, TV, phone and air-conditioning, though at the lower end they can be pretty characterless. Don't expect much space either; thanks to the city's notoriously high real estate prices, everything is packed in with the greatest efficiency. At this level, you'll find far better value and more atmosphere at one of the traditional, family-run **ryokan** in the outer districts.

For help unravelling Tokyo's addresses, see p.42.

AKASAKA

Akasaka Prince 赤坂プリンス

Map 4, D1. 1-2 Kioichō, Chiyoda-ku ⓣ3234-1111, ⓕ3262-5163, ⓦ*www.princehotels.co.jp/english/* Akasaka-mitsuke Station.

Forty-storey Tange Kenzō-designed tower with stunning views, though the cool grey and white interior is a bit chilly, and the rooms could do with some modernization. ❽.

Akasaka Tōkyū Hotel 赤坂東急ホテル

Map 4, E2. 2-14-3 Nagatachō, Chiyoda-ku ⓣ3580-2311, ⓕ3580-6066. Akasaka-mitsuke Station.

Affectionately known as "the pyjama building" because of its pink and white stripes, this hotel offers rooms at the lower

STAYING IN A RYOKAN

One of the highlights of a visit to Tokyo is staying in a **ryokan**, a family-run inn where you'll be expected to follow local custom from the moment you arrive.

Just inside the front door there's usually a row of **slippers** ready for you to change into. The bedrooms have rice-straw matting (*tatami*) on the floor and little else beyond a low table and dresser, plus a few cushions. The **bedding** is stored behind sliding doors during the day and laid out in the evening. In top-class establishments this is done for you, but elsewhere be prepared to tackle your own. There'll be a mattress (which goes straight on the *tatami*) with a sheet, a soft quilt to sleep under and a pillow stuffed with rice husks.

All *ryokan* provide a *yukata*, a loose cotton robe tied with a belt, and a short jacket in cold weather. The *yukata* can be worn in bed, when going to the bathroom and for wandering about the *ryokan* – many Japanese take an outdoor evening stroll in their *yukata* and wooden shoes (*geta*), kept in the entrance hall. It's important always to wrap the left side over the right; the opposite is used to dress bodies at a funeral. The traditional Japanese bath (*furo*) is a luxurious experience with its own set of rules (see p.27). There are usually separate **bathrooms** for men and women. If there's only one, either there'll be designated times for males and females, or guests take it in turn – it's perfectly acceptable for couples and families to bathe together, though there's not usually a lot of space.

Evening **meals** tend to be early, at 6pm or 7pm. Smarter *ryokan* generally serve meals in your room, while communal dining is the norm in cheaper places. **At night**, some *ryokan* lock their doors pretty early, so check before going out – they may let you have a key.

level of this price bracket, with screens on the windows lending a Japanese touch to otherwise standard Western comfort. ❼–❽

Akasaka Yōkō Hotel 赤坂陽光ホテル

Map 4, B9. 6-14-12 Akasaka, Minato-ku Ⓣ3586-4050, Ⓕ3586-5944, Ⓦ *www.yokohotel.co.jp* Akasaka Station.
Affordable, mid-range hotel in a red-brick building, with a smart marble lobby, simple rooms and cheaper singles. ❺–❻.

Capitol Tōkyū Hotel キャピトル東急ホテル

Map 4, G5. 2-10-3 Nagatachō, Chiyoda-ku Ⓣ3581-4511, Ⓕ3581-5882, Ⓦ *www.capitoltokyo.com* Kokkaigijido-Mae Station.
Adjacent to Hie-jinja, Tōkyū's flagship hotel blends Japanese and Western styles successfully, though some might find the overall ambience a little dark. There's a small traditional garden, an outdoor pool in the summer and several restaurants and bars. ❽–❾.

Marroad Inn Akasaka マロウドイン赤坂

Map 4, A9. 6-15-17 Akasaka, Minato-ku Ⓣ3585-7611, Ⓕ3585-7191. Akasaka Station.
Good-value business hotel offering plain rooms with desk and TV. The cheaper rooms have one double bed rather than two singles. The in-hotel Chinese restaurant does a ¥1000 dinner. ❺.

New Ōtani ニューオータニ

Map 4, D1. 4-1 Kioichō, Chiyoda-ku Ⓣ3265-1111, Ⓕ3221-2619, Ⓦ *www.newotani.co.jp/tokyo/en/* Akasaka-mitsuke Station.
Enormous luxury hotel, where the original star-shaped building is now dwarfed by the adjacent tower block. Features include a beautiful landscaped garden, 37 restaurants and bars, a tea ceremony room, an art gallery (see p.64), sports centre, swimming pools and tennis courts, a bookshop and post office. ❼–❽.

ASAKUSA AND AROUND

Asakusa View Hotel 浅草ビューホテル

Map 5, E2. 3-17-1 Nishi-Asakusa, Taitō-ku Ⓣ3847-1111, Ⓕ3842-2117. Tawaramachi Station.

Asakusa's grandest hotel is all sparkling marble and chandeliers, and the rooms have expansive views from the higher floors. A reasonable buffet lunch is available at the top-floor bar, and there's also a shopping arcade and a swimming pool (¥3000). ❼.

New Kōyō ニュー紅陽

Map 2, I2. 2-26-13 Nihonzutsumi, Taitō-ku Ⓣ3873-0343, Ⓕ3873-1358, Ⓦ*www.newkoyo.com* 179 Minowa Station.

Not the most convenient location, ten minutes' walk from the nearest subway station, but popular among budget travellers and job-hunters for its ultra-cheap single rooms (no doubles), it's worth paying a little extra for a four-mat room (¥2700), though even they are pretty cell-like. Reasonably clean communal baths, toilets and kitchen, plus coin laundry, Internet access and bike rental. ❶.

Ryokan Shigetsu 旅館浅草指月

Map 5, G4. 1-31-11 Asakusa, Taitō-ku Ⓣ3843-2345, Ⓕ3843-2348, Ⓦ*www.shigetsu.com* Asakusa Station.

This elegant and surprisingly affordable *ryokan* is *the* place to stay in Asakusa. Just off bustling Nakamise-dōri, inside, kimono-clad receptionists and tasteful art pieces set the mood. Rooms are in Western- or Japanese-style, small but all en suite. There's a Japanese bath and a good restaurant. The only down side is the 11pm curfew. ❺–❻.

Taitō Ryokan 台東旅館

Map 5, D5. 2-1-4 Nishi-Asakusa, Taitō-ku Ⓣ3843-282, Ⓦ*www.libertyhouse.gr.jp* Tawaramachi Station.

Atmospheric, if somewhat dilapidated, wooden *ryokan* that's turning into a quasi-*gaijin* house, thanks to its central location, cheap prices and enthusiastic owner. Only seven *tatami* rooms (none en-suite), so you'll need to book ahead. No smoking. ❸.

Hotel Top Asakusa ホテルトップ浅草

Map 5, F5. 1-5-3 Asakusa, Taitō-ku ©3847-2222, Ⓕ3847-3074. Asakusa Station.

Fairly modest business hotel well located on Asakusa's main street and with English-speaking staff. The small but comfortable rooms all have TV and telephone. ❺.

EBISU AND MEGURO

Hotel Excellent ホテルエクセレント

Map 6, C2. 1-9-5 Ebisu-nishi, Shibuya-ku Ⓣ5458-0087, Ⓕ5458-8787. Ebisu Station.

Standard business hotel that's not flash, but certainly reasonably priced for such a handy location. Singles go for ¥8700. ❺.

Meguro Gajoen 目黒牙城苑

Map 6, E7. 1-8-1 Meguro, Meguro-ku Ⓣ5434-3837, Ⓕ5434-3931, Ⓦ*www.megurogajoen.co.jp* Meguro Station.

No luxury is spared in the rooms (all suites) of this hotel attached to an amazing wedding hall. A choice of either Western or Japanese fittings, the Japanese rooms are the best with their own sauna, *hinoki* wood baths and tiny gravel gardens outside the windows. ❽–❾.

Hotel Watson ホテルワトソン

Map 6, E6. 2-26-5 Kami Osaki, Shinagawa-ku Ⓣ3490-5566, Ⓦ*www.htl-watson.co.jp* Meguro Station.

Decent-sized rooms with TV and mini-bar, at this sleek

business hotel with friendly management. Near the *Blues Alley Japan* club (see p.242) and *tonkatsu* restaurant *Tonki* (see p.185). Has singles for just under ¥10,000. ❻.

Westin Tokyo ウエスティン東京

Map 6, E4. 1-1-4 Mita, Meguro-ku Ⓣ 5423-7000, Ⓕ 5423-7600, Ⓦ *www.westin.co.jp* Ebisu Station.

In the Yebisu Garden Palace development, this opulent addition to Tokyo's luxury hotel scene is decorated in Art Nouveau style and fairly priced for what you get. There's a health club and plenty of restaurants and bars. ❽.

GINZA AND AROUND

Hotel Alcyone ホテルアルシオン

Map 7, G7. 4-14-3 Ginza, Chūō-ku Ⓣ 3541-3621, Ⓕ 3541-3263, Ⓦ *www.hotel-alcyone.co.jp* Higashi-Ginza Station.

In a prime location just round the corner from the Kabuki-za and five minutes' walk from Tsukiji. Ignore the gawdy Seventies decor in the lobby and head straight for the smart *tatami* rooms, which are good value at around ¥10,000, or less, per person. There's a communal bath in the basement and an attached Swiss restaurant. ❻.

Ginza Tōbu Hotel 銀座東武ホテル

Map 7, E8. 6-14-10 Ginza, Chūō-ku Ⓣ 3546-0111, Ⓕ 3546-8990, Ⓦ *www.tobu.co.jp/english/hotel/ginza.html* Higashi-Ginza Station.

Top-range business hotel that maintains a personal touch, just five minutes' walk southeast of the main Ginza Yon-chome crossing. Its rooms are a decent size, well furnished and reasonably priced. Services include a business centre, bar and restaurants. ❽.

Imperial Hotel 帝国ホテル

Map 7, C8. 1-1-1 Uchisaiwai-chō, Chiyoda-ku Ⓣ3504-1111, Ⓕ3581-9146, Ⓦ*www.imperialhotel.co.jp* Hibiya Station.

Facing the Imperial Palace, this prestigious hotel offers spacious rooms, with good views from the newer and slightly pricier tower. Services include a business centre, amenity lounge for late/early arrivals, baby-sitting, swimming pool (¥1000), thirteen top-class restaurants, four bars, a tea-ceremony room (¥1500) and a shopping arcade. ❽.

Palace Hotel パレスホテル

Map 7, A3. 1-1-1 Marunouchi, Chiyoda-ku Ⓣ3211-5211, Ⓕ3211-6987, Ⓦ*www.palacehotel.co.jp* Ōtemachi Station.

One notch down from the *Imperial* (see above), this top-class hotel also overlooks the palace gardens though it's a little less convenient. Rooms are fair-sized and comfortably furnished, with minibar, TV and all the standard amenities. There are seven restaurants and three bars, plus a shopping arcade, business centre and well-stocked bookshop. ❽.

Royal Park Hotel ロイヤルパークホテル

Map 2, G5. 2-1-1 Kakigarachō, Chūō-ku Ⓣ3667-1111, Ⓕ3667-1115, Ⓦ*www.royalparkhotels.co.jp/nihonbashi* Suitengūmae Station.

Swish business hotel conveniently located next to Tokyo City Air Terminal (TCAT) and above the Hanzōmon subway line. The rooms are quite stylish, and facilities include restaurants and bars, business centre, pool and gym. ❽.

Yaesu Fujiya Hotel 八重洲富士屋ホテル

Map 7, E5. 2-9-1 Yaesu, Chūō-ku Ⓣ3273-2111, Ⓕ3273-2180, Ⓦ*www.yaesufujiya.com* Tokyo Station.

Opposite the east entrance to Tokyo Station, offering professional service and convenience rather than great value for money. The cheaper rooms are small but perfectly decent. ❻–❼.

Yaesu Terminal Hotel

八重洲ターミナルホテル

Map 7, E3. 1-5-14 Yaesu, Chūō-ku ⓣ 3281-3771, ⓕ 3281-3089. Nihombashi Station.

Welcoming business hotel offering good rates (from under ¥17,000 for a double) for such a central location, though cheaper rooms are cramped. It's also in an appealing area, tucked among lively backstreets just northeast of Tokyo Station. ❻.

HARAJUKU & SHIBUYA

Creston Hotel クレストンホテル

Map 12, A1. 10-8 Kamiyamachō, Shibuya-ku ⓣ 3481-5800, ⓕ 3481-5515, ⓦ *www.crestonhotel.co.jp*. Shibuya Station.

Upmarket business hotel with larger than normal rooms and a discrete club-like atmosphere. Near NHK at the quiet end of Shibuya and a ten-minute walk from the nearest station. ❼.

Excel Hotel Tōkyū エクセルホテル東急

Map 12, D6. 1-12-2 Dōgenzaka, Shibuya-ku ⓣ 5457-0109, ⓕ 5457-0309, ⓦ *www.tokyo.co.jp/inn* Shibuya Station.

Well set-up for business travellers, with high-tech fixtures and contemporary furnishings in the rooms, this new skyscraper hotel, atop the Shibuya Mark City complex, is a fine choice. It has good restaurants with amazing views and is better value than the nearby and now dowdy-looking *Shibuya Tōkyū Inn*. ❼.

Hotel Florasian Aoyama フロラシオン青山

Map 8, G4. 4-17-58 Minami Aoyama, Minato-ku ⓣ 3403-1541, ⓕ 3403-5450. Omotesandō Station.

High standard Western-style rooms and a convenient location, five-minutes from Omotesandō, in a quiet residential area. Singles from ¥7500. ❻.

Harajuku Trimm 原宿トリム

Map 8, B3. 6-28-6 Jingūmae, Shibuya-ku Ⓣ3498-2101, Ⓕ3498-1777. Meiji-jingūmae Station.

Good-value business hotel in a yellow brick building, five minutes' walk along Meiji-dōri towards Shibuya from the crossing with Omotesandō. Rooms have beds that are slightly larger than usual. ❺.

National Children's Castle Hotel こどもの城ホテル

Map 12, I3. 5-53-1 Jingūmae, Shibuya-ku Ⓣ3797-5677, Ⓕ3406-7805. Shibuya Station.

On the sixth and seventh floors of this complex devoted to kids' entertainment (but you don't have to have children to stay here), offering large and comfy rooms, and inexpensive singles with no windows. ❺–❻.

Shibuya Business Hotel 赤坂プリンス

Map 12, F4. 1-12-5 Shibuya, Shibuya-ku Ⓣ3409-9300, Ⓕ3409-9378. Shibuya Station.

Apart from a capsule hotel, this is the cheapest deal you'll find in this pricey but happening part of town – thus it often gets booked up. It's in a quiet location behind the post office. ❺.

Shibuya Tōbu Hotel 渋谷東武ホテル

Map 12, D1. 3-1 Udagawachō, Shibuya-ku Ⓣ3476-0111, Ⓕ3476-0903, Ⓦ*www.tobu.co.jp/hotel/shibuya/index.html* Shibuya Station.

Pleasant chain hotel near Shibuya's department stores, with friendly service and a good range of restaurants. One of the few hotels where the single rooms are brighter than the doubles. ❻.

IKEBUKURO

Hotel Clarion ホテルクレリオン

Map 9, C3. 2-3-1 Ikebukuro, Toshima-ku ⓣ5396-0111, ⓕ5396-9815. Ikebukuro Station.

International-class hotel with more character than its local rivals. Rooms are equipped with minibar, satellite TV and in-house movies. It's well priced (at the bottom of this range) and well located, a couple of minutes' walk west of Ikebukuro Station. ❼.

Dai-ichi Inn Ikebukuro 第一イン池袋

Map 9, E3. 1-42-8 Higashi-Ikebukuro, Toshima-ku ⓣ3986-1221, ⓕ3982-4128, ⓦ*www.daiichihotels.com/hotel/ikebukuro* Ikebukuro Station.

This mid-range business hotel on the east side of Ikebukuro Station offers mainly single and twin rooms. They're old-fashioned in style but reasonably priced and comfortable, with mini-bar, phone and TV. There's a discount if you book online. ❻.

Kimi Ryokan 貴美旅館

Map 9, B2. 2-36-8 Ikebukuro, Toshima-ku ⓣ3971-3766, ⓕ3987-1326. Ikebukuro Station.

Book well ahead for this excellent-value institution on Tokyo's budget scene. Inside it has the flavour of an old *ryokan*, though the *tatami* rooms are box-like. It's a little tricky to find, in the backstreets of west Ikebukuro. 1am curfew. ❸.

Hotel Metropolitan ホテルメトロポリタン

Map 9, C5. 1-6-1 Nishi-Ikebukuro, Toshima-ku ⓣ3980-1111, ⓕ3980-5600, ⓦ*www.itbc.co.jp/hotel* Ikebukuro Station.

Ikebukuro's plushest hotel is managed by the Holiday Inn group and has all the facilities you'd expect, including limousine bus connections to Narita Airport, nine restaurants and an outdoor pool (summer only, ¥1000). The rooms are well priced for central Tokyo. ❼.

Hotel Theatre ホテルテアトル

Map 9, F4. 1-21-4 Higashi-Ikebukuro, Toshima-ku ⓣ3988-2251. Ikebukuro Station.

Small, pleasant hotel with some English-speaking staff. The rooms are cheerfully decorated and a touch better furnished than average at this price. ❺.

KANDA AND AROUND

Fairmont Hotel フェヤーモントホテル

Map 10, C6. 2-1-17 Kudan-Minami, Chiyoda-ku ⓣ3262-1151, ⓕ3264-2476. Kudanshita Station.

Relaxed hotel on a quiet side street overlooking the Imperial Palace moat, within easy reach of Yasukuni-jinja and Kitanomaru-kōen. Bedrooms are plain, but light and airy – the best have park views. ❼.

Hilltop Hotel 山の上ホテル

Map 10, F4. 1-1 Kanda-Surugadai, Chiyoda-ku ⓣ3293-2311, ⓕ3233-4567. Ochanomizu Station.

Perched on a little rise above Meiji University, this small 1930s hotel, formerly the commissioned officers' quarters under the Occupation and then haunt of famous writers (notably Mishima), makes up for its rather inconvenient location with Art Deco touches and a friendly welcome. Oxygen and negative ions are pumped around the premises. ❼.

Sakura Hotel サクラホテル

Map 10, E5. 2-21-4 Kanda-Jimbōchō ⓣ3261-3939, ⓕ3264-2777, ⓦ*www.sakura-hotel.co.jp* Jimbōchō Station.

You can't miss this cherry-pink building a couple of blocks

south of Yasukuni-dōri. The rooms are boxy and none are en-suite, but they're spotless and good-value for such a central location: choose between singles, bunk-bed twins, and cheaper dormitory bunks. You'll need to reserve well in advance. ❹.

Tokyo YMCA Hotel 東京ＹＭＣＡホテル

Map 10, G6. 7 Kanda-Mitoshirochō, Chiyoda-ku Ⓣ3293-1911, Ⓕ3293-1926, Ⓔ*pr@tokyo.ymca.or.jp* Ogawamachi Station.
Surprisingly smart accommodation at reasonable prices, with singles and twins but no doubles. Rooms are functional but reasonably spacious and guests can use the YMCA pool (¥1575). Discount for YMCA members. ❻.

YMCA Asia Youth Centre

YMCAアジアユースセンタ

Map 10, E4. 2-5-5 Sarugakuchō, Chiyoda-ku Ⓣ3233-0611, Ⓕ3233-0633, Ⓔ*ayc@ymcajapan.org* Suidōbashi Station.
Both men and women can stay at this hostel, where weekend rates are cheaper than weekday ones; there's a small discount for YMCA members. The rooms, mostly single, are a bit worn but all come with bathroom and TV. ❸–❹.

ODAIBA AND TOKYO BAY

Hotel Inter-Continental Tokyo Bay

ホテルインターコンチネンタル東京ベイ

Map 2, F11. 1-16-2 Kaigan, Minato-ku Ⓣ5404-2222, Ⓕ5404-2111, Ⓦ*www.interconti.com* Hinode Station.
Luxury hotel with views across the bay to the Rainbow Bridge and inland to Tokyo Tower, and rooms decorated in earthy tones. Ten minutes' walk from Hamamatsuchō Station or two minutes' from Hinode Station on the Yurikamome monorail. ❽.

Le Meridien Grand Pacific
ホテルパシフィック東京

See Odaiba map, p.136. 2-6-1 Daiba, Minato-ku ⓣ5500-6711, ⓕ5500-4507, ⓦ*www.lemeridien-asiapacific.com/* Daiba Station.
The traditional European style of this luxury hotel's interior sits somewhat uncomfortably with the futuristic architecture of Odaiba, but the rooms are fair value and there are lots of facilities, including a gallery with changing exhibitions. ❽–❾.

Hotel Nikkō Tokyo ホテル日航東京

See Odaiba map, p.136. 1-9-1 Daiba, Minato-ku ⓣ5500-5500, ⓕ5500-2525. Daiba Station.
With more contemporary style than Le Meridien opposite, the Nikkō scores more points for the beautiful modern works of art on its walls, and great views of the Rainbow Bridge and the city. Rooms have small balconies. Its bay view restaurants get packed on weekends ❽.

Tokyo Bay Ariake Washington Hotel
東京湾有明ワシントンホテレ

See Odaiba map, p.136. 3-1 Ariake, Minato-ku ⓣ5564-0111, ⓕ5564-0525. Kokusai-tenjijō Seimon Station.
Best value for the Odaiba area, this upmarket chain hotel has decent sized rooms with singles from ¥9950. You'll also find here *Georgetown*, a good buffet restaurant and *ji-biru* bar. ❻.

ROPPONGI AND AROUND

ANA Hotel Tokyo 東京全日空ホテル

Map 11, G2. 1-12-33 Akasaka, Minato-ku ⓣ3505-1111, ⓕ3505-1155, ⓦ*www.anaanet.or.jp/anahotels/e/* Tameiki Sannō Station.
Stylish hotel with attentive staff, swimming pool and spacious

public areas, conveniently located midway between Akasaka and Roppongi. It's got good views in any direction, but especially towards Tokyo Tower, and has a wide range of bars and restaurants. ❽.

Asia Centre of Japan ホテルアジア会館

Map 11, C1. 8-10-32 Akasaka, Minato-ku Ⓣ3402-6111, Ⓕ3402-0738. Aoyama Itchōme or Nogizaka Stations.

A bargain for this area, so it fills up quickly. Rooms are small, neat, and Western-style – the cheaper ones have no bath. There's a café and a garden restaurant. Singles start from ¥5100. ❹–❺.

Hotel Ibis ホテルアイビス

Map 11, D4. 7-14-4 Roppongi, Minato-ku Ⓣ3403-4411, Ⓕ3479-0609, Ⓦ*www.ibis-hotel.com* Roppongi Station.

A stone's throw from Roppongi crossing, the cheapest doubles are small but bright and have TV and fridge. The lobby is on the fifth floor, where there are Internet terminals and the friendly staff speak English. ❺–❼.

Hotel Mentels ホテルメンテルス六本木

Map 11, B5. 1-11-4 Nishi-Azabu, Minato-ku Ⓣ3403-7161, Ⓕ3403-9723. Roppongi Station.

Standard business hotel with old-fashioned, reasonably sized rooms. The location, right on Roppongi-dōri and close to Nishi-Azabu crossing, is ideal for those who want to party. The cheapest singles are under ¥10,000. ❺–❻.

Hotel Ōkura ホテルオークラ

Map 11, H2. 2-10-4 Toranomon, Minato-ku Ⓣ3582-0111, Ⓕ3582-3707, Ⓦ*www.hotelokura.co.jp/tokyo/* Kamiyachō Station.

A favourite of the style gurus, who adore its retro chic, the Ōkura has long been one of Tokyo's classiest operations. Try to stay in the main building, which has several restaurants and a tea ceremony room, rather than the newer South Wing. Also has its own oriental art museum (see p.68). ❼–❽.

Roppongi Prince Hotel

六本木プリンスホテル

Map 11, F3. 3-2-7 Roppongi, Minato-ku ⓣ3587-1111, ⓕ3587-0770, ⓦ*www.princehotels.co.jp/english/* Roppongi Station.
Popular with celebrities, the main feature in this hotel, designed by top architect Kurokawa Kisho and set in a quiet area of Roppongi, is its atrium and amoeba-shaped swimming pool, overlooked by the guest rooms. ❼.

Tokyo Prince Hotel 東京プリンスホテル

Map 11, I6. 3-3-1 Shiba Koen, Minato-ku ⓣ3432-1111, ⓕ3434-5551, ⓦ*www.princehotels.co.jp/english/* Onarimon Station.
Close to Tokyo Tower and Zōjō-ji temple, with good-sized rooms. Several in-house restaurants, and in the summer an outdoor pool and beer garden. ❼.

SHINAGAWA AND AROUND

Keihin Hotel 京品ホテル

Map 2, D13. 4-10-20 Takanawa, Minato-ku &3449-5711, ⓕ3441-7230. Shinagawa Station.
Small, old-fashioned hotel directly opposite the west entrance of Shinagawa Station. The cheaper rates mean you have to pay to use the TVs in the room and the bathrooms are tiny. It has some Japanese-style rooms. The cheapest singles are ¥8000. ❺.

Le Meridien Pacific Tokyo ホテルパシフィック東京

Map 2, D13. 3-13-3 Takanawa, Minato-ku ⓣ3445-6711, ⓕ3445-5733, ⓦ *www.lemeridien-asiapacific.com/* Shinagawa Station.
Also a minute's walk from the west entrance of Shinagawa Station, this hotel is one of the better deals in the luxury hotel bracket. It has good size rooms, Japanese gardens, an outdoor pool and several restaurants and bars. ❼.

New Ōtani Inn Tokyo ニューオータニ東京

Map 2, D14. 1-6-2 Osaki, Shinagawa-ku ⓣ3779-9111, ⓕ3779-9181. Ōsaki Station.
Upmarket business hotel with efficient service and some rooms reserved for non-smokers and women. Conveniently right beside the Yamanote line and part of the Ōsaki New City shops and restaurants complex. ❼.

New Takanawa Prince Hotel 新高輪プリンスホテル

Map 2, D13. 3-13-1 Takanawa, Minato-ku ⓣ3442-1111, ⓕ3444-1234, ⓦ *www.princehotels.co.jp/english/* Shinagawa Station.
Directly behind *Le Meridien,* this is the best of the three *Prince* hotels in Shinagawa. The lobby overlooks the elegant gardens created for Prince Takeda, a member of the imperial family, and there's a swimming pool in summer. ❽.

Ryokan Sansuisō 旅館山水荘

Map 2, C13. 2-9-5 Higashi-Gotanda, Shinagawa-ku ⓣ3441-7475, ⓕ3449-1944. Gotanda Station.
Simple, homely, Japanese-style accommodation at this spotless *ryokan*. Most of the *tatami* rooms are without en-suite bath and there is no food available. A five-minute walk from the station, near the Gotanda Bowling Centre. Singles start at ¥4900. ❹–❺.

Takanawa Tōbu Hotel 高輪東武ホテル

Map 2, D13. 4-7-6 Takanawa, Minato-ku Ⓣ3447-0111, Ⓕ3447-0117. Shinagawa Station.
Small but sleek business hotel, where rates include Western-style buffet breakfast in the ground-floor café. Five minutes' walk up the hill from the station. ❻–❼.

SHINJUKU

Central Hotel Shinjuku
セントラルホテル新宿

Map 13, G5. 3-34-7 Shinjuku, Shinjuku-ku Ⓣ3354-6611, Ⓕ3355-4245. Shinjuku Station.
The elegant lobby sets the tone at this classy, boutique-style hotel, in a very convenient location for the shops and nightlife. It also has no-smoking rooms. ❻.

Hotel Century Southern Tower
ホテルセンチユリートワ

Map 13, F7. 2-2-1 Yoyogi, Shinjuku-ku Ⓣ5354-0111, Ⓕ5354-0100, Ⓦ *www.southerntower.co.jp* Shinjuku Station.
Part of the new Odakyū Southern Tower complex, this smart, stylish hotel has better value room rates than many of its older rivals in Nishi-Shinjuku. ❼.

Keiō Plaza Intercontinental Hotel
京王プラザイナターコンチネンタルホテル

Map 13, C5. 2-2-1 Nishi-Shinjuku, Shinjuku-ku Ⓣ3344-0111, Ⓕ3345-8269, Ⓦ *www.keioplaza.co.jp* Shinjuku Station.
Long since knocked off its perch as the tallest, most glamorous

hotel in Shinjuku, the *Keiō* nevertheless retains some of its original cachet. Rooms on the western side have great views across to the Tokyo Metropolitan Government Building. ❽.

Park Hyatt Tokyo パークハイアット東京

Map 13, A7. 3-7-1-2 Nishi-Shinjuku, Shinjuku-ku ⓣ5322-1234, ⓕ5322-1288, ⓦ*www.parkhyatttokokyo.com* Tochō-mae Station.
The flagship of the Park Hyatt chain, this is the last word in designer luxury. The ultra-spacious rooms feature original art works, huge marble baths, and laser and CD players. The chic restaurants, bars and health and fitness centre, which occupy the pinnacles of Tange Kenzō's tower, have breathtaking views on all sides. ❾.

Shinjuku Prince Hotel 新宿プリンスホテル

Map 13, F2. 1-30-1 Kabukichō, Shinjuku-ku ⓣ3205-1111, ⓕ3205-1952, ⓦ*www.princehotels.co.jp/english/* Shinjuku Station.
Thin brown tower at the top end of this price range, right on Kabukichō's doorstep. The lobby is in the basement while the guest rooms start from the tenth floor. Rooms are functional, with glittering night views. ❼.

Shinjuku Washington Hotel 新宿ワシントンホテル

Map 13, C7. 3-2-9 Nishi-Shinjuku, Shinjuku-ku ⓣ3343-3111, ⓕ3340-1804. Tochō-mae Station.
Good-value upmarket business hotel in the building with the porthole windows. The lobby is on the third floor, where automated check-in machines (as well as humans) dish out electronic key cards for the compact, well-equipped rooms. ❻.

Tokyo Hilton Hotel 東京ヒルトンホテル

Map 13, A3. 6-6-2 Nishi-Shinjuku, Shinjuku-ku ⓣ3344-5111, ⓕ3342-6094, ⓦ*www.hilton.com* Tochō-mae Station.

In the slinky, wave-like building behind the more traditional skyscrapers of Nishi-Shinjuku. Rooms have nice Japanese design touches, such as *shōji* (paper screens) on the windows. Renowned for its buffet breakfast or lunch (¥2900) and afternoon tea spreads (¥1700). ❽–❾.

UENO AND AROUND

Ryokan Katsutaro 旅館勝太郎

Map 14, C4. 4-16-8 Ikenohata, Taitō-ku Ⓣ3821-9808, Ⓕ3821-4789, Ⓦ*www.pacificmall.com/ryokan/ryokan.htm* Nezu Station.

Within walking distance of Ueno Park, this is a good alternative if the *Sawanoya* is full (see below). It's a homely place with seven, slightly faded *tatami* rooms, some with bath, and laundry facilities. ❹.

Hotel Pine Hill ホテルパインヒル上野

Map 14, D8. 2-3-4 Ueno, Taitō-ku Ⓣ3836-5111, Ⓕ3837-0080. Ueno-Hirokōji Station.

Best value among the clutch of ordinary, mid-range business hotels in central Ueno. Rooms are small but fulfil the basic needs. ❻.

Sawanoya Ryokan 澤の屋旅館

Map 14, A3. 2-3-11 Yanaka, Taitō-ku Ⓣ3822-2251, Ⓕ3822-2252, Ⓦ*www.sawanoya.com* Nezu Station.

Welcoming *ryokan* with good-value, traditional *tatami* rooms, all with wash basin, TV, telephone and air-conditioning, though only two are en suite. The owner, Sawa-san, is something of a local character, and his son performs lion-dances for guests. The surrounding streets are worth exploring and Ueno Park is within walking distance, while central Tokyo is only a few stops down the Chiyoda Line. ❹.

Suigetsu Hotel Ohgaisou 水月ホテル鴎外荘

Map 14, C4. 3-3-21 Ikenohata, Taitō-ku ⓣ3822-4611, ⓕ3823-4340. Nezu Station.
One of very few mid-range hotels with a Japanese atmosphere. Its three wings, containing a mix of Western and *tatami* rooms, are built around the Meiji-period house and traditional garden of novelist Mori Ōgai, and there are two traditional baths – in marble or lacquered cypress. Prices are reasonable, especially for the Japanese-style rooms, as long as you specify no meals. ❹–❺.

Ueno First City Hotel 上野フアーストシチイホテル

Map 14, C9. 1-14-8 Ueno, Taitō-ku ⓣ3831-8215, ⓕ3837-8469. Yushima Station.
Spruce, reasonably priced and friendly little business hotel on the western edge of Ueno offering a choice of Japanese- and Western-style rooms, all en suite. Take exit 6 of Yushima Station, turn right and right again at the traffic lights. ❺.

CAPSULE HOTELS

Further down the price scale are Tokyo's **capsule hotels**, rows of coffin-like tubes with just enough room to sit up in, containing a mattress, with a TV and radio built into the plastic surrounds. The "door" consists of a plastic curtain – which won't keep out the loudest snores – and you're completely sealed away from the outside world and daylight, making alarm clocks a necessity for waking up early. Capsule hotels are generally clustered around major train stations and cater mainly to salarymen – often in various states of inebriation – who've missed the last train. Staying in a capsule provides a quintessentially Japanese experience, but they won't suit everyone – claustrophobics and anyone over two metres tall should give them a miss – and note also that the majority are for men only.

Though generally for just the one night, it is possible to reserve ahead should you wish to stay longer.

Capsule Inn Akasaka かぷせるイン赤坂

Map 4, B8. 6-14-1 Akasaka, Minato-ku ⓣ3588-1811. Akasaka Station.

Men-only, clean capsule hotel, with a large lounge and communal bathrooms. There are 280 capsules, so you shouldn't have a problem if you turn up late at night without a booking. Check in from 5pm; check out by 10am. ❷.

Capsule Hotel Riverside カプセルホテルリバーサイド

Map 5, H6. 2-20-4 Kaminarimon, Taitō-ku ⓣ3844-1155, ⓕ3841-6566. Asakusa Station.

Smart, friendly capsule hotel for men and women (who get fifteen capsules on a separate floor) in the thick of Asakusa. Located beside Azumabashi, facing the river, up a slightly off-putting staircase. Basic English spoken. Check in from 3pm. ❷.

Capsule Land Shibuya カプセルランド渋谷

Map 12, B7. 1-19-14 Dōgenzaka, Shibuya-ku ⓣ3464-1777, ⓕ3464-7771. Shibuya Station.

Recently refurbished men-only capsule hotel, easy to find at the top of the Dōgenzaka slope. Also has semi-double rooms for singles (including women) and couples, but they're very cramped. ❷.

Fontaine Akasaka フオンテーン赤坂

Map 4, D5. 4-3-5 Akasaka, Minato-ku ⓣ3583-6554. Akasaka-mitsuke Station.

Respectable capsule hotel and sauna, in the heart of Akasaka, that takes both men and women. Check in from 5pm. ❷.

Green Plaza Shinjuku グリーンプラザ新宿

Map 13, F1. 1-29-2 Kabukichō, Shinjuku-ku ⓣ3207-5411. Shinjuku Station.

The lobby is on the fourth floor for this large men-only capsule hotel (has room for 660), with friendly staff and a good fitness and sauna area. The roof-top spa baths cost extra. ❷.

YOUTH HOSTELS

Apart from capsule hotels, the cheapest option for budget travellers is to stay in one of Tokyo's two city-centre **youth hostels**. They're both clean and efficient and have excellent facilities, though impose an evening curfew and, usually, a maximum stay of three nights. Japan Youth Hostels also has a contract with Sky Court hotels to provide higher standard accommodation at favourable rates.

Hotel Sky Court Asakusa ホテルスカイコート浅草

Map 5, I3. 6-35-8 Asakusa, Taitō-ku ⓣ3875-4411, ⓕ3875-4941, ⓦ*www1.ocn.ne.jp/~hsky21* Asakusa Station.

Standard business hotel ten minutes' walk north of Asakusa Station where HI members pay a discounted rate of ¥5000 per night for a single en-suite room. They also offer free email access and there's no curfew. ❸.

Tokyo International Youth Hostel

東京国際ユースホステル

Map 10, B3. 18F, Central Plaza Bldg, 1-1 Kaguragashi, Shinjuku-ku ⓣ3235-1107. Iidabashi Station.

On a clear winter's day, you can see Fuji from this smart hostel above Iidabashi Station. Each bunk (¥3100 per night) has its own curtains and lockers, and there are fine Japanese baths, international phones, laundry facilities and a small members' kitchen – or breakfast and dinner available for a modest fee. Youth Hostel membership is not required, but they'll ask for some form of ID. Reception is open 3–9.30pm and there's a 10.30pm curfew. To find the hostel, exit B2 from the subway brings you straight up into the lift lobby; or, from the JR station's west exit, turn right into the Ramla Centre and keep straight ahead. ❷.

Tokyo Yoyogi Youth Hostel

東京代々木ユースホステル

Map 2, A7. 3-1 Kamizonochō, Shibuya-ku ⓣ3467-9163, ⓕ3467-9417. Sangubashi Station.

Small, comfortable single rooms only (¥3000 member/¥4000 non-member) at this hostel which is part of the pastel-coloured Olympic Youth Centre. It lacks atmosphere, but there are TVs and hot-water dispensers in the common rooms, laundry facilities and various cheap places to eat in the other parts of the centre. Guests must be out between 9am and 4pm, and there's a (none-too-strict) 10pm curfew. You'll need to book well in advance as rooms are limited. ❶.

LONG-TERM ACCOMMODATION

The recent recession has caused rents in Tokyo to drop slightly and it's said that landlords are becoming more flexible on the question of "key money" (usually one or two months' non-refundable rent when you move in). However, you're still up against the sheer weight of numbers when looking for **long-term accommodation**, not to mention endemic prejudice towards renting to non-Japanese. Be prepared for a long haul to get your own place.

Most newcomers start off in what's known as a **gaijin house** – a privately owned house or apartment consisting of shared or private rooms with communal kitchen and bathroom. They're usually rented by the month, though if there's space, weekly or even nightly rates may be available. Tokyo has a wide range of such places, from total fleapits to practically luxurious, though the best places are nearly always full. Among recommendations are *Taitō Ryokan* (Ⓣ & Ⓕ3843-2822, Ⓦ*www.libertyhouse.gr.jp*) which runs a good operation in Asakusa and *Sakura House* (Ⓦ*www.sakura-house.com*), with properties near Shinjuku among other areas. For other options scan the English-language press, particularly Tokyo Classified and Tokyo Noticeboard, or contact the Kimi Information Centre (8F, Oscar Bldg, 2-42-3 Ikebukuro Ⓣ3986-1604, Ⓕ3986-3037, Ⓦ*www2.dango.ne.jp/kimi*) which runs a useful letting agency. Monthly rates start from ¥30,000 to 40,000 per person for a shared room and ¥50,000 to 60,000 for a single. A deposit may also be required.

To find your own **apartment** it helps enormously to have a Japanese friend or colleague to act as an intermediary, or you could try an agent such as Kimi (see above). When you've found a place, apart from the first month's rent you should be prepared to pay a deposit of one to two months' rent in addition to key money and a month's rent in commission to the agent. Rentals in Tokyo start at ¥50,000–60,000 per month for a one room box.

Eating

Deciding what to **eat** in Tokyo can be a bewildering experience, and not just because you might be at a loss working out what's on the menu, or even on your plate. The problem is that with at least 80,000 **restaurants** in central Tokyo (compared to New York's 15,000 and London's mere 6000), you're swamped with choice. Virtually every type of cuisine is on offer, from African to Vietnamese, not to mention endless permutations of Japanese favourites, such as sushi, *rāmen*, *tempura* and *yakitori*. On top of this food crazes come and go, with *mukokuseki* food, a previously popular mix of global styles and ingredients, being eclipsed by a return to authentic Chinese and Korean, and bagels currently the snack *de jour*.

The good thing about so much choice is that there's no need to panic about prices; Tokyo has a plethora of **shokudō** (cafeterias), and cheap **noodle bars** dishing up curry rice – the Japanese equivalent of beans on toast. You'll also find plenty of **izakaya** (pub-style restaurants) and chain restaurants, where locals go when they need to fill up. **Bentō shops**, serving set boxes of food, are also plentiful, especially at lunchtime in shopping areas. Note, also, that several places listed in the Cafés and Teahouses,

Drinking and Live Music sections serve good food and are worth checking out at meal times.

The traditional Japanese **breakfast** is a gut-busting combination of miso soup, fish, pickles and rice, though many Japanese now prefer a quick *kōhii* and *tōsuto* (coffee and toast), served at most cafés on the "morning service" menu. Hardly anyone lingers over **lunch**, usually taken around noon. You could grab a sandwich, but they rarely bear any relation to ones back home and are best avoided in favour of a hearty meal at a restaurant, all of which offer set menus (called *teishoku*), usually around ¥1000 for a couple of courses, plus a drink, and rarely topping ¥2000 per person. At any time of day you'll catch people snacking in stand-up noodle bars – often found around train stations – and beside the revolving conveyor belts of cheap sushi shops. **Dinner**, the main meal of the day, can be eaten as early as 6pm (with many places taking last orders around 9pm), although Tokyo is better served than most places in Japan when it comes to late-night dining. With traditional Japanese cuisine you'll usually get all your courses at the same time, but at more formal places rice and soup are always served at the end of the meal.

With a few honourable exceptions (*Mominoki House* and *Crayon House* in Harajuku and *Shizenkan II* in Shibuya) finding truly vegetarian food can be difficult, so get a copy of *Vegetarian & Microbiotic Restaurants in Tokyo* from the TIC (see p.38).

To keep abreast of the latest restaurants, browse through the weekly freesheet *Tokyo Classified*, the monthly *Tokyo Journal*'s cityscope listings and the bi-monthly magazine *Eat*. The best Web site is the Tokyo Food Page (Ⓦ *www.bento.com/tokyofood.html*). Tokyo Q (Ⓦ *www.nokia*

.co.jp/tokyoq/) also has a useful database of restaurants, plus weekly reviews and *izakaya* recommendations. The *Zagat Survey of Tokyo Restaurants* (¥1500) is the most up-to-date restaurant guide; you can also check out their listings at Ⓦ *www.zagat.com/index.asp?localeID=5*

SNACKS AND FAST FOOD

Burger addicts need never go hungry in Tokyo, with branches of *McDonald's*, *KFC* and the local *Mos Burger*, *Love Burger* and *Lotteria* in virtually every neighbourhood. *Mos Burger*'s menu is the most interesting of the lot, featuring rice burgers (compacted rounds of rice sandwiching beef, pork, chicken or fish), carrot juice and green konyaku (a root vegetable) jelly. It's worth noting that *Mr Donut*'s menu includes Chinese dim sum (known in Japan as *yum cha*), as well as coffee and doughnuts. Decent **Japanese fast-food** chains include *Yoshinoya*, which serves up *gyūdon* (stewed strips of beef on rice), and *Tenya*, with its low-cost *tempura* and rice dishes; outlets of both places can be found near most main JR and subway stations.

At any time of the day or night, **convenience stores** such as Seven-Eleven, AM/PM and Lawson sell a wide range of snacks and meals which can be heated up in the shop's microwave or reconstituted with hot water. For more upmarket goodies, head for the basement food halls of the major department stores.

RESTAURANTS AND IZAKAYA

Tokyo has several **restaurant chains** worth checking out. For **Indian** food, *Moti*, with outlets in Roppongi and Akasaka, and *Samarat*, in Roppongi, Shibuya, Shinjuku and Ueno, are long-time local favourites. For good **Italian** dishes, head for *Capricciosa*, with branches all over the city

ESSENTIALS

Asa-gohan	Breakfast	朝ご飯
Hiru-gohan	Lunch	昼ご飯
Ban-gohan	Dinner	晩ご飯
Bentō	Boxed meal	弁当
Gohan	Rice	ご飯
Pan	Bread	パン
Niku	Meat	肉
Butaniku	Pork	豚肉
Gyūniku	Beef	牛肉
Toriniku	Chicken	鳥肉
Sakana	Fish	魚
Kai	Shellfish	貝
Tamago	Egg	卵
Kudamono	Fruit	果物
Yasai	Vegetables	野菜
Ninniku	Garlic	にんにく
Satō	Sugar	砂糖
Shio	Salt	塩
Tofu	Bean curd	豆腐

Places to eat

Aka chōchin	Pub-style restaurant with red lanterns outside	赤ちょうちん
Izakaya	Pub-style restaurant	居酒屋
Kissaten	Café	喫茶店
Resutoran	Restaurant	レストラン
Robatayaki	Restaurant specializing in charcoal-grilled foods	ろばた焼
Shokudō	Cafeteria	食堂

Meals

Chāhan	Fried rice	チャーハン
Kaiseki ryōri	Expensive Japanese haute cuisine	懐石料理
Karē	Mild curry served with rice	カレー
Nabe	Stew	鍋
Oden	Fish cakes and vegetables simmered in broth	おでん
Okonomiyaki	Savoury pancakes	お好み焼
Rāmen	Chinese-style noodles	ラーメン
Sashimi	Thinly sliced raw fish	刺身
Shabu-shabu	Thin beef slices cooked in broth	しゃぶしゃぶ
Soba	Thin buckwheat noodles	そば
Sushi	Vinegared rice topped with raw fish	寿司
Tempura	Lightly battered seafood and vegetables	天ぷら
Teriyaki	Food cooked in soy sauce and sweet sake	照焼
Udon	Thick wheat noodles	うどん
Yakitori	Chicken bits grilled on skewers	焼き鳥

Drinks

Biiru	Beer	ビール
Jūsu	Fruit juice	ジュース
Kōcha	Black tea	紅茶
Kōhii	Coffee	コーヒー
Matcha	Powdered green tea	抹茶
Miruku	Milk	ミルク
Mizu	Water	水
Nihon-shu	Rice wine (sake)	日本酒
Sake	Japanese alcohol	酒
Sencha	Green tea	煎茶

EATING ETIQUETTE

In most restaurants, before you start eating you'll be handed an *oshibori*, a damp, folded hand towel, usually steamed hot, but sometimes cold in summer. Use the towel to clean your hands and then fold it for the waiter to remove later. When the food arrives, you can wish your companions *bon appétit* by saying *itadakimas*.

Chopsticks (*hashi*) come with their own set of rules. Don't stick them upright in your rice – an allusion to death. If you're taking food from a shared plate, turn the chopsticks around and use the other end to pick up. Never cross your chopsticks when you put them on the table and don't use them to point at things. When eating soupy noodles you can enjoy a good slurp, and it's fine to drink directly from the bowl.

When you want the **bill**, say *o-kanjō kudasai* (bill please); the usual form is to pay at the till on the way out. Tipping is not expected, but it's polite to say *gochisō-sama deshita* (that was delicious) to the waiter or chef.

– its sign is in elongated *katakana* on a green, red and white background. *La Verde* is another Italian operation that gets good reviews. The *Seiryūmon* Taiwanese/Chinese restaurants are notable for their outlandish decor rather than the authenticity of their food.

Among the **Japanese chains** to look out for are *Tapa*, a lively **izakaya** specializing in *Ōzara* (big plate) cuisine; *Sushisei*, a classy sushi restaurant with branches in Tsukiji, Akasaka and Roppongi; *Kushinobo*, the folk craft-decorated, *kushikatsu* (deep fried morsels on skewers) restaurants, and *Tsunahachi*, which is *the* place for *tempura*. The *La Bohème* (Italian), *Zest* (Mexican) and *Monsoon* (Asian) chains are all run by the same company and can be relied on for value and late-night dining in chic settings; you'll find branches in Harajuku, Shibuya, Nishi-Azabu and Daikanyama.

If you can't decide what to go for, make your way to the restaurant floors of the major **department stores**, where you'll generally find a wide choice of cuisines and dining atmospheres under one roof, often with plastic food displays in the windows and daily specials. Also don't overlook the good-value **family restaurants**, which serve both Western and Japanese dishes and have easy-to-choose-from picture menus. The main ones are *Royal Host* (in Harajuku, Shinagawa and Takodanobaba among other locations), *Anna Millers*, famous for its dessert pies (in Hiro-o, Roppongi and Shinagawa), and *Jonathan's* (in Asakusa and Harajuku).

Where we give telephone numbers for the restaurants listed, it's advisable to book ahead, though you may need a Japanese speaker to help out. The listings give the closest subway or train station to the restaurant.

RESTAURANT PRICES

Restaurants have been graded as **inexpensive** (under ¥1000 for a meal without alcohol); **moderate** (¥1000–4000); **expensive** (¥4000–6000) and **very expensive** (over ¥6000). **Tipping** is not expected, but some restaurants and bars serving food, especially those in hotels, add on a **service charge** (typically 10 percent). Consumption tax may be included in advertised prices, but not always. Make sure you have cash to hand; payment by **credit cards** is becoming more common, but is generally restricted to upmarket restaurants and hotels.

AKASAKA

Blue Sky ブルースカイ

Map 4, D1. 17F, *New Ōtani*, 4-1 Kioichō, Chiyoda-ku ☎3238-0028. Akasaka-mitsuke Station.
Daily 11.30am–2.30pm & 5–10pm. Moderate to expensive.
This revolving restaurant at the top of one of the hotel's towers serves up a range of cuisines, including a Chinese buffet, and Japanese and Italian dishes. Best visited at night, when the neon-lit skyline view is at its most romantic.

Jangara じゃんがららあめん

Map 4, F5. Sotobori-dōri, Akasaka, Minato-ku. Akasaka Station.
Mon–Fri 11am–3pm, 5pm–12.30am. Inexpensive.
Funky noodle bar, near the entrance to Hie-jinja, serving up large bowls of *rāmen* in three types of soup: fish, mild and light, and greasy garlic, from ¥550, and beer at ¥450. Also in Akihabara, Ginza and Harajuku, with two branches on Omotesandō.

Jidaiya 時代屋

Map 4, E5. 3-14-3 Akasaka, Minato-ku ☎3588-0489. Akasaka Station.
Mon–Sat 6pm–4pm. Expensive.
Charming farmhouse-style *izakaya* in the heart of Akasaka, all dark wood, *tatami* and traditional ornaments. There's an English menu to help you select between the wide range of dishes, including a wild boar stew for ¥4000 and *kaiseki*-style course for ¥8000.

Los Platos ロスプラトス

Map 4, A9. 6-13-11 Akasaka, Minato-ku ☎3505-5225. Akasaka Station.
Mon–Sat 2pm–11pm. Expensive
Just off Akasaka-dōri, a 5min walk west of the subway exit, is

this authentic Spanish restaurant serving up *tapas* (from ¥1000 a plate or ¥4000 a set course) and *paella*. Has an English menu.

Sushisei 寿司清

Map 4, E4. 3-11-4 Akasaka, Minato-ku ☎3582-9503. Akasaka Station.

Mon–Fri 11.30am–2pm & 5–10.30pm, Sat 4.30–10pm. Moderate.

Famous sushi restaurant chain, where you may have to wait to be served at busy times. Choose from a hearty selection of fish slices at a fraction of the usual cost – roughly ¥3000 per head (less for lunch). Among other places there are also branches in Tsukiji (☎3541-7720) and Roppongi (☎3401-0578).

West Park Café ウエストパークカフエ

Map 4, E3. 2F, Akasaka Tōkyū Plaza, 2-14-3 Nagatachō, Chiyoda-ku. Akasaka-mitsuke Station.

Mon–Fri 11.30am–11pm, Sat & Sun 11.30am–3pm. Inexpensive to moderate.

Reasonably authentic American style deli-café, with an outdoor terrace and an airy interior. Good for light meals, and for their weekend brunch. The original branch is a 5min walk west of Yoyogi-kōen at 23-11 Moto-Yoyogichō.

Yakinikku Karebiya 焼肉カルビ屋

Map 4, E5. 3-12-7 Akasaka, Minato-ku. Akasaka Station.

Daily 11am–3am. Moderate.

One of the better value of Akasaka's several Korean barbecue restaurants, run by a friendly English-speaking manager. There's a picture menu and lunch deals for ¥800. Dinner courses, including soup, rice, salad, beef and pickles, are ¥2000.

Yama no Chaya 山の茶屋

Map 4, G4. 2-10-6 Nagatachō, Chiyoda-ku ☎3581-0656. Akasaka Station.

Mon–Sat 11.30am–1.30pm & 6–7pm (last orders). Very expensive.

If you're going to splash out on traditional Japanese cuisine, you could do a lot worse than this teahouse restaurant set in a wooded glade next to the Hie-jinja. It's been serving a delicately prepared set menu (¥10,000 for lunch, ¥18,000 for dinner) based around *unagi*(eel) for the last seventy years.

ASAKUSA

Chin'ya ちんや

Map 5, G5. 1-3-4 Asakusa, Taitō-ku. Asakusa Station.
Daily except Wed 11.45am–9pm. Moderate to expensive.
Founded in 1880, this traditional *shabu-shabu* and *sukiyaki* restaurant offers basic menus from ¥3000. It occupies seven floors, with cheaper, more casual dining in the basement.

Daikokuya 大黒家

Map 5, F4. 1-38-10 Asakusa, Taitō-ku. Asakusa Station.
Daily except Thurs 11.20am–8.30pm. Moderate.
It's best to avoid the lunchtime rush at this Meiji-era *tempura* restaurant, located in an attractive old building opposite Dembō-in garden. The speciality is *tendon*, a satisfying bowl of shrimp, fish and prawn *tempura* on a bed of rice (from ¥1400). The *tatami* room upstairs tends to be less hectic.

Kushi-suke クシスケ

Map 5, G5. 1-2-12 Asakusa, Taitō-ku. Asakusa Station.
Mon–Fri noon–11pm, Sat, Sun & hols 5–11pm. Inexpensive to moderate.
Relaxed *yakitori* bar hidden down an alley northeast of Kaminarimon. They serve well-priced *yakitori* lunch sets, or try their rice bowls (from around ¥800).

Owariya 尾張屋

Map 5, G5. 1-1-3 Asakusa, Taitō-ku. Asakusa Station.
Daily except Wed 11.30am–8.30pm. Inexpensive to moderate.
A deceptively ordinary-looking place that's been dishing up delicious *soba* in all its variations for over a century – the only give-away is some classy calligraphy around the walls. Prices range from just ¥550 to ¥2000. Selective English menu.

Sometaro 染太郎

Map 5, D5. 2-2-2 Nishi-Asakusa, Taitō-ku. Tawaramachi Station.
Daily noon–10pm. Inexpensive.
Homely restaurant specializing in *okonomiyaki*, cheap and filling savoury pancakes which you cook on a hotplate. A good-size bowl costs from ¥400, depending on your choice of ingredients, or try your hand at *yakisoba* (fried noodles), from ¥550; there's a book of English instructions and plenty of friendly advice. To find it, look for a tiny, bamboo-fenced garden and lantern half way up the street.

EBISU AND MEGURO

Cardenas Charcole Grill カーデイナスチヤコールグリル

Map 6, C2. 1-12-14 Ebisu Nishi, Shibuya-ku ⓣ 5428-0779. Ebisu Station.
Mon–Fri 11.30am–2pm, 5.30pm–2am, Sat & Sun 5.30pm–2am. Expensive.
Dramatic, multi-level basement space showcases some of Tokyo's best contemporary fusion cuisine – the fish cakes in *uni* sauce look like spiky sea urchins and taste fantastic. Steaks are expensive, but the other grilled dishes needn't break the bank. The same company also run the relaxed *Fummy's Grill* (see below),

Restaurant Cardenas (☎5447-1287) in Hiro-o and *Cardenas Chinois* (☎5766-1737), in Nishi-Azabu, serving stylish Chinese dishes.

Ebisu Tower 恵比寿タワー

Map 6, E4. Yebisu Garden City. Ebisu Station.
Daily 11.30am–9pm. Moderate to expensive.

Two floors of restaurants with great views across the city. Try *Yebisu* on the 39th floor, a classy *yakitori-ya* with sets for around ¥1000, or *Chibo*, a fun Ōsaka-style *okonomiyaki* restaurant on the 38th. The Indian restaurant *Ajanta* also does a lunch buffet for ¥1480.

Fummy's Grill フミーズグリル

Map 6, F2. 2-1-5 Ebisu, Shibuya-ku ☎3473-9629. Ebisu Station.
Daily 11.30am–2pm & 6pm–2am. Moderate to expensive.

Innovative cooking in a casual setting with an open terrace. Dishes that take their inspiration from around the Pacific Rim are prepared in an open kitchen. This is nouvelle cuisine without the skimpy portions, and with a good wine list to boot. There's a weekend brunch for ¥1300.

Good Honest Grub グドホンエストぐラブ

Map 6, C3. 1-11-11 Ebisu Minami, Shibuya-ku. Ebisu Station.
Mon–Fri 11.30am–midnight, Sat & Sun 8.30am–midnight.
Inexpensive to moderate.

Relaxed, brightly decorated place that serves up just what the name says – chunky sandwiches, big salads and sizeable plates of pasta. The fruit shakes are good and they also have organic wine.

Kotobuki Diner ことぶきダイナ

Map 6, G1. 5-3 Hiro-o, Shibuya-ku ☎3473-5463. Hiro-o Station.
Daily 5.30pm–2am. Moderate.

Lively, modern *izakaya* on two floors, popular with expats, and with ground-floor bar open to the street in the summer. They specialise in *yakitori* but there are plenty of other dishes, too.

Kushinobo 串の坊

Map 6, D2. 6F, Atre, 1-5-5 Ebisu, Shibuya-ku. Ebisu Station. Daily 11.30am–9pm. Inexpensive to moderate.

The lunch sets from under ¥1000 are great value at this *kushikatsu* restaurant – lots of interesting deep-fried nibbles on skewers are served up in a cosy folk-craft-decorated setting. Other branches around the city include Roppongi (2F, 7&7 Bldg, 7-14-18 Roppongi) which specializes in *fugu*, Shibuya (5F J&R Bldg, 33-12 Udagawachō), and Shinjuku (6F Isetan Kaikan, 3-15-17 Shinjuku).

Ninniku-ya にんにく屋

Map 6, E2. 1-26-12 Ebisu, Shibuya-ku ☎3445-9055. Ebisu Station. Mon–Sat 6.30–10.30pm. Moderate to expensive.

Tokyo's original garlic restaurant is still one of the best. Virtually everything on the menu is cooked with the pungent bulb, and the buzzing atmosphere in the long dining room with large shared wooden tables can't be beaten. Expect to wait for a table at the weekends.

Taillevent Robuchon タイユバンロブション

Map 6, E4. Yebisu Garden Place, 1-13-1 Mita, Meguro-ku ☎5424-1338. Ebisu Station.

Mon–Sat noon–2.30pm & 6–9.30pm. Very expensive.

Two of Paris's most celebrated restaurants have attached their names to this operation in the meticulous reproduction of a Louis XV-style chateau. The meals are theatrical creations with designer-label price tags. Start saving up for dinner, which is at least ¥20,000 per head.

Tonki とんき

Map 6, E6. 1-1-2 Shimo Meguro, Meguro-ku. Meguro Station. Daily except Tues 4–10.45pm. Moderate.

Tokyo's most famous *tonkatsu* restaurant, where a seemingly telepathic team makes order of chaos. There's usually a queue outside this main branch, west of the station. Try the *teishoku*, which comes with soup, rice, cabbage, pickles and tea for ¥1500. The annexe on the eastern side of the station, across the plaza on the second floor of the corner building, is open for lunch.

GINZA AND AROUND

Atariya 当リヤ

Map 7, E6. 3-5-17 Ginza, Chūō-ku. Ginza Station.
Mon–Sat 4.30–10.15pm. Moderate.

One of the more reasonable places to eat in Ginza, this small, workaday restaurant behind Mikimoto store has English menus and makes a good introduction to *yakitori* bars.

Chiang Mai チェンマイ

Map 7, C7. 1-6-10 Yūrakuchō, Chiyoda-ku ⓣ3580-0456. Hibiya Station.
Daily except Sat 11.30am–11pm. Inexpensive to moderate.

Cosy, relaxed Thai restaurant with excellent-value set lunches and a wicked *tom yam* soup. If this place is full try the more formal *Siam* round the corner.

Edo-gin 江戸銀

Map 7, G8. 4-5-5 Tsukiji, Chūō-ku ⓣ3543-4401. Tsukiji Station.
Mon–Sat 11am–9.30pm. Moderate to expensive.

Over one hundred chefs slice fish for hordes of customers who pack out this main shop and its three satellite shops. The portions are reckoned to be among the largest in the city, and certainly make the traditional one-bite technique of eating sushi difficult. The ¥1000 *teishoku* is the best bet for lunch.

Farm Grill ファムグリル

Map 7, E9. 2F, Ginza Nine 3, 8-6 Ginza, Chūō-ku ☎5568-6156. Shimbashi Station.

Daily 11.30am–11pm. Moderate.

Pay as you enter for this popular California-style buffet located under the expressway. It's ¥1600 for lunch or ¥2600 for dinner, both with a 2hr time limit. Drinks are not included, but in the evening you can opt for a ¥1050 *nomihodai* including wine, whisky, coffee and a choice of fifty cocktails. There's also a well-stocked wine bar with wine by the glass from ¥200 and bar snacks. Reservations recommended on Friday evenings.

Nair's ナイルレストラン

Map 7, F7. 4-10-7 Ginza, Chūō-ku. Higashi-Ginza Station.

Mon & Wed–Sat 11.30am–9.30pm, Sun & hols 11.30am–8.30pm. Moderate.

A Tokyo institution since 1949, now offering Kerala home-cooking. Maybe not the best Indian around, but the food's tasty and reasonably cheap for Ginza, especially at lunch time (¥1400 per head). In the evening, count on ¥2000–3000.

Shin Hi No Moto 新日の基

Map 7, C6. Yūrakuchō 1-chōme, Chiyoda-ku. Yūrakuchō or Hibiya Stations.

Daily 5pm–midnight. Moderate.

Lively, traditional *izakaya* under the tracks just south of Yūrakuchō Station. One of the few places to stock the excellent Sapporo Red Star beer, or cheap, strong *shōchū* (grain liquor). The manager's English, so tell him your budget, and count on at least ¥1500 per head. The speciality is seafood, straight from Tsukiji market.

Taimeiken たいめいけん

Map 7, F2. 1-2-10 Nihombashi, Chūō-ku. Nihombashi Station.
Mon–Sat 11am–9pm, closed Sun & hols. Inexpensive to moderate.

One of Tokyo's original Western-style restaurants, famous for dishing up *omu-raisu* (rice-stuffed omelette) in the film *Tampopo*. Downstairs is a cheap and cheerful cafeteria serving large portions of curry rice, *tonkatsu* and noodles, with a more expensive restaurant above. Selective English menu.

Tenmaru 天〇

Map 7, E8. 6-9-2 Ginza, Chūō-ku. Ginza Station.
Mon–Sat 11.30am–3pm & 5–9.30pm, Sun 11am–9pm. Moderate.

Consistently good *tempura* restaurant in a basement just off Chūō-dōri. Expect to spend at least ¥2000 a head. English menu available.

Torigin 鳥ぎん

Map 7, D7. B1, 5-5-7 Ginza, Chūō-ku. Ginza Station.
Daily 11.30am–10pm. Inexpensive to moderate.

Bright, popular restaurant serving *yakitori* and *kamameshi* (kettle-cooked rice with a choice of toppings), tucked down an alley two blocks east of Ginza's Sony Building among a whole clutch of cheeky rivals. Good for a snack or a full meal, particularly if you opt for *kamameshi* or a weekday lunch set, both from around ¥800. The English menu makes things a lot easier.

Tsukiji Tama-zushi 築地玉寿司

Map 7, E8. Ginza Rabi-ten, 5F, 6-9-5 Ginza, Chūō-ku. Ginza Station.
Sushi Bar 6F daily 11.30am–10pm; Sushi Corner 4F Mon–Sat 5.30pm–2am, Sun & hols to 10pm. Moderate.

Despite the plush surroundings, prices are very reasonable at this restaurant on three floors with a glitzy sushi bar on the sixth floor and a more soothing, Japanese-style "sushi corner" on the fourth. Plates cost between ¥100 and ¥500 for the basic *nigiri-zushi*.

Uzo Shio うず潮

Map 7, C7. 1-1-13 Yūrakuchō, Chiyoda-ku. Hibiya Station.
Daily 11am–10pm. Inexpensive.

Hone your *kaitenzushi* (conveyor-belt sushi) skills in this friendly sushi bar under the train tracks. If you look lost, they'll give you English guidelines on how it works, including how to order soup, make tea and so on. Prices start at ¥150 per plate.

Yaneura やねうら

Map 7, D8. B1, 6-8-7 Ginza, Chūō-ku. Ginza Station.
Mon–Fri 4–10pm, Sat, Sun & hols 1–9pm. Inexpensive to moderate.

Large, lively *okonomiyaki* joint (do-it-yourself pancakes) that draws a young crowd and the occasional *gaijin* (English menu available). Bowls of ingredients cost around ¥800, but you'll need at least two for a decent meal – or you can order extra toppings and side-dishes. They do good-value eat-all-you-can deals at around ¥1300 on weekends (1–5pm) and ¥200 more on Mondays (4–8pm); there's a 2hr time limit.

HARAJUKU AND AOYAMA

Angkor Wat アンコールワット

Map 13, G7. 1-38-13 Yoyogi, Shibuya-ku ⓣ3370-3019. Yoyogi Station.
Mon–Fri 11am–2pm & 5–11pm, Sat & Sun 5–11pm. Moderate.

Best Cambodian restaurant in Tokyo, a five-minute walk west of Yoyogi Station; look for the pottery elephant outside the entrance on a side street. Tell the waiters your price limit and let them bring you a selection of dishes (¥3000 per head is plenty). The sweetly spicy salads, soups and vegetable rolls are all excellent.

Aux Bacchanales オーバクナル

Map 8, C1. 1-6-1 Jingūmae, Shibuya-ku. Meiji-Jingūmae Station. Daily 10am–midnight. Moderate.

Nicest of the French-style bistros that have taken over Harajuku, with tables spilling onto the pavement, and surly French waiters to complement the *steak frites*. Drinks at the bar are cheaper, but who would want to miss the passing parade on Meiji-dōri?

Chao Bamboo チャオバンブー

Map 8, C3. 6-1-5 Jingūmae, Shibuya-ku. Omotesandō Station. Daily 11am–11pm. Moderate.

Same management as the larger – but inferior – *Bamboo* further up Omotesandō, but this one specializes in cheap and tasty Southeast Asian street food, served at outdoor tables. There's a photo menu and you'd be hard-pressed to spend more than ¥2000.

Crayon House クレヨンハウス

Map 8, E4. 3-8-15 Kita-Aoyama, Minato-ku. Omotesandō Station. Daily 11am–10pm. Moderate.

Of the two restaurants in this natural food shop, just off Omotesandō and around the corner from the Hanae Mori Building, the one to go for is the café *Hiroba* serving a hearty lunch buffet for ¥1200.

Fujimamas フジママズ

Map 8, C3. 6-3-2 Jingūmae, Shibuya-ku ⑦5485-2262. Meiji-Jingūmae Station.
Daily noon–3pm & 6–11pm. Moderate.

One of the current "in" places to graze. A spacious, two-level interior and a bit more style than substance to the east-west fusion food, but generally good value and the menu (desserts are headed up "Oh, I just couldn't ... but I will!") is a hoot.

Heirokuzushi 平禄寿司

Map 8, D4. 5-8-5 Jingūmae, Shibuya-ku. Meiji-Jingūmae Station.
Daily 11am–9pm. Inexpensive.

A new company has recently taken over this perennially popular *kaitenzushi* (conveyor-belt sushi) restaurant in a prime position on Omotesandō. Plates range from ¥120 to ¥240, but on the 2nd Tues of every month, everything is priced ¥120. It also does take-away which is good for picnics in Yoyogi-kōen.

La Bohème ラボエム

Map 8, C3. 2F, Jingūbashi Bldg, 6-7-18 Jingūmae, Shibuya-ku.
Meiji-Jingūmae Station.
Daily 11.30am–5pm. Moderate.

The original – and nicer – of the two *La Bohème* that are now in Harajuku (the other is on Omotesandō), serving European cuisine in a mock-Mediterranean atmosphere at reasonable prices. The Mexican restaurant *Zest* and the bar *Oh! God* are in the same building.

Las Chicas ラスチカス

Map 8, D5. 5-47-6 Jingumae, Shibuya-ku ⓣ3407-6865.
Omotesando Station.
Daily 11am–11pm. Moderate.

On a summer's night there are few nicer places to dine than in *Las Chicas*' enchanting courtyard, where fairy lights twinkle in the trees. The Asian-fusion cuisine is supported by some fine antipodean wines. In this same complex hidden away on Harajuku's quiet backstreets there's also a spacious indoor restaurant, a lively bar (with Internet terminals) and a hair salon.

Mominoki House モモノキハウス

Map 8, D1. 2-18-5 Jingūmae, Shibuya-ku ⓣ3405-9144. Meiji-Jingūmae Station.
Mon–Sat 11am–11pm. Moderate.

Lots of natural ingredients are used at this eclectic macrobiotic restaurant on the quiet north side of Harajuku. Plants, paintings and jazz add to the atmosphere. A good lunch can be had for around ¥1500, but prices rise steeply at dinner.

News Deli ニューズデリ

Map 8, E5. 3-6-26 Kita-Aoyama, Minato-ku. Omotesandō Station. Mon–Thurs 9am–midnight, Fri 9am–2am, Sat 11am–2am, Sun 11am–11pm. Inexpensive to moderate.

A lively atmosphere with good music and magazines to go with the wide range of deli-type food and snacks. Take-out available and good breakfast (¥680) and lunch deals (¥900).

Le Papillon de Paris ラパピヨンドパリ

Map 8, E4. Hanae Mori Bldg, 3-6-1 Kita-Aoyama, Minato-ku ⓣ3407 7461. Omotesandō Station.

Daily 11.30am–2.30pm & 5.30–9.30pm. Expensive.

A hushed atmosphere prevails at one of the more authentic of Tokyo's French restaurants. Only the crispest linen and finest china and crystal grace these tables, a suitable accompaniment for the well-prepared dishes. Famous for its good-value Sunday brunch (11am–2.30pm, ¥3500, without service and tax).

Pizza Express ピザエクスプレス

Map 8, C2. 4-30-3 Jingūmae, Shibuya-ku ⓣ5775-3894. Meiji-Jingūmae Station. Daily 11am–11pm. Moderate.

The UK-based upmarket pizza chain strikes out on Harajuku's most high profile corner. There's live jazz on Mondays and Thursdays 7–9pm. If you don't fancy pizza, check out the funky Asian-influenced *Elephant Bar* next door.

Rojak ロジやク

Map 8, G7. 6-3-14 Minami-Aoyama, Minato-ku ⓣ3409-6764. Omotesandō Station.

Daily noon–4pm & 6pm–midnight. Moderate – expensive.

A lush jungle scene is painted on one long-drop wall, there's a very cosy library-style bar with sofas and the Asian/organic menu is very appealing and not overpriced. Tucked down a cul-de-sac near the *Blue Note Tokyo* jazz club.

Soul 魂

Map 8, E5. 3-12-3 Kita-Aoyama, Minato-ku ⓣ5466-1877. Omotesandō Station.

Daily 11.30am–2pm & 6pm–midnight. Moderate.

Stylish *izakaya*, popular with young Japanese, and specializing in *mukokuseki*. The menu is in Japanese only, but you can point at the large plates of food on the counter to order. Expect to spend around ¥3000 per person. It's on the road beside the Kinokunya supermarket – look for the red lights.

Toriyoshi 鳥良

Map 8, C2. 4-28-21 Jingūmae ⓣ3470-3901. Meiji-Jingūmae Station.

Daily 6–11pm. Moderate.

Ultra-modern chicken restaurant that serves the bird in all manner of ways, from stew to *yakitori* and raw as *sashimi*. *Tori sembei* crackers, made out of deep-fried chicken skin, are worth trying. There are lots of other restaurants worth checking out on the same backstreet running parallel to Meiji-dōri.

un café ウンカフェ

Map 8, D6. B2, Cosmos Aoyama Bldg, 5-53-67 Jingūmae, Shibuya-ku ⓣ5469-0275. Omotesandō Station.

Daily 11.30am–11pm. Moderate.

Tucked away in the sunken plaza behind the United Nations University building (hence the punning name), this sleek operation has a hip, post-modern atmosphere. The menu ranges from simple dishes such as spaghetti and salads to beef carpaccio on savoury couscous or seared tuna steaks. There are tables on the plaza, making this an ideal alfresco dining spot in summer.

IKEBUKURO AND AROUND

Akiyoshi 秋吉

Map 9, B4. 3-30-4 Nishi-Ikebukuro, Toshima-ku. Ikebukuro Station. Daily 5pm–midnight. Inexpensive.

Unusually large *yakitori* bar with a lively atmosphere and a helpful picture-menu. You might have to queue at peak times for the tables, but there's generally space at the counter.

Malaychan マレーチャン

Map 9, B4. 3-22-6 Nishi-Ikebukuro, Toshima-ku. Ikebukuro Station. Mon-Sat 11am–2.30pm & 5–11pm, Sun & hols 11am–11pm. Inexpensive to moderate.

Popular unpretentious Malay restaurant dishing up decent food, from grilled fish on banana leaf and *mee goreng* to winter steam boats. The beer pitchers are good value, or throw in a Singapore Sling and you can still eat well for around ¥2000. Weekday lunch menus from ¥800.

Mawaru Sushi Hana-kan まわる寿し花館

Map 9, E7. 3-13-10 Minami-Ikebukuro, Toshima-ku. Ikebukuro Station.
Daily 11am–11pm. Inexpensive to moderate.

Big *kaitenzushi* with stools and family tables around the revolving counter. Plates cost from ¥120 to ¥500 for two pieces of sushi, and they also do take-out sushi *bentō*.

Mekong メコン

Map 9, B4. B1, 3-26-5 Nishi-Ikebukuro, Toshima-ku. Ikebukuro Station.
Daily except Tues lunchtime 11.30am–2.30pm & 5–11pm. Moderate.

The decor may not be much to rave about, but the tastes and aromas will take you straight back to Thailand. The lunchtime buffet is a steal at ¥1050; at other times you can eat well for around ¥2000 a head from their picture-menu.

Saigon サイゴン

Map 9, F3. 3F, 1-7-10 Higashi-Ikebukuro, Toshima-ku. Ikebukuro Station.
Mon–Fri noon–2.30pm & 5–10.30pm, Sat, Sun & hols 11.30am–10.30pm. Inexpensive to moderate.
Friendly, no-frills place serving authentic Vietnamese food, even down to the *333* beer. *Banh xeo* (sizzling pancake with a spicy sauce) or *bunh bo* (beef noodle soup) are recommended, with a side-dish of *nem* (spring rolls) if you're really hungry. Weekday lunchtime sets are excellent value at ¥750.

300B (Sanbyaku B) 三百ビ

Map 9, B3. 3-29 Nishi-Ikebukuro, Toshima-ku. Ikebukuro Station.
Mon–Fri 11.45am–11.30pm, Sat, Sun & hols 3–11pm. Moderate.
There are two *300B*s on opposite sides of the road but make sure you find this one (no.1) for the dried whale's penis hanging in the entrance. These are big, bubbling *izakaya*, popular with a young crowd for the cheap prices and good food.

speakeasy スピーキージー

Map 9, G4. B2, 1-21-1 Higashi-Ikebukuro, Toshima-ku. Ikebukuro Station.
Mon–Thurs & Sun 5.30–11.30pm, Fri & Sat to 4am. Moderate.
Cocooned deep in the bowels of Ikebukuro is this spacious, low-lit take on a very cool New York drinking dive circa 1929. They serve modern *izakaya*-style food for around ¥2000 a head and their own beer, with plans for an in-house microbrewery. Liveliest on Friday and Saturday nights, when there's a DJ.

KANDA AND RYŌGOKU

Botan ぼたん

Map 10, G5. 1-15 Kanda-Sudachō, Chiyoda-ku. Awajichō Station. Mon–Sat 11.30am–9pm (last order 8pm). Closed Sun & hols. Very expensive.

Chicken *sukiyaki* is the order of the day at this atmospheric old restaurant tucked in the backstreets of Kanda. There's no choice and it's certainly not cheap (just over ¥7000 a head) but this is the genuine article, where the chicken, vegetables and *tofu* simmer gently over individual braziers in small rooms.

La Bretagne ルブルターニュ

Map 10, B3. 4-2 Kagurazaka, Shinjuku-ku. Iidabashi Station. Tues–Sat 11.30am–10.30pm, Sun 11.30am–9pm. Moderate.

Attractive French-run restaurant offering authentic crepes and buckwheat *galettes* down a little dead-end street, with tables outside. Also serves salads, lunchtime sets (around ¥1500) and daily specials.

Mukashiya むかしや

Map 10, A3. 5-12 Kagurazaka, Shinjuku-ku. Iidabashi Station. Mon–Fri 5–11pm, Sat & hols 5–10.30pm, closed Sun. Moderate.

Big, old-style *izakaya* with a rustic flavour. The speciality food is *yakitori* – try their own *Mukashi-yaki*, made of soya bean skins, or choose from the English menu.

Tomoegata 巴潟

Map 10, Ryogoku inset. 2-17-6 Ryōgoku, Sumida-ku. Ryōgoku Station.

Daily 11.30am–10pm. Inexpensive to moderate.

In the heart of sumo territory, this is one of the best places to sample the wrestlers' protein-packed stew, *chanko-nabe*. For ¥3000 you can have the full-blown meal cooked at your table, though the smaller, ready-made version is pretty substantial (lunch only; ¥840). Easy to spot from its parade of colourful flags.

Yabu Soba やぶそば

Map 10, G5. 2-10 Kanda-Awajichō, Chiyoda-ku. Awajichō Station. Daily 11.30am–8pm. Inexpensive to moderate.

Connoisseurs travel a long way to slurp their noodles and listen to the distinctive sing-song cries of *Yabu Soba*'s cheerful waiting staff. Prices start at ¥600, from a short menu of *soba* and *udon* dishes.

ROPPONGI, AZABU-JŪBAN, NISHI AZABU AND HIRO-O

Bikkuri Sushi びっくり寿司

Map 11, E4. 3-14-9 Roppongi, Minato-ku. Roppongi Station. Daily 11am–5am. Inexpensive.

Conveyor-belt sushi on the corner of Gaien Higashi-dōri, opposite the Roi Building. The long opening hours help clubbers keep their energy levels up. Dishes start at ¥130.

Hard Rock Café ハードロックカフェ

Map 11, E4. 5-4-20 Roppongi, Minato-ku. Roppongi Station. Mon–Thurs 11.30am–2am, Fri & Sat until 4am, Sun until 11.30pm. Moderate to expensive.

You won't miss the giant gorilla clamped onto the side of this rock'n'roll burger joint that needs no introduction. Very noisy, very lively, very Roppongi.

Havana Café ハバナカフェ

Map 11, D3. 4-12-2 Roppongi, Minato-ku. Roppongi Station. Daily 11.30am–5am. Moderate.

More of a Cajun than a Cuban lilt to the menu at this brightly decorated café away from the main Roppongi drag. The portions are large, the prices reasonable and there's a happy hour from 5pm to 7pm.

Homework's ホームワークス

Map 6, F2. 5-1-20 Hirō, Shibuya-ku. Hiro-o Station.
Daily 11am–9pm, Sun 11am–6pm. Moderate.

Decent burgers – the chunky, home-made variety – and top chips at this popular pitstop at the end of Hiro-o's main shopping street. There's another branch at 1-5-8 Azabu-Jūban, Minato-ku, ten minutes' walk south of the Roppongi crossing (Map 11, E6).

Ichioku 一億

Map 11, D3. 4-4-5 Roppongi, Minato-ku. Roppongi Station.
Daily 5pm–3am, Sun until 11pm. Moderate.

At the Nogizaka end of Roppongi, look for the green, yellow and red front of this funkily decorated *mukokuseki izakaya*. Many swear by the cheese *gyoza*s and *tofu* steaks, but there's plenty more to choose from on the table top picture-menu. Dishes are made from organically grown vegetables.

Inakaya 田舎家

Map 11, D3. 7-8-4 Roppongi, Minato-ku ⓣ3405-9866. Roppongi Station.
Daily 5–11pm. Very expensive.

Food preparation as theatre at this justly famous *robatayaki*, where the chefs kneel on a raised dais amid a carnival of raw ingredients, screaming out the names of the cooked dishes that they pass to customers on wooden spatulas. A meal can easily clock up at ¥10,000 per person, but you'll have a memorable night. Also at 3-12-7 Akasaka, Minato-ku (ⓣ3586-3054).

Kisso

吉左右

Map 11, F5. B1, Axis Bldg, 5-17-1 Roppongi, Minato-ku ⓣ3582-4191. Roppongi Station.

Mon–Sat 11.30am–2pm & 5.30–10pm. Very expensive.

A fine place to sample *kaiseki-ryori*. Modern furnishings with traditional touches like the giant *ikebana* displays. Lunch sets are a bargain at ¥1200 to ¥2500; the evening courses, including at least nine different dishes, start at ¥8000.

Lilla Darlarna

リラダラルイナ

Map 11, E5. 5-9-19 Roppongi, Minato-ku ⓣ3478-4690. Roppongi Station. Mon–Sat noon–3pm & 6–9.30pm. Moderate.

Decorated like something out of a Hans Christian Andersen fairytale book, this intimate Swedish restaurant offers yummy meatballs with lingonberry jam, gravlax and other Scandinavian dishes. Fine lunch deals and the set dinner is ¥3500.

Noodles

ヌデレス

Map 11, F7. 2-21-7 Azabu-Jūban, Minato-ku ⓣ3452-3112. Azabu-Jūban Station.

Mon–Fri 6pm–4am, Sat & Sun 11.30am–2.30pm & 6pm–4am. Moderate.

Noodle dishes for the smart set, with some interesting variation such as sauteed foie gras with noodles (¥2000). The portions are big, which makes sharing a good idea and keeps the cost down.

Shimauta Paradise

島唄楽園

Map 11, D4. 4F, Seishidō Bldg, 7-14-10 Roppongi ⓣ3470-2310. Roppongi Station.

Mon–Sat 5–11pm. Moderate to expensive.

Lively restaurant near Roppongi Crossing, serving Okinawan cuisine – pickled sea cucumber, stewed pigs' trotters, fermented squid with tofu, etc. Wash it down with a flask of *shōchū* (distilled grain alcohol) diluted with warm water or

Orion beer from Japan's southern islands. When there's live music, there's a ¥1000 cover charge.

To the Herbs トゥーザハーブス

Map 11, B5. 1-13-13 Nishi-Azabu, Minato-ku ⓣ3497-4200. Roppongi Station.
Daily 11.30am–5am. Moderate.
Decent Italian food (crispy pizza, flavoursome pasta sauces) at this attractive wooden building near the crossing. Among other outlets, the one in Mejiro (ⓣ3499-2900), west of the station, specializes in spaghetti. There's also a handy branch in Ginza, next to the Kabuki-za (ⓣ5565-9800).

Volga ボルガ

Map 11, H5. 3-5-14 Shiba Koen, Minato-ku ⓣ3433-1766. Kamiyachō Station.
Daily 11am–2.30pm & 5–11pm. Expensive.
Outside is a camp onion-domed facade, inside it's like entering a set from *Dr Zhivago*, all heavy velvet and gilt. There are 27 different types of vodka, and a menu that embraces standard Russian dishes such as *borsch* and *piroshki*. It often has live music.

SHIBUYA

Lunchan Aoyama ランチヤンバー&グリル青山

Map 12, I3. 1-2-5 Shibuya, Shibuya-ku ⓣ5466-1398. Shibuya Station.
Mon–Sat 11.30am–11pm, Sun 11am–10pm. Expensive.
Glitzy and overblown for this quiet corner of Shibuya, but still worth swinging by. Large servings of California-style cuisine, including Caesar salad, ribs and cheesecakes. Sunday brunches are a justifiable indulgence.

Miyoko 妙高

Map 12, F3. 1-17-2 Shibuya, Shibuya-ku ⓣ3499-3450. Shibuya Station.

Mon–Sat 11am–11pm. Moderate.

You really can't go wrong with these hearty metal bowls of Yamanashi-ken flat *udon* noodles in a rich *nabe* stew – just the ticket on a chilly day. Or try the cold noodle dishes in summer. Look for the water wheel outside.

New York Kitchen ニューヨークキッチン

Map 12, D2. Mulbery Bldg, 1-17 Jinnan, Shibuya-ku. Shibuya Station.

Daily 11am–11pm. Inexpensive.

Stylish deli-café, just off Kōen-dōri around the corner from the Tobacco and Salt Museum (see p.119), with a good-value self-service food bar for about ¥500 per plate. Also does bagels and has an outdoor terrace opposite.

Sail O's Chinese Deli Café セルオズチヤイニズデリカフエ

Map 12, D6. 4F, Shibuya Mark City, Shibuya-ku. Shibuya Station.

Daily 11am–11pm. Inexpensive–moderate.

Fluffy white stuffed dumplings are the speciality at this appealingly designed pitstop in the East building of the Shibuya Mark City complex. For dessert try the custard ones.

Shizenkan II 自然館パート２

Map 12, G7. Royal Bldg, 3-9-2 Shibuya, Shibuya-ku. Shibuya Station.

Mon–Sat 11.30am–8pm. Moderate.

Health-food restaurant and shop, on the Ebisu side of Shibuya Station, serving a decent set lunch for ¥1000, with lots of brown rice and small vegetable dishes.

Shun Sai 旬彩

Map 12, D6. 25F, Shibuya Excel Hotel Tōkyū, 1-12-2 Dōgenzaka, Shibuya-ku. Shibuya Station.

Daily 11.30am–2pm & 6–10pm. Very expensive.

Once you've dragged your eyes away from the glorious view, you'll notice the exquisite *kaiseki-ryori* cuisine being served at this stylish hotel restaurant. A *bentō* lunch starts at ¥1800, while dinner courses are from ¥6500 upwards.

SHINJUKU AND AROUND

Ban Thai バンタイ

Map 13, F2. 1-23-14 Kabukichō, Shinjuku-ku ⓣ3207-0068. Shinjuku Station.

Daily 11.30am–3pm & 5–11pm. Moderate.

Shinjuku's most famous Thai restaurant is on the third floor of a building surrounded by the screaming neon strip joints of Kabukichō, and serves authentic dishes at moderate prices. For a quieter atmosphere, head out to their other branch (1-15-1 Tamagawa, Setagaya-ku ⓣ5716-3771), in a Thai wooden palace by the Tamagawa river. Both venues have live music.

Cambodia カンボジヤ

Map 2, B4. 2F, Yoshino Bldg, 3-10-14 Takada, Toshima-ku ⓣ3209-9320. Takadanobaba Station.

Mon–Sat 11.30am–2pm & 5–11pm. Moderate.

Popular Cambodian café, serving a spicy variation on *okonomiyaki* pancakes and Khmer-style curries. From the station, head east along Waseda-dōri for two blocks then turn north; the restaurant is on the second floor just after the comic bookstore.

Canard カナード

Map 13, I3. B1, Sankocho Haimu, 5-17-6 Shinjuku, Shinjuku-ku ⓣ3200-0706. Shinjuku Sanchōme Station.

Tues–Sun 11.30am–2pm & 6–10.30pm. Moderate to expensive.

Delicious French cooking in this cramped basement down an alley opposite the Marui Interior department store on Meiji-dōri. Set menus from ¥2800 at night; you'll pay extra for some dishes, such as the melt-in-the-mouth *tarte tatin*. Arrive early for the set lunch since the restaurant fills up quickly.

Daidaiya 橙家

Map 13, F5. 3F, Shinjuku Nowa Bldg, 3-37-12 Shinjuku, Shinjuku-ku. Shinjuku Station

Daily 5pm–1am (last order midnight). Expensive.

In a city of stunning restaurant interiors, this one really knocks your socks off. The food is "nouvelle Japonaise", with items such as foie gras on lotus root cakes, as well as a good sushi and *tempura* selection. Check out the original branch at 2F, Ginza Nine Bldg, 8-5 Saki, Ginza-nishi ⓣ5537-3566, and the newest and most luxurious in the Belle Vie complex (ⓣ3588-5087) above Akasaka Mitsuke Station.

Kakiden 柿伝

Map 13, F5. 3-37-11 Shinjuku, Shinjuku-ku ⓣ3352-5121. Shinjuku Station.

Daily 11am–9pm. Very expensive.

One of the best places in Tokyo to sample *kaiseki-ryori*. There's a lunch for ¥4000, but you won't regret investing in the eighteen course dinner for ¥8000. From 6 to 8pm there's a live performance on the thirteen-stringed *koto*. It's on the eighth floor of the Yasuyo Building next to the My City complex on the east side of the station.

Ken's Chanto Dining

ケンズチヤントダイツニグ

Map 13, G4. B1, FF Bldg, 3-26-8 Shinjuku, Shinjuku-ku ⓣ5363-0336. Shinjuku Station.

Daily 11.30am–2.30pm & 5pm–midnight. Expensive.

Upstairs is a casual café, but it's downstairs that things get interesting at this Korean-influenced modern Japanese restaurant. A very elegant contemporary setting with a giant central table and dishes such as *kimchee*-stuffed cabbage rolls and tuna *sashimi* with organic vegetables.

New York Grill ニューヨークグリル

Map 13, A7. Park Hyatt Tower, 3-7-1-2 Nishi Shinjuku, Shinjuku-ku ⓣ5323-3458. Shinjuku Station.

Daily 11.30am–2.30pm & 5.30–10.30pm. Expensive to very expensive.

Treat yourself at this 52nd-floor restaurant with fantastic views, enormous portions of food, stylish decor and a bustling vibe. The airy dining space is dominated by four huge New York theme paintings, or you can sit looking into the glass-fronted kitchen, where the head chef is English. The ¥4620 lunch, with a wide buffet, is well worth the splurge. Booking is essential.

Pas à Pas パザパ

Map 2, C6. 5 Funamachi, Shinjuku-ku ⓣ3357-7888. Yotsuya Sanchōme Station.

Mon–Sat noon–1.30pm & 6–9pm. Moderate.

On a side street close to the station, this unpretentious shoebox operation is credited with setting off the trend towards good-value, bistro-style food. The scrumptious three-course set menus are ¥1500 for lunch and ¥2500 for dinner. They also run *Metro de Paris*, 1-17-1 Shinjuku ⓣ3357-5655, one block north of Shinjuku Gyoen.

Rera Chise レラチセ

Map 2, C4. 2-1-19 Nishi-Waseda, Shinjuku-ku ⓣ3202-7642. Waseda Station. Mon–Sat 5–11pm. Moderate.

Off the beaten track, but there's a warm welcome at this cosy basement, Tokyo's only restaurant serving the food of the *Ainu* - Japan's aboriginal people. Lots of salmon and deer-meat dishes. Hosts occasional music performances and other events.

Seiryumon 青龍門

Map 13, G4. 3/4F, Shinjuku Remina Bldg, 3-17-4 Shinjuku, Shinjuku-ku ⓣ3355-0717. Shinjuku-Sanchōme Station. Mon–Fri 5.30am–4am, Sat 11.30am–4am, Sun 11.30am–11.30pm. Moderate to expensive.

The theme at this branch of the theatrical Chinese-café chain is Shanghai opium den circa 1840; you dine inside cages and there's a mock secret entrance to the restaurant. Fun if you're in a group.

Shion しおん

Map 13, G3. 3-25 Shinjuku, Shinjuku-ku. Shinjuku Station. Daily 11.30am–11pm. Inexpensive.

Around the corner from the bar *Kirin City* on the west side of Shinjuku, this is one of the city's most popular conveyor-belt sushi operations. The quality varies but the plates are cheap at ¥100 or ¥200 each.

Tsunahachi つな八

Map 13, G5. 3-31-8 Shinjuku, Shinjuku-ku. Shinjuku Station. Daily 11am–10pm. Moderate.

This main branch of the famous *tempura* restaurant almost always has a queue outside, though you're more likely to get a seat quickly if you settle for the upstairs rooms away from the frying action. Everything is freshly made and even with the ¥1100 set – including soup, rice and pickles – you'll be full.

ODAIBA

Positive Deli ポセチブデリ

See Odaiba map, p.136. 3F, Mediage, 1-7-1 Daiba. Daiba Station. Daily 11am–11pm.

Although packed with eating options, very few of Ōdaiba's restaurants compare favourably with what's available elsewhere in the city. However, this retro-70s deli serving gourmet Australian food and wines is worth a look. A whole roast chicken platter is good value at ¥1600, and in summer there's outdoor seating overlooking the bay.

UENO AND AROUND

Agra アーグラー

Map 14, E8. 2F, 4-7-2 Ueno, Taitō-ku. Okachimachi Station. Mon–Sat 11.30am–10pm, Sun & hols to 9pm. Inexpensive to moderate.

It's a bit of a squeeze in this tiny Indian behind AB-AB department store; look for the pavement sign board. Their curries include generous amounts of meat, fish or vegetables, starting at around ¥1000 per dish (including rice or nan bread), or there's a choice of good-value lunch and dinner sets.

Freshness Burger フレシツユスバーガー

Map 14, F7. 6-16-13, Ueno, Taitō-ku. Ueno Station. Daily 8am–11pm. Inexpensive.

If you're looking for a quick snack, or a picnic to take into the park, try this cheerful hamburger joint next to Marui – or there's seating upstairs. Look out for other branches around the city, too. Burgers start at under ¥300 with crunchy side salads from ¥220.

Goemon 五石門

Map 2, F3. 1-1-26 Hon-Komagome, Bunkyo-ku, ⓣ3811-2015. Hon-Komagome Station.
Mon–Fri noon–2pm & 5–10pm, Sat noon–8pm. Expensive to very expensive.
Cooking with tofu raised to a fine art in a delightful setting straight out of a woodblock print. Dine in one of the wooden pavilions fronting the rock garden and gurgling fountain, if possible. The set menu for lunch starts at ¥2700, while dinner is from ¥5500.

Hantei はん亭

Map 14, A4. 2-12-15 Nezu, Bunkyō-ku. Nezu Station.
Tues–Sat noon–2.30pm & 5–10.30pm, Sun & hols noon–2.30pm & 4–9.30pm. Moderate to expensive.
Stylish dining in a beautiful, three-storey wooden house. There's only one dish, *kushiage* – deep-fried skewers of crunchy sea food, meat and vegetables with special dipping sauces – served in combination plates, six at a time: ¥2700 for the first plate; ¥1300 thereafter, until you say stop.

Musashino むさしの

Map 14, D8. 2-8-11 Ueno, Taitō-ku. Ueno-Hirokōji Station.
Daily 11.30am–10pm. Moderate.
Ueno is famed for its *tonkatsu* (breaded pork cutlets). Prices are reasonable for a thick, succulent slab at this traditional restaurant behind bamboo screens and pot plants. Choose between standard "rose" or fillet, at around ¥1500 including soup, rice and pickles.

Sasa-no-yuki 笹乃雪

Map 14, G1. 2-15-10 Negishi, Taitō-ku. Uguisudani Station.
Daily except Mon 11am–9pm. Moderate.
Three centuries ago, the chef here was said to make tofu like

"snow lying on bamboo leaves"; both the name and the quality have survived, though the old wooden house is now marooned among flyovers. Inside, it's nowhere near as fancy as *Goemon* (see p.207), but calm prevails over the *tatami* mats as you feast on delicately flavoured silk-strained tofu. There are three menus (from ¥1600 for three varieties of tofu), with the emphasis on flavour rather than quantity.

Unagi Ben-kei うなぎベンけい

Map 14, E8. 4-5-10 Ueno, Taitō-ku. Ueno-Hirokōji or Okachimachi Stations.

Daily 11.30am–9.15pm, closed third Mon of month. Moderate.

Eel (*unagi*) is the order of the day at this informal, traditional restaurant on three floors – try their *unagi donburi* lunchtime set for a taster (¥1050; Mon–Sat). But they also do well-priced *sukiyaki* and *shabu shabu* meals (from ¥1260 for lunch), as well as *tempura*, *sashimi* and so forth. English menu available.

Cafés and teahouses

Finding an inexpensive cuppa in Tokyo was once like searching for the Holy Grail, but since the **café scene** was revolutionized in the early 1990s by the launch of several cheap chain coffee shops (see box), this has all changed. The mass-colonization of Tokyo by the Seattle-based *Starbucks* has further accelerated this trend and increased the choice.

The fever for overpriced **French-style sidewalk cafés** has cooled, but if you want to people-watch with the beautiful people, Omotesandō in Harajuku and Kyu-yamate-dōri in Daikanyama are still the places to hang out. Also don't miss sampling at least one of Tokyo's old-style **kissaten**, where the emphasis is on service and creating an interesting, relaxing space. You'll pay more, but many of these places, such as Shinjuku's *La Scala*, have become institutions.

Teahouses are much thinner on the ground, though Japanese green tea and sweets are undergoing something of a revival, as a low-calorie, traditional alternative to coffee and cake, and there are several places in Tokyo where you

TOKYO'S CHAIN CAFES

Of the many **chain cafés** now liberally spread around the city, *Renoir* and *Almond*, with its famous branch at Roppongi crossing, are the long-time survivors. However, with their stuck-in-the-seventies decor, these places are now overshadowed by the bright upstarts, such as *Café Veloce*, *Doutor*, and *Mr Donut*. These serve straight-forward "blend" (medium strength) coffee and tea from as little as ¥180, and offer a decent range of pastries, sandwiches and other snacks, particularly so *Mr Donut*, one of the few places to offer free coffee refills; they're ideal for breakfast or a quick snack. The chain cafés *Giraffe* and *Pronto* also transform into bars in the evening, serving reasonably priced alcoholic drinks and nibbles.

From just one outlet in 1996, *Starbucks* now seems to be everywhere; for sheer location power check out the branch overlooking the crossing at Shibuya Station. Unlike at other branches, this one only serves the more expensive, large-size coffees. For a less mercenary approach nip across to another recent foreign import, *Segafredo Zanetti*, in the Shibuya Mark City complex (there are others in Hiro-o, Shinagawa and Shinjuku). This famous Italian-brand coffee shop has more Euro-chic and serves decent *panini* sandwiches, beer and pear schnapps. Not to be outdone, the local biggie *Doutor* has its very stylish flagship branch in Shibuya, just north of Tower Records.

can participate in a traditional tea ceremony, or simply sip *matcha* (powdered green tea) in refined surroundings.

Cafés are usually open for breakfast and keep late hours, shutting at around 11pm or later if they serve alcohol. Teahouses, by contrast, are strictly a daytime affair. The listings below give the nearest subway or train station.

CAFÉS

Andersens　アンデルセン

Map 8, F5. 5-1-26 Aoyama, Minato-ku. Omotesandō Station.
Tokyo outpost of Hiroshima's famed Swedish-style bakery. An excellent range of pastries and sandwiches and a reasonably priced sit-down café, a good option for breakfast and lunch. Closed third Monday of the month.

Ben's Café　ベンスカフエ

Map 2, B4. 1-29-21 Takadanobaba, Shinjuku-ku. Takadanobaba Station.
Anytime is a good time to visit this laid-back New York style café with its splendid range of coffees, other drinks and snacks. But come on Sunday at 6pm for the open-mike poetry readings that pull in the crowds and are quite fun. Also has an Internet terminal.

Caffé@Idée　カフエ@イデー

Map 8, G7. 6-1-16 Minami-Aoyama, Minato-ku. Omotesandō Station.
On the top floor of a trendy interior design store. Popular for lunch; the food is Italian influenced and there are good desserts. In the evening it becomes a bistro and there's a cigar bar.

Café Comme Ça　カフエコムサ

Map 13, G4. 3-26 Shinjuku, Shinjuku-ku. Shinjuku Station.
In the trendy Five Foxes' Store and serving delicious cakes. Stark concrete surfaces are enlivened by paintings of Buddhist deities and piles of coloured powder as bright at the clothes downstairs.

Café du Monde かフエヂユモンド

Map 9, C4. Spice 2 Bldg, 1-10-10 Nishi-Ikebukuro, Toshima-ku. Ikebukuro Station.
Bright, modern New Orleans coffee shop specializing in authentic chicory coffee and *beignets* (doughnuts fried in cotton-seed oil) to eat with various dipping sauces.

Café de Ropé かフエデロペ

Map 8, C3. 6-1-8 Jingūmae, Shibuya-ku. Meiji-Jingūmae Station.
Old-timer, still hanging in there, but looking a bit tired compared to snazzier Harajuku cafés. Also serves alcohol and snacks. Its position on Omotesandō and floor-to-ceiling glass windows make it ideal for people-watching.

Café Michelangelo かフエミクランジエロ

Map 6, A2. 14-5 Hachiyama-chō, Shibuya-ku. Daikanyama Station.
One of the most "Parisienne" of Tokyo's faux French brigade of cafés. Take a wicker chair facing on to Kyū-Yamate-dōri, order an espresso and watch the passing parade.

Café Rodney かフエロデニ

Map 8, E3. 4-4-16 Jingūmae, Shibuya-ku. Omotesandō Station.
Ultra-cute, primary-coloured joint, designed by Rodney Alan Greenblat, creator of the Parappa the Rappa video game. The gentle sense of humour invades the English menu which suggests this "could be the best coffee". Bagels, light meals and micro-brew beers are also on offer.

Craightons クレイトンズ

Map 11, E4. 3-12-6 Roppongi, Minato-ku. Roppongi Station.
The drink company UCC's upmarket operation is fairly classy, with a self-service area on the ground floor and table service upstairs. Wide range of freshly ground coffees to choose from and very late hours.

Deux Maggots デウマゴ

Map 12, A4. B1, Bunkamura, 2-24-1 Dōgenzaka, Shibuya-ku. Shibuya Station.

This bistro, a joint venture with the famous literary café in Paris, has tables in a cool atrium – a good spot from which to take in the various levels of the Bunkamura. Set lunches from ¥1300.

éf エフ

Map 5, H6. 2-19-18 Kaminarimon, Taito-ku. Asakusa Station.

It's worth popping along to *éf* if only for the miraculous survival of the *kura* (traditional store house) hidden at the back which now houses a very eclectic gallery. The café also does decent lunch sets for around ¥900. 11am–8pm. Closed Tues.

La Scala ラスカラ

Map 13, G2. 1-14-1 Kabukichō, Shinjuku-ku. Shinjuku Station.

Like the setting for a David Lynch movie (with the customers to match), *La Scala* is all velvet drapes, chandeliers, wooden beams and cosy corners. The so-so drinks, needless to say, are overpriced, but the atmosphere, drenched in classical music, is priceless.

A Piece of Cake アピースオブケーキ

Map 8, G7. 6-1-19 Minami-Aoyama, Minato-ku. Omotesandō Station.

Looking onto the small, funky sculpture garden in front of the Okumoto Taro Memorial Museum (he's the designer of the cartoon-like statue in front of Shibuya's Children's Castle). Very laid back and some interesting menu choices including traditional Indian *chai* and mulled wine.

Perbacco ペルバッコ

Map 8, C3. 5-10-1 Jingūmae, Shibuya-ku. Meiji-Jingūmae Station.
Stylish Italian café, with a few pavement tables, on Omotesandō. The focaccia sandwiches are a good lunchtime nibble and the ice cream is an expensive treat at ¥375 a scoop.

Yoku Moku ヨックモック

Map 8, G5. 5-3-3 Minami-Aoyama, Minato-ku. Omotesandō Station.
Hushed café in tune with the elegant sensibilities of this designer-shop end of Omotesandō. Also has a shop selling nicely packaged but expensive cakes, biscuits and chocolates.

TEAHOUSES

Boku Seki 木石

Map 8, D2. Boku Seki, 3-20 Jingūmae, Shibuya-ku, Meiji-Jingūmae Station.
Walk through the bamboo gate and past the tiny garden, slip off your shoes and sit on the *tatami* to enjoy *Boku Seki's* traditional green tea and cake. Peruse photos of the owner's King Charles spaniel Jackie at the same time. Very Harajuku. Weds-Sun noon–7.30pm.

Café Artifagose カフエアリトフアゴス

Map 6, B2. 20-23 Daikenyama, Shibuya-ku. Daikanyama Station.
The "concept" is bread, cheese and, er, tea. Still, this café has a prime *al fresco* spot in the heart of ritzy Daikanyama and offers a wide range of fine Darjeeling and other teas plus excellent cheese.

Happōen ハ芳園

Map 2, D12. 1-1-1 Shirokanedai, Minato-ku. Shirokanedai Station.
The most charming of the capital's traditional teahouses set in

gardens. The large wooden house itself was moved here from the Yokohama home of a rich silk trader. *Matcha* and *wagashi* is ¥800 and served by ladies in kimono.

New Ōtani ニューオータニ

Map 4, D1. 4-1 Kioichō, Chiyoda-ku. Akasaka-mitsuke Station.
On the seventh floor of the main tower, the tea ceremony room *Seisei-an* (Thurs–Sat 11am–4pm) has a soothing, traditional atmosphere. Ladies in kimonos carry out the rituals, and you pay ¥1050 for a bowl of *matcha* and a Japanese sweet.

Hotel Ōkura ホテレオークラ

Map 11, H2. 2-10-4 Toranomon, Minato-ku. Kamiyachō Station.
The tea ceremony (Mon–Sat 11am–4pm; ¥1050) at this top-class hotel follows the formula and etiquette of the Edo Senke school of practice, which was developed in the new capital Edo during the seventeenth century.

The Peak Lounge ザピークラウンジ

Map 13, A7. Park Hyatt Hotel, 3-7-1-2 Nishi-Shinjuku, Shinjuku. Tochō-mae Station.
Leafy clumps of tall bamboo thrive in the greenhouse-like lounge on the 41st floor of the luxurious *Park Hyatt Hotel*. On clear days, high tea (¥2500) is accompanied by views across to Mount Fuji.

Suzuki 寿々木

Map 8, B1. 1-15-4 Jingūmae, Shibuya-ku. Harajuku Station.
Tucked behind teeming Takeshita-dōri but a million miles away in atmosphere, this shop specializing in *okashi* sweets has *tatami* rooms, *fusuma* screens and manicured gardens to gaze upon. A frothy *matcha* and one pick from the sweets costs ¥900.

Thé Chinois Madu テチンワズマドウ

See Odaiba map, p.136. Venus Fort, Palette Town, Ōdaiba. Aomi Station.

One of the few good reasons for braving the crowds at Venus Fort is this small but authentic Chinese-style teashop, attached to the Madu homeware store.

THE WAY OF TEA

Whenever you sit down in a restaurant or visit a Japanese home, you'll be offered a small cup of slightly bitter green tea, *ocha* (honourable tea), which is always drunk plain. Teas are graded according to their quality. *Bancha*, the cheapest, is for everyday drinking and, in its roasted form, is used to make the smoky *hōji-cha*, or mixed with popped brown rice for the nutty *genmaicha*. Medium-grade *sencha* is served in upmarket restaurants or to favoured guests, while top-ranking, slightly sweet *gyokuro* (dewdrop) is reserved for special occasions.

Tea was introduced to Japan from China in the ninth century and was popularized by Zen Buddhist monks who appreciated its caffeine kick during their long meditation sessions. Gradually, tea-drinking developed into a formal ritual known as *cha-no-yu*, the **tea ceremony**, whose purpose is to heighten the senses within a contemplative atmosphere. In its simplest form the ceremony takes place in a *tatami* room, undecorated save for a hanging scroll or display of *ikebana* (traditional flower arrangement). Using beautifully crafted utensils of bamboo, iron and rustic pottery, your host will whisk *matcha* (powdered green tea) into a thick, frothy brew and present it to each guest in turn. Take the bowl in both hands, turn it clockwise a couple of inches and drink it down in three slow sips. It's then customary to admire the bowl while nibbling on a dainty sweetmeat (*wagashi*), which counteracts the tea's bitter taste.

Drinking

Tokyo has a vast and vibrant bar scene – you certainly won't have to settle for pubs pulsating with karaoke crooning. However, the distinction between bars, clubs, live music venues (known as live houses) and restaurants can be hazy. If there is live music you'll often be paying for it through higher drinks prices or a cover charge, so it's always worth checking what the deal is before walking in. Some places, such as Ebisu's *What the Dickens* and Takadanobaba's *The Fiddler* (both listed under Live Music), are also great bars and serve fine food.

All the major breweries have their own reliable chains of **izakaya** (Japanese pubs). These are generally quite large and lively, and serve a good range of drinks and bar snacks. Look out for branches of *Kirin City* in Harajuku and Shinjuku; for *Suntory Shot Bar* in Roppongi; and Sapporo's *Lion Beer Hall* in Ebisu, Ginza, Ikebukuro and Shinjuku among other places. *Izakaya* open at around 6pm and shut down around midnight.

For **bars with a view**, the major hotels are hard to beat, though you'll need to dress up to feel comfortable amid the gold-card crowd. In summer, **outdoor beer gardens** flourish – look out for red lanterns and fairy lights on the roofs of buildings or in street-level gardens and plazas.

Try to sample at least one of Tokyo's **nomiya**, cramped, smoky bars where you'll see salarymen letting loose. Often no more than a short counter and a table, *nomiya* are usually run by a *mama-san*, who both charms and terrorizes her customers, and is less likely to rip you off if you speak some Japanese (but even that's no guarantee). The best *nomiya* are under the tracks at **Yūrakuchō**, along Shinjuku's **Shomben Yokochō** (piss alley) and **Golden Gai**, and **Nonbei Yokochō**, the alley running alongside the JR rail tracks, just north of Shibuya Station. These bars stay open as long as there are customers. If you're looking for a more *gaijin*-friendly scene **Roppongi** still can't be beat for a night out, but be prepared to witness some pretty sleazy behaviour.

In recent years, the "Big Four" Japanese breweries (Asahi, Kirin, Sapporo and Suntory) have had their monopoly on domestic sales eroded by foreign imports and deregulation of the industry, which has encouraged local **microbreweries** to expand their operations. In Japanese the new

DRINKING ETIQUETTE

• If you're out drinking with Japanese, remember to pour your colleagues' drinks, but never your own; they'll take care of that. In fact, you'll usually find your glass being topped up after every couple of sips, making it difficult to judge how much you've imbibed.

• You can make a toast by lifting your glass and saying "kampai".

• In small bars, regular customers keep a bottle of their favourite tipple behind the counter with their name on it.

• In *nomiya* and small bars you'll probably be served a small snack or a plate of nuts with your first drink, whether you've asked for it or not; this is often the flimsy excuse for the cover charge added onto the bill at the end.

brews are called *ji-biiru* (regional beer), and there are now several places, some listed below, where you can sample them.

Tea and **coffee** drinkers are well catered for with a range of coffee and snacks bars, old-style coffee shops and traditional teahouses – we've listed the best on pp.209–216.

AKASAKA

Guts ガッツ

Map 4, B8. 7-9-7 Akasaka, Minato-ku. Akasaka Station.
Mon–Sat 5.30pm–5am, Sun 5.30pm–3am.
Modern *izakaya* opposite the *Akasaka Yōkō Hotel*. The menu promises Japanese *tapas*, which means the usual nibbles, but it's all well done and not too pricey (although there is a ¥300 cover charge). Shame about the name, really.

Torattoria とらつとりあぼーる

Map 4, E5. 3-6 Akasaka, Minato-ku. Akasaka Station.
Daily 11am–5am.
Café, with small tables covered with checked table cloths, until 5pm when it turns into a bar. Between 11am and 7pm a small beer is just ¥100, as good a reason as any for searching this place out.

EBISU AND HIRO-O

Billy Barew's Beer Bar Ebisu
ビリーバルウズビアバー

Map 6, C3. 2F, Ebisu AM Bldg, 2-1-11 Ebisu-Minami, Shibuya-ku. Ebisu Station.
Mon–Thurs 6pm–2am, Fri & Sat 6pm–4am, Sun 6pm–midnight.

New location on Komazawa-dōri, for this convivial bar. Boasts a menu of over 100 different beers from around the world at ¥1000 a bottle.

Casablanca de Vino カサバランカデビノ

Map 6, C3. 1-10-10 Ebisu-Nishi, Shibuya-ku. Ebisu Station.
Mon–Sat 11am–midnight.
Empty crates stacked together make up the tables at this small café/wine-bar (the corks come out after 5pm), just off Komazawa-dōri. They have a good range of vinos and a glass will only knock you back ¥500.

Hanesawa Beer Garden 羽沢ガーデン

Map 6, E1. 3-12-15 Hiro-o, Minato-ku, Hiro-o Station.
June–Sept 5–9pm.
Authentic beer garden, complete with lanterns and fish ponds, in the backstreets west of Hiro-o Station. Cool off with one of their famous, foamy *dai jokki* – big mugs of ale.

Smash Hits スマツウヒツ

Map 6, G2. B1, M2 Hirō Bldg, 5-6-26 Hiro-o, Minato-ku. Hiro-o Station.
Daily 7pm–3am.
Karaoke for exhibitionists in this basement bar designed as a mini-amphitheatre. With 12,000 English songs to choose from, plus many in other languages, too, you'll never be stuck for a tune. Entry is a hefty ¥3000 including two drinks. Closed 3rd Mon of month.

Symposion シンポシオン

Map 6, A2. 17-16 Sarugakuchō, Shibuya-ku. Daikanyama Station.
Daily 5.30pm–1am (last order 11pm).
This restaurant and bar is pure *belle époque* – you almost expect Toulouse-Lautrec and a troupe of Can Can girls to come high kicking through the art nouveau doors. Walk along Kyū-

yamate-dōri to the far end of the Hillside Terrace complex and have a wad of cash at the ready.

Yebisu Beer Station
恵比寿ビヤスターシヨン

Map 6, E4. Yebisu Garden Place. Ebisu Station.
Daily 11.30am–10pm.
Several bars and *izakaya* are spread across Sapporo's office and shopping development in their old brewery, and there's also a spacious beer garden, open all year round.

GINZA AND AROUND

Baden Baden バーでンバーでン

Map 7, C7. 2-1-8 Yūrakuchō, Chiyoda-ku. Yūrakuchō Station.
Mon–Fri 5–11pm, Sat 5–11.30pm, Sun & hols 4–9.30pm.
The best of several German beer restaurants, selling Hofbrauhaus on draught and a decent selection of schnapps. The food's not bad either – serious platters of franks, cheese and potatoes. Located under the railway tracks.

Double-Decker Bus ダブルデカバース

Map 7, B9. 1-7-1 Nishi-Shimbashi, Minato-ku. Toranomon Station.
Mon–Fri noon–2pm & 5pm–4am, Sat 5–10pm.
Café by day, bar by night, this shabby-chic London double decker seems to have run aground in Tokyo en route from Aldwych. A G&T (¥800) on the upper deck is just the ticket.

Lion ライオン

Map 7, E4. 7-9-20 Ginza, Chūō-ku. Ginza Station.
Daily Mon–Sat 11.30am–11pm, Sun & hols 11.30am–10.30pm.
This baronial beer hall, flagship of the Sapporo chain, is a beautiful 1930s period piece, with its dark tiles and mock wood-

panelling. Above the bar, a classic scene of harvest maidens worked in mosaics forms the centrepiece. There are light meals on offer, and more substantial fare in the restaurant upstairs.

Town Cryer タウンクライヤ

Map 7, B2. 6F, Tokyo Sankei Bldg, 1-7-2 Ōtemachi, Chiyoda-ku.
Ōtemachi Station.
Mon–Fri 11.30am–10pm.

Rub shoulders with financial types and journos at this "genuine British pub" (well, it's got beams and horse brasses).

KARAOKE

The Japanese were partial to a good singsong long before **karaoke**, literally "empty orchestra", was invented, possibly by an Ōsaka record store manager in the early 1970s. The machines, originally clunky eight-track tape players with a heavy duty microphone, have come a long way since then and are now linked up to videos, screening the lyrics crooned along to, and featuring a range of effects to flatter the singer into thinking their caterwauling is harmonious. Not for nothing have karaoke machines been dubbed the "electronic *geisha*".

In the mid-1980s, the whole industry, which earns ¥1 trillion a year, was boosted by the debut of the **karaoke box**, a booth kitted out with a karaoke system and rented out by groups or individuals wanting to brush up on their singing technique. These boxes have proved particularly popular with youngsters, women and families who shied away from the smoky small bars frequented by salarymen that were the original preserve of karaoke. Amazingly, research has shown that the introduction of karaoke has coincided with a significant drop in the number of drunks taken into protective custody by the police, salarymen drinking less, rather than more, as they relax over a rousing rendition of *My Way*.

Run by the same team behind Ebisu's *What the Dickens*, which means the hearty meals can be relied on.

HARAJUKU AND SHIBUYA

Bar Aoyama バー青山

Map 12, I6. Daikyo Bldg, 4-5-9 Shibuya. Shibuya Station.
Daily 9pm–5am. ¥1000 on Sat.

Garage-sale chic at this arty bar which gets kicking from around midnight. Drinks start at ¥700. Every Saturday there's a techno/jungle club. The entrance, a grimy black metal door in the wall beside thundering Roppongi-dōri, is easily missed.

Bar Isn't It バーイズントイシト

Map 12, B4. B1, Hontis Bldg, 2-23-12 Dōgenzaka, Shibuya-ku.
Shibuya Station.
Daily 9pm–5am.

Opposite the Bunkamura is the second Tokyo outpost of the pack 'em in, serve 'em everything for ¥500 bar operation. Fri and Sat there's a ¥1000 entry charge including one drink and you'll need to show some ID.

Kranz クランズ

Map 12, B7. 2-11-1 Dōgenzaka, Shibuya-ku. Shibuya Station
Daily 24 hours.

Industrially chic café from 6am to 7pm, bar from 7pm to 6am. Serves some good imported bottled beers as well as gourmet coffees and organic bread. Handy as a chill-out spot after you've finished clubbing.

Oh! God オーガッど

Map 8, C3. 6-7-18 Meiji-jingūmae ⓣ 3406-3206. Meiji-Jingūmae Station.
Daily 6pm–6am.

Basement bar in the same complex as *La Bohème* and *Zest* restaurants. The real attraction is the free movies screened nightly. Nothing up to date (call for the programme), but worth checking out. Drinks start at around ¥700 and there are two pool tables. Another good post-club venue.

Pink Cow ピンクカウー

Map 8, B2. 1-10-1 Jingūmae, Shibuya-ku ⓣ5411-6777. Meiji-Jingūmae Station.

Tues–Sun 1pm–late; after 11pm ¥500 cover charge.

Buried in the backstreets off Omotesandō, *Pink Cow* is a haven for local artists and is decorated with their colourful works. Has a good range of imported wines and also runs a Friday night home-cooked buffet for ¥2000. Call for details of other regular events.

NORTH TOKYO

Asahi Sky Room アサヒスカイルーム

Map 5, I6. 22F, Asahi Bldg, 1-23-1 Azumabashi, Sumida-ku. Asakusa Station.

Daily 10am–9pm.

The famous Flamme d'Or building next door has its own modernistic beer hall, but the top-floor *Sky Room* wins out for night views over Asakusa. It's not expensive, but the uncomfortable seats won't make you want to linger.

Brussels ブラさルス

Map 2, E4. 3-16-1 Kanda-Ogawamachi, Chiyoda-ku. Jimbōchō Station.

Mon–Fri 5.30pm–2am, Sat 5.30–11pm.

Fifty varieties of Belgian beer to work through, either wedged in at the counter or in more spacious surroundings upstairs. Lively, student atmosphere and bar snacks.

Dubliners' ダブリナーズ

Map 9, C4. B1, 1-10-8 Nishi-Ikebukuro, Toshima-ku. Ikebukuro Station.
Daily 11.30am–11pm.
Plenty of elbow-room in this relaxed basement Irish pub, part of the Sapporo chain. There's Guinness and Kilkenny on draught, and dishes such as colcannon (mushy cabbage and potato stew) or cheese nachos. Happy hour Mon–Thurs 3–8pm.

Kamiya 神谷

Map 5, H6. 1-1-1 Asakusa, Taitō-ku. Asakusa Station.
Daily except Tues 11.30am–10pm.
Once the haunt of literary figures such as Nagai Kafū and Tanizaki Junichirō, *Kamiya* has been on the Asakusa scene since 1880. It's also famous for its *Denkibran* ("electric brandy"), first brewed in 1883; a small shot of gin, wine, curaçao and brandy, it's a potent tipple, though there's also a "weaker" version (30 degrees) for modern tastes (¥260 a glass). The ground floor's the liveliest and most informal; pay for your first round of food and drinks at the cash desk as you enter.

Tagoru タゴール

Map 2, D4. 3-5 Kagurazaka, Shinjuku-ku. Iidabashi Station.
Mon–Fri 6pm–2am, Sat & Sun 6pm–midnight.
Hang loose among the incense and ethnic fabrics of this quirky, cosy, cluttered bar – serving Chinese food and other snacks – before heading for somewhere with a bit more bite.

The Warrior Celt ザワリオールケルト

Map x, xx. 3F, Ito Bldg, 6-9-22 Ueno. Ueno Station.
Mon, Tues & Sun 5pm–midnight, Wed–Sat 5pm–5am.
Things can get pretty raucous at this good-time bar in the thick of Ueno. Prime ingredients are a fine range of beers, most notably Old Speckled Hen on tap, a nightly happy hour

(5–7pm), live bands on Fri & Sat (from 8.30pm) and, last but not least, Ladies' Night on Thurs (all drinks ¥500). Add fish and chips with real mushy peas – or a mean hummus – and you're away.

ROPPONGI

Acarajé Tropicana アカラジエトツロピカナ

Map 11, C5. B2, Edge Bldg, 1-1-1 Nishi-Azabu. Roppongi Station. Mon–Thurs 9pm–1am, Fri & Sat 9pm–2am. ¥1000 on weekends.

Large and popular Latin-American-style basement bar/restaurant just off Roppongi-dōri, which turns into a dance club on the weekend.

Bar Isn't It バーイズントイシト

Map 11, E4. 3F, MT Bldg, 3-8-18 Roppongi, Minato-ku ⓣ3746-1598. Roppongi Station.

Daily 6pm–5am. ¥1000 on Fri & Sat including one drink.

This bar's concept of ¥500 for all drinks and food plus space to move has found a natural home in Roppongi. There are beer-vending machines for when it's too crowded to get to the bar. Club nights are Fri & Sat and twice monthly on Thurs they have live comedy.

Castillo カステイロ

Map 11, D4. 6-1-8 Roppongi, Minato-ku. Roppongi Station. Mon–Sat 8pm–6am.

If you never got over the disco craze of the 1970s and 1980s this often hopping bar, with small dance floor, is the place to boogie – get on down to one of the tracks on their vast range of LPs.

Déjà vu デジヤブ

Map 11, E4. 3-15-24 Roppongi, Minato-ku. Roppongi Station. Daily 5pm–5am.

Long-running *gaijin* dive still packing them in at the weekends. The open front stops it getting too sweaty. Overshadowed these days by the *Gas Panic* bars next door.

Dusk Till Dawn ダスクチルダウン

Map 11, E4. 2F, Zonan Bldg, 3-13-8 Roppongi, Minato-ku. Roppongi Station.

Mon–Sat 6pm–late.

A convivial bar on the main drag, with a bit more space than most, a balcony at the back for some air and a huge TV screen. Happy hour is 6–9pm.

Gas Panic ガスパニック

Map 11, E4. 50 Togensha Bldg, 3-15-24 Roppongi. Roppongi Station.

Daily 6pm–5am.

Main outpost for one of Roppongi's most popular and grungiest bars. Suave it ain't, but virtually everyone passes through here at least once. Get ripped and enjoy. Happy hour is from 6pm to 9.30pm, when all drinks are ¥300. On Thursdays, all drinks cost ¥300 all night. The downstairs *Club 99* is open Thurs–Sat 8pm–6am.

Ginga Kogen Beer 銀河高原ビール

Map 11, E4. 3-8-15 Roppongi. Roppongi Station.

Daily 5pm–4am.

One of the larger regional breweries, which began in Sawa Uchi Mura in Iwate-ken, has opened this *izakaya* to promote its three types of beer: Weizen, Pilsner and Stout. Snack-type food (squid pizza, seaweed-topped spaghetti) is also available.

Quest クエスト

Map 11, E4. 2F, Nakano Bldg, 5-8-3 Roppongi, Minato-ku. Roppongi Station.

Daily 6pm–5am.

PACHINKO PARLOURS

Could one in four Japanese be wrong? That's the number of people who together spend a staggering ¥26.3 trillion a year on **pachinko**, a pinball game of limited skill that is one of Japan's major industries and top pastimes. It's easy to spot pachinko parlours; they look like mini Las Vegas casinos on steroids – all flashing lights and big neon signs. Inside, the atmosphere is no less in your face. The noise of thousands of steel balls clattering through the upright electronic bagatelles is deafening, yet rows of players sit mesmerized as they control the speed with which the balls fall through the machine. The aim is for the balls to drop into the right holes so more balls can be won and traded in for prizes, such as cigarette lighters and calculators. Although it's illegal for the parlours to pay out cash, there's always a cubby-hole close by where prizes can be exchanged for money, a charade that the authorities have long turned a blind eye to. The initial cost of indulging in this mechanized mayhem can be as little as ¥100 for 25 ball bearings; just remember to take your earplugs, too.

Pachinko parlours are open from around 10am, but they're busiest in the evenings when Tokyo's corporate warriors wind down.

"Your search is over for the perfect bar" they claim; maybe not yet, but they do have three free Internet terminals, sport on a big screen TV and Aussie-style meat pies. Half-price drinks for women Sun & Mon.

Trading Places トラデイングプレセズ

Map 11, E5. 5-16-52 Roppongi, Minato-ku. Roppongi Station. Daily 6pm–4am.

Just off the main drag, on the lower ground floor of the Forum building, this is one of the area's classier and more spacious watering holes. There's a long bar, good music and a happy hour from 6pm to 8pm.

SHINJUKU AND AROUND

Clubhouse クラブハウス

Map 13, I5. 3F, Marunaka Bldg, 3-7-3 Shinjuku, Shinjuku-ku. Shinjuku-sanchōme Station.

Tues–Thurs 5pm–midnight, Fri 5pm–late, Sat noon-late, Sun noon-midnight.

Gaijin-run sports bar that's big on space and atmosphere and has a policy of being cheaper than the Roppongi competition. Also a good place to eat – does fine fish and chips (¥800), a selection of vegetarian dishes and a Sunday brunch from noon to 4.30pm.

The Dubliners' ダブリナーズ

Map 13, G4. 2F, Shinjuku Lion Hall, 3-28-9 Shinjuku, Shinjuku-ku. Shinjuku Station.

Mon–Thurs 11.30am–11.30pm, Fri & Sat 11.30am–2am, Sun 11.30am–10pm.

Mock-Victorian decor, Irish stew on the menu, and, of course, Guinness and Kilkenny bitter on tap. Good for a quiet lunch or coffee as well as a rowdy night's drinking. Sometimes has live music midweek.

Footnik フツトニツク

Map 2, B3. B1, Marujo Bldg, 3-12-8 Takadanobaba, Shinjuku-ku. Takadanobaba Station.

Daily 5pm–1am, except Sat until 4am.

Tokyo's only bar devoted to soccer, run by enthusiast Yuji-san, who speaks English, pulls pints from a good range of imported beers on tap and serves decent, filling food. There's a game or two on the big screen every night, but for popular matches you'll have to pay an entry charge – for details check out their Web site (Ⓦ *www1.neweb.ne.jp/wb/footnik*). Japanese movies with subtitles are also occasionally screened.

Jetée ジュテ

Map 13, H3. 2F, 1-1-8, Kabukichō. Shinjuku Sanchōme Station. Mon–Sat 7pm–1am. ¥1000.

No more than eight people can fit in this second-floor cubbyhole decorated with movie posters and hand-painted bottle keeps (regulars' own bottles of booze). This quintessential Golden Gai bar is run by Kawai-san, a francophile mama-san with a passion for films and jazz. Don't bother turning up during May, when she decamps to the Cannes Film Festival.

Rolling Stone ローリングストーン

Map 13, I5. B1, Ebichu Bldg, 3-2-7 Shinjuku. Shinjuku Sanchōme Station.

Mon–Sun 9pm–5am. Mon–Thurs a ¥200 table charge is added to the bill (¥500 after midnight); ¥2000 cover charge on Fri & Sat, including two drinks.

Conversation is out, ear-splitting rock music is in at this long-running rock'n'roll bar. Every weekend it becomes a sweaty hell hole for those who can't think of anything better than shoving their way to the bar.

The Shamrock シヤムロク

Map 13, D6. B1, Seishin Bldg, 1-13-3 Nishi-Shinjuku, Shinjuku-ku Ⓣ 3348-4609. Shinjuku Station.

Mon–Thurs 11.30am–11pm, Fri & Sat 11.30am–midnight, Sun noon–midnight.

Another popular Irish bar near the main post office on the west side of the station. Has live music most Wednesdays; call for details. Happy hour for cocktails is 5–7pm. Worth checking out for a meal too, with lunch served daily noon–2pm.

Tōhōkenbunroku 東方見聞録

Map 13, I4. 3-6-7 Shinjuku, Shinjuku-ku. Shinjuku-sanchōme Station.
Daily 5pm–midnight.
Ultra-stylish chain *izakaya*, on the fourth floor above a pachinko parlour, with cosy wood and *tatami* booths around a radioactively green glass pond. The speciality is *yakitori* and if you order cold *sake* it will come in a large pottery cup overflowing into a saucer. There's a ¥300 cover charge. Two other branches in Shinjuku, one on the west side of the station on the second floor next to Yodobashi camera, the other on the fourth floor opposite *Lotteria* at 3-36 Shinjuku.

Vagabond バガボンド

Map 13, E3. 2F, 1-4-20, Nishi-Shinjuku. Shinjuku Station.
Mon–Sat 5.30–11.30pm, Sun till 10.30pm.
Local institution where Matsuoka-san plays the genial host to perfection, greeting guests and sometimes accompanying the jazz pianists who play every night from 7pm. The walls are decorated with strange and wonderful paintings collected by the owner from the days when he ran a Japanese restaurant in Paris. There's a ¥500 cover charge for table snacks, but the drinks are good value and the atmosphere priceless. Also has a new and quieter counter bar downstairs.

Yūan 由庵

Map 13, A7. B1, Shinjuku Park Tower, 7-1 Nishi-Shinjuku, Shinjuku-ku. Tochōmae Station.
Mon–Sat 11.30am–3pm & 5–10pm.
Elegantly decorated *izakaya* in the basement of the trendy Shinjuku Park Tower. The set lunches (¥1000–¥13000) are excellent value and although it's much more expensive at night, it's still worth dropping by to linger over a chilled glass of *sake* at their low wooden tables and dine off the rustic pottery.

TOKYO BAY

T.Y. Harbor Brewery T.Y.ハーバーブルレリ

Map 2, E14. Bond St, 2-1-3 Higashi Shinagawa, Shinagawa-ku. Tennoz Isle Station.
Mon–Sat 5–11pm.
Rave reviews for the beer at this microbrewery with less successful attached Californian restaurant, housed in a converted Bayside warehouse – one of the few places in Tokyo with a waterside view. The freshly made real ales include Amber Ale, Porter, Wheat Beer and California Pale Ale. Take the monorail from Hamamatsuchō to get here.

Sunset Beach Brewing Company さンせトビーチブルインカユンパニ

See Odaiba map, p.136. 1-6-1 Decks Tokyo Beach, Odaiba. Odaiba Kaihin Kōen Station.
Daily 11am–3.30pm & 5–11pm.
The real attraction is the view across Tokyo Bay of the Rainbow Bridge. For glasses of the two types on offer it's ¥600 at the stand-up bar, while inside the large beer hall, an average, all-you-can-eat buffet will cost you around ¥1400 for lunch, ¥3000 for dinner. Take the monorail from Shimbashi to get here.

Nightclubs

Tokyo is as important a pit stop on the international clubbing scene as London and New York, and you'll find all the latest sounds covered, from acid jazz to techno, trance and drum 'n' bass. Overseas DJs and event organizers regularly jet in to gig at the top clubs, while local superstars, such as the United Future Organization (UFO), take their brand of music abroad. Among the top DJs at the moment is Ko Kimura, whose brand of hard house has a devoted gay following (see p.235).

While some clubs weather the vagaries of fashion better than others, you'd be wise to check the **local media** before heading out. *Tokyo Classified* is a good source and their Web site (Ⓦ *www.tokyoclassified.com/welcome.html*) has even more listings. *Tokyo Q*'s Web site (Ⓦ *www.tokyoq.com*) also has weekly recommendations, but some of their listings are now out-of-date. Also check the Web site of Club Information Agency (Ⓦ *www.ciajapan.com*) and look for their free monthly booklet of flyers at clubs and shops, such as Tower Records. Most major clubs also have their own Web site detailing their monthly schedules.

At all clubs there'll be a **cover charge**, typically around ¥3000, which usually includes tickets for your first couple of drinks. With the exception of *Velfarre* (see p.238), most clubs don't get going until after 11pm, especially at weekends, and stay open to around 4 or 5am (this is despite the fact that it's technically illegal for clubs to permit dancing after midnight). After-hours parties on Sunday mornings from 5am are also becoming popular - ones to check out are those at the *Liquid Room*, *Maniac Love* and *Velfarre*. If you're not sure where to go, head first to one of the popular *gaijin* bars in Roppongi (see p.226) or Ebisu (see p.219), where you can plug into the local vibe and plan your next move.

If clubbing isn't your scene, check out Tokyo's many other nightlife options. Live music listings begin on p.239, and for computer whizz kids with itchy fingers there are Sega games centres in Shinjuku (see p.104) and Odaiba (see p.140). And wherever you go in Tokyo you'll never be far from a pachinko parlour (see box on p.228), where you can try your hand at Japan's unique and noisy form of pinball.

CLUBS

Bed ベド

Map 9, B3. B1, 3-29-9 Nishi-Ikebukuro ⓣ03/3981-5300. Ikebukuro Station.

Daily 10pm–5am. ¥2000 including two drinks.

Welcome newcomer to Ikebukuro nightlife. A mix of hip hop, reggae, r&b, and the occasional drum 'n' bass keeps things jumping until 5am.

Blue ブルー

Map 8, G7. B1/2, NYK Bldg, 6-2-9 Minami-Aoyama, Minato-ku. Omotesandō Station.

Opening hours variable; call ⓣ3797-1581. ¥2500 including two drinks.

A hazy blue glow over the door halfway down Kotto-dōri, next to a classy jewellers, is the only give-away to this cool acid-jazz joint. Two levels – one for chilling, one for dancing – and sessions from the renowned acid-jazz/drum 'n' bass UFO DJs.

Club Asia クラブアジア

Map 12, A6. 1-8 Maruyamachō, Shibuya-ku Ⓦ *www.clubasia.co.jp* Shibuya Station.

Daily 11pm–5am. Varies with event, but generally ¥2500 including two drinks.

Long-running club, in the heart of the Dōgenzaka love hotel district, with several dance floors and an attached *al fresco* Asian restaurant. Popular place for special events.

Code コド

Map 13, G1. 4F, Shinjuku Toho Kaikan, 1-19-9 Kabukichō, Shinjuku-ku Ⓦ *www.sonet.ne.jp/CYBERJAPAN* Shinjuku Station.

Opening hours vary with event. ¥2500–3000 entry.

With room for 2000 people, *Code* is one of Japan's biggest clubs, with three dance floors. Turn up on Fridays to see the noted house DJ Ko Kimura go through his paces. Hosts gay nights, often on Sunday.

Fai フアイ

Map 8, E6. B2, 5-10-1 Minami-Aoyama, Minato-ku Ⓦ *www.fai-aoyama.com/i* Omotesandō Station.

Daily 11pm–4am. ¥2000 including two drinks.

Cosy, easy-listening lounge bar, on the corner of Aoyama-dōri and Kotto-dōri, where the kids go wild to everything from Abba to Latin, soul and jazz. Food available and no entrance charge before 11pm.

Harlem ハーレム

Map 12, A6. Dr Jeekan's Bldg, 2-4 Maruyamachō, Shibuya-ku Ⓦ *www.harlem.co.jp* Shibuya Station.

Opening hours and prices vary with event.

Spacious two-floor club specializing in hip-hop, rap and r&b.

Currently one of the hottest options in this club-saturated part of town.

Lexington Queen レクシントンクイーン

Map 11, E4. Daisan Goto Bldg, 3-13-14 Roppongi, Minato-ku. Roppongi Station.

Daily 8pm–5am. ¥4000 (¥3000 for women) including two drinks.

Ageing Bill Hersey, Tokyo Weekender's society columnist, is on hand to be photographed with VIPs at this dinosaur of a Roppongi disco for the rich and famous. Avoid if you in any way value your street cred.

Liquid Room リクイードルム

Map 13, F1. 7F, Shinjuku HUMAX Pavilion, 1-20-1 Kabukichō, Shinjuku-ku ⓦ *www.liquidroom.net* Shinjuku Station.

Opening times and admission prices vary with event.

All kinds of music genres on the decks at this trendy live house and club in the heart of Shinjuku; in the past Massive Attack have played here. Also a favourite spot for various gay club nights. Check local media and flyers for details.

Luners ルーナス

Map 11, E6. 1-4-5 Azabu-Jūban, Minato-ku ⓦ *www.luners.co.jp/* Azabu-Jūban Station.

Opening hours and admission varies with event.

Basement club near the Singapore Embassy, hosting a mixed bag of events including the fun gay/drag club nights organized by *The Ring* (see p.249).

Maniac Love マニアツクラブ

Map 8, E6. 5-10-6 Minami-Aoyama, Minato-ku ⓦ *www.maniaclove.com* Omotesandō Station.

Mon–Thurs 10pm–4am, Fri 9pm–5am, Sat 9pm–Sun 10am. ¥2000 weekdays, ¥2500 Fri & Sat; ¥1000 Sun from 5am, plus unlimited coffee.

Small but happening basement club just off Kotto-dōri, playing everything from ambient and acid jazz to hard house and garage. Hardcore clubbers come for its early morning raves.

Milk みるく

Map 6, C2. B1, Roob 6 Bldg, 1-13-3 Ebisu-Nishi, Shibuya-ku. Ebisu Station.

Daily 8pm–4am. ¥3000 including two drinks.

A cross between a club and a live house, *Milk* packs in a lively crowd and is currently one of Tokyo's hippest indie-style hangouts. The regular Britpop nights are worth watching out for.

Mix ミクス

Map 8, E5. 3-6-19 Kita-Aoyama, Minato-ku Ⓦ *www.at-mix.com* Omotesandō Station.

Daily 7pm–5am. ¥2000 including two drinks; free on Sun.

This long narrow basement space on Aoyama-dōri hosts an arty crowd at weekends who don't seem to mind being squashed in like sardines. The music is an infectious mix of soul and reggae.

New Pylon Roppongi ニューパイーロン六本木

Map 11, D4. Colosseum Hall TSK Bldg, 7-15-30 Roppongi, Minato-ku Ⓦ *www.club-pylon.com* Roppongi Station.

Fri & Sat from 9pm. ¥3500 (¥3000 for women).

Yet another relocation for this one-time Shibuya-based club. Three floors of music, offering something for practically everyone.

328 (San-nippa) 三二八

Map 11, B5. 3-24-20 Nishi Azabu. Roppongi Station.

Mon–Thurs 8pm–4am, Fri & Sat 8pm–5am, Sun 8pm–3am. ¥2000 including two drinks.

Long-standing DJ bar in a basement right on the Hirō side of the Nishi Azabu crossing, next to the police box. More laid-back than many other late-night Roppongi options.

Sugar High シユガーハイ

Map 12, B6. 3F, Yubun Bldg, 2-16-3 Dōgenzaka, Shibuya-ku. Shibuya Station.

Daily 7pm–5am. Admission varies with event.

Small but *gaijin*-friendly DJ bar hosting a range of events, which affect the entry charge. Aphex Twin have played here in the past. Happy hour 7–9pm.

Velfarre ベルフアーレ

Map 11, D4. 7-14-22 Roppongi, Minato-ku Ⓦ *www.velfarre.avex.co.jp* Roppongi Station.

Thurs & Sun 6pm–midnight, Fri & Sat 6pm–1am. ¥5000 (¥4000 for women, ¥500 extra for men on Fri & Sat).

Monolithic club, which cost its sponsors ¥4 billion. Expensive to get in but you will get up to three drinks and food depending on the night. Often packed by 9pm since it shuts relatively early. Sometimes hosts recovery parties at the weekends.

Yellow イエロー

Map 11, B5. 1-10-11 Nishi-Azabu, Minato-ku Ⓦ *www.space-lab-yellow.com/* Roppongi Station.

Mon–Sat 8.30pm–3am. ¥2000–4000 including two drinks.

Look for the blank yellow neon sign and head down to the basement to discover one of Tokyo's most enduring and trendy clubs, playing a range of music on different nights. It's mainly techno and house at weekends, when cover charges are highest.

Live music

Tokyo has an incredibly varied appetite for music from all corners of the globe, as a trip to any of the city's major CD emporiums will prove. It's not surprising, therefore, that top acts are keen to include the capital on their schedules. On many nights of the week you can take your pick from live performances of anything from Beethoven to Beatles tribute bands, via traditional Japanese ballads and contemporary jazz.

Pop and rock are usually played in "live houses", most of which are little more than a pub with a small stage. There are several larger venues where top local and international acts do their thing, and when the likes of Madonna or U2 come to town they're always to be found at the cavernous Tokyo Dome in Suidōbashi, affectionately known as the "Big Egg". Tickets for concerts can be bought through ticket agencies – see the Directory, p.293.

In 1997 several major performance halls opened and there are usually one or two **concerts** of Western **classical** music every week, either by one of Tokyo's several resident symphony orchestras or a visiting group, as well as occasional performances of **opera**. **Tickets**, available from the relevant box office or a ticket agency (see p.299), are pricey (starting at around ¥3000) and are often scooped up as soon as they go on sale. However, a limited number of cheap seats (sometimes half-price) often go on sale on the day of the performance – be prepared to queue.

If you get the chance, try and catch a concert of **traditional Japanese music**, played on instruments such as the *sakuhachi* (flute), the *shamisen* (a kind of lute that is laid on the ground), and *taiko* (drum). Top groups to watch out for include Kodo, the theatrical drumming ensemble, who occasionally play at the Bunkamura in Shibuya.

ROCK AND POP

Cavern Club カバーンクラブ

Map 11, E4. 5-3-2 Roppongi, Minato-ku. Roppongi Station.
Mon–Sat 6pm–2.30am, Sun 6pm–midnight. ¥1500.

No prizes for guessing what kind of music is played here. A meticulous re-creation of the Beatles' Liverpool venue, with pretty decent Beatles cover bands providing the entertainment.

Club Quattro クラブクアトロ

Map 12, C4. 5F, Quattro Bldg, 32-13 Udagawachō, Shibuya-ku ⓣ3477-8750. Shibuya Station.
Opening hours and cover charge depend on the act.

Intimate indie rock venue in a loft-like space, which hosts local and international acts, as well as up-and-coming bands and artists.

Crocodile クロコダイル

Map 12, F1. 6-18-8 Jingūmae, Shibuya-ku ⓣ3499-5205. Meiji-Jingūmae Station.
Daily 6pm–2am. ¥2000-3000.

Everything from samba to blues and reggae at this well-established basement space on Meiji-dōri between Harajuku and Shibuya. Also broadcasts gigs live on the Internet (check them out at Ⓦ*www.music.co.jp/~croc/*). Shows start at around 8pm.

Cyber サイバー

Map 8, F2. B1, 1-43-14 Higashi-Ikebukuro, Toshima-ku ⓣ3985-5844. Ikebukuro Station.

Usually opens from around 4–6pm. From ¥2000, depending on who's playing.

Dark, throbbing rock dive among the soaplands and love hotels north of Ikebukuro Station. Though the bands are variable, you might strike lucky – and there's not a lot else on in Ikebukuro. *Cyber* also runs the Explosion record label.

The Fiddler フエドラー

Map 2, B4. B1, 2-1-2 Takadanobaba, Shinjuku-ku, ⓣ3204-2698 ⓦ*www.thefiddler.com* Takadanobaba Station.

Mon–Thurs & Sun 6pm–3am, Fri & Sat 6pm–5am.

At the intersection of Waseda and Meiji-dōri this British pub, also known as the Mean Fiddler, has rock and blues bands playing most nights to students from the nearby university. It serves fish and chips, shepherd's pie and other comfort food, and pints of Guinness and Bass go for around ¥900.

On Air East & On Air West オンエア

Map 12, A6. 2-3 Maruyamachō, Shibuya-ku ⓣ5458-4646. Shibuya Station.

Opening hours and cover charge variable.

Major international acts often play at these twin venues, opposite each other slap in the middle of Shibuya's love hotel district.

Roppongi Pit Inn 六本木ピットイン

Map 11, E4. B1, Shiaki Bldg, 3-17-7 Roppongi, Minato-ku ⓣ3585-1063. Roppongi Station.

Daily 7.30pm–midnight. Around ¥3500.

Same concept as the *Shinjuku Pit Inn* (see p.243), but with a broader range of performers, including rock and fusion artists.

What the Dickens ワツトザデイケンズ

Map 6, C2. 4F, Roob 6 Bldg, 1-13-3 Ebisu-Nishi, Shibuya-ku. Ebisu Station.

Tues–Sat 5pm–2am, Sun 5pm–midnight.

Live music every night at this Olde England pub complete with beams and candle-lit nooks. Guinness and Bass Pale Ale are on tap at ¥950 a pint, ¥600 a half. The food – a range of hearty pies served with potatoes, veggies and bread – is excellent and costs ¥1500 or less.

JAZZ AND BLUES

Birdland ビルドランド

Map 11, E4. Square Bldg, 3-10-3 Roppongi, Minato-ku ⓣ3478-3456. Roppongi Station.

Mon–Thurs & Sun 6pm–midnight, Fri & Sat until 1am. ¥1500.

Candles light up this traditional jazz joint in the basement of a building that also offers far rowdier clubs. ¥1500 minimum drink order, plus service charge of ten percent.

Blue Note ブルーノト

Map 8, F7. 6-3-16 Minami-Aoyama, Minato-ku ⓣ5485-0088. Omotesandō Station.

Mon–Sat 5.30pm–1am. Around ¥6000 including one drink.

Tokyo's premier live jazz venue attracts world-class performers, with shows at 7 and 9.30pm.

Blues Alley Japan ブルースアリー日本

Map 6, E6. B1, Meguro Station Hotel, 1-3-14 Meguro, Meguro-ku ⓣ5496 4381. Meguro Station.

Daily 7.30–11pm. Cover charge depends on the acts.

This offshoot of the Washington DC blues and jazz club occupies a small basement space near the station. Food is also available.

New York Bar ニューヨークバー

Map 13, A7. Park Hyatt Hotel, 3-7-1-2 Nishi-Shinjuku, Shinjuku-ku. Shinjuku Station.

Daily 6pm–midnight. ¥2000 cover charge, free if you eat at the New York Grill.

Top-class live jazz plus a glittering night view of Shinjuku are the attractions of this sophisticated bar attached to the *Park Hyatt's New York Grill*.

Shinjuku Pit Inn 新宿ピットイン

Map 13, I5. B1, Accord Shinjuku Bldg, 2-12-4 Shinjuku ⓣ3354-2024. Shinjuku Station.

Daily 7.30–10.30pm. ¥4000 cover charge.

Serious jazz at this long-standing club, which has been the launch pad for many top Japanese performers and also attracts overseas artists.

CLASSICAL MUSIC AND OPERA

Casals Hall カザルスホール

Map 10, F4. 1-6 Kanda-Surugadai, Chiyoda-ku ⓣ3294-1229. Ochanomizu Station.

Major venue for chamber music, piano recitals and small ensembles inside the Ochanomizu Square Building, designed in a "shoebox" shape by top architect Arata Isozaki.

Orchard Hall オーチやードホール

Map 12, A4. 2-24-1 Dōgenzaka, Shibuya-ku ⓣ3477-9111, ⓦ*www.bunkamura.co.jp* Shibuya Station.

Large, traditional concert hall in the Bunkamura Centre, up the slope from central Shibuya.

New National Theatre 新国立劇場

Map 2, A7. 1-20 Honmachi, Shinjuku-ku ⓣ5352-9999,

www.nntt.jac.go.jp Hatsudai Station.
Just behind Opera City, the New National Theatre comprises three stages specially designed for Western performance art, including opera, ballet, dance and drama.

NHK Hall NHKホール

Map 2, A9. 2-2-1 Jinnan, Shibuya-ku 3465-1751. Harajuku or Shibuya stations.
One of Tokyo's older auditoria for classical concerts, but still well rated and home to one of the city's top orchestras. Next to the NHK Broadcasting Centre, south of Yoyogi-kōen.

Suntory Hall サントリーホール

Map 11, G2. Ark Hills, 1-13-1 Akasaka, Minato-ku 3505-1001, *www.suntory.co.jp/suntoryhall* Roppongi or Tameike-Sannō stations.
Reputed to have the best acoustics in the city, with free lunchtime organ concerts held Monday to Friday, between 12.15 and 12.45pm.

Tokyo International Forum 東京国際フオーラム

Map 7, C5. 3-5-1 Marunouchi, Chiyoda-ku 5221-9000. Yūrakuchō Station.
The Forum's four multi-purpose halls include one of the world's largest auditoria, with over five thousand seats. Its aim is to be truly international, staging an eclectic mix of performance art, from opera to Kabuki.

Tokyo Opera City 東京オペラシチイ

Map 2, A7. 3-20-2 Nishi-Shinjuku, Shinjuku-ku 5353-9999, *www.tokyooperacity-cf.or.jp/en/index2.html* Hatsudai Station.
The stunningly designed concert hall at this new venue seats over 1600, and there's a more intimate recital hall too.

Gay Tokyo

Compared to other big Japanese cities, such as Ōsaka, Tokyo's gay and lesbian scene is relatively open and friendly, and it's completely out of the closet as far as the rest of the country is concerned. Even so, don't expect the same level of openness as in London, San Francisco or Sydney; gay life in Tokyo is a low-key affair and you certainly won't find same-sex couples parading their love on the streets.

It wasn't until 1995 that Tokyo got around to holding its first **gay pride march** – this has now blossomed into an annual event (every May) with over two thousand participants. The first spin-off lesbian march happened in October 1997. Also every May, the Tokyo International Lesbian and Gay Video and Film Festival attracts people from all over the country.

Shinjuku Nichōme is the epicentre of Tokyo's gay world, and bulges with bars and clubs – this is about as cruisey as things get for Japan. There are several gay events held at clubs around the city, including *Code*, *Liquid Room*, *Yellow* and *Pasha*, which regularly hosts the monthly women-only club night *Goldfinger* – see clubs p.248; *Tokyo Journal* has some details in its Cityscope listings, and the Tokyo Classified Web site is another good source of information (see p.39).

INFORMATION SERVICES

International Gay Friends is a networking group for gays which organizes support groups for men and women. To contact them, write to if/Passport, CPO 180, Tokyo 100-91, or call ⓣ5693-4569. Alternatively, the useful **GayNet Japan** Web site ⓦ*www.gnj.or.jp/gaynet/* covers most aspects of gay life in the country. **Asia Lesbian Wave** can be checked out at ⓦ*www.geocities.com/WestHollywood/Stonewall/1430*. A recommended Japanese source of information is the travel guide *Otoko Machi Map* – ask around in the gay neighbourhoods of Tokyo for where to buy it.

BARS & CLUBS

Ace エス

Map 13, I6. B2, Dai-ni Hayakawaya Bldg, 2-14-6 Shinjuku, Shinjuku-ku. Shinjuku-Sanchōme Station.
Thurs–Sun hours vary. ¥1000–¥3000 depending on the night.
House and garage still rule at this basement club (the old *Delight*) just next to the cruising park in Nichōme.

Arty Farty アーテイーフアーテイー

Map 13, I5. 2-4-17 Shinjuku, Shinjuku-ku. Shinjuku-Sanchōme Station.
Mon–Sat 9pm–5am, Sun 2pm–5am. No cover charge.
A youthful scene at this bar on the corner with decor that is a cross between New Mexico adobe chic and a Christmas grotto. Hosts gay/straight events on Sundays, when women are allowed in.

Club Dragon クラブドラゴン

Map 13, I5. B1, Accord Bldg, 2-14-4 Shinjuku, Shinjuku-ku.

Shinjuku-Sanchōme Station.
Mon–Sat 9pm–3am. ¥1000 including one drink. Women ¥2000 on Fri & Sat.

Techno and disco sounds drift up from this stripped-down dance club across the street from GB. The dress code favours leather and body-piercing, and women will feel more welcome during the week (it gets very hardcore at weekends).

Club Zip クラブジップ

Map 13, I5. 2-14-11 Shinjuku, Shinjuku-ku. Shinjuku-Sanchōme Station.
Daily 3pm–5am.

There's an English sign outside this classy and spacious bar, where it's possible to have a quiet drink without being ogled. No cover charge and beers are a reasonable ¥600 (¥500 during happy hour).

Fuji Bar フジバー

Map 13, I5. 2-12-16 Shinjuku, Shinjuku-ku. Shinjuku-Sanchōme Station.
Mon–Thurs & Sun 7.30pm–2.30am, Fri & Sat 7.30pm–4am.

Cosy karaoke bar in the basement of the building around the corner from GB (see below) that has a wide selection of English songs, in case you're in the singing mood (¥100 per song). The crowd is a gay/straight mix.

GB ジービー

Map 13, I5. B1, Business Hotel T Bldg, 2-12-3 Shinjuku, Shinjuku-ku. Shinjuku-Sanchōme Station.
Mon–Thurs 8am–2pm, Fri 8am–3am, Sat 8am–3am.

The initials stand for Ginger Bar (after Ginger Rogers) at this friendly, boys-only basement joint, with a good mix of Japanese and foreigners. Most *gaijin* come here first before exploring the more exotic corners of Nichōme.

Goldfinger ゴロドフインガ

Map 11,B6. Pasha Club, Nishi-Azabu, 6F, The Wall Bldg, 4-2-4 Nishi-Azabu, Minato-ku. Ⓦ *www.so-net.ne.jp/CYBERJAPAN* Roppongi Station.

Monthly 9pm–late. ¥3500 including two drinks.

English architect Nigel Coates's funky Wall Building is the monthly home for this long-running women-only club. Check their Web site or the CIA flyers (see p.233) for the dates it's scheduled.

Kinswomyn キンズウイミン

Map 13, I5. 3F, Dai-ichi Tenka Bldg, 2-15-10 Shinjuku, Shinjuku-ku. Shinjuku-Sanchōme Station.

Mon–Sat 7pm–3am.

Women-only bar, which has a more relaxed ambience (and lower prices) than many of Nichōme's other lesbian haunts. Drinks are ¥700 and there's no cover charge.

Lamp Post ランプポスト

Map 13, I5. 2-21-15 Shinjuku, Shinjuku-ku. Shinjuku-Sanchōme Station.

Daily 7pm–3am.

Everyone is welcome to come and listen to the live piano music at this small but convivial bar.

Koishi こいし

Map 8, F5. 5-19-15 Minami-Aoyama, Minato-ku. Omotesandō Station.

Mon–Sat 6.30–11pm.

Large portions of home-cooking-style food and drinks at this laid-back *izakaya* run by gay owners and frequented by the fashion and show-biz crowd who hang out at this stylish end of Omotesandō.

The Ring

ザリング

Various venues.

¥3500 including two drinks.

This was one of the first glam gay/straight dance parties to hit Tokyo in the early Nineties, and it's still going strong at various venues around the city. You'll usually find it held at *Luners* (see p.236).

Theatre and cinema

Though language can be a problem when it comes to exploring Tokyo's **performance arts**, colourful extravaganzas like Takarazuka or the more traditional Kabuki are enjoyable, and even the notoriously difficult Nō and Butō are worth trying once. Tokyo may not seem the obvious place to seek out a Shakespeare tragedy or an Ibsen revival, especially since **tickets** are expensive and hard to come by, but major international theatre groups often pass through on their foreign tours. **Information** about current or upcoming performances is available in the English-language press and from Tokyo TIC (see p.38). Alternatively, ring Teletourist (Ⓣ3201-2911; 24hr) for recorded details of what's on.

As far as **cinema** goes, you'll be spoilt for choice of multi-screens showing the latest Hollywood blockbuster – usually with Japanese subtitles – while a decent number of smaller cinemas show independent and art-house releases.

See *Directory*, p.299, for details of ticket agencies.

TRADITIONAL THEATRE

Kabuki is by far the most accessible of Japan's traditional performance arts and its dramatic plots, full of larger-than-life heroes, are easy to follow without understanding a word. Performances last three or four hours, but single-act tickets are available at the Kabuki-za (see below). Puppet theatre, **Bunraku**, predates Kabuki but shares many of the same story-lines. It's less exciting – the puppets need three people to manipulate them – but the artistry of the puppeteers is astounding. Even most Japanese find **Nō**, the country's oldest form of theatre, unfathomable. Its highly stylized, painfully slow movements and archaic language don't make for a rip-roaring theatrical experience, though it can be incredibly powerful. **Kyōgen**, short satirical plays with an earthy humour and simple plots, liven up the intervals. If you want to try Nō or Kyōgen, it's worth asking at the TIC about free performances by amateur groups.

Kabuki-za 歌舞伎座

Map 7, F7. 4-12-15 Ginza, Chūō-ku ⓣ5565-6000. Higashi-Ginza Station.

Tokyo's main Kabuki theatre stages two programmes every day during the first three weeks of the month, usually at 11am and 4.30pm. Prices start at around ¥2500 for the full programme, or you can buy one-act tickets (usually under ¥1000) at the theatre. Details, including a brief English synopsis, are available at the theatre or Tokyo TIC, and you can rent earphone guides (¥650, plus ¥1000 deposit; not available for one-act seats). A pair of binoculars is useful – inevitably the cheapest seats are way up at the back.

Kanze Nō-gakudō 観世能楽堂

Map 2, A9. 1-16-4 Shōtō, Shibuya-ku ⓣ3469-5241. Shibuya Station.

The home theatre of Kanze, the best-known of Tokyo's several Nō troupes, and one of the city's most traditional Nō theatres. Located north of the main Tōkyū department store.

Kokuritsu Gekijō 国立劇場

Map 2, E7. 4-1 Hayabusachō, Chiyoda-ku ☎ 3230-3000. Hanzōmon Station.

Tokyo's National Theatre puts on a varied programme of traditional theatre and music, including Kabuki, Bunraku, court music and dance. English-language programmes and earphones (¥650, plus ¥1000 deposit) are available, and tickets start at around ¥1500 for Kabuki and ¥4400 for Bunraku.

Kokuritsu Nō-gakudō 国立能楽堂

Map 2, B7. 4-18-1 Sendagaya, Shibuya-ku ☎ 3423-1331. Sendagaya Station.

Only built in 1983, the National Nō Theatre is a public venue which hosts various schools of Nō several times a month, five minutes' walk southwest of Sendagaya Station.

Shimbashi Embujō 新橋演舞場

Map 7, F9. 6-18-2 Ginza, Chūō-ku ☎ 3541-2600. Higashi-Ginza Station.

Large theatre on the eastern edge of Ginza staging a range of traditional dance, music and theatre.

CONTEMPORARY AND INTERNATIONAL THEATRE

Apart from Andrew Lloyd Webber musicals, the most famous theatrical experience you can have in Tokyo is **Takarazuka**, the all-singing, all-dancing, all-female revue which appears occasionally at the Takarazuka Theatre (see p.254). Keep an eye out as well for performances of **Butō** (or *Butoh*). This highly expressive dance form, inspired by visiting American performers in the early 1950s, is minimalist, introspective, and often violent or sexually explicit. It's not to everyone's taste – it's actually more popular abroad than in Japan – but not to be missed if you're interested in modern performance art. There are a handful of groups in Tokyo; events are listed in *Tokyo Journal*, or ask at the TIC.

Both Takarazuka and Butō have entered the mainstream, but there's plenty happening on the fringes. Tiny Alice and the Japan Foundation Forum are prime places to catch **avant-garde theatre,** while every autumn (mid-Oct to mid-Dec) the Tokyo International Festival of Performing Arts (Ⓦ *www1.biz.biglobe.ne.jp/~tif*) showcases the best on the current scene.

Tokyo is also on the circuit for many **international theatre** companies, who often appear at the Tokyo Globe or Shinjuku's New National Theatre (see opposite), though seats sell out months in advance for the bigger names. Easier to come by are tickets for the amateur dramatic group **Tokyo International Players**, which has been going for over a century, feeding off the ever-changing cast of foreign acting talent that passes through the city. Check the English-language press for details of their shows, mounted four of five times a year. Look out, too, for the Tokyo Comedy Store (Ⓦ *www.tokyocomedy.com*), which offers the city's best live improvisation and stand-up **comedy** (in English) twice a month on Thursdays in Roppongi's *Bar Isn't It* (see p.226); tickets cost ¥1500, including one drink.

Japan Foundation Forum

Map 4, F8. 1F, Akasaka Twin Tower, 2-17-22 Akasaka, Minato-ku Ⓣ 5562-3892, Ⓦ *www.jpf.go.jp/e/others/forum.html* Tameikesannō Station.

Established in 1994 to promote international cultural exchange, the Forum stages a variety of events including performances by international – mainly Asian – theatre groups. They also host contemporary art installations from time to time.

Le Theatre Ginza ラテアトル銀座

Map 7, F5. 1-11-2 Ginza, Chūō-ku ⓣ03535-5151. Ginza-Itchōme Station.

Luxury theatre next to the equally plush *Hotel Seiyō* which hosts quality avant-garde productions by international groups.

Shiki Gekijō しき劇場

Map 2, F10. 1-10-48 Kaigan, Minato-ku ⓣ0120-489-444, ⓦ*www.shiki.gr.jp*. Hamamatsuchō or Takeshiba stations.

Two modern theatres – named Spring and Autumn – one hosting big Western musicals (such as *The Lion King*), the other home-grown productions.

Takarazuka Gekijō 宝ずか劇場

Map 7, C7. 1-1-3 Yūrakuchō, Chūō-ku ⓣ5251-2001. Hibiya Station.

Mostly Hollywood musicals punched out by a huge cast in fabulous costumes to an audience of middle-aged housewives and star-struck teenage girls. The theatre, opposite the *Imperial Hotel*, also stages regular Takarazuka performances as well as conventional dramas.

Terpsichore テルプシコーレ

Map 1, D4. 3-49-15 Nakano, Nakano-ku ⓣ3383-3719. Nakano Station.

The most active of Tokyo's Butō venues, comprising a tiny theatre beside the tracks just west of Nakano Station.

Theatre Cocoon シヤターコくーン

Map 12, A4. 2-24-1 Dogenzaka, Shibuya-ku ⓣ3477-9111. Shibuya Station.

Part of Shibuya's Bunkamura arts centre, this modern theatre hosts some of Tokyo's more accessible fringe productions.

Tiny Alice タイニアリス

Map 13, I4. 2-13-6 Shinjuku-ku ⓣ3354-7307. Shinjuku-Sanchōme Station.

Well-known for its cutting-edge Japanese and Asian performance art, and for its summer theatre festival.

Tokyo Globe 東京グローブ

Map 2, B5. 3-1-2 Hyakuninchō, Shinjuku-ku ⓣ3360-1151. Shin-ōkubo Station.

A covered re-creation of the original London Globe Theatre which regularly hosts high profile theatre troupes including, inevitably, the Royal Shakespeare Company.

CINEMA

Tokyoites are avid cinema-goers, though a trip to the cinema (*Eiga-kan*) doesn't come cheap – ¥1800 or ¥2500 for *shiteseki* (reserved seats). The best time to catch a movie is on Cinema Day, generally the first day of the month, when all **tickets** cost ¥1000. You can cut the cost somewhat by buying discount tickets in advance from a ticket agency such as CN Playguide and Pia. Note that the last show is generally around 7pm, and that if it's a popular new release you'll need to be at the cinema well before the start time to get a decent seat, or sometimes any seat at all.

Of the city's several film festivals, the biggest is the **Tokyo International Film Festival** held every October at the Bunkamura (see p.255) and other cinemas around Shibuya. Although it's increasingly becoming a vehicle for promoting major releases from the US, this is still one the few opportunities you'll have for catching Japanese and world cinema with English subtitles, not to mention seeing some films that would never get a general release. For more information check out their Web site ⓦ*www.tokyo-filmfest.or.jp/e_indx.html*

Film **listings** are published sporadically throughout the week in *The Japan Times* and on Thursday in the *Daily Yomiuri*. *Tokyo Classified* and *Tokyo Journal* both carry listings reviews, and have good maps locating all the major cinemas.

Apart from those listed here, which tend to specialize in independent movies, there are many more cinemas to be found in Ginza, Ikebukuro, Shibuya and Shinjuku, mostly showing the latest Hollywood blockbuster. And don't forget the big screen experiences at Tokyo's two IMAX theatres, in Shinjuku and Ikebukuro.

Le Cinéma ルシネマ

Map 12, A4. Tōkyū Bunkamura, 2-30 Dōgenzaka, Shibuya-ku ⓣ3477-9111. Shibuya Station.

This upmarket filmhouse within the Bunkamura arts complex has two screens and is the main venue for the Tokyo International Film Festival (see above).

Cinema Rise シネマライズ

Map 12, C3. Spain-zaka, 1307 Udagawa-chō, Shibuya ⓣ3464-0052. Shibuya Station.

Sleek, avant-garde-looking cinema with two screens, which focuses on successful independent movies from around the world.

Ciné Saison Shibuya シネセソン渋谷

Map 12, C5. Prime Bldg, 2-29-5 Dōgenzaka, Shibuya-ku ⓣ3770-1721. Shibuya Station.

Comfy cinema which showcases a wide range of films, including classic revivals from the 1960s and 1970s.

Cinema Qualité シネマクアリテ

Map 13, G5. Musashinokan Bldg, 3-27 Shinjuku, Shinjuku-ku ⓣ3354-5670. Shinjuku Station.

Three screens at this complex on the east side of Shinjuku

Station behind the Mitsukoshi department store. Often screens classic revivals as well as independent European hits.

Haiyu-za Talkie Night 俳優タルキーニーと

Map 11, D4. Haiyu-za Gekijo, 4-9-2 Roppongi, Minato-ku ⓣ3470-2880. Roppongi Station.

Artsy cinema, east of the crossing, which shows independent flicks from Japan and abroad. Also has late-night shows and the British chain pub *Hub* in its lobby.

Hibiya Chanter 日比谷シヤンテ

Map 7, C7. Hibiya Chanter Bldg, 1-2-2 Yūrakuchō, Chiyoda-ku ⓣ3591-1511. Hibiya and Yūrakuchō stations.

Three large cinemas on different floors at this complex which screens many of the higher-profile American and British releases.

Iwanami Hall 岩波ホール

Map 10, E5. 2-1 Kanda-Jimbōchō, Chiyoda-ku ⓣ3262-5252. Jimbōchō Station.

Since 1968, Iwanami Hall has had a policy of screening non-commercial European films, from as unlikely places as Greece and Poland, as well as quirky Japanese movies.

National Film Centre 国立フイルムセンター

Map 7, F5. 3-7-6 Kyōbashi, Chūō-ku ⓣ3272-8600. Kyōbashi Station.

A treasure-trove for film lovers, with a gallery showing film-related exhibitions and two small cinemas screening retrospectives from their 17,000 archived movies. Most are Japanese classics, though occasionally they dust off their collection of foreign movies.

Shin-Bungei-za 新ぶんげいざ

Map 9, E6. Ikebukuro, Toshima-ku ⓣ3971-9422. Ikebukuro Station.

Recently re-opened retrospectives theatre that has matinee double bills. The ¥1300 six-month membership includes one ticket, a monthly newsletter and regular discounts on admission.

Theatre Ikebukuro シエタ池袋

Map 9, E6. Ikebukuro, Toshima-ku ⓣ3987-4311. Ikebukuro Station.

This place showcases films from Asia, Africa and Latin America, offering a ¥1000 one-year membership for discount admission.

Waseda Shochiku 早稲田松功

Map 2, B4. 1-5-16 Takadanobaba, Shinjuku-ku. Takadanobaba Station.

Popular with students from the nearby university, this cinema is cheaper (¥1300) and less fancy than others but still shows a decent selection of mainstream and non-commercial releases.

Yebisu Garden Cinema 恵比寿ガーデンシネマ

Map 6, E4. Yebisu Garden Place, 4-20 Ebisu, Shibuya-ku ⓣ5420-6161. Ebisu Station.

Two screens at this modern cinema in the Yebisu brewery development showing an interesting range of classy Hollywood and British releases.

Festivals

Whenever you visit Tokyo, chances are there'll be a religious festival (*matsuri*) taking place somewhere. Of the major events listed below, by far the most important is New Year, when most of the city closes down for a week (roughly Dec 28–Jan 3). Note that in some cases the dates might change, so be sure to double check before setting out.

Tokyo also hosts three grand **sumo tournaments** each year (see p.270), as well as **film** and **theatre festivals**. Several non-Japanese festivals which have also caught on include **Valentine's Day** (February 14), when women give men gifts of chocolate, while on **White Day** (March 14) men get their turn with chocolates (white, of course) perfume or racy underwear. Another import is **Christmas**, which is celebrated in Japan as an almost totally commercial event, with plastic holly and tinsel in profusion. **Christmas Eve**, in particular, is one of the most popular date nights of the year, when all the most expensive and trendiest restaurants are booked solid. By contrast, **New Year's Eve** is a fairly subdued, family-orientated event.

For a full list of public holidays, see p.25.

JANUARY

Ganjitsu (or Gantan)

January 1. National holiday. The first shrine-visit of the year (*hatsu-mōde*) draws the crowds to Meiji-jingū, Hie-jinja, Kanda Myōjin and other city shrines to pray for good fortune. Performances of traditional dance and music take place at Yasukuni-jinja.

Ippan Sanga

January 2. Thousands of loyal Japanese, and a few curious foreigners, troop into the Imperial Palace grounds to greet the emperor. The royal family appear on the balcony several times during the day from 9.30am to 3pm.

Dezomeshiki

January 6. Tokyo firemen in Edo-period costume pull off dazzling stunts atop long bamboo ladders. In Harumi, Tokyo Bay.

Seijin-no-hi (Adults' Day)

Second Mon in January. National holiday. Colourful pageant of twenty-year-old women, and fewer men, in traditional dress visiting city shrines to celebrate their entry into adulthood. At Meiji-jingū various ancient rituals are observed, including a ceremonial archery contest.

FEBRUARY

Setsubun

February 3 or 4. On the last day of winter by the lunar calendar, people scatter lucky beans around their homes and at shrines or temples to drive out evil and welcome in the year's good luck. The liveliest festivities take place at Sensō-ji, Kanda Myōjin, Zōjō-ji and Hie-jinja.

MARCH

Hina Matsuri (Doll Festival)

March 3. Families with young girls display beautiful dolls of the emperor, empress and their courtiers dressed in ancient costume. Department stores,

The TIC (see p.38) publishes a monthly round-up of festivals in and around the city.

hotels and museums often put on special displays at this time.

APRIL

Hana Matsuri

April 8. Buddha's birthday is celebrated in all Tokyo's temples, either with parades or quieter celebrations where a small statue of Buddha is sprinkled with sweet tea.

Kamakura Matsuri

Mid-April. Kamakura's week-long festival includes traditional dances, costume parades and horseback archery.

Jibeta Matsuri

Mid-April. In celebration of fertility and reproduction, an iron phallus is forged and giant wooden phalluses paraded around Kanayama-jinja in Kawasaki. Join the dancing crowds, including a group of demure transvestites, and have huge fun.

MAY

Kodomo-no-hi (Children's Day)

May 5. National holiday. The original Boys' Day now includes all children as

CHERRY BLOSSOM

With the arrival of spring in early **April**, a pink tide of **cherry blossom** washes north over Tokyo. The finest displays are Yasukuni-jinja, Ueno-kōen, Aoyoma Cemetery and the riverside Sumida-kōen, where every tree shelters a blossom-viewing party. Though best at night, under the light of hanging paper lanterns, this is also the rowdiest time as revellers, lubricated with quantities of sake, croon to competing karaoke machines.

families fly carp banners, symbolizing strength, outside their homes.

Kanda Matsuri

Mid-May. One of the city's top three festivals, taking place in odd-numbered years at Kanda Myōjin. People in Heian-period costume escort eighty gilded *mikoshi* (portable shrines) through the streets.

Tōshō-gū Haru Matsuri

May 17–18. Huge procession of one thousand armour-clad warriors and three *mikoshi*, commemorating the burial of Shogun Tokugawa Ieyasu in Nikkō in 1617.

Sanja Matsuri

Third weekend in May. Tokyo's most boisterous festival, when over one hundred *mikoshi* are jostled through the streets of Asakusa, accompanied by lion dancers, geisha and musicians.

JUNE

Sannō Matsuri

June 13–20. The last of the big three festivals (after Kanda and Sanja) takes place in even-numbered years, focusing on colourful processions of *mikoshi* through Akasaka.

JULY

Hanabi Taikai

Late July and August. The summer skies explode with thousands of fireworks, harking back to traditional "river-opening" ceremonies to mark the start of the summer boating season. The Sumida-gawa display is the most spectacular (view it from river-boats or Asakusa's Sumida-kōen on the last Sat in July), but those in Edogawa, Tamagawa, Arakawa and Harumi come close, or head out to Kamakura for their *hanabi taikai* on August 10.

AUGUST

Fukagawa Matsuri

Mid-August. Every three years Tomioka Hachiman-gū hosts the city's wettest festival, when spectators throw buckets of water over 54 *mikoshi* being shouldered through the streets. The next event is in 2002.

Obon

Mid-August. Families gather around their ancestral graves, and much of Tokyo closes down, though many neighbourhoods stage dances in honour of the deceased.

SEPTEMBER

Tsurugaoka Hachiman-gū Matsuri

September 14–16. Annual shrine-festival of Tsurugaoka Hachiman-gū in Kamakura. The highlight is a demonstration of horseback archery (*yabasume*) on the final day.

Ningyō Kuyō

September 25. A funeral service for unwanted dolls is held at Kiyomizu Kannon-dō in Ueno-kōen, after which they are cremated.

OCTOBER

Tōshō-gū Aki Matsuri

October 17. Repeat of Nikkō's fabulous procession held for the spring festival, minus the horseback archery displays.

NOVEMBER

Daimyō Gyōretsu

November 3. Re-enactment of a feudal lord's procession along the Tōkaidō (the great road linking Tokyo and Kyoto), accompanied by his doctor, accountant, tea master and road sweepers. At Sōun-ji, near Hakone-Yumoto.

Tori-no-ichi

Mid-November. Fairs selling *kumade*, bamboo rakes decorated with lucky charms, are held at shrines on "rooster days" according to the zodiacal calendar. The main fair is at Ōtori-jinja (Iriya Station).

Shichi-go-san

November 15. Cameras are out in force for the festival

when children aged 7, 5 and 3 don traditional garb to visit the shrines, particularly Meiji-jingū, Hie-jinja and Yasukuni-jinja.

DECEMBER

Gishi-sai

December 14. Costume parade in Nihombashi re-enacting the famous vendetta of the 47 *rōnin* (see p.129), followed by a memorial service for them at Sengaku-ji.

Hagoita-ichi

Dec 17–19. The build-up to New Year begins with a battledore fair outside Asakusa's Sensō-ji (see p.77).

Ōmisoka

December 31. Leading up to midnight, temple bells ring out 108 times (the number of human frailties according to Buddhist thinking), while thousands gather at Meiji-jingū, Hie-jinja and other major shrines to honour the gods with the first visit of the New Year. If you don't like crowds, head for a small local shrine.

Sports and martial arts

The Japanese take their sport very seriously, and it's not uncommon for parts of Tokyo to come to a complete standstill during crucial moments of a major baseball (*yakyu*) game as fans gather around television screens in homes, offices, shops, bars – even on the street. **Baseball** is the city's biggest sporting obsession, and it's rare to find anyone who doesn't support one of Tokyo's three main teams. Hot on baseball's heels is **soccer**, which since the launch of the professional J-League in 1993 has enjoyed phenomenal popularity and will only get more attention in the run up to the 2002 World Cup to be held in Japan (see box, p.268).

Sumo wrestling also has a high profile, with big tournaments (*bashō*) televised nationwide and wrestlers enjoying celebrity status. **Martial arts**, such as aikido, judo and karate, all traditionally associated with Japan, are far less popular, though Tokyo, with its numerous *dōjō* (practice halls), is the best place in the country to view or learn these ancient fighting ways. Many *dōjō* allow visitors in to watch practice sessions.

Check the local media, such as *The Japan Times* and *Tokyo Classified*, for details of events. To get tickets it's best to approach one of the major **advance ticket agencies**. Major games and events sell out fast, so a second approach is to go directly to the venue on the day and see if you can get a ticket from the box office or a tout outside; expect to pay well over the odds if it's a popular game.

For details of ticket agencies, see *Directory*, p.299.

BASEBALL

If you're in Tokyo during the **baseball** season (April to the end of October), think about taking in a professional match; even if you're not a fan, the buzzing atmosphere and audience enthusiasm can be infectious. As well as the professional leagues (of which there are two, Central and Pacific), there's the equally, if not more, popular All-Japan High School Baseball Championship, and you might be able to catch one of the local play-offs before the main tournament held each summer in Ōsaka; check with the tourist office for details.

Tickets, available from the stadia or at advance ticket booths, start at around ¥1500 and go on sale on Friday, two weeks prior to a game. For more information on Japan's pro-baseball leagues, check out the Web site on Ⓦ *www.inter.co.jp/Baseball/*.

Tokyo Dome (Big Egg) 東京ドーム

Map 10, D2. 1-3 Koraku, Bunkyō-ku ⓣ3811-2111. Suidōbashi Station.

Huge covered arena, affectionately nicknamed the Big Egg, home to both the Nippon Ham Fighters and Yomiuri Giants baseball teams, and a great place to take in a night game (*naitā*).

Jingū Stadium 神宮技場

Map 2, C8. 13 Kasumigaoka, Shinjuku-ku ⓣ3404-8999. Gaienmae Station.

The home ground of Tokyo's third professional baseball team, the Yakult Swallows, is one of the stadia grouped in Meiji-jingū's Outer Gardens.

SOCCER

The J-League, Japan's first professional football league, launched amid a multi-billion-yen promotional drive in 1993, has certainly captured the public's imagination and wallet with its glitzy and full range of associated merchandise. The game is going from strength to strength, with the league's ten teams at its inception having now multiplied to two leagues of 27 teams in total. Sixteen clubs play in the J1 league, 11 in the J2, all participate in the JL Yamazaki Nabisco Cup and there are a host of other cups and contests including the JOMO Cup, in which fans pick their dream teams from among all the J-League players.

Top footballers have been bought in from around the world (Gary Lineker was the star draw of the initial season) and, with the World Cup scheduled to be held in Japan and Korea in 2002 (see box), the game's continued popularity is assured. The local team is **FC Tokyo**, whose home ground is the new Tokyo Stadium near Chōfu, 5 minutes' walk from Tobitakyu on the Keiō line. For full details of the J-League in English, including match reports, check out the Web site at ⓦ *www.j-league.or.jp*.

National Stadium 国立競技場

Map 2, C7. 10 Kasumigaoka-chō, Shinjuku-ku ⓣ3403-1151. Sendagaya Station.

Big Japanese and international games are held at this huge oval

FIFA WORLD CUP 2002

In June 2002, 32 football teams will battle it out in Japan and South Korea for the **World Cup** – the seventeenth contest organised by the Fédération Internationale de Football Association (FIFA) since the first kick-off in 1930, and the first time the event has been held in two countries.

The tournament begins in Korea's Seoul Stadium on May 31 and climaxes at Japan's Yokohama International Stadium on June 30; each country will host 32 matches, with France (the current champions), Japan and Korea automatically qualifying. Tickets prices, set in US dollars, range from $60 to $150 for first round matches to $300 to $750 for the final. For ticket enquiries within Japan call ⓣ3287-1199 or check the Web sites listed below.

Of the ten stadia across Japan being used, four are relatively close to Tokyo. The **Yokohama International Stadium** (ⓦ*www.city.yokohama.jp/me/w-cup/english/index.html*) has seating capacity for 70,000, making it one of Japan's largest. It's located fifteen minutes' walk from Shin-Yokohama Station, on the main Tōkaidō Shinkansen line linking Tokyo, Kyoto and Ōsaka.

The 43,000-seater **Kashima Stadium** (ⓦ*www.pref.ibaraki.jp/prog/wldcup/English/index.htm*) is in Ibaraki-ken, around 80km east of the capital. To get here take a JR train to Kashima-jingū Station and then transfer to the Kashima Rinkai Tetsudo line to Kashima Soccer Stadium, the ground being a five minute walk from the station. Alternatively there will be direct bus services from the south exit of Tokyo Station to Kashima-jingū Station where, again, there'll be a local bus to the stadium.

Some 20km north of Tokyo is the 63,000 capacity **Urawa Stadium** (ⓦ*www.2002saitama.com/e-index.html*) in Saitama-ken. To get here hop on the Namboku subway line, making sure you're on a through train to the new Urawa-Misono Station on the Saitama Railway line. The stadium is a fifteen minute walk from the station.

The 50,000-seater Ecopa stadium in **Fukuroi** (Ⓦ *www2.shizuokanet.ne.jp/worldcup/english/index.html*) in Shizuoka-ken is 170km southwest along the coast from Tokyo. The fastest route is to take a Shinkansen to Kakegawa (1hr 51min on the Kodama service) train then transfer to the local JR Tōkaidō Honsen line to reach the new stadium station.

For details of the other six World Cup venues check out the Web sites for Kōbe (Ⓦ *www.city.kobe.jp/index-e.html*), Niigata (Ⓦ *www.pref.niigata.jp/worldcup/index-e.html*), Oita in Kyūshū (Ⓦ *www2.pref.oita.jp/10200/english/index.html*), Ōsaka (Ⓦ *www.city.osaka.jp/english/index.html*), Rifu in Miyaki-ken (Ⓦ *www.worldcup-miyagi.com/e/index.html*) and Sapporo (Ⓦ *www.worldcup-sapporo.com/*). In Korea, matches will be played in Chonju, Inchon, Kwangju, Pusan, Seogwipo, Seoul, Suwon, Taegu, Taejon and Ulsan.

JNTO has put out a useful guide with access information for all the venues. For more details on the games in Japan, check out the official Web site Ⓦ *www.jawoc.or.jp/index_e.htm*, and for those in Korea look up Ⓦ *www.2002worldcupkorea.org/*. For general information on the World Cup go to FIFA's site Ⓦ *www.fifa.com*

Note that inexpensive to moderately priced accommodation will be in heavy demand in Tokyo and the surrounding area, so if you are planning on using the capital as a base, make any hotel bookings well in advance (see *Accommodation*, p.147). If you're stuck for somewhere to stay or can't get tickets for a match, the sports bars of Roppongi are one place to head, as is Tokyo's one dedicated soccer bar, *Footnik* in Takadanobaba (see p.229).

stadium built for the 1964 Olympics and seating 75,000 people. Tickets costs from ¥2000.

SUMO

Sumo, Japan's national sport, was developed from divination rites performed at Shinto shrines – and it still retains its religious flavour. Two huge wrestlers, weighing on average 170 kilos each and wearing nothing but a hefty loincloth, face off in a small ring of hard-packed clay; the loser is the first to step outside the rope or touch the ground with any part of the body except the feet. Bouts are often over in seconds, but the pageantry and ritual make for a surprisingly absorbing spectacle.

Each year three major tournaments (*bashō*) take place in Ryōgoku's National Stadium (see below). At other times it's possible to watch practice sessions (*keiko*) at the stables (*heya*) where the wrestlers live and train. These sessions take place in the early morning (usually from around 5 or 6am to 10.30am) except during and immediately after a *bashō* or when the wrestlers are out of town; visitors are expected to watch in silence and women must wear trousers. A few stables accept visitors without an appointment, but it's safest to doublecheck first with the Tokyo TIC to make sure they're actually training that day. Recommended stables to try are: Dewanoumi Beya (2-3-15 Ryōgoku, Sumida-ku; ⓣ3631-0090) and Kasugano Beya (1-7-11 Ryōgoku, Sumida-ku; ⓣ 3631-1871); you can pick up Japanese-only maps of the stables from the Ryōgoku Station ticket window.

For further information about tournaments, tickets and related events, consult the Nihon Sumō Kyōkai Web site (ⓦ *www.sumo.or.jp*) or pick up a copy of *Sumo World* magazine (ⓦ *www.iac.co.jp/~sumowrld/*).

Kokugikan 国技館

Map 10, Ryoguku inset. 1-3-28 Yokoami, Kōtō-ku ☏3623-5111. Ryōgoku Station.

The National Sumo Stadium is the venue for Tokyo's three *bashō* during the middle fortnights of January, May and September. To buy tickets contact a ticket agency (see p.299) or, better still, line up early – before 9am – outside the stadium box office for one of the unreserved tickets sold on the day (¥2100); note that tickets are particularly hard to come by on the first and last days.

AIKIDO

Half a sport, half a religion, **aikido** translates as "the way of harmonious spirit", and blends elements of judo, karate and kendo into a form of self-defence without body contact. It's one of the newer martial arts, having only been created in Japan earlier last century and, as a rule, is performed without weapons. For a painfully enlightening and humorous take on the rigours of aikido training, read Robert Twigger's *Angry White Pyjamas* (see *Contexts*, p.358).

The International Aikido Federation 合気道本部道場

Map 2, B4. 17-18 Wakamatsuchō, Shinjuku-ku ☏3203-923. Around ten minutes by bus from the west exit of Shinjuku Station. You'll also find the Aikikai Hombu Dōjō at the same address and telephone number, where visitors are welcome to watch practice sessions.

JUDO

Probably the martial art most closely associated with Japan, **judo** is a self-defence technique that developed out of the

Edo-era style of fighting called jujutsu. Judo activities in Japan are controlled by the All-Japan Judo Federation (see below).

All-Japan Judo Federation

Map 2, E3. Kodokan, 1-16-30 Kasuga, Bunkyō-ku ☎3818-4199.
Reached from either Kasuga or Kōrakuen subway stations, this *dōjō* has a spectators' gallery open to visitors free of charge (Mon–Fri 6–7.30pm, Sat 4–5.30pm). There's also a hostel here where you can stay if you have an introduction from an authorized Judo body or an approved Japanese sponsor.

Nippon Budōkan Budo Gakuen 日本武道館

Map 10, C5. 2-3 Kitanomaru-kōen, Chiyoda-ku ☎3216-5143. Kudanshita Station.
Around fifty free martial arts exhibition matches are held at this large octagonal arena, an important centre for all martial arts, as well as judo. Within the Budōkan, there's also a school where you can catch practice sessions (Mon–Fri 5–8pm, Sat 2–6.30pm).

KARATE

Karate has its roots in China and was only introduced into Japan in 1922. Since then the sport has developed into many different styles, all with governing bodies and federations based in Tokyo.

Japan Karate Association

Map 2, C9. 4F Sanshin Bldg, 29-33 Sakuragaoka-chō, Shibuya-ku ☎5459 6226. Shibuya Station.
It's possible to watch classes at the world's largest karate association, usually held Mon–Sat 10.30–11.30am & 5–8pm, but it's best to call first.

Japan Karatedo Federation

Map 2, E6. 6F, 2 Nippon Zaidan Bldg, 1-11-2 Toranomon, Minato-ku ☎3503-6640. Toranomon Station.

This umbrella organization can advise on the main styles of karate and where you can best see practice sessions or take lessons. Call from Monday to Friday, between 9am and 5pm.

KENDO

Kendo (the way of the sword) is Japanese fencing using a long bamboo weapon (the *shinai*) or the metal *katana* blade. This fighting skill is the oldest in Japan, dating from the Muromachi period (1392-1573). It was developed as a sport in the Edo-period and is now watched over by the All-Japan Kendo Federation.

All-Japan Kendo Federation

Map 10, C5. Nippon Budōkan, 2–3 Kitanomaru-kōen, Chiyoda-ku ☎3211-5804/5. Kudanshita Station.

Practice sessions aren't generally open to the public here, but you might be lucky enough to catch the All-Japan Championships held in Tokyo each December, or the children's kendo competition in January, both held at the Budōkan.

Shopping

Cruising the boutiques and fashion malls, toting a couple of designer-label carrier bags, is such a part of Tokyo life that it's hard not to get caught up in the general enthusiasm. There are shops to suit every taste and budget, from swanky department stores to craft shops stuffed with all kinds of tempting curiosities, and from hushed antiques shops to rag-bag flea markets.

All these outlets are good places to hunt for **souvenirs**, from cheap and cheerful paper products to satin-smooth lacquer-ware or sumptuous wedding kimono. Keep an eye out, too, for vending machines and "¥100 Shops" (everything at ¥100), which can yield amazing gizmos for next to nothing. When it comes to **fashion**, head straight for Omotesandō, where you'll find world-famous names, such as Issey Miyake and Comme des Garçons, as well as funky, teenage tat in the lanes of Harajuku.

Naturally, Tokyo is a prime hunting ground for the latest **electronic gadgets**, hot off the designers' screens, and also for certain types of **electrical equipment** and **cameras**. Some **CDs** may be slightly less expensive than at home, and the selection of world music, jazz and techno in particular takes some beating. Foreign-language **books and magazines**, however, are less well represented and can be very pricey.

DUTY-FREE SHOPPING

Foreigners can buy **duty-free** items (that is, without consumption tax), but only in certain tourist shops and the larger department stores. Perishable goods, such as food, drinks, tobacco, cosmetics and film, are exempt from the scheme, and most stores only offer duty-free if your total spend on one day exceeds ¥10,000. The shop will either give you a duty-free price immediately or, in department stores especially, you pay the full price first and then apply for a refund at their "tax-exemption" counter. The shop will attach a copy of the customs document (*warriin*) to your passport, to be removed by customs officers when you leave Japan. Note that regulations vary for foreign residents, and also that you can often find the same goods elsewhere at a better price, including tax, so shop around first.

In general **opening hours** are from 10am to 7pm or 8pm. Most shops close one day a week, not always on Sunday, and smaller places often shut on public holidays.

Though it's always worth asking, few shops take **credit cards** and fewer still accept cards issued abroad, so make sure you have plenty of cash. See p.299 for details of **consumption tax**.

You'll find 24-hour convenience stores in most neighbourhoods, usually near the subway or train station. Lawson, Family Mart, AM/PM and Seven-Eleven have the widest geographical coverage.

ANTIQUE AND FLEA MARKETS

There's at least one **flea market** in Tokyo every weekend, though you'll need to arrive early for any bargains; see below for a round-up of the main venues. Alternatively, head for the permanent **antique halls**, also listed below, which gather several dealers under one roof, and where you'll come across fine, hand-painted scrolls, and intricate *netsuke* or samurai armour among a good deal of tat. Finally, for a really wide selection, consider visiting the **Heiwajima Antiques Fair**, which takes place over three days about five times a year (usually in Feb/March, May, June, Sept and Dec) at the Ryūtsū Centre (10am–6pm), one stop on the monorail from Hamamatsuchō to Haneda; ask at the TIC (see p.38) for the current schedule.

Antique Market

アンティークマーケットハナイモリビル

Map 8, E4. B1, Hanae Mori Building, 3-6-1 Kita-Aoyama, Minato-ku. Omotesandō Station.

Open 11am–8pm; some shops close on Thurs.

Permanent stalls selling an expensive assortment of Japanese and Western antiques. Each stall has its own speciality – woodblock prints, ceramics, jewellery and so on.

Hanazono-jinja 花園神社

Map 13, H3. 5-17-3 Shinjuku, Shinjuku-ku. Shinjuku-Sanchōme Station.

Regular Sunday flea market from dawn to dusk in the grounds of a shrine, on the west side of Shinjuku.

Nogi-jinja 乃木神社

Map 11, C2. 8-11-27 Akasaka, Minato-ku. Nogizaka Station.

Lively flea market held on the second Sunday of each month from dawn to dusk.

Tōgō-jinja 東郷神社

Map 8, C1. 1-5-3 Jingūmae, Shibuya-ku. Harajuku Station.

Daily 4am–3pm.

One of Tokyo's best flea markets held on the first, fourth and fifth (if there is one) Sundays of the month.

Tokyo Antiques Hall

東京ふ億クラフトアンヂアンテイークハルズ

Map 2, C3. 3-9-5 Minami-Ikebukuro, Toshima-ku. Ikebukuro Station. Daily except Thurs 11am–7pm.

Over thirty stalls, selling everything from boxes of dog-eared postcards to original *ukiyo-e* and magnificent painted screens.

ARTS, CRAFTS AND SOUVENIRS

While most department stores have a reasonable **crafts** section, it's a lot more fun rummaging around in Tokyo's specialist shops. The largest concentration is in **Asakusa** (see box on p.82), though a few still survive in the thick of Ginza and Nihombashi. If money is no object, head for the arcades in the big hotels, such as the *Imperial* (see p.155), *Ōkura* (see p.162) and *New Ōtani* (see p.151), where you can pick up luxury gifts, from Mikimoto pearls to Arita porcelain.

Bengara

べんがら

Map 5, H3. 2-35-11 Asakusa, Taitō-ku. Asakusa Station. Daily except Thurs 10am–6pm, Sun & hols 11am–6pm.

The best place in Tokyo to buy *noren*, the split curtain hanging outside every traditional shop or restaurant, usually bearing the company logo. There's a whole range of patterns, sizes and prices, or you can order your own design.

Beniya

ベニヤ

Map 12, I4. 2-6-8 Shibuya, Shibuya-ku. Shibuya Station. Daily except Thurs 10am–7pm.

If you're interested in folk crafts (*mingei*), check out this well-stocked shop with a broad range of crafts from around the country at prices to suit all budgets.

Fuji-Torii ふじとりい

Map 8, D3. 6-1-10 Jingūmae, Shibuya-ku. Meiji-Jingūmae Station. Closed Tues and third Mon of the month. Daily 11am–7pm.

Small and slightly more upmarket than the nearby Oriental Bazaar (see below) specializing in *ukiyo-e*, other works of art and antiques.

Itō-ya 伊東屋

Map 7, E6. 2-7-15 Ginza, Chūō-ku. Ginza Station.
Mon–Sat 10am–7pm, Sun & hols 10.30am–7pm.

This wonderful stationery store, with nine floors and two annexes, is great for a whole range of packable souvenirs. Itō-ya 3 specializes in traditional *washi* paper, calligraphy brushes, inks and so on. There are branches in Shibuya and Ikebukuro.

Mingeikan 日本民芸館

Map 2, A10. 4-3-33 Komaba, Meguro-ku. Komaba-Tōdaimae Station.
Tues–Sun 10am–5pm.

The gift shop of the Japan Folk Crafts Museum may be a bit out of the way, but they have original pottery and prints to die for and it's a fine source of souvenirs. If you're in town, don't miss their annual sale of new work (Nov 23–Dec 3).

Oriental Bazaar オリエンタルバザール

Map 8, D3. 5-9-13 Jingūmae, Shibuya-ku. Meiji-jingūmae Station.
Daily except Thurs 9.30am–6.30pm.

This popular, one-stop souvenir emporium sells everything from secondhand kimono to origami paper, all at reasonable prices.

Takumi 匠

Map 7, D8. 8-4-2 Ginza, Chūō-ku. Shimbashi Station.
Closed Sun & hols Tues–Sun 11am–7pm.
Small folk-craft shop chock-a-block with bags, baskets, pots, toys and fabrics.

Washikobo 和紙工房

Map 11, B5. 1-8-10 Nishi-Azabu, Minato-ku. Roppongi Station.
Mon–Sat 10am–6pm.
Delightful shop crammed to the rafters with traditional *washi* paper in all its manifestations, as well as traditional wooden toys – the ideal place to look for small, lightweight souvenirs.

S Watanabe 渡邊木版美術画補

Map 7, D8. 8-6-19 Ginza, Chūō-ku. Shimbashi Station.
Mon–Sat 9.30am–8pm.
Small, central shop specializing in woodblock prints at a range of prices. You'll find modern and traditional designs, including original *ukiyo-e* as well as reproductions of famous artists.

BOOKS AND MAGAZINES

Buying foreign-language books in Tokyo is likely to make a large impact on your wallet, but it can be enjoyable to browse the city's major **bookstores** (listed below). In most big hotels, you'll find bookshops stocking English-language books on Japan and a limited choice of fiction as well as imported newspapers and magazines. Bookworms should also rummage around the **secondhand bookstores** of Jimbōchō (see p.74), north of central Tokyo on the Hanzōmon, Mita and Shinjuku subway lines.

Aoyama Book Centre 青山ブックセンター

Map 11, D4. Roppongi Denki Bldg, 6-1-20 Roppongi, Minato-ku. Roppongi Station.

Mon–Sat 10am–5.30am, Sun 10am–10pm.

Top Roppongi hangout in the wee small hours when dazed clubbers can flick through a wide selection of Japanese and English books and magazines, including a good range of art books.

Jena イエナ

Map 7, E7. 5-6-1 Ginza, Chūō-ku. Ginza Station.

Mon–Sat 10.30am–8.30pm, Sun 11am–7.30pm.

Handily located in the heart of Ginza, Jena's third floor stocks a decent range of foreign-language books and magazines. It's distinguished by its helpful and knowledgeable staff as well as a fair selection for Japanese-language students.

Kinokuniya 紀伊国屋

Map 13, G7. Takashimaya Times Square, Annex Bldg, 5-24-2 Sendagaya, Shinjuku-ku. Shinjuku Station.

Daily 10am–8pm. Closed one Wed a month.

Kinokuniya's new seven-storey outlet offers the best selection of foreign-language books and magazines in Tokyo on its sixth floor, while its original shop on Shinjuku-dōri remains a favourite meeting spot.

Kitazawa 北沢

Map 10, E5. 2-5 Jimbōchō, Chiyoda-ku. Jimbōchō Station.

Mon–Sat 10am–6pm.

The best for English-language titles among dozens of secondhand stores in Jimbōchō. It's on Yasukuni-dōri, just west of the junction with Hakusan-dōri.

MANGA

All types of drawn cartoons, from comic strips to magazines, are known as **manga**, and together they constitute a multi-billion yen business that accounts for around a third of all published material in Japan. The best seller is *Shukan Shōnen Jump*, a weekly which regularly shifts five million copies, but there are hundreds of other titles, not to mention the popular daily strips in newspapers.

Although *manga* are targeted at a cross-section of society – and sometimes cater to less wholesome tastes – comic books are frequently used to explain complicated current affairs topics and to teach high-school subjects.

Manga have become a recognized art form and top artists are respected the world over. The "god of *manga*" **Tezuka Osamu** created *Astro Boy* and *Kimba, the White Lion* in the 1960s and went on to pen more challenging work such as the adventures of the mysterious renegade surgeon Black Jack and the epic war-time saga *Adorufu ni Tsugu* (*Tell Adolf*).

Manga are available just about everywhere, from train station kiosks to bookshops, and there's a useful Web site for the serious fan at ⓦ*www.kodanclub.com*.

Maruzen 丸善

Map 7, E2. 2-3-10 Nihombashi, Chūō-ku. Nihombashi Station.
Mon–Sat 10am–7pm, Sun & hols 10am–6pm.

Stocks a wide range of imported and locally produced books, with a strong showing in art and design, and magazines in a variety of languages. You can buy traditional *washi* paper in the basement and there's a small crafts gallery on the fourth floor.

On Sundays オンスンダズ

Map 8, F1. Watari-um Museum of Contemporary Art, 3-7-6 Jingūmae, Shibuya-ku. Gaienmae Station.
Tues–Sun 11am–8pm.

Tokyo's best choice of art, photography and architecture books, plus a fabulous selection of postcards in this stylish bookshop inside one of the city's more avant-garde galleries.

Tower Books タワーブックス

Map 12, E3. 7F, Tower Records, 1-22-14 Jinnan, Shibuya-ku. Shibuya Station.

Daily 10am–10pm.

The cheapest prices for imported books, magazines and papers. Tower Records in Shinjuku and Ikebukuro (see p.292) stock a more limited range.

CAMERAS

Shinjuku is Tokyo's prime area for **cameras** and photographic equipment, though **Ikebukuro** also has a solid reputation for new and secondhand deals at reasonable prices. We've listed a few of the best places to head for.

BIC Camera ビックカメラ

Map 9, E3. 1-41-5 Higashi-Ikebukuro, Toshima-ku. Ikebukuro Station.

Daily 10am–8pm.

BIC claims to offer the cheapest prices for its cameras, audio and electronic goods. This is their main store, immediately north of the station on Meiji-dōri, and there are four more scattered round east Ikebukuro, as well as branches in Shinjuku and Shibuya.

Camera no Kimura カメラのきむら

Map 9, C3. 1-18-8 Nishi-Ikebukuro, Toshima-ku. Ikebukuro Station.

Mon–Sat 8am–8pm, Sun & hols 10am–7pm.

This small store, tucked behind the Dai-Ichi Kangyō Bank, has a solid reputation for new and used cameras, with a wide variety of recent models.

Camera Sakuraya カメラサクラヤ

Map 13, E6. 3-17-2 Shinjuku, Shinjuku-ku. Shinjuku Station. Daily 10am–8pm.

Highly recommended rival to Yodobashi Camera (see below). Its main store is on Shinjuku-dōri near Isetan department store, with another branch in west Shinjuku across the road from Yodobashi. Branches in Shibuya and Ikebukuro amongst others.

Shimizu Shōkai

Map 7, E7. 4-3-2 Ginza, Chūō-ku. Ginza Station. Mon–Sat 10am–7pm, Sun 10.30am–6pm.

Reputable used camera specialist in the backstreets of Ginza two blocks west of Mikimoto's pearl shop.

Yodobashi Camera ヨドバシカメラ

Map 13, E6. 1-11-1 Nishi-Shinjuku, Shinjuku-ku. Shinjuku Station. Daily 9.30am–9pm.

Among Shinjuku's plethora of camera shops, this place usually offers decent reductions and stocks the broadest range; it claims to be the world's largest camera shop. There's also a smaller branch in Ueno.

DEPARTMENT STORES

You can find almost anything you're looking for in Tokyo's massive **department stores**, from the impressive basement food halls right up through fashion, crafts and household items to the restaurant floors. These places are more likely to have English-speaking staff and a duty-free service (see box on p.275) than smaller stores, though prices do tend to be slightly over the odds. Look out for sales, particularly for kimono sales, which are advertised several times a year in the English-language press and can offer great bargains.

Isetan 伊勢丹デパート

Map 13, H4. 3-14-1 Shinjuku, Shinjuku-ku. Shinjuku Station.
Daily except Wed 10am–7.30pm.
Stocks well-designed local goods and has a reputation for promoting up-and-coming fashion designers.

Matsuya 松屋デパト

Map 7, E7. 3-6-1 Ginza, Chūō-ku. Ginza Station.
Daily 10am–8pm.
More downmarket than many other big department stores, Matsuya has a decent choice of traditional crafts and household goods at competitive prices. Also in Asakusa (map 5, H5).

Matsuzakaya 松坂屋デパト

Map 14, D9. 3-29-5 Ueno, Taitō-ku. Ueno-Hirokōji Station.
Mon–Sat 10am–7.30pm, Sun & hols 10am–7pm.
Three-hundred-year-old store with a not-surprisingly fusty air, similar in style to Matsuya. Also in Ginza (map 7, E8).

Mitsukoshi 三越デパト

Map 7, E1. 1-4-1 Nihombashi-Muromachi. Mitsukoshi-mae Station.
Daily 10am–7pm.
Tokyo's most prestigious store is elegant, spacious and renowned for its high-quality merchandise – including a good range of traditional household items, such as lacquerware and pottery, as well as kimono, *obi* and other accessories. Branches in Ginza (map 7, E7), Ikebukuro (map 9, F4) and Ebisu (map 6, E4).

Seibu 西武デパト

Map 9, E5. 1-28-1 Minami-Ikebukuro, Toshima-ku. Ikebukuro Station.
Daily 10am–8pm.
Sprawling department store with a reputation for innovation,

especially its fashion offshoot, Parco, whose racks and shelves groan with state-of-the-art ephemera; you'll find Parco here in Ikebukuro, though the Shibuya stores are more manageable (see p.288).

Takashimaya 高島屋デパト

Map 7, F3. 2-4-1 Nihombashi, Chūō-ku. Nihombashi Station. Daily 10am–7pm.

Like Mitsukoshi, Takashimaya has a long and illustrious past. Though it appeals to decidedly conservative tastes, it's a good place to look for traditional household items. Also in Shinjuku (map 13, G7).

Tōbu 東武デパト

Map 9, D4. 1-1-25 Nishi-Ikebukuro, Toshima-ku. Ikebukuro Station. Daily 10am-8pm.

Japan's largest department store is mainly of interest for its excellent basement food halls on two levels and dozens of restaurants in its Spice and Spice 2 annexes.

Tōkyū Hands 東危ハーンズ

Map 12, C3. 12-10 Udagawachō, Shibuya-ku. Shibuya Station. Daily 10am–8pm, except second and third Wed of the month.

An offshoot of Tōkyū department store, specializing in every imaginable hobby, from rock climbing to crochet. It's a great place to look for quirky souvenirs. Also in Ikebukuro (map 9, G4) and at Takashimaya Times Square in Shinjuku (map 13, G7).

FASHION

All Tokyo's big department stores have several floors devoted to **clothes**, from **haute couture** to more modest wear at affordable prices, albeit rather uninspired. Instead, the epicentre of Japanese fashion is **Omotesandō**, where designers' showrooms make for great window shopping, even if you don't have money to burn. Nearby, the boutiques of **Harajuku** and **Shibuya** cater to a younger crowd, searching out the latest in recycled grunge gear. Daikanyama, a ritzy neighbourhood west of Shibuya (see p.124), is a good place to check out up-and-coming Japanese designers.

The more studenty Shimo-Kitazawa, also a short train ride from Shibuya, specializes in funky boutiques, some selling secondhand clothes where you can scoop big-name labels at bargain prices – and keep an eye open, too, for creations by local art and design students.

Finding clothes that fit is becoming easier as young Japanese are, on average, substantially bigger-built than their parents, and foreign chains tend to carry larger sizes. **Shoes**, however, are more of a problem. Some stores do stock bigger sizes; Washington shoe shops and ABC-Mart are usually a good bet, though the women's selection is pretty limited and you'll be hard pressed to find anything for average Western-size men. One of the best places to hunt for bargain shoes is Higashi-Shinjuku, especially around the Studio Alta fashion supermarket, and Ueno's Ameyoko-chō market.

ABC-Mart ABCマート

Map 14, E7. 4-7-1 Ueno, Taitō-ku. Okachimachi Station.
Daily 10am–8pm.

"International Shoes Gallery" on Ameyoko-dōri specializing in import brands at reasonable prices. There are branches in all the main city centres.

Bathing Ape ベーシングエプ

Map 8, C2. B1, 4-28-22 Jingūmae, Shibuya-ku. Meiji-Jingūmae Station.
Daily 11am–8pm.

More a trendy gallery, with sneering sales staff, plasma screens displaying the trade mark camouflage design of ape heads and a giant poster for their primary inspiration, *Planet of the Apes*. A T-shirt, as worn by pop stars, will set you back ¥6000.

Comme des Garçons コムデギャルソン

Map 8, F5. 5-2-1 Minami-Aoyama, Minato-ku. Omotesandō Station. Daily 11am–8pm.

High fashion for men and women by world-famous designer Rei Kawakubo in this beautiful store which is more like an art gallery than a clothes shop.

Five Foxes' Store ファイブフオクズストル

Map 13, G4. 3-26 Shinjuku, Shinjuku-ku. Shinjuku Station. Mon–Sat 11am–11pm, Sun 11am–8pm.

Stylish showcase for the bright and affordable fashion brand-of-the-moment *Comme ça de Mode* – there's a large section in Seibu's *Loft* department store in Shibuya (map 12, D3) and at the *Touch Your All* building in Harajaku.

Hysteric Glamour ヒステリクグラマ

Map 8, B5. 6-23-2 Jingūmae, Shibuya-ku. Meiji-Jingūmae Station. Daily 11am–8pm.

More sales staff with attitude at this premier outlet for the premier Japanese youth brand (there are over 50 other shops around the country). The look is very 60s/70s Americana, all rather retro-kitsch.

Issey Miyake 三宅一生

Map 8, F5. 3-18-11 Minami-Aoyama, Minato-ku. Omotesandō Station.

Daily 11am–8pm.

One of the top names in world fashion, famous for his elegant, eminently wearable designs. Across the road from Comme des Garçons.

Laforet ラフォオレ

Map 8, C2. 1-11-6 Jingūmae. Meiji-Jingūmae Station.
Daily 11am–8pm.
One of Tokyo's first "fashion buildings", packed with trendy boutiques, many catering to the fickle tastes of Harajuku's teenage shopping mavens. Wander through and catch the zeitgeist.

Movida モビダ

Map 12, D3. 21-1 Udagawachō, Shibuya-ku. Shibuya Station.
Daily 10am–8pm.
Ultra cool sister-establishment to Parco, showcasing up-and-coming local designers alongside well-known international labels such as Jean Paul Gaultier.

Muji

Map 8, G2. 2-12-18 Kita-Aoyama, Minato-ku. Gaienmae Station.
Daily 10am–8pm.
There are branches of this internationally famous "no-brand" fashion and lifestyle chain across Tokyo, but this outlet, built from salvaged wood and steel, is one of the most stylish.

Parco パルコ

Map 12, C2. 15-1 Udagawachō, Shibuya-ku. Shibuya Station.
Daily 10.30am–8.30pm.
Dozens of boutiques in Parts 1 and 2 of this store, belonging to the Seibu chain (see department stores, p.284), specialize in trend-setting, youth-orientated fashion.

Pink Dragon ピンクドラゴン

Map 12, F2. 1-23-23 Shibuya. Shibuya Station.
Daily 11am–8pm.
Amazing array of stylish, kitsch 1950s clothes and ephemera with men's clothing upstairs and the Miracle Woman designer

threads downstairs. The Art Deco building, just off Meiji-dōri, is easily identified by the giant golden egg outside.

Shiseido Cosmetic Garden
資生堂コスメチクガーデン

Map 8, C3. Harajuku Piazza Bldg, 4-26-18 Jingūmae, Shibuya-ku. Meiji-jingūmae Station.
Tues–Sun 11am–7.30pm, closed every other Tues.
Not a shop as such, but an "immersive brand space" where you can try Shiseido products for free and seek advice from beauty consultants, some of whom speak English. Japanese speakers shouldn't miss the Beauty Navigator which snaps your skin-tone and then gives you a virtual makeover.

UniQlo ユニクロ

Map 8, B3. 6-10-8 Jingūmae, Shibuya-ku. Meiji-jingūmae Station.
Daily 11am–9pm.
The Japanese version of Gap has exploded over Tokyo proving that cheap can still be cool. The clothes are simple but good quality – mostly plain cotton fabrics – and come in a wide range of colours, if not huge sizes. Branches in all Tokyo's main shopping centres.

Washington ワシントン

Map 7, E7. 5-7-7 Ginza, Chūō-ku. Ginza Station.
Daily 10.30am–8pm.
The main store of an upmarket shoe-shop chain which carries a reasonable selection of sizes to fit Western feet.

ELECTRICAL AND ELECTRONIC EQUIPMENT

Akihabara (see p.72) boasts Tokyo's biggest concentration of stores selling **electronic goods**. Anything you can plug in or turn on is available from a bewildering array of stores split into several outlets – each one a megastore of up to seven floors apiece – selling overlapping product ranges. Fortunately, they're mostly concentrated along a small stretch of Chūō-dōri and its sidestreets, all within walking distance of Akihabara Station (on the JR Yamanote and Hibiya subway lines). Nowadays you'll also find plenty of discount stores in **Shinjuku**, **Ikebukuro** and **Shibuya**.

Before buying electrical goods, do compare prices – many shops are willing to bargain – and make sure there's the appropriate voltage switch (the Japanese power supply is 100v). For English-language instructions, after-sales service and guarantees, stick to export models, which you'll find mostly in the stores' duty-free sections.

Laox ラオックス

Map 10, H4. 1-2-9 Soto-Kanda, Chiyoda-ku. Akihabara Station. Mon–Sat 10am–8pm, Sun & hols 10am–7.30pm.

One of the most prominent names and probably the best place to start: prices are reasonable, they have a well-established duty-free section with English-speaking staff, and their nine stores sell everything from pocket-calculators to plasma-vision TVs.

T-Zone Minami T-Zoneミナミ

Map 10, H3. 4-3-3 Soto-Kanda, Chiyoda-ku. Akihabara Station. Mon–Sat 10.30am–8pm, Sun & hols 10am–7.30pm.

Specialist computer store recommended for its broad range of English-language software and games, both on the second floor, where you'll also find its duty-free section.

Yamagiwa ヤマギワ

Map 10, H4. 4-1-1 Soto-Kanda, Chiyoda-ku. Akihabara Station. Mon–Fri 10.30am–8pm, Sat, Sun & hols 10am–8pm.

Another highly-rated store with a duty-free section on the sixth floor, selling a broad range of products.

RECORDS AND CDS

Tokyo's tastes in **CDs and records** are nothing if not eclectic, boosting an already mammoth output of home-grown pop and ballads. In recent years foreign outlets including HMV, Virgin and Tower Records have busted into the market with huge selections, listening stations and, crucially, lower prices for imported CDs, typically under ¥2000. CDs produced for the home market, with translated lyrics and extra tracks, are more expensive, but it's also worth looking out for special Japan-only issues which will still be cheaper here than at home.

Disk Union ディスクユニオン

Map 13, H5. 3-31-4 Shinjuku, Shinjuku-ku.
Mon–Sat 11am–8pm, Sun 11am–7pm.

Along with Recofan (see below), Disk Union has about the broadest selection of secondhand records and CDs – if not necessarily the cheapest prices – in more than twenty stores scattered around Tokyo; some stores specialize, so ask for the genre you're interested in. There are several stores in Ochanomizu (map 10, F4) and Shibuya's Udagawachō (map 12, C4) as well as Shimo-Kitazawa.

HMV HMV

Map 12, D4. 24-1 Udagawachō, Shibuya-ku. Shibuya Station.
Daily 10am–10pm.

This is the main outlet of the British music store and a good place to look if you can't find what you want in the nearby Tower Records. Good selection of discs, videos and DVDs. HMV has the highest number of outlets in central Tokyo, with other branches in Laforet in Harajuku (map 8, C2), Shinjuku's Takashimaya Times Square (map 13, G7), ABAB in Ueno (map 14, E8), Ginza (map 7, D6) and the Metropolitan Plaza in Ikebukuro (map 9, C5).

Recofan　　レコファン

Map 12, C3. 4F, Shibuya BEAM, 31 Udagawachō, Shibuya-ku. Shibuya Station.
Daily 11.30am–9pm.
A mixed bag of new and used records and CDs, both imported and locally produced, at bargain prices. Three branches in Shibuya and two in Shimo-Kitazawa, plus other outlets around the city.

Tower Records　　トワーレコドズ

Map 12. E3. 1-22-14 Jinnan, Shibuya-ku. Shibuya Station.
Daily 10am–10pm.
Currently Tokyo's biggest music store, with six floors of CDs, records and related paraphernalia, including videos and games. There are also branches in Shinjuku and Ikebukuro (map 2, B2).

Virgin Megastore　　ベルジンメガストルー

Map 13, H5. B1, Marui Fashion Building, 3-30-6 Shinjuku, Shinjuku-ku. Shinjuku-Sanchōme Station.
Daily except Wed 11am–10pm.
Virgin concentrates its energies in its flagship Shinjuku store, with a smaller outlet in Nishi-Ikebukuro's Marui store (map 9, B3).

Directory

AIRLINES Most airline offices are located in the Yūrakuchō, Toranomon and Marunouchi districts of central Tokyo. Air Canada ⓣ03/3586-3891, ⓦ*www.aircanada.ca*; Air China ⓣ5251-0711, ⓦ*www.airchina.com.cn*; Air France ⓣ3475-2211, ⓦ*www.airfrance.com*; Air New Zealand ⓣ3287-6311, ⓦ*www.airnewzealand.com*; Air Nippon ⓣ03/5435-0333, ⓦ*www.ana.co.jp*; Air Pacific ⓣ03/3435-1377, ⓦ*www.airpacific.com*; Alitalia ⓣ3592-3970, ⓦ*www.alitalia.it/eng*; All Nippon Airways ⓣ0120–029333, ⓦ*www.ana.co.jp*; American Airlines ⓣ3214-2111, ⓦ*www.americanairlines.com*; Asiana Airlines ⓣ03/3582-6600, ⓦ*www.flyasiana.com*; British Airways ⓣ3593-8811, ⓦ*www.britishairways.com*; Canadian Airlines ⓣ3281-7426, ⓦ*www.CdnAir.ca*; Cathay Pacific ⓣ3504-1531, ⓦ*www.cathaypacific.com*; China Airlines ⓣ3436-1661, ⓦ*www.china-airlines.com*; Delta ⓣ5404-3200, ⓦ*www.delta.com*; Dragonair ⓣ3506-8361, ⓦ*www.dragonair.com*; Eva Air ⓣ03/5408-3500, ⓦ*www.evaair.com*; Finnair ⓣ0120–700915, ⓦ*www.finnair.com*; Garuda Indonesia ⓣ3240-6161, ⓦ*www.garuda-indonesia.com*; Iberia ⓣ3578-3555, ⓦ*www.iberia.es*; Japan Airlines ⓣ0120–255931, ⓦ*www.jal.co.jp*; Japan Air System ⓣ0120–711283, ⓦ*www.jas.co.jp*; KLM ⓣ3216-0771, ⓦ*www.klm.com*; Korean Air ⓣ5443-3311, ⓦ*www.koreanair.com*; Lufthansa

Ⓣ 3578-6777, Ⓦ *www.lufthansa.com*; Malaysia Airlines Ⓣ 3503-5961, Ⓦ *www.malaysianairlines.com*; Northwest Ⓣ 3533-6000, Ⓦ *www.nwa.com*; Philippine Airlines Ⓣ 3593-2421, Ⓦ *www.philippineair.com*; Qantas Ⓣ 3593-7000, Ⓦ *www.qantas.com*; Sabena Ⓣ 3585-6151, Ⓦ *www.sabena.com*; SAS Scandinavian Airlines Ⓣ 0120–678101, Ⓦ *www.scandinavian.net*; Singapore Airlines Ⓣ 3213-3431, Ⓦ *www.singaporeair.com*; South African Airways Ⓣ 3470-1901 Ⓦ *www.saa-usa.com*; Swissair Ⓣ 3212-1016, Ⓦ *www.swissair.com*; Thai International Ⓣ 3503-3311, Ⓦ *www.thaiair.com*; United Airlines Ⓣ 0120–114466, Ⓦ *www.united.com*; Virgin Atlantic Ⓣ 3499-8811, Ⓦ *www.virginatlantic.com*

AIRPORT INFORMATION
Narita Airport Ⓣ 0476/34-5000; Haneda Airport Ⓣ 5757-8111 (both in English). See p.34 for more details.

AIRPORT TAX International departure tax from Narita is now included in the price of the air ticket.

AMERICAN EXPRESS 4-30-16 Ōgikubo, Suginami-ku Ⓣ 0120–020666 (Mon–Fri 9am–7pm). Travel service centre with a 24hr ATM for American Express card holders only.

BANKS AND EXCHANGE
Authorized "Foreign Exchange Banks" are located in the Yūrakuchō district, southwest of Tokyo Station and along most major shopping streets; Tokyo Mitsubishi Bank handles the widest range of currencies. Standard banking hours are Mon–Fri 9am–3pm. There are exchange bureaux in both terminals of Narita Airport (Terminal 1: 6.30am–11pm; Terminal 2: 7am–10pm). For more on banks, see p.23.

BIKE RENTAL Rental Acom (Shinjuku Ⓣ 3350-5081 or Shimbashi Ⓣ 3432-8522, both open daily 10am–7pm) has bikes, and just about anything else you could need, to rent. For a minimum of two days an ordinary bike is ¥2100 and a mountain bike ¥4200. You'll need to present your passport and make an advance booking in Japanese.

CAR RENTAL The main rental companies are Avis ⓣ5550-1015; Hertz ⓣ0120–489882, ⓦ*www.hertz-car.co.jp*; Nippon ⓣ3468-7126; Nissan ⓣ5424-4111; Orix ⓣ3779-0543 and Toyota ⓣ0070-8000-10000. All have branches around the city and at Narita and Haneda airports, and English-speaking staff. Prices start at around ¥6500 per day for the smallest car, plus ¥1000 insurance.

CREDIT CARDS For lost credit cards call the following 24hr toll-free numbers: American Express ⓣ0120–020120; Mastercard ⓣ00531-11-3886; Visa International ⓣ0120–133173.

DISABLED TRAVELLERS In comparison with most British and US cities, Tokyo is far less friendly towards disabled travellers. Few train or subway stations are furnished with lifts or escalator access, with the exception of the new Toei Ō-Edo Line which is fully equipped with lifts, ramps and escalators from ground level to the platforms. It's usually possible to organize assistance at stations, but you'll need a Japanese-speaker to make the arrangements. Most trains designate one or two "Silver Seats" close to the doors in each carriage for the disabled, elderly and pregnant women. New, Western-style hotels are the most likely to have fully accessible rooms, while recently constructed shops, museums and other public buildings are usually equipped with ramps, wide doors and accessible toilets. Taxi drivers rarely help wheelchair-users travelling alone. Three companies offer taxis with lifts: Busyū Kotsū Corporation ⓣ0423/25-8611, Keihin Unsō Co. Ltd ⓣ3790-0117 and Miyazono Taxi ⓣ5991-2944.

ELECTRICITY 100 volts AC, at 50 cycles in Tokyo. Plugs are generally American-style (two flat pins), and most appliances designed for 117 volts will work perfectly well. Travellers from Britain (240 volts) will need both an adapter and a transformer. Major hotels provide razor sockets at both 110 and 220 volts.

EMBASSIES Australia, 2-1-14 Mita, Minato-ku ⓣ5232-4111; Canada, 7-3-58 Akasaka, Minato-ku ⓣ3408-2101; China, 3-4-33 Moto-Azabu, Minato-ku ⓣ3403-3380; France, 4-11-44

Minami-Azabu, Minato-ku ☎5420-8800; Germany, 4-5-10 Minami-Azabu, Minato-ku ☎3473-0151; Ireland, 2-10-7 Kōjimachi, Chiyoda-ku ☎3263-0695; Israel, 3 Nibanchō, Chiyoda-ku ☎3264-0911; Italy, 2-5-4 Mita, Minato-ku ☎3453-5291; Netherlands, 3-6-3 Shiba-kōen, Minato-ku ☎5401-0411; New Zealand, 20-40 Kamiyamachō, Shibuya-ku ☎3467-2271; South Africa, 2-7-9 Hirakawachō, Chiyoda-ku ☎3265-3366; Spain, 1-3-29 Roppongi, Minato-ku ☎03/3583-8531; UK, 1 Ichibanchō, Chiyoda-ku ☎3265-5511; USA, 1-10-5 Akasaka, Minato-ku ☎3224-5000.

EMERGENCIES Police ☎110; fire and ambulance ☎119. Phone Jhelp.com ☎0120–461997, *www.jhelp.com* for a 24hr English-language toll-free service, or try the English-language helpline of Tokyo Metropolitan Police on ☎3501-0110 (Mon–Fri 8.30am–5.15pm). Tokyo English Life Line (TELL; *www.tell.gol.com*) provides telephone counselling on their helpline ☎3968-4099 (daily 9am–4pm ☎ 7–11pm).

HOSPITALS AND CLINICS To find an English-speaking doctor and the hospital or clinic best suited to your needs, phone the Tokyo Medical Information Service (☎5285-8181; Mon–Fri 9am–8pm); they also provide emergency medical translation services. Otherwise, two major hospitals with English-speaking doctors are St Luke's International Hospital, 9-1 Akashichō, Chūō-ku ☎3541-5151, and Tokyo Adventist Hospital, 3-17-3 Amanuma, Suginami-ku ☎3392-6151; their reception desks are open Mon–Fri 8.30–11am for non-emergency cases. Among several private clinics with English-speaking staff, try Tokyo Medical and Surgical Clinic, 32 Mori Building, 3-4-30 Shiba-kōen, Minato-ku ☎3436-3208 (by appointment only), or the International Clinic, 1-5-9 Azabudai, Minato-ku ☎3582-2646.

IMMIGRATION To renew your tourist or student visa, apply to the Tokyo Regional Immigration Bureau (2F, 1-3-1 Ōtemachi, Chūō-ku Mon–Fri 9am–noon & 1–6pm; ☎3286-5241), signed from Ōtemachi Station.

INTERNET ACCESS You can log on for free at: Net Time Mobile Square, Tokyo Sankei Building, 1-7-2 Otemachi; Marunouchi Café, 3-2-3 Marunouchi (closed Sun); and the bar Quest, 2F, Nakano Building, 5-8-3 Roppongi. Of the places that charge, Manga Sabo, B2 Mitsuba Building, Shibuya (opposite HMV and beneath the Tōkai Bank), is one of the cheapest (¥420 per hr) and is open 24hr. Bagus (6F, Sanzen Building, 28-6 Udagawachō), also in Shibuya, comes close with rates at ¥470 per hour. Though it's more expensive at ¥210 per twenty minutes, Kinko's, the 24hr one-stop office service centre, has branches scattered all over Tokyo; call their toll-free number (Ⓣ0120–001966) to find the one nearest you.

LANGUAGE COURSES Tokyo has numerous language schools offering intensive and part-time courses. Among the most established are Berlitz, 2F, Akasaka Capital Bdg, 1-7-19 Akasaka Ⓣ3584-4211 and Kokusai Gakuin, 12F, 2-15-1 Dōgenzaka Ⓣ3770-5344. For details of other schools, contact the Association of International Education Japan, 4-5-29 Komaba, Meguro-ku Ⓣ5454-5216, Ⓕ5454-5236, Ⓦ*www.aiej.or.jp* See also Scholarships below.

LEFT LUGGAGE There are lockers of various sizes at all mainline stations, charged on a daily basis (¥300–600), for up to a maximum of three days. Most hotels will keep bags for a few days. Otherwise, you can leave them at Tokyo Station's baggage room for up to fifteen days, at a daily rate of ¥410 for the first five days and ¥820 per day thereafter; you'll find it at the far southeast end of the station, beyond the Express Bus ticket office.

LOST PROPERTY Ask a Japanese-speaker to help you call the following offices: Taxis Ⓣ3648-0300; JR trains Ⓣ3231-1880; Eidan subways Ⓣ3834-5577; Toei buses and subways Ⓣ3815-7229; Metropolitan Police Lost and Found Office Ⓣ3814-4151. For credit card losses, see above.

PHARMACIES The American Pharmacy, Hibiya Park Building,

1-8-1 Yūrakuchō (Mon–Sat 9.30am–8pm, Sun & hols 10am–6.30pm), and Boots, 5-4-3 Ginza, just east of the Sony building (daily 10am–9pm), both have English-speaking pharmacists and a good range of general medical supplies.

POLICE Call ☎ 110 for the police in an emergency, or telephone their English-language helpline ☎ 3501-0110 (Mon–Fri 8.30am–5.15pm).

POST OFFICE The central post office lies southwest of Tokyo Station (Mon–Fri 9am–7pm, Sat 9am–5pm, Sun & hols 9am–12.30pm; 24hr service for stamps and parcels). Poste restante can be collected from the basement (Mon–Fri 8am–8pm, Sat 8am–5pm, Sun & hols 9am–12.30pm); remember to take along your passport. Their postal address is 2-7-2 Marunouchi, Chiyoda-ku, Tokyo 100-8799. The "International ATMs" (see p.22) are accessible Mon–Fri 7am–11pm, Sat, Sun & hols 9am–7pm. The International Post Office, 2-3-3 Ōtemachi (Mon–Fri 9am–7pm, Sat 9am–5pm, Sun & hols 9am–12.30pm) is a bit less convenient but usually quieter. There are sub-post offices in all major centres and at both terminals of Narita Airport. For English-language information about postal services, call ☎ 5472-5851.

PUBLIC BATHS Soak up the atmosphere at one of the following *sentō* (public baths), some of which are classified as *onsen*, hot-spring baths filled with mineral-rich water. For the cheaper baths, take soap, shampoo and a towel – or buy them at the door. See p.27 for tips on bathing etiquette. Two very traditional bathhouses are Asakusa Kannon Onsen (2-7-26 Asakusa; daily 6.30am–6pm; ¥700), just west of Sensō-ji, and Ueno's Rokuryu (3-4-20 Ikenohata; Tues–Sun 3–11pm; ¥400), which is tucked down an alley behind the *Suigetsu Hotel Ohgaisou* (see p.168). For a no-nonsense neighbourhood soak, try Jakotsu-yu (1-11-11 Asakusa; daily except Tues 1pm–midnight; ¥400) or Ginza-yu (1-12-2 Ginza; Mon–Sat 3–11pm; ¥400). Finally, there's the Azabu-Jūban Onsen (1-5-22 Azabu-Jūban), where the casual ground-floor baths offer better value (¥400; 3–11pm) while upstairs is a much classier affair (¥1260; 11am–9pm).

SCHOLARSHIPS Japan's Ministry of Education, Science, Sports and Culture (Monbusho) offers three types of annual scholarships to foreign students. These are available to those who wish to further their knowledge of Japanese or Japanese studies, for those who want to undertake an undergraduate degree, and for those who wish to become a research student at a Japanese university. The scholarships include return airfare, tuition fees and a generous monthly allowance. For more details contact your nearest Japanese embassy or consulate.

TAXES A consumption tax (*shōhizei*) of five percent is levied on virtually all goods and services in Japan, including restaurant meals and accommodation. Sometimes this tax will be included in the advertised price, sometimes not, so, for large amounts, check first. Note that any service charges will be calculated after the tax has been added.

TAXIS The major taxi firms are Daiwa ⓣ3503-8421; Hinomaru Limousine ⓣ3212-0505, ⓦ*www.hinomaru.co.jp*; Kokusai ⓣ3491-6001; and Nihon Kōtsū ⓣ3586 2151.

TICKET AGENCIES To get tickets for theatre performances, films, concerts and sporting events, it's best, in the first instance, to approach one of the major advance ticket agencies. *Ticket Pia* (ⓣ5237-9999) can be found in the main city areas, such as Ginza, Ikebukuro, Shibuya and Shinjuku. Or try phoning Lawson (ⓣ3569-9900) or CN Playguide (ⓣ5802-9999). Major events sell out quickly, but you can go directly to the venue on the day and see if you can get a ticket from the box office or a tout outside (though expect to pay over the odds with the latter).

TIME ZONES Tokyo is nine hours ahead of Greenwich Mean Time (so at noon in London, it's 9pm in Tokyo), fourteen hours ahead of New York, seventeen hours ahead of Los Angeles and two hours behind Sydney. There is no daylight saving, so during British Summer Time, for example, the difference drops to eight hours.

TRAINS For English-language information on train services throughout Japan, call the JR East-Infoline (Ⓣ3423-0111; Mon–Fri 10am–6pm).

TRAVEL AGENTS For international tickets try one of the following English-speaking agents. Note that we've listed just the head-office numbers, though they all have several branches – see adverts in the English press. A'cross Travellers Bureau (Shinjuku Ⓣ3340-6471, Ⓦ*www.across-travel.com*); Hit Travel (Ebisu Ⓣ3473-9040); No. 1 Travel (Shinjuku Ⓣ3200-8871, Ⓦ*www.no1-travel.com*). The main domestic travel agents are: Japan Travel Bureau (JTB) Ⓣ5620-9500, Ⓦ*www.jtb.co.jp*, with dozens of branches all over Tokyo; Nippon Travel Agency Ⓣ3572-8744 and Kinki Nippon Tourist Ⓣ3263-5522. The contact numbers are for their foreign tourist departments.

WORKING Finding employment is relatively simple, especially if you have the right qualifications (a degree is essential) and appropriate visa. The main places to look for job adverts are Monday's edition of *The Japan Times*, the free weekly magazines *Tokyo Classified* and *Tokyo Notice Board*, and Web sites – two of the best are Ⓦ*www.Hijobs.co.jp* and Ⓦ*www.jobsinjapan.com* The most common job available to foreigners is teaching English, with the big employers being the national school chains, such as Berlitz, Shane, GEOS, ECC and NOVA. Some have recruiting drives abroad; look in your local media under teaching opportunities or overseas work. It's also worth investigating the government-sponsored Japan Exchange and Teaching (JET) programme, which places Assistant Language Teachers (ALTs) in secondary schools. For further details of the scheme and application forms, UK citizens should contact the JET Programme Desk (Ⓣ020/478-2010), whilst residents of the US, Canada, Australia and New Zealand should contact their nearest Japanese consulate or embassy (see p.295).

Other options include rewriting or editing Japanese documents, modelling, bar work and hostessing, although the dangers of the latter have been demonstrated by the case of Lucie Blackman, a Briton who went missing from a hostess bar and was subsequently found murdered.

Those more interested in the business world should contact the Kaisha Society, c/o OneWorld, 3-3-2 Higashi Azabu, Minato-ku, Tokyo 106 (ⓦ*www.kaisha.gol.com*), a support and discussion organization for foreigners working in Japan.

Whatever work you're looking for, a smart set of clothes and following general rules of social etiquette will give you an advantage.

OUT OF THE CITY

Nikkō and around

If you make one trip from Tokyo, it should be to the pilgrim town of **Nikkō**, 128km north of the capital, where Japan's most impressive shrine complex, **Tōshō-gū**, is set amid splendid mountains and surrounded by outstanding hiking trails. The antithesis of the usually austere Shinto shrines – and often considered overbearingly gaudy – multi-coloured Tōshō-gū is the dazzling jewel of Nikkō; year round, masses of Japanese tourists dutifully tramp around the complex, which includes the **Futarasan-jinja** shrine and Buddhist temple **Rinnō-ji**. Also worth investigating on a day-trip here is the **Nikkō Tōshō-gū Museum of Art**, a traditional wooden villa decorated with some beautifully painted screens.

The best way of reaching Nikkō is on a Tōbu-Nikkō **train** from Asakusa in Tokyo (the station is in the basement of the Matsuya department store, connected by tunnel to Asakusa subway station). *Kaisoku* (rapid) trains make the journey in around two hours and cost ¥1330 one way. For the marginally faster *kyuko* (express) trains you pay a surcharge of ¥1220, and for the "Kegon" *tokkyū* (limited express), which takes one hour and 45 minutes, a total of ¥2750. Unless your train is a direct one for Nikkō, you'll need to change at Shimo-Imaichi.

BUYING TICKETS AT NIKKŌ

You can save money if you buy the right **ticket** for the temples and shrines in Nikkō. If you intend to see Rinnō-ji, Tōshō-gū and Futarasan-jinja you should buy the ¥900 *nisha-ichiji* (two shrines, one temple) **combination ticket**, which includes entrance to the Taiyōin-byō mausoleum, but not the roaring dragon hall (*Honji-dō*) nor the area containing the sleeping cat (*Nemuri-neko*) carving and Ieyasu's tomb at Tōshō-gū. It's worth paying the extra for these excluded sights, as you'll still be better off than if you buy separate tickets at each temple and shrine. The combination ticket can be bought from booths beside the Sanbutsu-dō hall in Rinnō-ji and outside the Omotemon gate to Tōshō-gū.

Nikkō is also served by JR trains, but this route, which takes longer and costs more than the Tōbu line, only makes sense if you have a JR rail pass (see *Introducing the city*, p.34). Take a Shinkansen from either Tokyo or Ueno stations to Utsunomiya, a journey of fifty minutes, where you must change to the JR Nikkō line for a local train taking forty five minutes to reach the Nikkō terminus, a minute's walk east of the Tōbu Station.

Inside the Tōbu Station is an **information desk** (daily 8.30am–5pm; ⓣ0288/53-4511), where the assistant speaks a little English and can supply maps and leaflets on the area. The main **tourist information centre** is the Nikkō Kyōdo Centre (daily 8.30am–5pm; ⓣ0288/54-2496), on the main road from the station to Tōshō-gū complex; assistants here can make accommodation bookings.

THE APPROACH TO TŌSHŌ-GŪ

From Nikkō's train stations, hop on a bus or walk uphill along the main street for fifteen minutes to reach Tōshō-gū. At the top of the gently sloping road you'll pass one of Nikkō's most famous landmarks, the red **Shin-kyō bridge** – currently covered up, being completely rebuilt over the next few years, though the original arched wooden structure first went up in 1636. Legend has it that when the Buddhist priest Shōdō Shōnin first visited Nikkō in the eighth century, he was helped across the Daiya-gawa river at this very spot by the timely appearance of two snakes, who formed a bridge and then vanished once he'd crossed.

For the main shrine and temple complex take the left-hand uphill path across from the bridge to emerge in front of the main compound of **Rinnō-ji**, a Buddhist temple founded in 766 by Shōdō Shōnin, whose statue stands on a rock at the entrance. The large red hall, Sanbutsu-dō, houses three giant gilded statues: the thousand-handed Kannon, the Amida Buddha and the fearsome horse-headed

TOKUGAWA IEYASU'S MONUMENT

Nikkō has been a holy place in both the Buddhist and Shinto religions for over a thousand years, but its fortunes only took off seriously with the death of **Tokugawa Ieyasu** in 1616. In his will, the shogun requested that a shrine be built in his honour at Nikkō. The shrine was completed in 1617, but was deemed not impressive enough by Ieyasu's grandson, Tokugawa Iemitsu, who ordered work to begin on today's elaborate mausoleum.

The new shrine, **Tōshō-gū**, was completed in 1634 and the jury has been out on its ostentatious design ever since. The flamboyant decoration was not just an aesthetic choice; the shogun, always with an eye on quelling rebellion, wanted to stop rival lords amassing money, so ordered the *daimyō* to pay for the shrine materials and the thousands of craftsmen needed to build it.

Kannon. It's worth paying to view these awe-inspiring figures from directly beneath their lotus-flower perches – entry is included in the combination ticket (see p.306).

TŌSHŌ-GŪ 東照宮

The broad, tree-lined Omotesandō leads up to the main entrance to Tōshō-gū, just to the east of Rinnō-ji. Pass under a giant stone *torii* gate and on the left you'll see an impressive red and green five-storey pagoda. Straight ahead is the Omotemon gate, the entrance to the main shrine precincts, where you'll need to hand over a section of your combination ticket or Tōshō-gū only ticket (¥1250).

Inside the precincts, turning left will take you past the **Three Sacred Storehouses** (*Sanjinko*) on the right, and the **Sacred Stables** (*Shinkyōsha*) on the left. Camera-crazy tourists are usually snapping away in front of the stables, keen to capture one of the many famous painted wooden carvings within Tōshō-gū – the "hear no evil, see no evil, speak no evil" **monkeys**, which symbolize the three major principles of Tendai Buddhism. The route leads to steps up to the dazzling **Yōmeimon** (Sun Blaze Gate), with wildly ornate carvings and intricate decoration. Even more striking are the detailed panels on the flanking walls, which are adorned with fantastic flowers and birds. A belfry and drum tower stand alone amid pools of pebbles in front of the gate. Behind the drum tower is the **Honji-dō** (¥50), a small hall which is part of Rinnō-ji temple and inside of which is a ceiling painting of a "roaring dragon". A priest will demonstrate how to make the dragon roar by standing beneath its head and clapping to create an echo.

It's better to pay the small charge to see the roaring dragon than fork out ¥430 for the less impressive sleeping cat

(*Nemuri-neko*), just above the Sakashitamon gate to the right of the inner precinct beyond the Yōmeimon – you'd easily miss this minute carving if it wasn't for the gawping crowd. Two hundred stone steps lead uphill from the gate to the surprisingly simple **tomb of Ieyasu**, amid a glade of pines, and about the only corner of the shrine where the crowds are generally absent.

Directly in front of the Yōmeimon is the less fussy white and gold **Karamon**, a locked gate beyond which is the Haiden, or hall of worship. The side entrance to the hall is right of the Sakashitamon, and you'll need to remove your shoes and stop taking photographs. Inside, you can walk down into the *honden*, the shrine's central hall, still decorated with its beautiful original paintwork.

NIKKŌ TŌSHŌ-GŪ MUSEUM OF ART AND AROUND 日光博物館

Daily April–Oct 9am–5pm; Nov–March 9am–4pm; ¥800.

Around the back of the shrine complex, to the left as you walk out of the Omotemon gate, is the **Nikkō Tōshō-gū Museum of Art**. This traditional wooden mansion, dating from 1928, is the former head office of the shrine. Inside, the sliding doors and screens were decorated by the top Japanese painters of the day and together constitute one of the most beautiful collections of this type of art anywhere in the country.

Not far east of here are the grounds of **Meiji-no-Yukata**, the early twentieth-century holiday home of the American trade representative F. W. Horne. The various houses amid the trees are now fancy restaurants (see p.312), but it's worth wandering around even if you don't eat here to take in the pretty gardens and sylvan setting.

Two memorable dates to visit Nikkō are May 17 for Tōshō-gū's springtime Grand Festival, with its colourful procession of 1200 costumed priests and warriors, ancient music and dances and *yabusame* (horseback archery), and October 17, when the whole show is restaged, minus the archery.

FUTARASAN-JINJA AND TAIYOIN-BYO 二荒山神社と大猷院廟

If Tōshō-gū hasn't left you too visually exhausted, press on to some of the other temples and shrines in the surrounding woods. At the end of right-hand path next to Tōshō-gū's pagoda, the **Futarasan-jinja**, with its simple red colour scheme, comes as a relief to the senses. The shrine is dedicated to the deity of Mount Nantai, the volcano whose eruption created nearby Lake Chuzenji-ko. There are some good paintings of animals and birds on votive plaques in the main hall, and the attached garden (¥200) is a quiet retreat with a small teahouse serving *macha* green tea and sweets for ¥350. You can also inspect the *bakemono tōrō*, a "phantom lantern" made of bronze in 1292 and said to be possessed by demons.

Bypassed by the tourist melee is the charming **Taiyōin-byō** (entry included in the combination ticket), which contains the mausoleum of the third shogun, Tokugawa Iemitsu, who died in 1651. This complex was deliberately designed to be less ostentatious than Tōshō-gū and is much more impressive because of this. Look out for the green god of wind and the red god of thunder nestling in the alcoves behind the Nitenmon gate and the beautiful Karamon (Chinese-style gate) and fence surrounding the gold and black lacquer inner precincts.

LAKE CHUZENJI-KO AND THE KEGON FALLS 中禅寺湖と華厳滝

Some 10km east of Nikkō lies the scenic **Lake Chuzenji-ko** and, flowing from it, the breathtaking **Kegon Falls**. Both were created thousands of years ago when nearby Mount Nantai erupted and its lava plugged the valley. The lift to the viewing platform at the base of the falls (daily: March, April & Nov 8am–5pm; May–Sept 7.30am–6pm; Oct 7.30am–5pm; Dec–Feb 9am–4.30pm; ¥530) is east across the car park behind the bus station; don't be put off by the queues of tour groups – a much shorter line is reserved for independent travellers. The lift drops 100m through the rock to the base of the falls, where you can view over a ton of water per second cascading from the Ojiri River which flows from the lake.

Note that the twisting, one-way road from Nikkō to Chuzenji clogs with bumper to bumper traffic during *kōyō* in mid-October, the prime time for viewing the magnificent autumn foliage. Buses for the journey leave from both train stations, cost ¥1100 one way and can easily take two or even three hours, depending on the amount of congestion.

ACCOMMODATION

Narusawa Lodge

1 Tokorono ⓣ & ⓕ 0288/54-1630.

Delightful *minshuku*, surrounded by flowers and set well away from the tourist throng. The *tatami* rooms are lovely, shared bathrooms are spotless and the family who run it are very friendly and speak a little English. If you stay more than one night, the price drops by ¥300 per person. ❷.

Nikkō Daiyagawa Youth Hostel

1075 Naka Hatsuishi-machi ☎ 0288/54-1974.

From the main approach to the shrine, English signposts lead to this cosy hostel near the river. Excellent meals, which you must pre-book, and dorms with bunk beds. ❶.

Nikkō Kanaya Hotel

1300 Kami-Hatsuishi-machi ☎ 0288/54-0001; Ⓕ 53-2487.

Nikkō's top Western-style hotel has some cheaper rooms with en-suite shower or just a toilet, but rates skyrocket during peak holiday seasons. ❼.

Nikkō-shi Koryu Sokushin Centre

2854 Tokorono ☎ 0288/54-1013.

Upmarket public hostel on the far side of the Daiya-gawa from the town, uphill from the high school. The *tatami* rooms are excellent and have lovely views of the town. It also has Western-style rooms, a laundry and a small kitchen for self-caterers. There's a 10pm curfew. ❷–❹

Pension Green Age Inn

10-9 Nishi-sandō ☎ 0288/53-3636; Ⓕ 53-1000.

Eccentric decorations enliven this small, great-value Western-style hotel close to Tōshō-gū and featuring a communal *onsen* bath made from pine. ❺.

Turtle Inn Nikkō

2-16 Takumi-chō ☎ 0288/53-3168; Ⓕ 53-3883.

Popular pension run by an English-speaking family, in a quiet location next to the Daiya-gawa river and near the main shrines, with small *tatami* rooms, common bathrooms and a cosy lounge. Evening meal at ¥2000 is a good deal, but breakfast is pricey at ¥1000 per person. ❸.

EATING AND DRINKING

Nikkō and Chuzenji both offer various dining options for when you feel a little peckish – our recommendations are listed below.

Nikkō

Hippari Dako

Top of Route 119 to Tōshō-gū, Nikkō.

Inexpensive *yakitori* and noodle café – look for the giant kite outside. Beer and sake are also served. Open daily 11am–7pm.

Kanaya Hotel

1300 Kami-Hatsuishi-machi.

A meal in the hotel's elegant second-floor dining room will set you back at least ¥3500 for lunch, ¥6000 for dinner, while the first-floor *Maple Leaf* coffee shop is cheaper, but less glamorous. Best bet is the *Yashio* Japanese restaurant, behind the coffee shop, which has set lunches for under ¥2000. Open daily 11am–8pm.

Meiji-no-Yukata

200m east of Tōshō-gū, ⓣ0288/53-3751.

The main restaurant here is the cheapest, if you go for a la carte and don't mind shelling out ¥1500 for curry rice. Best to dig deeper and sample the exquisite *shojin-ryōri* vegetarian course (¥3500) in the traditional *Gyoshintei*, where the waitresses wear kimono and you can gaze out on a lovely garden. The Art Nouveau *Fujimoto* is very elegant, French-influenced and expensive. Booking is advisable. Open daily 11am–8pm.

Milky House

2-2-3 Inari-machi.

This convivial coffee shop, serving inexpensive snacky meals and beer, also doubles up as an Internet café charging ¥500 for 30 minutes. Open daily 10am-10pm.

Suzuya

Stand-alone restaurant just before you cross over the bridge up the slope from the Kosugi Hoan Museum of Art. This is a good place to sample *yuba-ryōri*; the set lunch is ¥1300 and includes *tempura*, rice, noodles and rolled tofu. Open daily 11am–3pm.

Chuzenji

Chez Hoshino

This stylish European-style restaurant, with a real log fire in winter, faces the lake. Three-course lunch with coffee is ¥2500 per person; dinner is more expensive, but individual dishes start at ¥1000.

Tsugaya

Opposite the Chuzenji bus station, this casual restaurant serves a good selection of set Japanese meals and has English-speaking staff. Expect to pay around ¥2000.

Fuji Five Lakes

The best reason for heading 100km west from Tokyo towards the area known as **Fuji Five Lakes** is to climb **Mount Fuji**, Japan's most sacred volcano and, at 3776m, its highest mountain. At its most beautiful from October to May, when the summit is crowned with snow, Fuji-san, as it's respectfully known by the Japanese, has long been worshipped for its latent power (it last erupted in 1707) and near-perfect symmetry. The climbing season runs from July to September, but even if you don't fancy making the rather daunting ascent, just getting up close to what has to be Japan's most famous national symbol is a memorable experience.

The area's transport hub of **Fuji-Yoshida**, with its wonderfully atmospheric shrine, **Fuji Sengen-jinja**, and nearby state-of-the-art amusement park, is worth checking out. During the summer, the **five lakes** – the Yamanaka-ko, Kawaguchi-ko, Sai-ko, Shōji-ko and Motosu-ko – are packed with urbanites fleeing Tokyo.

The simplest way to reach the Fuji Five Lakes area is to take a **bus** (¥1700) from the Shinjuku bus terminal in Tokyo, on the west side of the train station; in good traffic, the trip takes around one hour and 45 minutes and during the climbing season there are frequent services, including at least three a day that run directly to the fifth station. The

train journey from Shinjuku Station involves transferring from the JR Chūō line to the Fuji Kyūkō line at **Ōtsuki**, from where a local train chugs first to Fuji-Yoshida and then on to Kawaguchi-ko. On Sundays and public holidays there is an early-morning direct train from Shinjuku which does the trip in just over two hours.

The best place for **tourist information** is the Fuji-Yoshida Tourist Information Service (daily 9am–5.30pm; ⓣ0555/22-7000), to the left as you exit Fuji-Yoshida Station. A comprehensive system of buses will help you **get around**, but fares are high and if you are considering touring the area it's worth buying the Fuji Kyūkō Wide Free Pass (¥3500) at Shinjuku or as soon as you arrive at Ōtsuki: this is valid for three days and covers all rail travel and buses around the five lakes, plus tickets for the cable car and lake cruise at Kawaguchi-ko.

FUJI-YOSHIDA 富士吉田

Fuji-Yoshida lies so close to Mount Fuji that when the dormant volcano eventually blows her top the residents will be toast. For the time being, however, this small, prosperous town acts as the traditional departure point for journeys up Mount Fuji, with frequent buses leaving for Fuji-san's fifth station (see box, p.317) from outside the railway station.

The volcano aside, the town's main attraction is its Shinto shrine. To get there, head southwest from the station uphill along the main street, Honchō-dōri – this will take you past several **pilgrims' inns** (*oshi-no-ie*). These old lodging houses, where pilgrims used to stay before climbing Mount Fuji, are set back from the road, their entrances marked by narrow stone pillars. When the road hits a junction, turn left and you'll soon see the giant *torii* and a broad gravel pathway lined with stone lanterns leading to **Fuji Sengen-jinja**, a large, colourful shrine set in a small forest. The

CLIMBING MOUNT FUJI

"A wise man climbs Fuji once. A fool climbs it twice" – so goes the Japanese proverb. Don't let the sight of children and grannies trudging up lull you into a false sense of security; this is a tough climb.

There are several **routes** up the volcano, with the ascent divided into sections known as **stations**. Most people take a bus to the Kawaguchi-ko fifth station (*go-gome*), where a Swiss chalet-style giftshop marks the end of the road about halfway up the volcano. The traditional hike, though, begins at Fuji-Yoshida; walking from here to the fifth station takes around five hours, and another six hours to reach the summit. Many choose to climb at night to reach the summit by dawn; during the season the lights of climbers' torches resemble a line of fireflies trailing up the volcanic scree.

Essential items to carry include at least one litre of water and some food, a torch and batteries, a raincoat and extra clothes; however hot it might be at the start of the climb, the closer you get to the summit the colder it becomes, with temperatures dropping by as much as 20°C and sudden rain and lightning strikes not uncommon. You can rest en route at any of seventeen huts, most of which provide dorm accommodation from around ¥5000 per night for just a bed (no need for a sleeping bag), and ¥7000 with dinner. It's essential to book in advance (☎0555/22-1948).

Once at the summit, it will take you around an hour to make a circuit of the crater. Otherwise you can take part in the time-honoured tradition of making a phone call or mailing a letter from the post office.

Mount Fuji's official climbing season, when all the facilities on the mountain are open, including lodging huts and pay phones at the summit, runs from July 1 to August 27.

main shrine (*honden*) has been designated an important cultural asset because of its age (it was built in 1615) and beauty. Look round the back for the jolly, brightly painted wooden carvings of the deities Ebisu, the fisherman, and Daikoku, the god of wealth, good humour and happiness, who appears content to let a rat nibble at the bales of rice he squats upon.

These fun-loving gods would certainly approve of **Fujikyō Highland** (Mon–Fri 9am–5pm, Sat 9am–7pm, Sun and hols 9am–6pm; closed third Tues of month, except Aug; ¥1000 entry only; ¥4300 one-day pass), a vast amusement park, one train stop west of Fuji-Yoshida, featuring the truly terrifying roller coaster Fujiyama.

ACCOMMODATION

Fuji-Yoshida Youth Hostel

2-339 Shimo Yoshida Honchō, Fuji-Yoshida-shi ⓣ0555/22-0533.

Basic hostel, twenty minutes' walk from Fuji-Yoshida Station. English is spoken and meals are available. ❷.

Kawaguchi-ko Youth Hostel

2128 Funatsu, Kawaguchi-ko-machi ⓣ0555/72-1431; ⓕ72-0630.

Five minutes' walk southwest of Kawaguchi-ko Station, with *tatami* rooms and bunks, and bikes for rent. ❷.

Petit Hotel Ebisuya

3647 Funatsu, Kawaguchi-ko-machi ⓣ0555/72-0165.

Next to Kawaguchi-ko Station, with splendid views of Fuji from some of its *tatami* rooms. The café downstairs serves hearty set meals. ❺.

Taikoku-ya

Honchō-dōri, Fuji-Yoshida ⓣ0555/22-3778.

Original pilgrims' inn on the main road with traditional *tatami* rooms and an ornamental garden. Couples preferred. ❻.

EATING AND DRINKING

The best place to **eat** is **Fuji-Yoshida**, which is renowned for its thick *teuchi udon* noodles, made and served in people's homes at lunchtime only. Head for the convivial *Hanaya* towards the top of Honchō-dōri, which serves just three types of dishes: *yumori* noodles in a soup, *zaru* cold noodles and *sara* warm noodles dipped in hot soup. At **Kawaguchi-ko** the best option is a picnic lunch from the lakeside Seven-Eleven store. During the climbing season, you can buy pricey snacks and stamina-building dishes, such as curry rice, from the huts on Mount Fuji.

Hakone

The lakeland and mountain area of **Hakone**, 90km west of Tokyo, is a favourite day-trip from the capital – especially for locals. In under two hours, you can be in the most beautiful hilly countryside, unwinding in one of the many *onsen*, hopping on a cable car to take in the breathtaking scenery, or simply walking in nature, and – weather permitting – catching some great views of nearby Mount Fuji. There's so much to do that an overnight stop is best, though you should aim to come during the week to avoid the crowds.

The traditional day route through Hakone runs anti-clockwise through the Fuji-Hakone-Izu National Park from Hakone-Yumoto, over Mount Sōun, across the length of Lake Ashi-ko to Moto-Hakone and back to the start.

The most enjoyable way of getting around is to take a combination of trains from Shinjuku Odakyū Station, on the west side of Shinjuku Station, thus breaking up the journey into a series of mad-cap rides. To do this, buy either the three-day **Hakone Free Pass** (¥5500) or two-day **Hakone Weekday Pass** (¥4700) valid Monday to Thursday, not including public holidays – both cover a return journey on the Odakyū line from Shinjuku to Odawara, and unlimited use of the Hakone–Tōzan line, Hakone–Tōzan funicular railway, cable car, pirate boat across the lake and most local buses. The pass will also get you discounts at many of the region's attractions. For ¥870 extra one way, you can take the more comfortable "Romance Car" directly through to Hakone-Yumoto in one hour and thirty minutes. If you have a JR rail pass, the fastest route is to take a Shinkansen to Odawara, from where you can catch either a train or bus into the national park area.

HAKONE-YUMOTO 箱根湯元

Hakone-Yumoto, the small town nestling in the valley at the gateway to the national park, is marred by scores of concrete-block hotels and souvenir shops, but does have some great **onsen**, ideal for relaxing after a day's sightseeing around the park. Best of the lot is **Tenzan Notemburo** (daily 9am–11pm; ¥900), a luxurious public complex some 2km southwest of the town. The main building has outdoor baths, including waterfalls and bubble baths, in a series of rocky pools. Men also have a clay hut sauna, and for ¥200 extra on weekdays (¥900 on weekends) both men and women can use the wooden baths in the building across the car park. A free shuttle bus runs to the baths from the bridge just north of Hakone-Yumoto Station.

Hakone-Yumoto is a good place to **eat**; try the *udon* noodles at *Kodanaki*, on the main road south from the station. There are also three good-value restaurants at the Tenzan Notemburo, serving rice, *shabu-shabu* (sautéed beef) and *yakiniku* (grilled meat) dishes.

MIYANOSHITA AND AROUND 宮の下

The Hakone-Tōzan switchback railway zig-zags for nearly 9km alongside a ravine from Hakone-Yumoto to the village of Gōra. The best place to alight – and stay overnight – is the village *onsen* resort of **Miyanoshita**. As well as hot springs, the village has decent antique shops along its main road, and several hiking routes up 804-metre **Mount Sengen** on the eastern flank of the railway – one path begins just beside the station. At the top, you'll get a fabulous view of the gorge below.

Miyanoshita's real draw is its handful of splendid **hotels**.

Accommodation

Fujiya Hotel

Ⓣ0460/2-2211; Ⓕ2-2210.
Plush Western-style hotel in the grand old style with lots of Japanese touches. The rooms are good value, especially from Sunday to Friday, when foreign guests qualify for a cheaper rate. ❻.

Naraya Inn

Ⓣ0460/2-2411; Ⓕ7-6231.
Wonderfully traditional *ryokan* founded in the sixteenth century. Guests sleep in mini-villas and there are several *onsen* baths dotted around the compound. ❼.

Motonamikan

Ⓣ0460/2-3158.
Formerly known as *Pension Yamaguchi*, this delightful place is five minutes' walk downhill from Miyanoshita Station. Rates include Western-style meals. ❻.

Eating

The *Fujiya*'s *Orchid Lounge* is great for afternoon tea, while its ornate French restaurant is an excellent, if pricey, choice for lunch or dinner. The *Picot Bakery* on the main road outside the *Fujiya* is a good place to pick up bread and cakes for breakfast or lunch.

HAKONE OPEN-AIR MUSEUM 彫刻の森美術館

Two more stops along the railway will bring you to Chōkoku-no-Mori Station, where the nearby **Hakone Open-Air Museum** (daily: March–Nov 9am–5pm; Dec–Feb 9am–4.30pm; ¥1600) features all manner of sculptures – from works by Rodin and Giacometti to Michelangelo reproductions and bizarre modern formations – scattered across its landscaped grounds, which have lovely views to the sea. There's an enclave of pieces by Henry Moore, a Picasso Pavilion, with over two hundred paintings, lithographs, ceramics and sculptures, and four galleries featuring works by Chagall, Miró and Renoir alongside modern Japanese artists such as Ryuzaburo Umehara and Takeshi Hayashi.

The best place for **lunch** is the *Gyōza Centre* (daily 11.30am–3pm & 5–8pm), on the main road between the Hakone Open-Air Museum and Gōra, where a set meal costs ¥1155. There's usually a long line of customers waiting to sample the delicious home-made dumplings (*gyōza*).

GŌRA AND ŌWAKUDANI 強羅と大湧谷

Apart from lunch (see above) there's little reason to stop at **Gōra** except to transfer from the railway to a funicular tram (¥410), which takes only ten minutes to cover the short but steep distance to **Sōunzan**, the start of the cable car across Mount Sōun.

From Sōunzan, the **cable car** (¥1330 one way) floats like a balloon on its thirty-minute journey over the mountain to the Tōgendai terminal, beside Lake Ashi-ko, stopping at a couple of points along the way. The first stop, **Ōwakudani**, is the site of a constantly bubbling and steaming valley formed by a volcanic eruption three thousand years ago.

You can learn more about this at the informative **Ōwakudani Natural History Museum** (daily 9am–4pm; ¥400), downhill from the cable car station. There's an entertaining diorama model of a volcano that flashes, rumbles and glows red at the point of eruption. To see the real thing, hike up the valley through the lava formations to the bubbling pools, where eggs are boiled until they are black before being scoffed by every visiting Japanese tourist.

Accommodation

Fuji Hakone Guesthouse

912 Sengokuhara ⓣ0460/4-6577; ⓕ4-6578.

Run by the English-speaking Takahashi-san, with *tatami* rooms, and *onsen* water piped into a communal bath. Breakfast only. Take bus #4 from the east exit of Odawara Station. ❹.

Hakone Sengokuhara Youth Hostel

912 Sengokuhara ⓣ0460/4-8966; ⓕ4-6578.

Directly behind the above *Fuji Hakone Guesthouse* in a lovely wooden building, with Japanese-style rooms. Private rooms available for ¥5000 per person. ❷.

ASHI-KO AND AROUND 芦ノ湖

The Tōgendai cable car terminus is at the northern end of the bone-shaped Lake **Ashi-ko**, from where, if the weather is good, you'll get fantastic views of **Mount Fuji**. The most enjoyable thing to do here is board one of the colourful, cartoon-like "pirate ships" (¥840) that sail the length of the lake in thirty minutes.

The boats dock at Hakone-machi, where the **Hakone Barrier** (daily 9am–4.30pm; ¥200) was once where all traffic on the Tōkaidō, the feudal-era road linking Kyoto and Edo, had to pass. What stands here today is a reproduction, enlivened by waxwork displays which provide the historical background. Stroll north of the barrier around the wooded promontory, past the bland reconstruction of the Emperor Meiji's Hakone Detached Palace, to take in the views of the lake.

Running for roughly 1km beside the road from the Hakone Barrier to the lakeside village of **Moto-hakone** is part of the original Tōkaidō road, shaded by 420 cryptomeria trees. Across the lake, a vermilion *torii* gate stands in the water just north of Moto-Hakone – this scene is celebrated in many a *ukiyo-e* print and modern postcard. The gate belongs to the **Hakone Gongen** and is the best thing about this small Shinto shrine, set back in the trees, where samurai once came to pray.

Accommodation

Hakone Lake Villa Youth Hostel

ⓣ0460/3-1610.

In a secluded spot above Lake Ashi-ko, with *tatami* and Western-style dorms, a bath filled with *onsen* water and good-value meals. ❷.

Hakone Prince Hotel

ⓣ0460/3-1111; ⓕ3-7616.

Prime location on the east side of Ashi-ko and offering a multitude of facilities. ❼.

Moto-Hakone Guest House

ⓣ0460/3-7880; ⓕ4-6578.

A short bus ride (get off at Ashinokoen-mae) or stiff ten-minute walk up the hill from the village, offering spotless, Japanese-style rooms, with singles at ¥5000. Breakfast only. ❹.

BACK TO HAKONE-YUMOTO 箱根湯元

From either Moto-Hakone or Hakone-machi you can take a **bus** back to Hakone-Yumoto. Far more rewarding, however, is the eleven-kilometre **hike** along part of the

Tōkaidō, which after the first couple of kilometres is all downhill and takes around four hours. The route begins five minutes up the hill from the Hakone Tōzan bus station in Moto-Hakone, where large paving stones are laid through the shady forests. When the path comes out of the trees and hits the main road, you'll see the **Amazake-jaya teahouse**, where you can rest, just as travellers have done for centuries, and sip a restorative cup of the rice drink amazake, with some pickles.

From the teahouse, the path shadows the main road to the small village of **Hatajuku**, where since the ninth century craftsmen have perfected the art of *yosegi-zaiku*, or marquetry. These wooden boxes, toys and other objects inlaid with elaborate mosaic patterns make great souvenirs and there are workshops throughout the village, including one right where the path emerges onto the main road.

Hatajuku is a good place to pick up the bus for the rest of the way to Hakone-Yumoto if you don't fancy hiking any further. From here the path descends to the Sukumo-gawa river and past several old temples, as well as the Tenzan Notemburo (see p.321), before ending up in the centre of Hakone-Yumoto.

Kamakura

The small, relaxed town of **Kamakura** is trapped between the sea and a circle of wooded hills, one hour's train ride – 50km – south of Tokyo, and is steeped in history. For a brief, tumultuous period (1192–1333), this was Japan's political and military centre under a shogunate which was nominally answerable to the emperor in Kyoto.

The town's most famous sight is the **Daibutsu**, a glorious bronze Buddha surrounded by trees and sea air, though the ancient Zen Buddhist temples of **Engaku-ji** and **Kenchō-ji** are equally compelling. Not that Buddhism has a monopoly; among several colourful Shinto shrines, the foremost is **Tsurugaoka Hachiman-gū**, which dominates central Kamakura. You can take in most of these sights on a busy day-trip from Tokyo, but Kamakura more than justifies a longer stay.

The easiest way of getting to Kamakura is on the JR Yokosuka Line from Tokyo Station. **Trains** run every ten or twenty minutes, and stop at Kita-Kamakura – a good place to start your explorations – before pulling into the main Kamakura Station a few minutes later; make sure you board a Yokosuka– or Kurihama–bound train to avoid changing at Ōfuna. **Local buses** leave from in front of Kamakura Station, and there's a **bike rental** outlet up the slope behind the tourist office (daily 8.30am–5pm).

The small **tourist information** window (daily 9am–5/6pm; ⓣ0467/22-3350) is immediately outside Kamakura Station's east exit; they have English-speaking staff but only a limited range of maps and brochures, so call at the Tokyo TIC (see p.38) before setting off.

KITA-KAMAKURA 北鎌倉

The most satisfying of Kamakura's major Zen temples, founded in 1282, **Engaku-ji** (daily: April–Oct 8am–5pm; Nov–March 8am–4pm; ¥200) lies hidden among ancient cedars immediately south of Kita-Kamakura Station. The layout follows Chinese Zen principles – a pond and bridge (now cut off by the train tracks), followed by a succession of austere buildings. Beyond a magnificent two-storied gate, the temple's most important building is the dainty Shari-den, which is said to contain a tooth of the Buddha.

Continuing southeast along the main road, **Tōkei-ji** (daily: April–Oct 8.30am–5pm; Nov–March 8.30am–4pm; ¥100), founded as a nunnery in 1285, is a pleasing cluster of buildings set in flower-filled gardens, and is popularly known as the "Divorce Temple". Until the mid-nineteenth century this was one of the few places where wives could escape domestic ill-treatment. Husbands could be summoned to resolve the dispute or, ultimately, sign the divorce papers at the end of three years. Some of these documents are preserved in the Treasure House (¥300), while, at the back of the temple, there's a mossy cemetery for both famous and forgotten nuns.

Further along the valley, a lane turns right just before the train tracks, past Jōchi-ji's unusual Chinese-style gate. This is the start of the **Daibutsu Hiking Course**, a ridge-path (2km) which makes an enjoyable approach to the great Buddha (see p.331). Even if you're not going that far, it's well worth taking a diversion to see the captivating cave-shrine dedicated to the goddess **Zeniarai Benten** ("Money-Washing Benten"). The entrance is via a short tunnel into a natural amphitheatre filled with a forest of *torii* wreathed in incense and candle-smoke. According to legend, money washed in the cave's sacred spring is guaranteed to double.

Back on the main road, it's another five-minute walk to the greatest of Kamakura's Zen temples, **Kenchō-ji** (daily 8.30am–4.30pm; ¥300). Again, there's a strong Chinese influence: the main complex begins with a towering gate, beyond which a grove of gnarled juniper trees, said to have grown from seeds brought from China, hides the nicely dilapidated Butsu-den (the Buddha Hall). Instead of Buddha, however, the hall's main image is of Jizō, the bodhisattva who leads souls to salvation, seated on a lotus throne. Behind, the Hattō (Lecture Hall), which numbers among Japan's largest wooden, Buddhist buildings, is under restoration and will be closed until 2003.

South of Kenchō-ji lies **Ennō-ji** (daily: March–Nov 9am–4pm; Dec–Feb 9am–3,30pm; ¥200), a temple with a wonderful collection of ferocious statues – the red-faced King of Hell and his ten cohorts. From here it's only a short walk to the back entrance of Tsurugaoka Hachiman-gū.

TSURUGAOKA HACHIMAN-GŪ 鶴岡八幡宮

Since 1063, **Tsurugaoka Hachiman-gū** has been the guardian shrine of the Minamoto clan, the founders of the Kamakura shogunate. Though most of the present buildings are much more recent, their striking red paintwork, the parade of souvenir stalls and the constant bustle of people create a buzzing, festive atmosphere. The main approach is from the south, along a grand avenue running die-straight from the sea to a vermilion-lacquered *torii* and three humpbacked bridges. From here a promenade leads between two lotus-filled ponds to an ancient gingko tree and a flight of steps, where the third Kamakura shogun was murdered by his vengeful nephew in 1219. At the top stands the shrine itself, an attractive collection of buildings set amongst trees, which is dedicated to Hachiman, the God of War. Like all Shinto shrines, however, you can only peer in.

Instead, head back down the steps and left past a beautiful, black-lacquered shrine, to find the modern **Kamakura National Treasure Hall** (Tues–Sun 9am–4pm; ¥300). This one-room museum has a stunning collection of Kamakura– and Muromachi–period art (1192–1573), mostly gathered from the Zen temples.

SUGIMOTO-DERA AND HŌKOKU-JI 杉本寺と報国寺

These two modest temples on the quiet, eastern side of town are among Kamakura's most enchanting sights. To get there takes roughly thirty minutes on foot from Hachiman-gū, or ten minutes by bus from Kamakura Station (bus #23, #24 or #36 from stand 5; ¥170). The bus drops you outside **Sugimoto-dera** (daily 8am–4.30pm; ¥200), a small, thatched temple at the top of a foot-worn staircase; founded in 734, this is Kamakura's oldest temple. Inside its smoke-blackened hall, take a look behind the main altar where three statues of *Jūichimen Kannon*, the eleven-faced Goddess of Mercy, are enshrined. The images were carved by famous monks and all are at least one thousand years old. According to legend, they survived a fire in 1189 by miraculously taking shelter behind a nearby tree; *Sugimoto* means "under the cedar".

On the opposite side of the main road, **Hōkoku-ji** (daily 9am–4pm; ¥200) is best known for its grove of evergreen bamboo. A walk through the dappled forest of gently curved stems, where tinkling water spouts and the soft creaking of the wind-rocked canes muffles the outside world, is an extraordinarily soothing experience.

THE DAIBUTSU AND HASE-DERA 大仏と長谷寺

Hase, on the west side of Kamakura, is home to the magnificent Daibutsu (the "Great Buddha") and a 1300-year-old statue of Kannon, the Goddess of Mercy. Both these sights are within walking distance of Hase Station, on the private Enoden Line; trains leave from platforms on the west side of Kamakura Station every ten to fifteen minutes (¥190; 5min).

Japan's second largest bronze Buddha, **Daibutsu** (daily: April–Sept 7am–6pm; Oct–March 7am–5.30pm; ¥200) can seem disappointing at first, but as you get closer the magic begins to take hold. The eleven-metre-tall figure sits on a stone pedestal, a broad-shouldered figure lost in meditation, his face and robes streaked grey-green by centuries of sun, wind and rain.

The image is of Amida Nyorai, the Buddha who receives souls into the "Western Paradise". It was cast in 1252 under the orders of the first Kamakura shogun, Minamoto Yoritomo, and is made of bronze plates bolted together around a frame – you can climb inside for ¥20. Amazingly, the Daibutsu has withstood fires, typhoons, tidal waves and even the Great Earthquake of 1923.

On the way back to Hase Station, it's worth visiting **Hase-dera** (daily March–Sept 8am–5pm; rest of year to 4.30pm; ¥300), a temple on a hill to the west of the road, with good views over Kamakura Bay. According to legend, this temple was founded in 736 when an eleven-faced Kannon washed ashore nearby. The goddess is supposedly one of a pair carved from a single camphor tree in 721 by a monk in the original Hase, near Nara in western Japan; he placed one in a local temple and pushed the other out to sea. Today the "Kamakura Kannon" – just over 9m tall and gleaming with gold leaf – resides in an attractive building at the top of the temple steps. This central hall is flanked by two smaller buildings: the right hall houses a large Amida Buddha, carved in 1188 for Minamoto Yoritomo, while the left is a small treasure hall (daily 9am–4pm). Ranks of doll-like Jizō statues are a common sight in Hase-dera; these sad little figures, often wearing woollen mufflers, commemorate stillborn or aborted children.

ACCOMMODATION

Kamakura Kagetsuen Youth Hostel

27-9 Sakanoshita Ⓣ 0467/25-1238; Ⓕ 25-1236.

Small hostel with aged bunk-bed dormitories on the seafront, ten minutes' walk from Hase Station. No meals and there's an 11pm curfew. ❷.

Hotel Mori

3F, 1-5-21 Komachi Ⓣ 0467/22-5868; Ⓕ 25-6954.

Round the corner from the station on the main drag, offering bright, clean decent-sized twin or triple rooms with TV and en-suite bathrooms. ❻.

Shangrila Tsuruoka

3F, 1-9-29 Yukinoshita Ⓣ 0467/25-6363; Ⓕ 25-6456.

Small, friendly hotel hidden above a shopping mall. Though a bit fussy, the rooms are light, well kept and perfectly adequate. ❺.

Hotel Tsurugaoka Kaikan

2-12-27 Komachi Ⓣ 0467/24-1111; Ⓕ 24-1115.

Glitzy, old-fashioned hotel on the road to the Tsurugaoka shrine, with English-speaking staff and Japanese and Western-style rooms. Specify if you don't want meals. ❼.

EATING

Chaya-kado

1518 Yamanouchi.

Homely *soba* restaurant handily located in Kita-Kamakura, on the main road just north of Kenchō-ji. Prices start at ¥700. Open daily 10am–5pm.

Fudo-chaya

2-2-21 Yukinoshita.

Down a lane west of Hachiman-gū, this quirky restaurant next to a tiny cave-shrine is recommended for its ambience rather than its limited selection of noodle dishes from around ¥700. Daily except Thurs 11am–5pm.

Hachi-no-ki

7 Yamanouchi ⓣ 0467/22-8719.

Famous old restaurant beside Kenchō-ji, serving Buddhist vegetarian *shōjin-ryōri*, with a newer branch opposite Tōkei-ji. Whichever you opt for, prices start at around ¥3500 for a set menu, and it's advisable to book.

Sometaro

2F, 3-12-11 Hase.

Traditional restaurant near Hase-dera specializing in *okonomiyaki* (do-it-yourself savoury pancakes). A bowl of ingredients costs around ¥900. Open daily 11.30am–9pm.

Tsukui

11-7 Onarimachi.

Another cheap, friendly *okonomiyaki* and *yakisoba* joint down a stone-paved alley on the west side of Kamakura Station. Prices from around ¥900. English menu. Daily except Tues noon–10pm.

Watami

3F, 1-6-17 Komachi.

Lively, modern *izakaya* near the station with a helpful picture-menu. Most dishes are under ¥400 and you can feast for ¥1500–2000 per head excluding drinks. Mon–Thurs & Sun 4pm–midnight; Fri & Sat 4pm–5am.

Kawagoe

Only 40km north of Tokyo in Saitama-ken is the old castle town of **Kawagoe**, an interesting and highly enjoyable day-trip. Although it doesn't look promising on arrival, Kawagoe's compact area of sights, around 1km north of the main station, is faithfully described as a "Little Edo", and can easily be toured in a few hours, although once you've browsed the many traditional **craft shops** and small museums, checked out the venerable temple complex **Kita-in**, and paused to sample the town's culinary delights you'll probably find the day has flown by.

On Oct 14 and 15 Kawagoe's grand matsuri is held, one of the liveliest festivals in the Tokyo area involving some 25 ornate floats (called *dashi*), and hundreds of costumed revellers.

Kawagoe's fortunes owe everything to its strategic position on the Shingashi River and Kawagoe-kaidō, the ancient highway to the capital. The town's merchants prospered, accumulating enough wealth to build the fire-proof **kurazukuri**, the black, two-storied shop-houses the town is now famous for. At one time there were over two hundred of these houses, but their earthenware walls didn't prove quite so effective against fire as hoped (nor were they much use in the face of Japan's headlong rush to modernization). Even so, some thirty still remain, with sixteen prime examples clustered together along Chūō-dōri, around 1km north of the JR and Tōbu stations, protected as Important Cultural Properties.

Of the choice of three **train** lines to Kawagoe, the fastest service is the express on the Tōbu line from Ikebukuro (32min; ¥450); you can either get off at Kawagoe Station, also on the slower JR Saikyo line, or Tōbu Kawagoe-shi, which is marginally closer to Chūō-dōri. Seibu Shinjuku line trains run from Shinjuku to Hon-Kawagoe Station (43min; ¥470), which is the most convenient of the lot for the kurazukuri. Also, immediately east of the main square in front of the Seibu terminus is a bicycle rental shop (¥700 for the day), handy if you plan to see all of Kawagoe's somewhat scattered sights.

The staff at the **tourist information** office (daily 9am–4pm; ⓣ0492/46-2027) at Kawagoe Station don't speak English but they can provide you with a map of town and an English pamphlet on the sights.

ALONG CHŪŌ-DŌRI

Along Chūō-dōri, around 200 metres before the main enclave of kurazukuri, you'll pass a small shrine, **Kumano-jinja**, beside which is a tall storehouse containing a magnificent *dashi* float; this is your only chance to inspect one up close outside of the annual festival. At the next major crossroads, on the left hand side, is the old Kameya *okashi* (sweet) shop, warehouse and factory. These buildings now house the **Yamazaki Museum of Art** (daily except Thurs 9.30am–5pm; ¥500), dedicated to the works of Meiji-era artist Gaho Hashimoto. Some of his elegant screen paintings hang in the main gallery, while in the converted *kura* (storehouses) are artistic examples of the sugary confections once made here. If this gets your mouth watering, you'll be glad to know entry includes a cup of tea and *okashi*.

Heading up Chūō-dōri, you'll pass several craft shops including Machikan which specializes in knives and swords (costing anything from ¥20,000 to ¥800,000), and Sōbiki Atelier which sells woodwork. On the left, take a moment to duck into **Choki-in**, a temple with a statue of an emaciated Gandara-style Buddha in its grounds along with a pretty lily pond and sculpted bushes and trees. Back on the main street, the **Kurazukuri Shiryōkan** (Tues–Sun 9am–5pm; ¥100) is a museum housed inside an old tobacco wholesaler's, one of the first kurazukuri to be rebuilt after the great fire of 1893. In the living quarters you can squeeze around the tiny twisting staircase that leads from the upper to the ground level, and in one of the *kura*, view woodblock prints of the fires that ravaged the town alongside turn-of-the-century fire fighting uniforms.

On the right, opposite the museum, you can't miss the **Toki-no-Kane**, the wooden bell tower, rebuilt in 1894, that was used to raise the alarm when fires broke out. Now an electric motor powers the bell that rings four times daily. Take the turning on the left after the bell tower and follow it down until you reach **Yoju-in**, another handsomely wrought temple with pleasant grounds. Just north of here is the **Kashiya Yokochō**, or confectioner's alley, a picturesque pedestrian street still lined with several colourful sweet and toy shops - another great place to browse for souvenirs.

It's a five-hundred-metre hike east of the kurazukuri, along the main road, to reach the scant remains of Kawagoe Castle, now mainly parkland and the grounds of the senior high school, but still containing the vast **Honmaru-goten**, the former residence of the *daimyō*. Inside is a museum (Tues–Sun 9am–5pm; ¥100) containing mainly archeological artefacts, but it's the building itself, dating from 1848, that is the main attraction, with its Chinese-style gabled roof, spacious *tatami* rooms and gorgeous painted screens.

Heading south from the castle grounds you'll soon arrive at **Naritasan Betsu-in**, an unremarkable shrine which comes to life on the 28th of each month when it hosts a busy flea market.

KITA-IN

If your time in Kawagoe is limited you should prioritize **Kita-in**. This main temple complex of the Tendaishu Buddhist sect, 500m southeast of the kurazukuri, is notable because it contains the only remaining structures from Edo Castle, now the site of Tokyo's Imperial Palace. There's been a temple on these grounds since 830 AD, and it gained fame when the first Tōkugawa shogun Ieyasu declared the head priest Tenkai Sōjō a "living Buddha". Such was the reverence in which the priests here were held, that when the temple was burnt down in 1638, the third shogun Iemitsu donated an annex palace from Edo castle as a replacement building. The wooden building was dismantled and reassembled at Kita-in next to the main temple.

You have to pay an entry fee (¥400) to view the palace buildings, but it's well worth it. The room with a painted ceiling of floral designs is believed to be where Iemitsu was born. Serene gardens surround the palace and a covered wooden bridge leads across into the temple's inner sanctum, decorated with a dazzling golden chandelier.

The entry fee also includes access to the **Gōhyaku Rakan**, a remarkable grove of stone statues. Although the name translates as 500 Rakans, there are actually 540 of these enigmatic dwarf disciples of Buddha, no two alike. The different expressions on their faces are fascinating; it's also fun to search for the statue which bears the Chinese symbols of your birth year. As if this isn't sufficient, Kita-in also has its own mini **Tōshō-gū**, enshrining the spirit of Tokugawa Ieyasu and similarly decorated in bright colours and elaborate carvings as its famous cousin in Nikkō.

EATING

Kawagoe is so close to Tokyo that there's no need to stay the night. It is, however, worth indulging in the town's fine range of **dining** options. The local speciality is *unagi* (eel); a couple of good rustic places to try this rich dish are *Ogatō* and *Ogagiku*, both a short walk southeast of the kurazukuri. *Kotobukian* beside Kita-in is renowned for its *soba* (buckwheat noodles), as is *Kinbue* on Chūō-dōri. Also don't leave town without sampling its sweet potato beer, Setsumaimo Lager, an original brew using a plentiful local ingredient, and available at several restaurants and shops and *Oni*, an atmospheric *izakaya*, five minutes' walk north of Tōbu Kawagoe-shi Station.

Yokohama

On its southern borders Tokyo merges into **Yokohama**, Japan's second-largest city and a major international port. It's far more relaxed than the capital, with an airy, seafront feel and a cosmopolitan vibe. Local people are proud of their international heritage; in 1858, as Japan opened up to the outside world (see History, p.351), Yokohama was one of the first ports in which foreigners were allowed to trade. Most of the city's sights are related to the former foreign settlements, from the European-style residences, church spires and bijou tea shops of **Yamate** to the lively alleys and restaurants of **Chinatown**. But Yokohama is also styling itself as a city of the future – its Landmark Tower is Japan's tallest building and the focus of **Minato Mirai 21**, a half-completed "harbour-city of the twenty-first century".

The cheapest way of getting here is on a Tōkyū-Tōyoko **train** from Shibuya Station, calling at Yokohama Station before terminating at the more central Sakuragichō Station (every 5 min; 40min). Coming from Tokyo Station, there's a choice between the faster Tōkaidō Line and Yokosuka Line (both every 5–10min; 30min) or the Keihin-Tōhoku Line (every 5–10min; 40min). All three are JR lines; the first two terminate at Yokohama Station while the latter is more convenient if you're continuing to Sakuragichō, Kannai or beyond.

There are **information** centres with English-speaking staff in the underground concourse outside the east exit of

Yokohama Station (daily 10am–6pm; ⓣ045/441-7300) and outside Sakuragichō Station's east exit (daily 9am–6pm, Aug to 8pm; ⓣ045/211-0111).

Yokohama is reasonably spread out, so using the **local trains** saves time. JR trains run every five to ten minutes (minimum fare ¥130) between Yokohama, Sakuragichō, Kannai and southerly Ishikawachō stations. Alternatively, Sea-Bass **ferries** shuttle between Yokohama Station (from beside Sogō department store) and Yamashita-kōen (¥600; 15min) via Minato Mirai (¥340), with departures every fifteen minutes (10am–7pm). From Yamashita-kōen there are a variety of **sightseeing cruises** round the harbour; prices start at ¥900 for forty minutes.

MOTOMACHI AND YAMATE 元町と山手

South of central Yokohama, trains on the JR Keihin-Tōhoku from Tokyo stop at Ishikawachō Station before plunging into a series of tunnels beneath **Yamate**. From the station walk southeast down the fashionable shopping street of **Motomachi**, which used to serve the city's expats and still exudes a faint European flavour. At the far end, paths lead up onto a promontory with panoramic views of the harbour and the graceful Bay Bridge.

Just inland, you'll find the **Foreigners' Cemetery**, where, since 1854, over 4500 people from more than forty countries have been buried. Walking south from the cemetery's gate will take you past a handsome row of houses, including the turreted Yamate Jubankan – now a French restaurant – and the city's oldest wooden building, next door. The latter, erected in 1909, contains the **Yamate Museum** (daily 11am–4pm; ¥200), worth a quick look for its collection of nineteenth-century satirical cartoons in English. Just beyond, the square tower of **Christ Church**, founded in 1862 but rebuilt in 1947, adds a village-green touch to the neighbourhood, which is still a popular residential district for Yokohama's expatriate community.

CHINATOWN AND YAMASHITA-KŌEN 中華街と山下公園

Back down on the levels, the streets of **Chinatown** are packed with colourful trinket shops and bustling restaurants whose aromas are hard to resist. Founded in 1863, this is the largest of Japan's Chinatowns, though today only around 2000 ethnic Chinese live here. The focus of community life, and the area's only specific sight, is **Kanteibyō** (daily 10am–8pm; free), a shrine dedicated to Guan Yu, a former warlord and guardian deity of Chinatown. Inside, a long-haired Guan Yu sits on the main altar, gazing over the heads of supplicants petitioning for health and prosperity. The whole area erupts with dragon dances, fireworks and parades around Chinese New Year (late January or early February) and Chinese National Day (October 1).

From Chinatown it's a short stroll down to the harbour front, with its Marine Tower (106m) and a pleasant seafront park, **Yamashita-kōen**. A retired passenger liner, built in 1930 for the Yokohama–Seattle service, lies moored beside the ferry pier; it now serves, rather ignominiously, as a "floating amusement ship". At the south end of Yamashita-kōen, the **Doll Museum** (Tues–Sun July & Aug 10am–7pm; rest of year 10am–5pm; ¥300) offers a more diverting display of Japanese folk and classical dolls.

KANNAI 関内

The traditional centre of Yokohama, **Kannai** still has some of its original Western-style buildings, plus a couple of museums. Walking north from Yamashita-kōen, you first pass the **Silk Museum** (Tues–Sun 9am–4.30pm; ¥500), a rather dry celebration of the industry on which Yokohama's fortunes were built in the late nineteenth century. Nearby is the best of the city's many historical museums, the **Yokohama Archives of History** (Tues–Sun 9.30am–5pm; ¥200). As you enter, take a quick look at the attractive brick building in the central courtyard – it originally served as the British Consulate in the 1930s. Other European-style facades in the area include the biscuit-coloured **Customs House**, near the harbour, and the graceful **Port Opening Memorial Hall** a few blocks inland. Lastly, the **Kanagawa Prefectural Museum** (Tues–Sun 9.30am–5pm; ¥300), in north Kannai, is worth looking at but not going in. The building was completed in 1904 as the headquarters of the Yokohama Bank and boasts one of the city's most ornate Western-style facades.

MINATO MIRAI 21 (MM21) みなとみらい２１

On Yokohama's northern skyline a collection of futuristic skyscrapers pinpoint the **Minato Mirai 21** (MM21) development. A mini-city of hotels, apartment blocks, offices and cultural facilities will eventually occupy nearly two square kilometres of reclaimed land and disused dockyards, with its own subway line and state-of-the-art waste disposal and heating systems. Building work will continue into 2005, with the subway scheduled for completion the year before, but already the bulk of the hotels, conference facilities, shopping malls and museums are in place. Next will come the office blocks, exhibition halls and waterfront parks to fill the empty plots behind.

Landmark Tower and around

For the moment access to MM21 is via Sakuragichō Station, from where a covered moving walkway whisks you towards the awesome, 296-metre tall **Landmark Tower**. Inside, take the world's fastest lift for an ear-popping, forty-second ride up to the 69th-floor **Sky Garden** (daily 10am–9pm; July–Sept 10am–10pm; ¥1000). On clear days superb views of Mount Fuji more than justify the observatory's steep entry fee. Alternatively, you can enjoy a coffee for about the same price in the opulent *Sirius Sky Lounge* on the 70th floor of the tower's *Royal Park Hotel*.

A water-filled dock in front of Landmark Tower is now home to the *Nippon-maru* sail training ship, part of the **Yokohama Maritime Museum** (Tues–Sun: March–June & Sept–Oct 10am–5pm; July & Aug 10am–6.30pm; Nov–Feb 10am–4.30pm; ¥600). The *Nippon-maru*, built in 1930, sailed the equivalent of 45 times round the world. You can explore the entire vessel, from the engine room to the captain's cabin.

East of the Landmark Tower lie a succession of swanky shopping malls, the sail-shaped *Intercontinental Hotel* and, on an adjacent island, the slowly revolving **Cosmo Clock 21** (daily except Thurs: mid-March to July & Sept–Nov, Mon–Fri 11am–9pm, Sat & Sun 11am–10pm; Aug daily 11am–10pm; Dec to mid-March, Mon–Fri 11am–8pm, Sat & Sun 11am–9pm ¥700). With a capacity of 480 passengers, this 112-metre **Ferris wheel** claims to be the world's largest; one circuit takes around fifteen minutes, allowing plenty of time to admire the view.

Yokohama Museum of Art and the Industrial Museum

MM21's two major museums are to be found in the blocks immediately north of Landmark Tower. In the **Yokohama**

Museum of Art (daily except Thurs 10am–6pm; ¥500; varying prices for special exhibitions), mostly twentieth-century Japanese and Western art is set off to fine effect by designer Tange Kenzō's cool, grey space. The nearby **Mitsubishi Minato Mirai Industrial Museum** (Tues–Sun 10am–5.30pm; ¥500; ⓦ *www.mhi.co.jp/e_museum/ef_home.html*) illustrates technological developments, from today's power generators and oil platforms to the space stations of tomorrow. There are plenty of models and interactive displays, with English-speaking staff on hand if needed, but the biggest draw is the Sky-Walk Adventure, a helicopter simulator, on the second floor. After a short flying lesson, you get to take the virtual chopper swooping and soaring over Fuji or down into the Grand Canyon for a stomach-wrenching fifteen-minute ride.

ACCOMMODATION

Echigoya Ryokan

2F, 1-14 Ishikawachō, Naka-ku ⓣ045/641-4700; ⓕ641-8815.

Homely *ryokan* with no-frills Japanese-style rooms. One of the few budget places in central Yokohama. ❹.

Kanagawa Youth Hostel

1 Momijigaoka, Nishi-ku ⓣ045/241-6503.

Aged and overpriced, but its dormitory beds are the cheapest option in town. ❶.

Navios Yokohama

Sinkō-chō, Naka-ku ⓣ045/633-6000, ⓕ633-6001.

Best-value option in Yokohama, if you don't mind the slightly inconvenient location seven minutes' walk from Sakuragichō Station. ❻.

Hotel New Grand

10 Yamashitachō, Naka-ku ⓣ045/681-1841, ⓕ681-1895.

This 1920s' hotel still retains its original elegance in the old wing. Satellite TV and en-suite bathrooms are standard, and there are harbour views from some rooms. ❽.

Sakuragichō Washington Hotel

Sakuragichō 1-chōme, Naka-ku ⓣ045/683-3111, ⓕ683-3112.
Spanking new addition to the *Washington* chain, right next to Sakuragichō Station, with relatively spacious rooms above a shopping mall. ❻.

EATING

Heichinrou

149 Yamashitachō ⓣ045/681-3001.
Large, popular Cantonese restaurant recommended for its good-value, weekday lunch deals (from ¥1400) and *dim sum* sets (from ¥700 per plate; up to 4.30pm). Reservations recommended at the weekend. Open daily 11am–10.15pm.

Manchinrou

153 Yamashitachō ⓣ045/681-4004.
Famous restaurant serving Guangdong cuisine. Noodle and fried rice dishes start at around ¥1100 and lunch sets at ¥2700. English spoken and bookings recommended. Open daily 11am–10pm.

Peking Hanten

79-5 Yamashitachō.
Beijing restaurant, with lunchtime menus from ¥1000. English menu available. Open daily 11.30am–2am.

Shei Shei

138 Yamashitachō.
Small Szechuan restaurant serving a great weekday set lunch (¥500), and where you share tables at busy times. Open daily 11.30am–2pm & 5–8.30pm.

Suro Saikan Honkan

190 Yamashitachō.
Popular for its reliable Shanghai cuisine. Weekday lunch sets start at under ¥700 and courses from around ¥3000, but count on at least ¥4000 in the evening. Open daily 11.30am–10pm.

CONTEXTS

A brief history of Tokyo

Today's restless metropolis, sprawling round the western shores of Tokyo Bay, began life as a humble fishing village lost among the marshes of the Sumida-gawa, called **Edo**. Tokyo's founding date is usually given as 1457, the year when Ōta Dōkan, a minor lord, built his modest castle on a bluff overlooking the river. However, a far more significant event occurred in 1590 when the ambitious warlord **Tokugawa Ieyasu** established his power-base in this obscure castle-town, far from the emperor in Kyoto. For more than a century Japan had been torn apart by social and political unrest, but in little over a decade Ieyasu had reunited the country and taken the title of shogun, effectively a military dictator. Though the emperor continued to hold court in Kyoto, from now on Japan's real centre of power lay in Edo.

Under the Tokugawa

The **Tokugawa** dynasty set about creating a city befitting their new status, initiating massive construction projects which have continued, for one reason or other, to the present day. By 1640 Edo Castle was the most imposing in all Japan, complete with a five-storey central keep, a double moat and a complex, spiralling network of canals. Instead of perimeter walls, however, there were simple barrier gates and then a bewildering warren of narrow, tortuous lanes, sudden dead-ends and unbridged canals to snare unwelcome intruders. At the same time drainage work began on the surrounding marshes, where embankments were raised to protect the nascent city against flooding.

The shogun protected himself further by requiring his *daimyō* (feudal lords) to split the year between their provincial holdings and Edo, where their families were kept as virtual hostages. Maintaining two households with two sets of retainers, travelling long distances and observing prescribed ceremonies on the way, left them neither the time nor money to raise a serious threat. But the *daimyō* also enjoyed numerous privileges: within Edo they were granted the most favourable land to the west of the castle, in the area known as **Yamanote**. Artisans, merchants and others at the bottom of the established order, meanwhile, were confined to **Shitamachi**, a low-lying, overcrowded region to the east. Mid-eighteenth-century Edo was the world's largest city, with a population well over one million, of whom roughly half were squeezed at an astonishing 70,000 people per square kilometre into Shitamachi. Though growing less distinct, this division between the "high" and "low" city is still apparent today.

Life in the low city

During more than two hundred years of peace, the shogunate grew increasingly conservative and sterile, while life down in Shitamachi was buzzing. Peace had given rise to an increasingly wealthy merchant class and a vigorous, often bawdy subculture where the pursuit of pleasure was taken to new extremes. In Shitamachi, where rank counted for little, the arbiters of fashion were the irrepressible, devil-may-care *Edo-ko*, the "children of Edo", with their earthy humour and delight in practical jokes. Inevitably, there was also a darker side to life and the *Edo-ko* knew their fair share of squalor, poverty and violence. Licensed brothels, euphemistically known as "pleasure quarters", flourished, and child prostitution was common.

Shitamachi's tightly packed streets of thatch and wood dwellings usually suffered worst in the great fires which broke out so frequently they were dubbed *Edo no hana*, the "flowers of Edo". In January 1657, the **Fire of the Long Sleeves** laid waste to three-quarters of the buildings and killed an estimated hundred thousand people. Subsequent precautions included earth firewalls, manned watchtowers and local fire-fighting teams, who were much revered for their acrobatic skills and bravery. However, the fires raged on and the life expectancy of an Edo building averaged a mere twenty years.

Opening the doors

Since the early seventeenth century Japan had been a **closed country**. Distrusting the success of earlier Christian missionaries and fearful of colonization by their European backers, the shogun banned virtually all contact with the outside world. Within this vacuum, by the early nineteenth century the highly conservative shogunate had become a weak and inept regime. When it failed to deal effectively with **Commodore Perry**, the American who insolently sailed his "Black Ships" into Edo Bay in 1853 and 1854 to secure trading rights, the shoguns' days were numbered. Opposition forces gradually rallied round the emperor until, after a brief civil war, the fifteenth Tokugawa shogun surrendered in November 1867. A few months later, in what came to be called the **Meiji Restoration**, power was fully restored to the emperor, and in 1869 Emperor Meiji took up permanent residence in the city now known as **Tokyo**, Japan's "eastern capital".

Modernization

The first years of **Meiji rule** saw another, very different revolution. Determined to modernize, Japan embraced the ideas and technologies of the West with startling enthusiasm. Tokyo stood at the centre of innovation: brick buildings, electric lights, trams, trains and then cars all made their first appearance here, greeted with a lively curiosity by the townspeople. Within a few decades the castle lost its outer gates and most of its grounds, canals were filled in or built over and the commercial focus shifted to Ginza, while Shitamachi's wealthier merchants decamped for the more desirable residential areas of Yamanote, leaving the low city to sink into slow decline.

Beneath its modern veneer, though, Tokyo remained largely a city of wood, still regularly swept by fire. When massive tremors rocked the city at midday on September 1, 1923, blazes sparked by thousands of cooking-fires and fanned by strong winds caused the greatest damage. Earthquakes were nothing new, but what came to be known as the **Great Kantō Earthquake** was worse than anything that had gone before. Half of Tokyo, by then a city of some two million, was destroyed, while a hundred thousand people lost their lives.

The war and its aftermath

The city rose from its ashes and for a while development continued apace, but nationalism was on the rise and before long Tokyo, like the rest of Japan, was gearing up for war. The first bombs hit the city in April 1942, followed by more frequent raids throughout 1944 as the Allied forces drew closer, reaching a crescendo in March 1945. During three days of sustained **incendiary bombing** an estimated hundred thousand people died, most of them on the night of March 9, when great swathes of the city burnt to the ground. The physical devastation surpassed even that of the Great Earthquake: Meiji-jingū, Sensō-ji and Edo Castle were all destroyed, Shitamachi all but obliterated, and from Hibiya it was possible to see clear across the eight kilometres to Shinjuku.

From a pre-war population of nearly seven million, Tokyo in 1945 was reduced to around three million residents in a state of near-starvation. This time, however, regeneration was fuelled by an influx of American dollars and food aid under the **Allied Occupation** led by General MacArthur. A **Security Pact** was signed between the two nations allowing the US to keep bases in Japan in exchange for providing military protection. Not surprisingly, the liveliest sector of the economy during this period was the blackmarket, first in Yūrakuchō and later in Ueno and Ikebukuro. Then, in 1950, the Korean War broke out and suddenly central Tokyo was undergoing extensive redevelopment on the back of a manufacturing boom, while immigrants flooded in from the provinces to fill the factories.

The boom years

With economic recovery well on the way, political tensions surfaced in the late 1950s. Anti-American **demonstrations** occurred sporadically throughout the decade, but in May 1960 more serious rioting broke out over ratification of the revised Security Pact. The crisis passed, though student discontent continued to rumble on for a long time – so much so that in 1968 the authorities closed Tokyo University for a year – and heavily armed riot police became a familiar sight on the streets. But the situation was never allowed to threaten the major event of the post-war period when, on October 10, 1964, Emperor Hirohito opened the eighteenth **Olympic Games**, the first in Asia, which was welcomed by many Japanese as a sign of long-awaited international recognition. Visitors to the games, for their part, were surprised by the previously war-torn country's rapid transformation, epitomized by the stunning Shinkansen trains zipping between Tokyo and Kyoto.

Like the rest of the industrialized world, Tokyo suffered during the oil price crisis of the 1970s, but by the following decade her economy was the envy of the world. The late-1980s **boom** saw land prices in Tokyo reach dizzying heights, matched by excesses of every conceivable sort, from gold-wrapped sushi to mink toilet-seat covers. The heady optimism was reflected in building projects such as the Metropolitan Government offices in Shinjuku, the Odaiba reclamation and the vast development of Makuhari Messe on the east side of Tokyo Bay.

Into the new millennium

By 1992, the bubble had burst. The sudden sobering-up and subsequent loss of confidence was compounded by revelations of deep-seated political corruption and by the AUM Shinrikyō terrorist group releasing deadly sarin gas on Tokyo commuter trains in 1995 – a particularly shocking event which left twelve dead and thousands injured.

The official announcement of **recession** in 1998, coupled with the plummeting value of the yen and rising unemployment, saw the ruling Liberal Democratic Party (LDP) take a drubbing in the August 1998 upper-house elections, though they managed to stay in power as part of a right-wing coalition. Newspaper headlines during the late 1990s continued to make sobering reading as a seemingly endless stream of exposed financial misdealings led to resignations and suicides. By February 1998, a manual on how to commit suicide had sold an incredible 1.1 million copies and over 30,000 people – the majority middle-aged men facing unemployment – killed themselves that year, followed by a record 33,000 in 1999.

While the **new millennium** has brought glimmerings of a **recovery** in the economy – hardly surprising after ¥125 trillion has been pumped into it through various government packages – the unemployment rate remains stubbornly around a previously unthinkable five percent. And the number of spectacular **business failures** continues, most notably the venerable Sogō department-store chain which in July 2000 became Japan's second biggest corporate bankruptcy, with almost ¥2 trillion in debts.

As **new-technology** and Internet-based companies take off and **deregulation** of various industries continues, the more gung-ho commentators are beginning to talk of a "third great opening" for Japan, following on from the economic impetuses provided by the Black Ships in 1853 and General MacArthur during the Occupation. On the streets, meanwhile, new buildings continue to go up at a dizzying speed, teen fashions are as wild and funky as always and the Tokyo buzz remains as addictive as ever.

Books

Many of the titles below are published by Kodansha and Charles E Tuttle both in Japan and abroad. However, if you can, buy your books before your journey, since they're generally more expensive in Japan.

General non-fiction

Isabella Bird, *Unbeaten Tracks in Japan* (Virago). After a brief stop in Meiji-era Tokyo, intrepid Victorian adventurer Bird reaches parts of Japan not trampled by tourists.

Ian Buruma, *A Japanese Mirror*; *The Wages of Guilt* and *The Missionary and the Libertine* (Faber). This excellent Dutch writer examines Japan's popular culture in *A Japanese Mirror*. *The Wages of Guilt* compares how Germany and Japan have come to terms with their roles in World War II and is a fascinating travelogue into the bargain. *The Missionary and the Libertine* collects together essays on Japan-bashing, Hiroshima, Pearl Harbour, and more.

John Dower, *Embracing Defeat: Japan in the Aftermath of World War II* (Allen Lane/Penguin Press). Very accessible Pulitzer Prize winner looking at the impact of the American occupation on Japan. Dower concludes it had a fundamental and long-lasting effect on the country. First-person accounts of post war Tokyo and snappy writing bring the whole book alive.

Lesley Downer, *The Brothers* (Chatto & Windus). The Tsutsumi family are the Kennedys of Japan and their saga of wealth (which has done a lot to shape modern day Tokyo), illegitimacy and the fabled hatred of the two half brothers is made gripping reading by Downer. Also look out for *On the Narrow Road to the Deep North*, her book following in the footsteps of the poet Bashō and her new work *Geisha*.

Robin Gerster, *Legless in Ginza* (Melbourne University Press). A funny and spot-on account of the writer's two year residence at Japan's most prestigious university, Tokyo's Todai. Gerster is no dry academic, writing instead with a larakin Aussie verve and noticing things that many other ex-pat commentators ignore.

David Kaplan & Andrew Marshall, *The Cult at the End of the World* (Arrow). Chilling account of the nerve-gas attack on the Tokyo subway by the AUM cult in 1995. The gripping, pulp-fiction-like prose belies formidable research by the authors.

Alex Kerr, *Lost Japan* (Lonely Planet). A beautifully written and thoughtfully observed set of essays covering aspects of Kerr's life and passions, including Kabuki, art collecting and his time in the "bubble era" Tokyo of the 1980s.

Richard McGregor, *Japan Swings* (Allen & Unwin/Yen). One of the more intelligent books penned by a former Tokyo correspondent. McGregor sets politics, culture and sex in 1990s' post-bubble Japan in his sights, revealing a fascinating world of ingrained money, politics and shifting sexual attitudes.

Mark Schilling, *The Encyclopedia of Japanese Pop Culture* (Weatherhill). Forget sumo and samurai; Godzilla, pop idols and instant *ramen* are really where Japan's culture is at. Schilling's book is a spot-on guide to late-twentieth-century Japan.

Edward Seidensticker, *Low City, High City* (Tuttle) and *Tokyo Rising: The City Since the Great Earthquake* (Tuttle). Seidensticker, a top translator of Japanese literature, tackles Tokyo's history from its humble beginnings to the Great Kantō quake of 1923 in the first book and follows up well with a second volume focusing on the capital's postwar experiences.

Richard Tames, *A Traveller's History of Japan* (Windrush Press). This clearly written and succinct volume romps through Japan's history and provides useful cultural descriptions and essays.

Robert Twigger, *Angry White Pyjamas* (Indigo). The subtitle "An Oxford poet trains with the Tokyo riot police" gives you the gist, and although Twigger's writing is more prose than poetry, he provides an intense forensic account of the daily trials, humiliations and triumphs of becoming a master of aikido. Even if you're not into martial arts, it's worth picking up.

Rey Ventura, *Underground in Japan* (Jonathan Cape). The non-Caucasian *gaijin* experience in Japan is brilliantly essayed by Ventura, who worked with fellow Filipino illegal immigrants in the dockyards of Yokohama.

Paul Waley, *Tokyo: City of Stories* (Weatherhill). An intimate, anecdotal history of the capital, which delves into Tokyo's neighbourhoods, uncovering some fascinating stories in the process.

Guides and reference books

Jude Band, *Tokyo Night City* (Tuttle). Hip, streetwise guide to the capital's hot nightspots. Out of date, but still worth a gander for the attitude-shot writing.

Anne Hotta with Yoko Ishiguro, *A Guide to Japanese Hot Springs* (Kodansha). Over 160 *onsen*, including 25 within easy reach of Tokyo, are detailed in this indispensable guide for bath lovers, as well as the cultural history of natural hot water pursuits in Japan.

Thomas F Judge and Tomita Hiroyuki, *Edo Craftsmen* (Weatherhill). Beautifully produced portraits of some of Shitamachi's traditional craftsmen still working in the backstreets of Tokyo. A timely insight into a disappearing world.

John & Phyllis Martin, *Tokyo: A Cultural Guide to Japan's Capital City* (Tuttle). Informative guide designed around short walking tours of the capital.

Robb Satterwhite, *What's What in Japanese Restaurants* (Kodansha). Handy guide to all things culinary you'll encounter during your adventures in Japanese food and drink. The menus annotated with Japanese characters are particularly useful.

Enbutsu Sumiko, *Old Tokyo: Walks in the City of the Shogun* (Kodansha). Tokyo's old Shitamachi area is best explored on foot and Sumiko's guide, illustrated with block prints, helps bring the area's history alive.

Noriyuki Tajima, *Tokyo: A Guide to Recent Architecture* (Ellipsis). Compact, expertly written and nicely illustrated book that's an essential accompaniment on any modern architectural tour of the capital.

TokyoQ, *Annual Guide to the city* (Stonebridge Press). Spin off from the fine Web site, this handy slim volume is worth picking up for those extra titbits of info that only living in the city for eons gives you.

Japanese fiction

Alfred Birnbaum (ed), *Monkey Brain Sushi* (Kodansha). Eleven often quirky short stories by contemporary Japanese authors. A good introduction to modern prose writers.

Kawabata Yasunari, *Snow Country*; *The Izu Dancer*, etc (Tuttle). Japan's first Nobel Prize winner for fiction writes intense tales of passion usually about a sophisticated urban man falling for a simple country girl.

Mishima Yukio, *After the Banquet*; *Confessions of Mask*; *Forbidden Colours*; *The Sea of Fertility*, etc (Penguin/ Kodansha). Novelist Mishima sealed his notoriety by committing ritual suicide after leading a failed military coup in 1970. He left behind some of Japan's finest post-war novels. Themes of tradition, sexuality and militarism run through many of his works.

Miyuki Miyabe, *All She Was Worth* (Kodansha). When a young man's fiancée goes missing, a trail of credit-card debts and worse turns up. Clever whodunit set in contemporary Tokyo.

Murakami Haruki, *Underground*, *Norwegian Wood*, etc (Harvill).
One of Japan's greatest living novelists. See box, p.361.

Murakami Ryu, *Almost Transparent Blue*; *Sixty-nine* and *Coin Locker Babies* (Kodansha). Ryu is among the most feted of contemporary Japanese writers. *Almost Transparent Blue* is a tale of student life mixing reality and fantasy. *Sixty-nine* is Ryu's semi-autobiographical account of rebellious teenage passions of the late 1960s. *Coin Locker Babies* spins a tragedy about two boys dumped in adjacent coin lockers as babies.

Oe Kenzaburo, *Nip the Buds Shoot the Kids* (Kodansha); *A Personal Matter* (Tuttle); *A Healing Family* (Kodansha). Oe won Japan's second Nobel Prize for literature in 1994. *Nip the Buds* is a tale of lost innocence; *A Personal Matter* tackles the trauma of his disabled son, while *A Healing Family* catches up with Hikari thirty years later, documenting his trials and triumphs. Never an easy read, but always startlingly honest.

Yoshimoto Banana, *Kitchen*, *Lizard* and *Amrita* (Faber & Faber). Trendy (and somewhat overrated) thirty-something novelist whose quirky, lyrical style and odd stories have struck a chord with modern Japanese youth and overseas readers.

Japan in foreign fiction

Alan Brown, *Audrey Hepburn's Neck* (Sceptre). Beneath this tale of a young guy from the sticks adrift in big-city Tokyo, Brown weaves important themes, including the continuing impact of World War II and the confused relationships between the Japanese and *gaijin*. An evocative, enchanting fable of contemporary Japan.

James Clavell, *Shogun* (Dell). Blockbuster fictionalized account of Englishman Will Adams' life in seventeenth–century Japan as an adviser to Shogun Tokugawa Ieyasu.

Ian Fleming, *You Only Live Twice* (Pan). Bondo-san on the

MURAKAMI HARUKI

Conspiracies, suicidal women, futile love, disappearing elephants and talking sheep all feature in the wildly popular work of **Murakami Haruki**, one of the most entertaining Japanese writers around. Hailed as a post-war successor to the great novelists Mishima, Kawabata and Tanizaki, in 21 years he has published over a dozen novels, including the most recent, *Underground* (Harvill), a study of the 1995 Tokyo subway gas attack. Translated into some 30 languages, Murakami is being talked of as a future Nobel Prize laureate, yet the 51-year-old writer and marathon runner shuns the media spotlight and is happy that few people recognize him.

Many of Murakami's books are set in Tokyo, drawing on his time at Waseda University in the early 1970s and running his own jazz bar in Kokubunji, which became a haunt for literary types and, no-doubt, provided inspiration for his jazz-bar running hero in the bittersweet novella *South of the Border, West of the Sun*. He's back in Tokyo now, after spending large parts of his career abroad, including five years teaching in the US. The contemporary edge to Murakami's writing, which eschews the traditional cliches of Japanese literature, has been fuelled by his translation work of books by John Irving, Raymond Carver, Truman Capote and Paul Theroux among others.

A good introduction to Murakami is *Norwegian Wood* (Harvill), a tender coming-of-age love story between two students that has sold over five million copies. The truly bizarre *A Wild Sheep Chase* and its follow-up *Dance Dance Dance* (both Harvill/Kodansha) are funny but disturbing modern-day fables, dressed up as detective novels. His best book is considered to be *The Wind-Up Bird Chronicle* (Harvill), a hefty yet dazzling cocktail of mystery, war reportage and philosophy.

trail of arch-enemy Blofeld in trendy mid-Sixties' Tokyo and the wilds of Kyūshū, assisted by Tiger Tanaka and Kissy Suzuki.

William Gibson, *Idoru* (Penguin). Love in the age of the computer chip. Cyberpunk novelist Gibson's sci-fi vision of Tokyo's high-tech future – a world of non-intrusive DNA checks at airports and computerized pop icons (the *idoru* of the title) – rings disturbingly true.

Dianne Highbridge, *In the Empire of Dreams* (Allen & Unwin). In this series of loosely connected short stories, Australian Highbridge focuses on the experiences of young women – all, bar one, ex-pats like the author – attempting to make a life in Japan. Evocative descriptions and some insights, but few surprises as Highland ticks off the issues from mixed marriages to the *gaijin* who find it impossible to leave.

Gavin Kramer, *Shopping* (Fourth Estate). British lawyer Kramer's zippy first novel is on the bleak side, but captures the turn-of-Millennium zeitgeist of Tokyo, where schoolgirls trade sex for designer labels and *gaijin* flounder in a sea of misunderstanding.

John David Morley, *Pictures from the Water Trade* (Flamingo). The sub-title, *An Englishman in Japan*, says it all as Morley's alter ego Boon crashes headlong into an intense relationship with demure, yet sultry Mariko in an oh-so-foreign world. Along the way, some imaginative observations and descriptions are made.

Peter Tasker, *Silent Thunder* (Orion/Tuttle). Top British financial analyst Tasker's first stab at fiction is a fun, throwaway thriller, with Bond-like set pieces and some lively Japanese characters, especially Mori, his down-at-heal gumshoe. Much better than the follow-up *Buddha Kiss*, although Tasker seems to have found his form again with his latest snappy read *Samurai Boogie*.

Glossary of Japanese terms

banzai Traditional Japanese cheer, meaning "10,000 years".

bashi Bridge.

basho Sumo tournament.

bodhisattva Buddhist who has forsaken *nirvana* to work for the salvation of all humanity.

-cho, or **machi** Subdivision of the city, smaller than a *ku*.

-chome Area of the city consisting of a few blocks.

dai Big or great.

daimyo Feudal lords.

-dori Main road.

Edo Pre-1868 name for Tokyo.

gaijin Foreigner.

gawa River.

geisha Traditional female entertainer accomplished in the arts.

geta Wooden sandals.

higashi East.

-ji Buddhist temple.

-jingu, or **-jinja** Shinto shrine.

Jizo Buddhist protector of children, travellers and the dead.

-jo Castle.

kampai "Cheers" when drinking.

kanji Japanese script derived from Chinese characters.

Kannon Buddhist Goddess of Mercy.

katakana Phonetic script used mainly for writing foreign words in Japanese.

kimono Literally "clothes" but usually referring to women's traditional dress.

kita North.

koban Local police box.

-koen/gyoen Public park.

-ku Principal administrative division of the city, usually translated as "ward".

matsuri Festival.

Meiji Period named after the Emperor Meiji (1868–1912).

mikoshi Portable shrine used in festivals.

minami South.

minshuku family-run lodge, similar to a bed-and-breakfast, cheaper than a *ryokan*.

mon Gate.

netsuke Small, intricately carved toggles for fastening the cords of cloth bags.

nishi West.

noren Split curtain hanging in shop and restaurant doorways.

obi Wide sash worn with kimono.

okanshi Japanese sweets.

onsen Hot spring, generally developed for bathing.

pachinko Vertical pinball machines.

ronin Masterless samurai.

ryokan Traditional Japanese inn.

samurai Warrior class who were retainers of the *daimyo*.

sento Neighbourhood public bath.

Shinkansen Bullet train.

Shinto Japan's indigenous religion, based on the premise that gods inhabit all natural things, both animate and inanimate.

Shitamachi Low-lying, working-class districts of east Tokyo, nowadays usually referring to Asakusa and Ueno.

shogun The military rulers of Japan before 1868.

shoji Paper-covered sliding screens used to divide rooms or cover windows.

soaplands a brothel.

sumi-e Ink paintings.

sumo Japan's national sport, a form of heavy-weight wrestling which evolved from ancient Shinto divination rites.

tatami Rice-straw matting, the traditional covering for floors.

-tera/-dera Buddhist temple.

torii Gate to a Shinto shrine.

ukiyo-e "Pictures of the floating world", colourful woodblock prints which became particularly popular in the late eighteenth century.

washi Japanese paper.

yakuza Professional criminal gangs.

yukata Loose cotton robe worn as a dressing gown in a *ryokan*.

INDEX

A

B

C

D

E

F

G

L

M

N

O

P

R

S

V

W

Y

Z

ROUGH GUIDES: Travel

Drum 'n' bass
THE ROUGH GUIDE
THE ROUGH GUIDE TO
Hip-hop
Techno
THE ROUGH GUIDE
Electronica
House
THE ROUGH GUIDE

100
Essential
CDs
Eight titles,
one name
ROUGH
GUIDES

Will you have enough stories to tell your grandchildren?
©2000 Yahoo! Inc.
Yahoo! Travel
Do You Yahoo!?

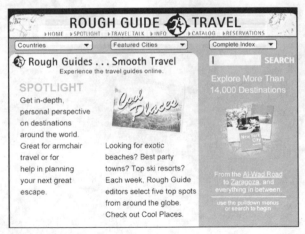

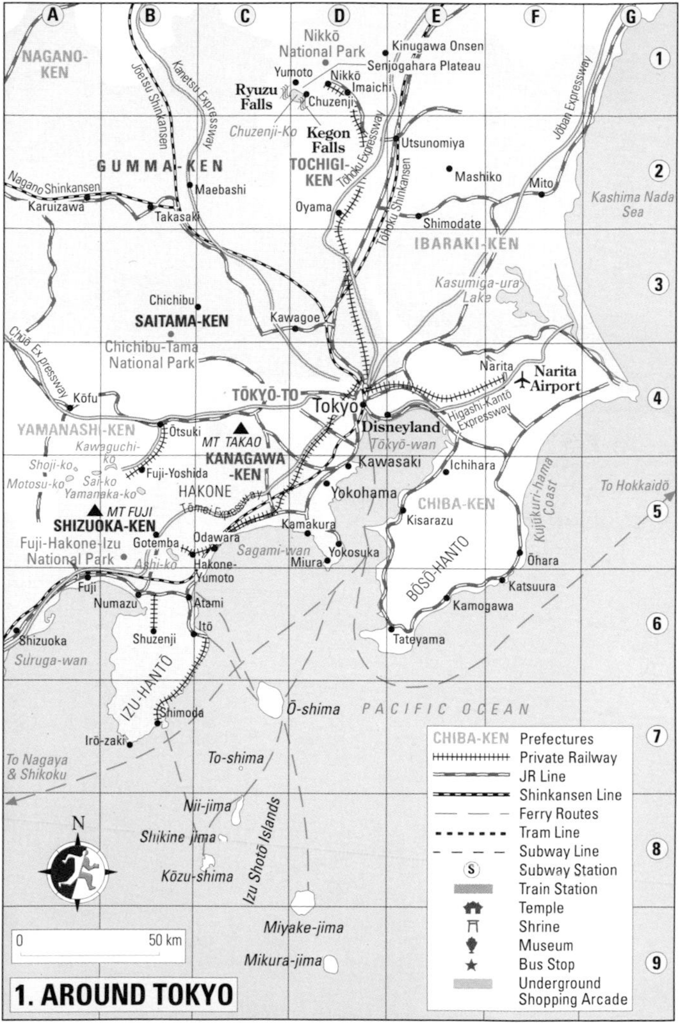
A
B
C
D
E
F
G
1
2
3
4
5
6
7
8
9
NAGANO-KEN
Nikkō National Park
Kinugawa Onsen
Senjogahara Plateau
Yumoto
Nikkō
Imaichi
Ryuzu Falls
Chuzenji
Chuzenji-Ko
Kegon Falls
Joetsu Shinkansen
Kanetsu Expressway
Tōhoku Expressway
Jōban Expressway
Utsunomiya
GUMMA-KEN
TOCHIGI-KEN
Mashiko
Mito
Kashima Nada Sea
Nagano Shinkansen
Maebashi
Karuizawa
Takasaki
Oyama
Tōhoku Shinkansen
Shimodate
IBARAKI-KEN
Kasumiga-ura Lake
Chichibu
SAITAMA-KEN
Kawagoe
Chichibu-Tama National Park
Chūō Expressway
Narita
Narita Airport
Kōfu
TŌKYŌ-TO
Tokyo
Higashi-Kantō Expressway
YAMANASHI-KEN
Ōtsuki
MT TAKAO
Disneyland
Tōkyō-wan
Kawaguchi-ko
Shoji-ko
KANAGAWA-KEN
Kawasaki
Ichihara
Fuji-Yoshida
Motosu-ko
Sai-ko
Yamanaka-ko
HAKONE
Yokohama
CHIBA-KEN
Kujūkuri-hama Coast
To Hokkaidō
MT FUJI
Tōmei Expressway
Kisarazu
SHIZUOKA-KEN
Kamakura
Fuji-Hakone-Izu National Park
Gotemba
Odawara
Sagami-wan
Yokosuka
BŌSŌ-HANTO
Ōhara
Ashi-ko
Miura
Hakone-Yumoto
Fuji
Katsuura
Numazu
Atami
Kamogawa
Itō
Shizuoka
Shuzenji
Tateyama
Suruga-wan
IZU-HANTŌ
Ō-shima
PACIFIC OCEAN
Shimoda
Irō-zaki
To Nagaya & Shikoku
To-shima
Nii-jima
Shikine jima
Kōzu-shima
Izu Shotō Islands
Miyake-jima
Mikura-jima
N
0
50 km
CHIBA-KEN Prefectures
Private Railway
JR Line
Shinkansen Line
Ferry Routes
Tram Line
Subway Line
S Subway Station
Train Station
Temple
Shrine
Museum
Bus Stop
Underground Shopping Arcade

1. AROUND TOKYO

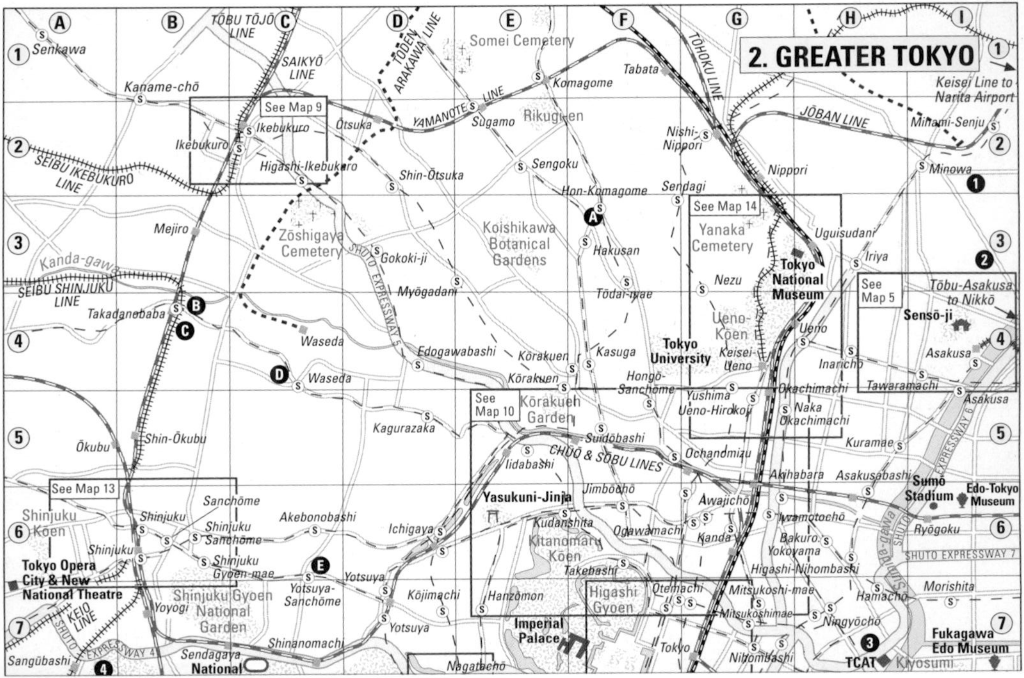
2. GREATER TOKYO
Keisei Line to Narita Airport
Tōbu-Asakusa to Nikkō
See Map 9
See Map 14
See Map 5
See Map 10
See Map 13
TŌBU TŌJŌ LINE
SAIKYŌ LINE
TODEN ARAKAWA LINE
YAMANOTE LINE
TŌHOKU LINE
JŌBAN LINE
SEIBU IKEBUKURO LINE
SEIBU SHINJUKU LINE
CHŪŌ & SŌBU LINES
KEIO LINE
SHUTO EXPRESSWAY 5
SHUTO EXPRESSWAY 4
SHUTO EXPRESSWAY 6
SHUTO EXPRESSWAY 7
Senkawa
Kaname-chō
Ikebukuro
Higashi-Ikebukuro
Ōtsuka
Shin-Ōtsuka
Sugamo
Komagome
Tabata
Nishi-Nippori
Nippori
Minami-Senju
Minowa
Sengoku
Hon-Komagome
Sendagi
Mejiro
Zōshigaya Cemetery
Somei Cemetery
Rikugi-en
Koishikawa Botanical Gardens
Hakusan
Yanaka Cemetery
Uguisudani
Iriya
Tokyo National Museum
Sensō-ji
Kanda-gawa
Gokoki-ji
Myōgadani
Tōdai-mae
Nezu
Takadanobaba
Waseda
Edogawabashi
Kōrakuen
Kasuga
Tokyo University
Ueno-Kōen
Keisei-Ueno
Ueno
Inaricho
Asakusa
Tawaramachi
Hongō-Sanchōme
Yushima
Ueno-Hirokoji
Okachimachi
Naka Okachimachi
Kōrakuen Garden
Kagurazaka
Suidōbashi
Ochanomizu
Kuramae
Ōkubu
Shin-Ōkubu
Iidabashi
Akihabara
Asakusabashi
Sumō Stadium
Edo-Tokyo Museum
Yasukuni-Jinja
Jimbōchō
Awajichō
Iwamotochō
Ryōgoku
Sumida-gawa
Shinjuku Kōen
Shinjuku
Sanchōme
Shinjuku Sanchōme
Akebonobashi
Ichigaya
Kudanshita
Ogawamachi
Kanda
Bakuro
Yokoyama
Kitanomaru Kōen
Tokyo Opera City & New National Theatre
Shinjuku Gyoen-mae
Yotsuya
Takebashi
Higashi-Nihombashi
Morishita
Yotsuya-Sanchōme
Kōjimachi
Hanzōmon
Higashi Gyoen
Otemachi
Mitsukoshi-mae
Hamachō
Shinjuku Gyoen National Garden
Yoyogi
Mitsukoshimae
Ningyōchō
Imperial Palace
Shinanomachi
Tokyo
Fukagawa Edo Museum
Sangūbashi
Sendagaya
National
Nagatachō
Nihombashi
TCAT
Kiyosumi

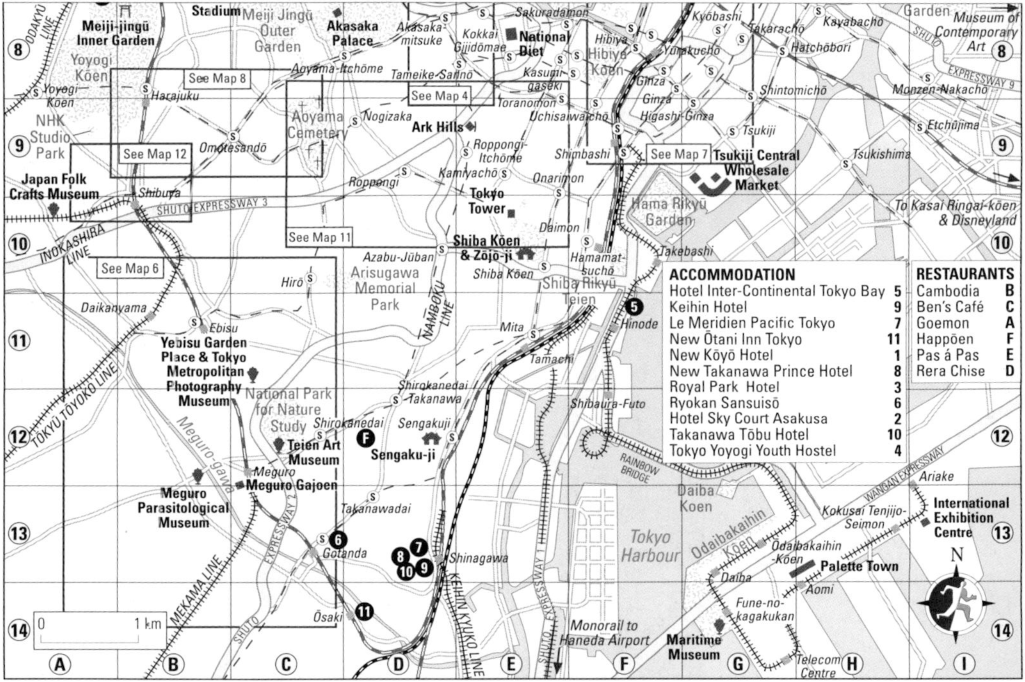
ACCOMMODATION
Hotel Inter-Continental Tokyo Bay 5
Keihin Hotel 9
Le Meridien Pacific Tokyo 7
New Ōtani Inn Tokyo 11
New Kōyō Hotel 1
New Takanawa Prince Hotel 8
Royal Park Hotel 3
Ryokan Sansuisō 6
Hotel Sky Court Asakusa 2
Takanawa Tōbu Hotel 10
Tokyo Yoyogi Youth Hostel 4
RESTAURANTS
Cambodia B
Ben's Café C
Goemon A
Happōen F
Pas á Pas E
Rera Chise D
Meiji-jingū Inner Garden
Stadium
Meiji Jingū Outer Garden
Akasaka Palace
National Diet
Museum of Contemporary Art
Yoyogi Kōen
NHK Studio Park
Japan Folk Crafts Museum
See Map 8
See Map 4
See Map 12
See Map 11
See Map 6
See Map 7
Aoyama Cemetery
Ark Hills
Tokyo Tower
Shiba Kōen & Zōjō-ji
Tsukiji Central Wholesale Market
Hama Rikyū Garden
To Kasai Ringai-kōen & Disneyland
Arisugawa Memorial Park
Shiba Rikyū Teien
Yebisu Garden Place & Tokyo Metropolitan Photography Museum
National Park for Nature Study
Teien Art Museum
Sengaku-ji
Meguro Gajoen
Meguro Parasitological Museum
Tokyo Harbour
Daiba Koen
Odaibakaihin Kōen
Rainbow Bridge
International Exhibition Centre
Palette Town
Maritime Museum
Monorail to Haneda Airport
Meguro-gawa
Odakyū Line
Inokashira Line
Tōkyū Tōyoko Line
Mekama Line
Namboku Line
Keihin Kyuko Line
Shuto Expressway 3
Shuto Expressway 2
Shuto Expressway 1
Shuto Expressway 9
Wangan Expressway
Yoyogi-Kōen
Harajuku
Omotesandō
Shibuya
Aoyama-Itchōme
Nogizaka
Akasaka-mitsuke
Tameike-Sannō
Kokkai Gijidōmae
Sakuradamon
Kasumigaseki
Toranomon
Uchisaiwaichō
Roppongi
Roppongi-Itchōme
Kamiyachō
Onarimon
Daimon
Azabu-Jūban
Shiba Kōen
Hamamatsuchō
Shimbashi
Hibiya
Yūrakuchō
Ginza
Higashi-Ginza
Kyōbashi
Takarachō
Kayabachō
Hatchōbori
Shintomichō
Tsukiji
Monzen-Nakachō
Etchūjima
Tsukishima
Takebashi
Hinode
Mita
Tamachi
Shibaura-Futo
Hirō
Daikanyama
Ebisu
Shirokanedai
Shirokanedai Takanawa
Sengakuji
Meguro
Takanawadai
Gotanda
Shinagawa
Ōsaki
Ariake
Kokusai Tenjijo-Seimon
Odaibakaihin-Kōen
Daiba
Aomi
Fune-no-kagakukan
Telecom Centre
N
0 1 km
A B C D E F G H I
8 9 10 11 12 13 14

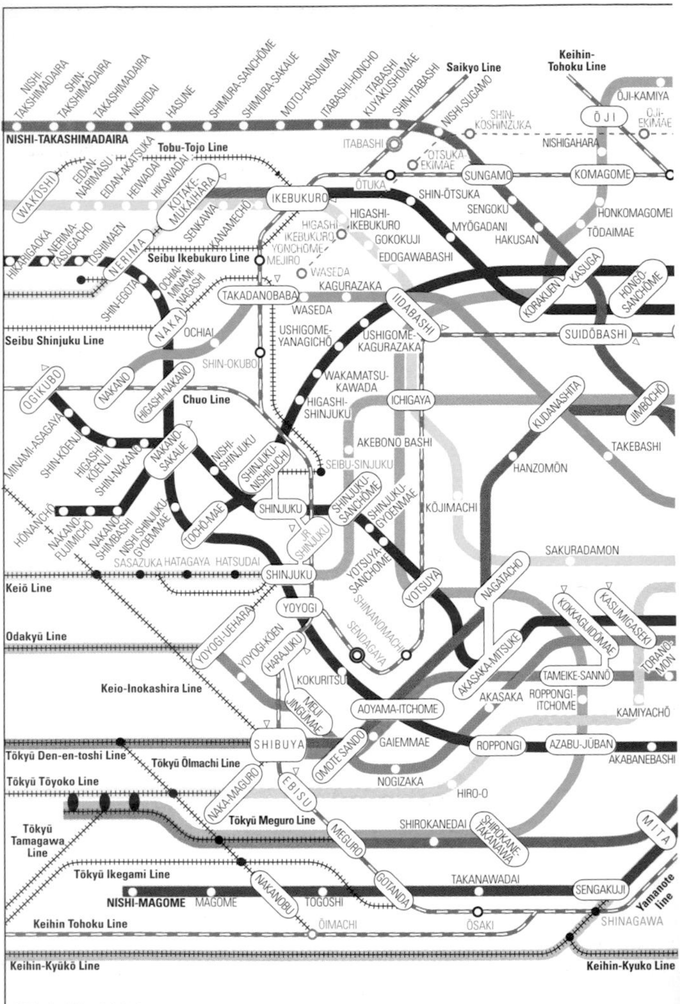
NISHI-TAKASHIMADAIRA
SHIN-TAKASHIMADAIRA
TAKASHIMADAIRA
NISHIDAI
HASUNE
SHIMURA-SANCHŌME
SHIMURA-SAKAUE
MOTO-HASUNUMA
ITABASHI-HONCHO
ITABASHI KUYAKUSHOMAE
SHIN-ITABASHI
Saikyo Line
NISHI-SUGAMO
Keihin-Tohoku Line
ŌJI-KAMIYA
SHIN-KOSHINZUKA
ŌJI
ŌJI-EKIMAE
NISHI-TAKASHIMADAIRA
Tobu-Tojo Line
ITABASHI
OTSUKA-EKIMAE
NISHIGAHARA
WAKŌSHI
EIDAN-NARIMASU
EIDAN-AKATSUKA
HEIWADAI
HIKAWADAI
KOTAKE-MUKAIHARA
ŌTUKA
SUNGAMO
KOMAGOME
IKEBUKURO
SHIN-ŌTSUKA
SENGOKU
HONKOMAGOMEI
SENKAWA
KANAMECHŌ
HIGASHI-IKEBUKURO
MYŌGADANI
HAKUSAN
TŌDAIMAE
HIKARIGAOKA
NERIMA-KASUGACHO
TOSHIMAEN
NERIMA
HIGASHI-IKEBUKURO YONCHOME
GOKOKUJI
Seibu Ikebukuro Line
MEJIRO
EDOGAWABASHI
KASUGA
KORAKUEN
HONGŌ-SANCHŌME
SHIN-EGOTA
OCHIAI-MINAMI-NAGASHI
WASEDA
TAKADANOBABA
KAGURAZAKA
IIDABASHI
WASEDA
NAKAI
USHIGOME-YANAGICHŌ
USHIGOME-KAGURAZAKA
SUIDŌBASHI
OCHIAI
Seibu Shinjuku Line
SHIN-OKUBO
OGIKUBO
NAKANO
HIGASHI-NAKANO
WAKAMATSU-KAWADA
Chuo Line
HIGASHI-SHINJUKU
ICHIGAYA
KUDANASHITA
JIMBŌCHŌ
MINAMI-ASAGAYA
SHIN-KŌENJI
HIGASHI-KŌENJI
SHIN-NAKANO
NAKANO-SAKAUE
NISHI-SHINJUKU
SHINJUKU-NISHIGUCHI
AKEBONO BASHI
TAKEBASHI
SEIBU-SINJUKU
HANZOMŌN
SHINJUKU
SHINJUKU-SANCHŌME
SHINJUKU-GYOENMAE
KŌJIMACHI
HŌNANCHŌ
NAKANO-FUJIMICHŌ
NAKANO-SHIMBASHI
NISHI SHINJUKU GYOENMAE
TOCHŌ-MAE
JR SHINJUKU
SASAZUKA
HATAGAYA
HATSUDAI
SHINJUKU
YOTSUYA-SANCHOME
YOTSUYA
SAKURADAMON
Keiō Line
SHINANOMACHI
NAGATACHO
YOYOGI
KOKKAGIJIDŌMAE
KASUMIGASEKI
Odakyū Line
YOYOGI-UEHARA
YOYOGI-KŌEN
HARAJUKU
SENDAGAYA
AKASAKA-MITSUKE
TORANOMON
TAMEIKE-SANNŌ
Keio-Inokashira Line
KOKURITSU
MEIJI JINGUMAE
AOYAMA-ITCHOME
AKASAKA
ROPPONGI-ITCHOME
KAMIYACHŌ
SHIBUYA
OMOTE SANDO
GAIEMMAE
ROPPONGI
AZABU-JŪBAN
AKABANEBASHI
Tōkyū Den-en-toshi Line
Tōkyū Ōimachi Line
Tōkyū Tōyoko Line
NAKA-MAGURO
EBISU
NOGIZAKA
HIRO-O
Tōkyū Meguro Line
SHIROKANEDAI
SHIROKANE-TAKANAWA
MITA
Tōkyū Tamagawa Line
MEGURO
Tōkyū Ikegami Line
NAKANOBU
GOTANDA
TAKANAWADAI
SENGAKUJI
Yamanote line
NISHI-MAGOME
MAGOME
TOGOSHI
Keihin Tohoku Line
ŌIMACHI
ŌSAKI
SHINAGAWA
Keihin-Kyūkō Line
Keihin-Kyuko Line

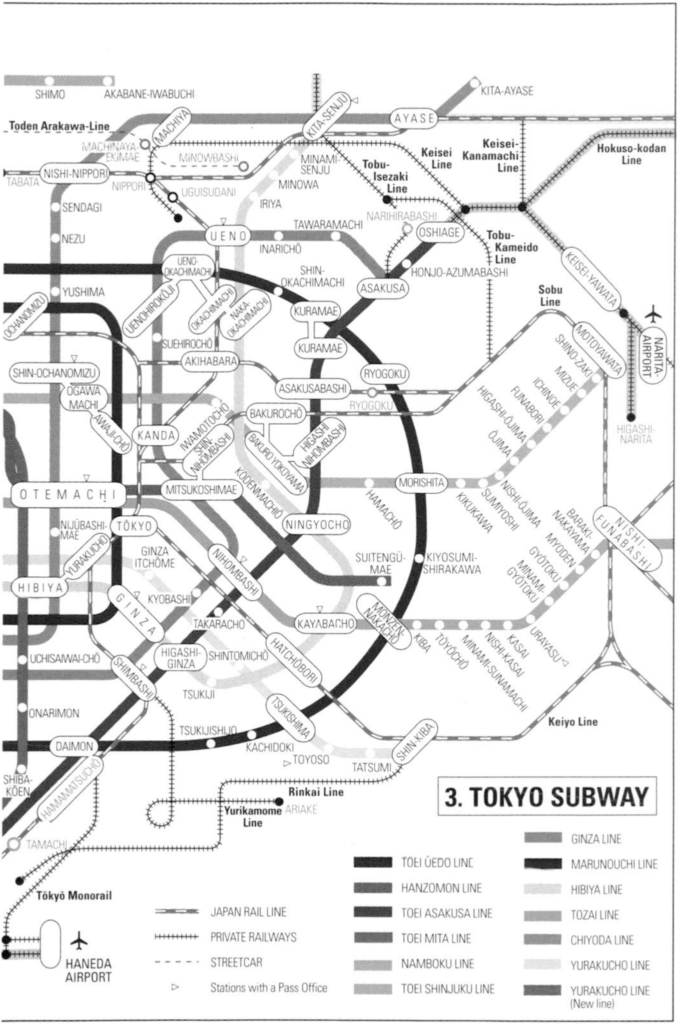
3. TOKYO SUBWAY
SHIMO
AKABANE-IWABUCHI
KITA-AYASE
Toden Arakawa-Line
MACHIYA
KITA-SENJU
AYASE
MACHINAYA-EKIMAE
MINOWBASHI
MINAMI-SENJU
Keisei Line
Keisei-Kanamachi Line
Hokuso-kodan Line
TABATA
NISHI-NIPPORI
NIPPORI
UGUISUDANI
MINOWA
Tobu-Isezaki Line
SENDAGI
IRIYA
NARIHIRABASHI
NEZU
UENO
TAWARAMACHI
OSHIAGE
Tobu-Kameido Line
INARICHŌ
UENO-OKACHIMACHI
SHIN-OKACHIMACHI
HONJO-AZUMABASHI
KEISEI-YAWATA
YUSHIMA
ASAKUSA
Sobu Line
OCHANOMIZU
UENOHIROKŌJI
OKACHIMACHI
NAKA-OKACHIMACHI
KURAMAE
NARITA-AIRPORT
MOTOYAWATA
SUEHIROCHŌ
KURAMAE
SHINO-ZAKI
AKIHABARA
RYOGOKU
MIZUE
SHIN-OCHANOMIZU
ASAKUSABASHI
ICHINOE
OGAWA MACHI
RYOGOKU
FUNABORI
HIGASHI-ŌJIMA
AWAJI-CHŌ
BAKUROCHŌ
HIGASHI-NARITA
KANDA
IWAMOTOCHŌ
ŌJIMA
SHIN-NIHOMBASHI
BAKURO YOKOYAMA
HIGASHI NIHOMBASHI
OTEMACHI
MITSUKOSHIMAE
KODENMACHŌ
MORISHITA
NISHI-ŌJIMA
HAMACHŌ
KIKUKAWA
SUMIYOSHI
NIJŪBASHI-MAE
TŌKYŌ
NINGYOCHO
BARAKI-NAKAYAMA
NISHI-FUNABASHI
MYODEN
YURAKUCHO
GINZA ITCHŌME
NIHOMBASHI
SUITENGŪ-MAE
KIYOSUMI-SHIRAKAWA
GYŌTOKU
MINAMI-GYŌTOKU
HIBIYA
GINZA
KYOBASHI
MONZEN-NAKACHO
TAKARACHO
KAYABACHO
KIBA
TŌYŌCHŌ
MINAMI-SUNAMACHI
NISHI-KASAI
KASAI
URAYASU
UCHISAIWAI-CHŌ
HIGASHI-GINZA
SHINTOMICHŌ
HATCHŌBORI
SHIMBASHI
TSUKIJI
ONARIMON
TSUKISHIMA
Keiyo Line
TSUKIJISHIJO
DAIMON
KACHIDOKI
SHIN-KIBA
TOYOSO
TATSUMI
SHIBA-KŌEN
HAMAMATSUCHŌ
Rinkai Line
Yurikamome Line
ARIAKE
TAMACHI
Tōkyō Monorail
HANEDA AIRPORT
JAPAN RAIL LINE
PRIVATE RAILWAYS
STREETCAR
Stations with a Pass Office
TOEI ŪEDO LINE
HANZOMON LINE
TOEI ASAKUSA LINE
TOEI MITA LINE
NAMBOKU LINE
TOEI SHINJUKU LINE
GINZA LINE
MARUNOUCHI LINE
HIBIYA LINE
TOZAI LINE
CHIYODA LINE
YURAKUCHO LINE
YURAKUCHO LINE (New line)

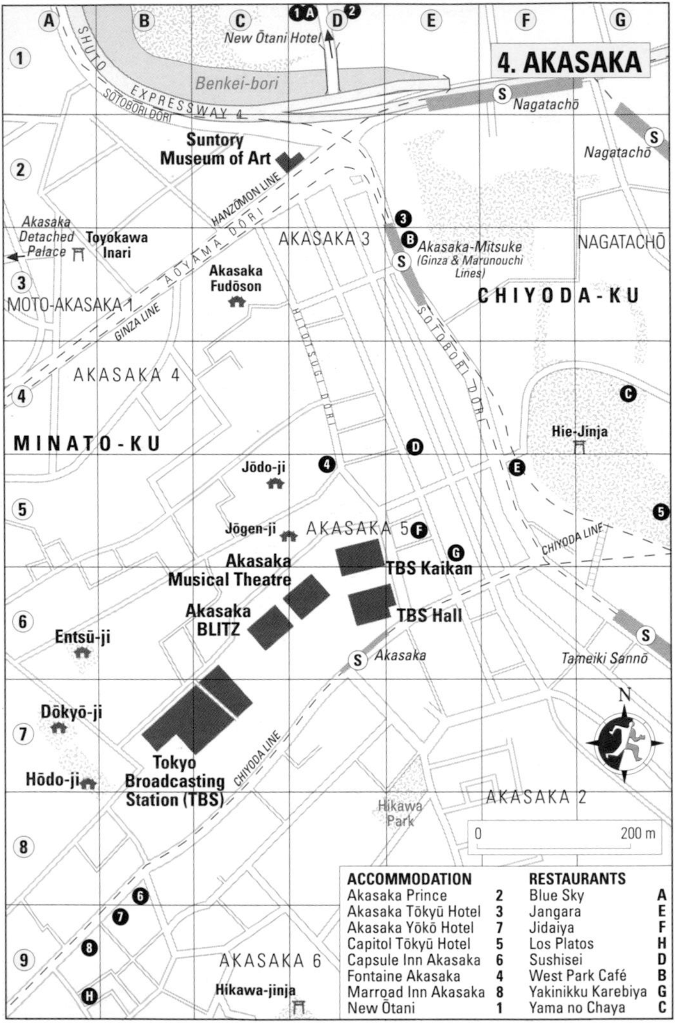

ACCOMMODATION		RESTAURANTS	
Akasaka Prince	2	Blue Sky	A
Akasaka Tōkyū Hotel	3	Jangara	E
Akasaka Yōkō Hotel	7	Jidaiya	F
Capitol Tōkyū Hotel	5	Los Platos	H
Capsule Inn Akasaka	6	Sushisei	D
Fontaine Akasaka	4	West Park Café	B
Marroad Inn Akasaka	8	Yakinikku Karebiya	G
New Ōtani	1	Yama no Chaya	C

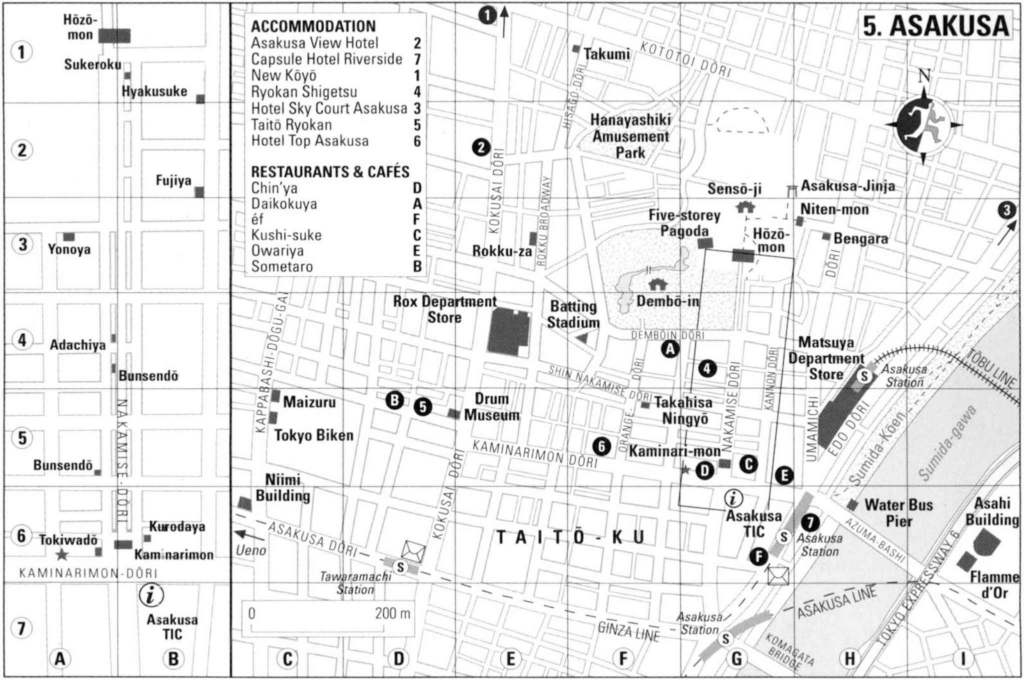
5. ASAKUSA
ACCOMMODATION
Asakusa View Hotel 2
Capsule Hotel Riverside 7
New Kōyō 1
Ryokan Shigetsu 4
Hotel Sky Court Asakusa 3
Taitō Ryokan 5
Hotel Top Asakusa 6
RESTAURANTS & CAFÉS
Chin'ya D
Daikokuya A
éf F
Kushi-suke C
Owariya E
Sometaro B
Hōzō-mon
Sukeroku
Hyakusuke
Fujiya
Yonoya
Adachiya
Bunsendō
Bunsendō
NAKAMISE-DŌRI
Tokiwadō
Kurodaya
Kaminarimon
KAMINARIMON-DŌRI
Asakusa TIC
Takumi
KOTOTOI DŌRI
HISAGO-DŌRI
Hanayashiki Amusement Park
KOKUSAI DŌRI
ROKKU BROADWAY
Rokku-za
Sensō-ji
Asakusa-Jinja
Niten-mon
Five-storey Pagoda
Hōzō-mon
Bengara
DŌRI
Dembō-in
Rox Department Store
Batting Stadium
DEMBOIN DŌRI
Matsuya Department Store
Asakusa Station
TŌBU LINE
KAPPABASHI-DŌGU-GAI
SHIN NAKAMISE DŌRI
DŌRI
Takahisa Ningyō
NAKAMISE DŌRI
KANNON DŌRI
UMAMICHI
EDO DŌRI
Sumida-Koen
Sumida-gawa
Maizuru
Tokyo Biken
Drum Museum
KAMINARIMON DŌRI
ORANGE
Kaminari-mon
Niimi Building
ASAKUSA DŌRI
Ueno
KOKUSAI DŌRI
Tawaramachi Station
TAITŌ-KU
Asakusa TIC
Asakusa Station
Water Bus Pier
AZUMA-BASHI
TOKYO EXPRESSWAY 6
Asahi Building
Flamme d'Or
ASAKUSA LINE
GINZA LINE
Asakusa Station
KOMAGATA BRIDGE
0
200 m
N

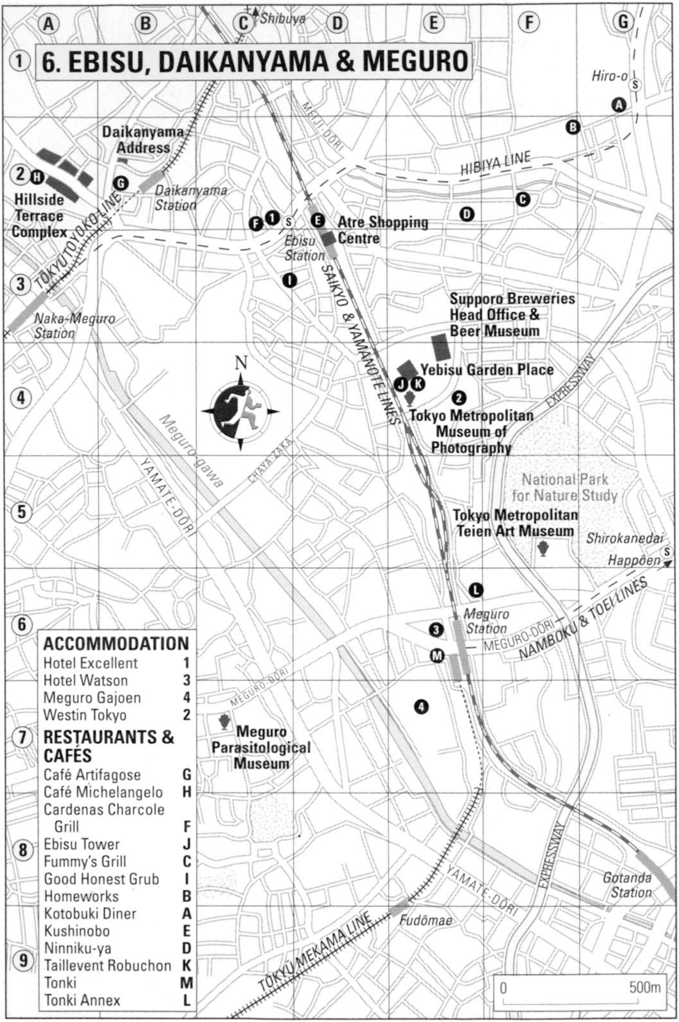
6. EBISU, DAIKANYAMA & MEGURO
A
B
C
D
E
F
G
1
2
3
4
5
6
7
8
9
Shibuya
Hiro-o
Daikanyama Address
Hillside Terrace Complex
Daikanyama Station
TŌKYŪ TOYOKO LINE
MEIJI-DŌRI
HIBIYA LINE
Atre Shopping Centre
Ebisu Station
SAIKYO & YAMANOTE LINES
Naka-Meguro Station
Supporo Breweries Head Office & Beer Museum
Yebisu Garden Place
Tokyo Metropolitan Museum of Photography
EXPRESSWAY
N
Meguro-gawa
CHAYA-ZAKA
YAMATE-DŌRI
National Park for Nature Study
Tokyo Metropolitan Teien Art Museum
Shirokanedai
Happōen
NAMBOKU & TOEI LINES
Meguro Station
MEGURO-DŌRI
Meguro Parasitological Museum
Gotanda Station
Fudōmae
TŌKYŪ MEKAMA LINE
0
500m
ACCOMMODATION
Hotel Excellent 1
Hotel Watson 3
Meguro Gajoen 4
Westin Tokyo 2
RESTAURANTS & CAFÉS
Café Artifagose G
Café Michelangelo H
Cardenas Charcole Grill F
Ebisu Tower J
Fummy's Grill C
Good Honest Grub I
Homeworks B
Kotobuki Diner A
Kushinobo E
Ninniku-ya D
Taillevent Robuchon K
Tonki M
Tonki Annex L

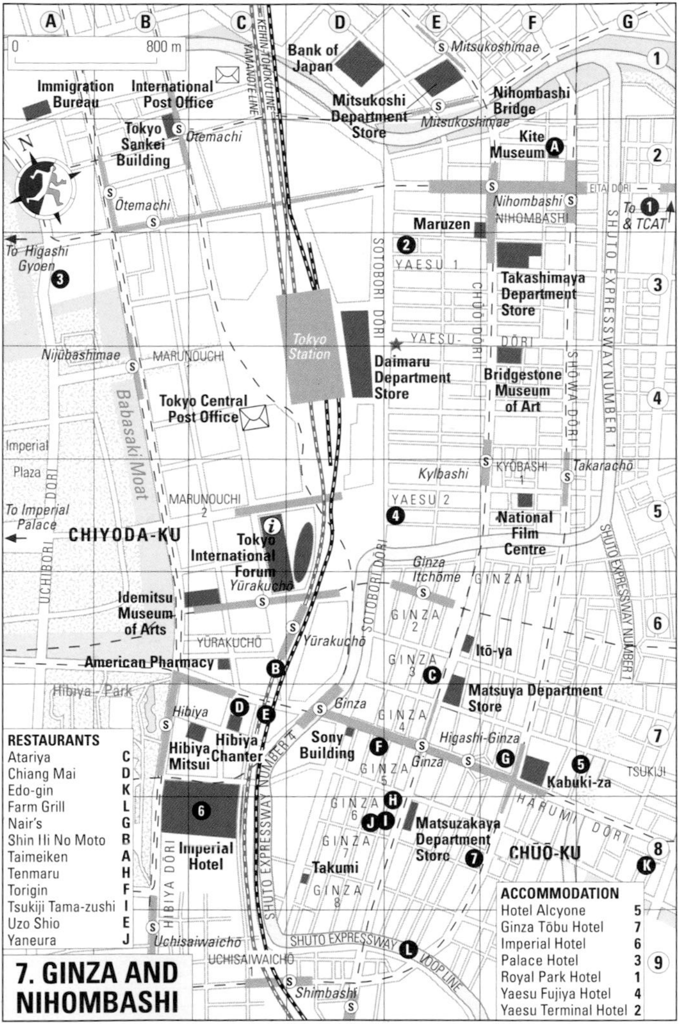
7. GINZA AND NIHOMBASHI
RESTAURANTS
Atariya C
Chiang Mai D
Edo-gin K
Farm Grill L
Nair's G
Shin Hi No Moto B
Taimeiken A
Tenmaru H
Torigin F
Tsukiji Tama-zushi I
Uzo Shio E
Yaneura J
ACCOMMODATION
Hotel Alcyone 5
Ginza Tōbu Hotel 7
Imperial Hotel 6
Palace Hotel 3
Royal Park Hotel 1
Yaesu Fujiya Hotel 4
Yaesu Terminal Hotel 2
0 800 m
Immigration Bureau
International Post Office
Tokyo Sankei Building
Ōtemachi
Bank of Japan
Mitsukoshi Department Store
Mitsukoshimae
Nihombashi Bridge
Kite Museum
EITAI DŌRI
Nihombashi
NIHOMBASHI
To & TCAT
Maruzen
YAESU 1
Takashimaya Department Store
SOTOBORI DŌRI
CHŪŌ DŌRI
YAESU-DŌRI
SHŌWA DŌRI
SHUTO EXPRESSWAY NUMBER 1
KEIHIN-TŌHOKU LINE
YAMANOTE LINE
To Higashi Gyoen
Tokyo Station
Daimaru Department Store
Bridgestone Museum of Art
Nijūbashimae
MARUNOUCHI
Babasaki Moat
Tokyo Central Post Office
Imperial Plaza
UCHIBORI DŌRI
Kylbashi
KYŌBASHI 1
Takarachō
MARUNOUCHI 2
YAESU 2
National Film Centre
To Imperial Palace
CHIYODA-KU
Tokyo International Forum
Yūrakuchō
Ginza Itchōme
GINZA 1
GINZA 2
GINZA 3
GINZA 4
GINZA 5
GINZA 6
GINZA 7
GINZA 8
Idemitsu Museum of Arts
YŪRAKUCHŌ
Itō-ya
American Pharmacy
Matsuya Department Store
Hibiya Park
Hibiya
Ginza
Sony Building
Higashi-Ginza
Hibiya Mitsui
Hibiya Chanter
Kabuki-za
TSUKIJI
HARUMI DŌRI
Imperial Hotel
Matsuzakaya Department Store
CHŪŌ-KU
Takumi
SHUTO EXPRESSWAY NUMBER 4
HIBIYA DŌRI
Uchisaiwaichō
UCHISAIWAICHŌ 1
SHUTO EXPRESSWAY LOOP LINE
Shimbashi

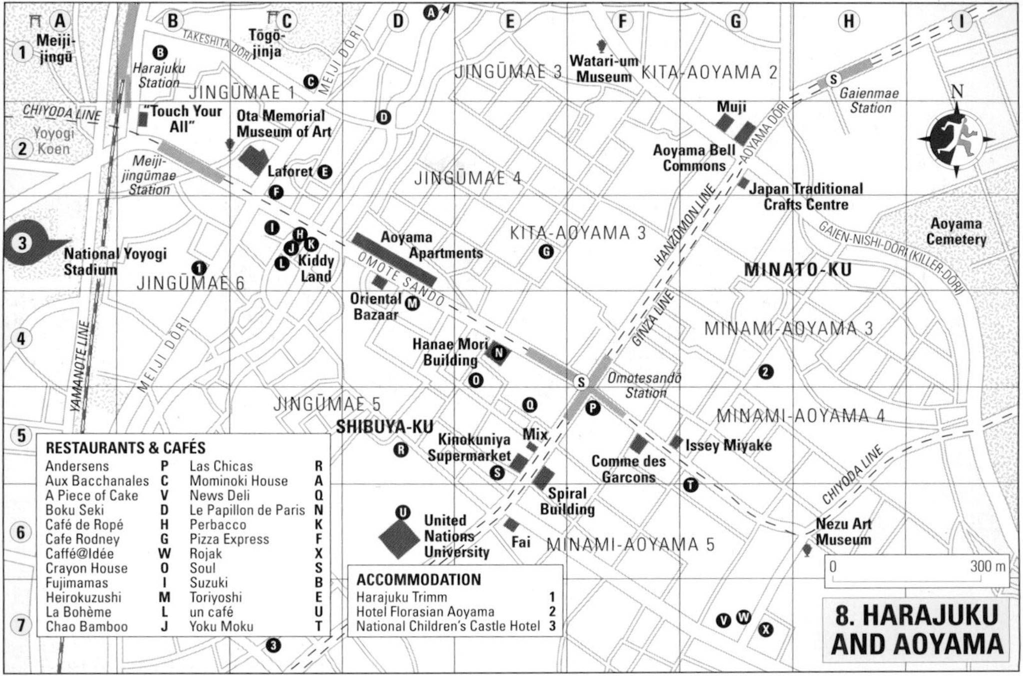
8. HARAJUKU AND AOYAMA
A B C D E F G H I
1 2 3 4 5 6 7
Meiji-jingū
Tōgō-jinja
Harajuku Station
TAKESHITA DŌRI
MEIJI DŌRI
JINGŪMAE 1
JINGŪMAE 3
JINGŪMAE 4
JINGŪMAE 5
JINGŪMAE 6
Watari-um Museum
KITA-AOYAMA 2
KITA-AOYAMA 3
Gaienmae Station
N
CHIYODA LINE
Yoyogi Koen
"Touch Your All"
Ota Memorial Museum of Art
Muji
Aoyama Bell Commons
AOYAMA DŌRI
Meiji-jingūmae Station
Laforet
Japan Traditional Crafts Centre
HANZŌMON LINE
GAIEN-NISHI-DŌRI (KILLER-DŌRI)
Aoyama Cemetery
National Yoyogi Stadium
Aoyama Apartments
Kiddy Land
OMOTE SANDŌ
MINATO-KU
Oriental Bazaar
GINZA LINE
MINAMI-AOYAMA 3
MINAMI-AOYAMA 4
MINAMI-AOYAMA 5
YAMANOTE LINE
Hanae Mori Building
Omotesandō Station
SHIBUYA-KU
Kinokuniya Supermarket
Mix
Issey Miyake
Comme des Garcons
Spiral Building
United Nations University
Fai
Nezu Art Museum
0 300 m
RESTAURANTS & CAFÉS
Andersens P
Aux Bacchanales C
A Piece of Cake V
Boku Seki D
Café de Ropé H
Cafe Rodney G
Caffé@Idée W
Crayon House O
Fujimamas I
Heirokuzushi M
La Bohème L
Chao Bamboo J
Las Chicas R
Mominoki House A
News Deli Q
Le Papillon de Paris N
Perbacco K
Pizza Express F
Rojak X
Soul S
Suzuki B
Toriyoshi E
un café U
Yoku Moku T
ACCOMMODATION
Harajuku Trimm 1
Hotel Florasian Aoyama 2
National Children's Castle Hotel 3

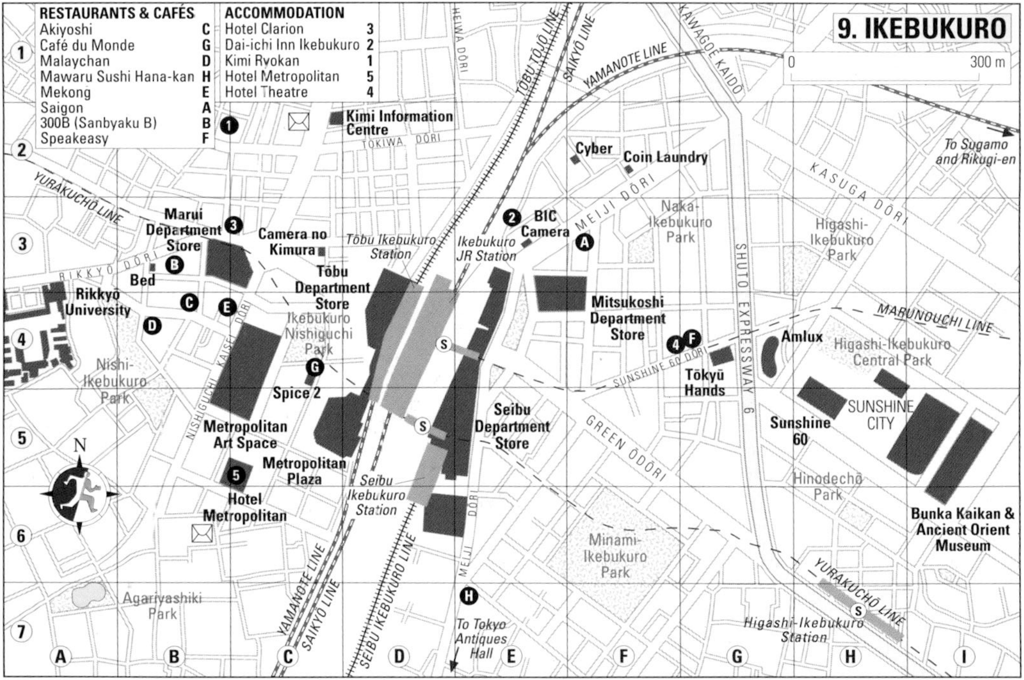
9. IKEBUKURO
0
300 m
RESTAURANTS & CAFÉS
Akiyoshi C
Café du Monde G
Malaychan D
Mawaru Sushi Hana-kan H
Mekong E
Saigon A
300B (Sanbyaku B) B
Speakeasy F
ACCOMMODATION
Hotel Clarion 3
Dai-ichi Inn Ikebukuro 2
Kimi Ryokan 1
Hotel Metropolitan 5
Hotel Theatre 4
Kimi Information Centre
TOKIWA DŌRI
HEIWA DŌRI
TŌBU TŌJŌ LINE
SAIKYŌ LINE
YAMANOTE LINE
KAWAGOE KAIDŌ
To Sugamo and Rikugi-en
Cyber
Coin Laundry
KASUGA DŌRI
YURAKUCHŌ LINE
Marui Department Store
Camera no Kimura
Tōbu Ikebukuro Station
Ikebukuro JR Station
BIC Camera
MEIJI DŌRI
Naka-Ikebukuro Park
Higashi-Ikebukuro Park
SHUTO EXPRESSWAY 6
RIKKYŌ DŌRI
Bed
Rikkyō University
Tōbu Department Store
Mitsukoshi Department Store
MARUNOUCHI LINE
Amlux
Higashi-Ikebukuro Central Park
Ikebukuro Nishiguchi Park
KAISEI DŌRI
NISHIGUCHI
SUNSHINE 60 DŌRI
Tōkyū Hands
Nishi-Ikebukuro Park
Spice 2
SUNSHINE CITY
Sunshine 60
Seibu Department Store
GREEN ŌDŌRI
Metropolitan Art Space
Metropolitan Plaza
Hotel Metropolitan
Seibu Ikebukuro Station
Hinodechō Park
Bunka Kaikan & Ancient Orient Museum
Minami-Ikebukuro Park
SEIBU IKEBUKURO LINE
Agariyashiki Park
To Tokyo Antiques Hall
Higashi-Ikebukuro Station
N
A
B
C
D
E
F
G
H
I
1
2
3
4
5
6
7

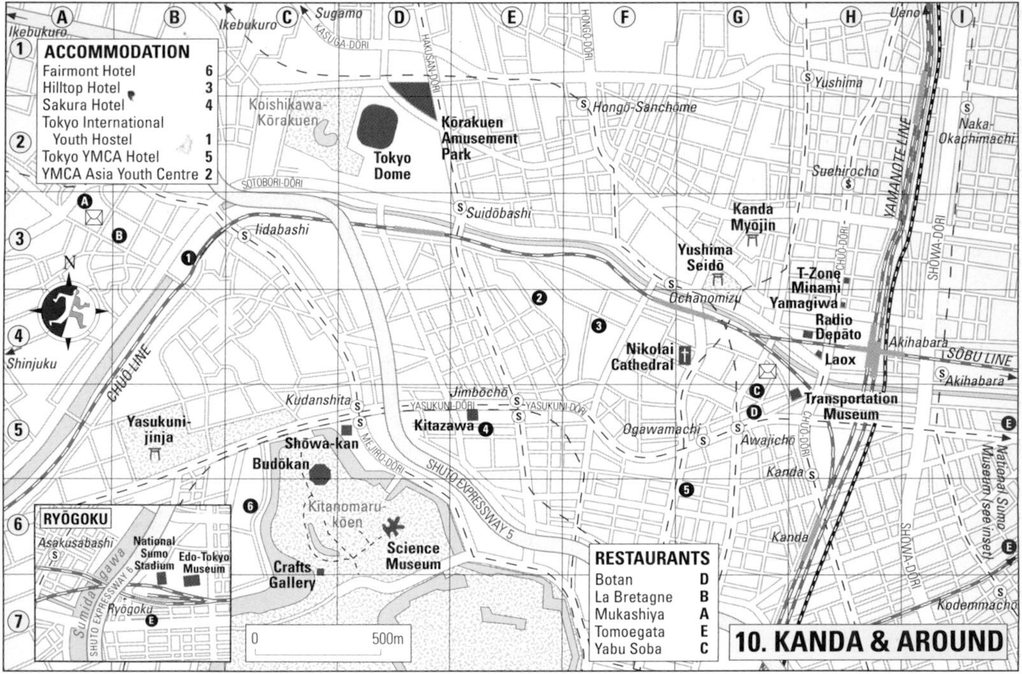
10. KANDA & AROUND
ACCOMMODATION
Fairmont Hotel 6
Hilltop Hotel 3
Sakura Hotel 4
Tokyo International Youth Hostel 1
Tokyo YMCA Hotel 5
YMCA Asia Youth Centre 2
RESTAURANTS
Botan D
La Bretagne B
Mukashiya A
Tomoegata E
Yabu Soba C
Ikebukuro
Sugamo
Ueno
Shinjuku
Koishikawa-Kōrakuen
Tokyo Dome
Kōrakuen Amusement Park
Suidōbashi
Iidabashi
Hongō-Sanchōme
Yushima
Suehirocho
Naka-Okachimachi
Kanda Myōjin
Yushima Seidō
Ochanomizu
T-Zone Minami
Yamagiwa
Radio Depāto
Laox
Akihabara
Nikolai Cathedral
Transportation Museum
Jimbōchō
Kitazawa
Kudanshita
Yasukuni-jinja
Shōwa-kan
Budōkan
Kitanomaru-kōen
Science Museum
Crafts Gallery
Ogawamachi
Awajichō
Kanda
Kodemmacho
National Sumo Museum (see inset)
CHŪŌ LINE
SŌBU LINE
YAMANOTE LINE
HAKUSAN-DŌRI
KASUGA-DORI
HONGŌ-DŌRI
SOTOBORI-DŌRI
CHŪŌ-DŌRI
SHŌWA-DŌRI
YASUKUNI-DŌRI
MEJIRO-DŌRI
SHUTO EXPRESSWAY 5
RYŌGOKU
Asakusabashi
National Sumo Stadium
Edo-Tokyo Museum
Ryōgoku
Sumidagawa
SHUTO EXPRESSWAY 6
0 500m

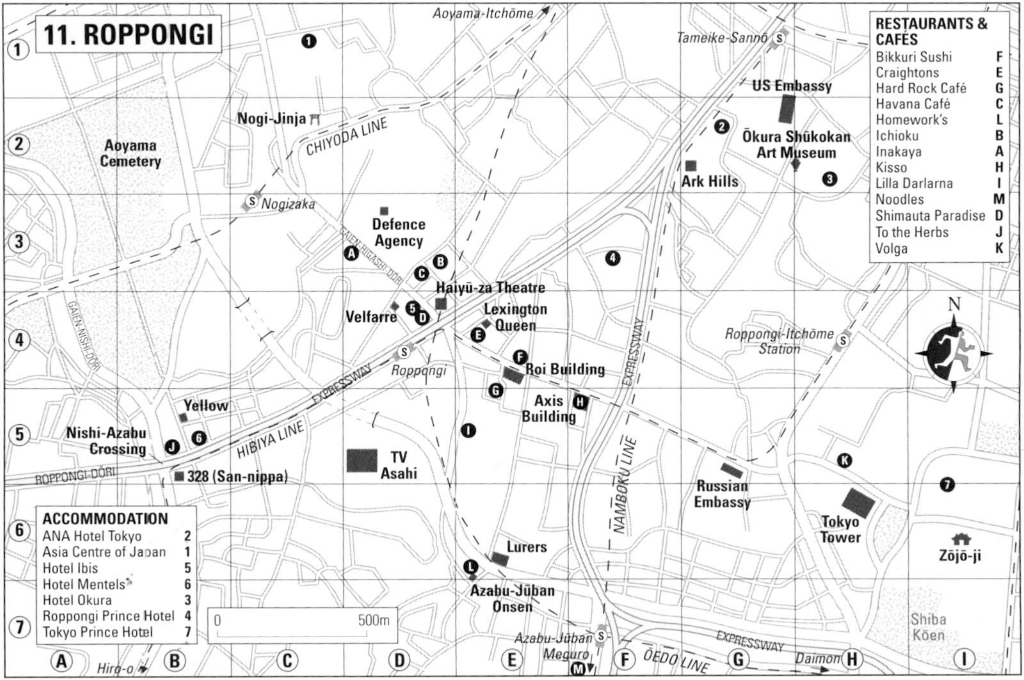

11. ROPPONGI
RESTAURANTS & CAFÉS
Bikkuri Sushi F
Craightons E
Hard Rock Café G
Havana Café C
Homework's L
Ichioku B
Inakaya A
Kisso H
Lilla Darlarna I
Noodles M
Shimauta Paradise D
To the Herbs J
Volga K
ACCOMMODATION
ANA Hotel Tokyo 2
Asia Centre of Japan 1
Hotel Ibis 5
Hotel Mentels 6
Hotel Okura 3
Roppongi Prince Hotel 4
Tokyo Prince Hotel 7
Aoyama-Itchōme
Tameike-Sannō
US Embassy
Nogi-Jinja
Ōkura Shūkokan Art Museum
Aoyama Cemetery
CHIYODA LINE
Ark Hills
Nogizaka
Defence Agency
GAIEN-HIGASHI-DŌRI
GAIEN-NISHI-DŌRI
Haiyū-za Theatre
Velfarre
Lexington Queen
Roppongi-Itchōme Station
Roppongi
EXPRESSWAY
Roi Building
Axis Building
Yellow
Nishi-Azabu Crossing
HIBIYA LINE
TV Asahi
ROPPONGI-DŌRI
328 (San-nippa)
NAMBOKU LINE
Russian Embassy
Tokyo Tower
Lurers
Zōjō-ji
Azabu-Jūban Onsen
Azabu-Jūban
Meguro
ŌEDO LINE
Daimon
Shiba Kōen
Hiro-o
0
500m
N

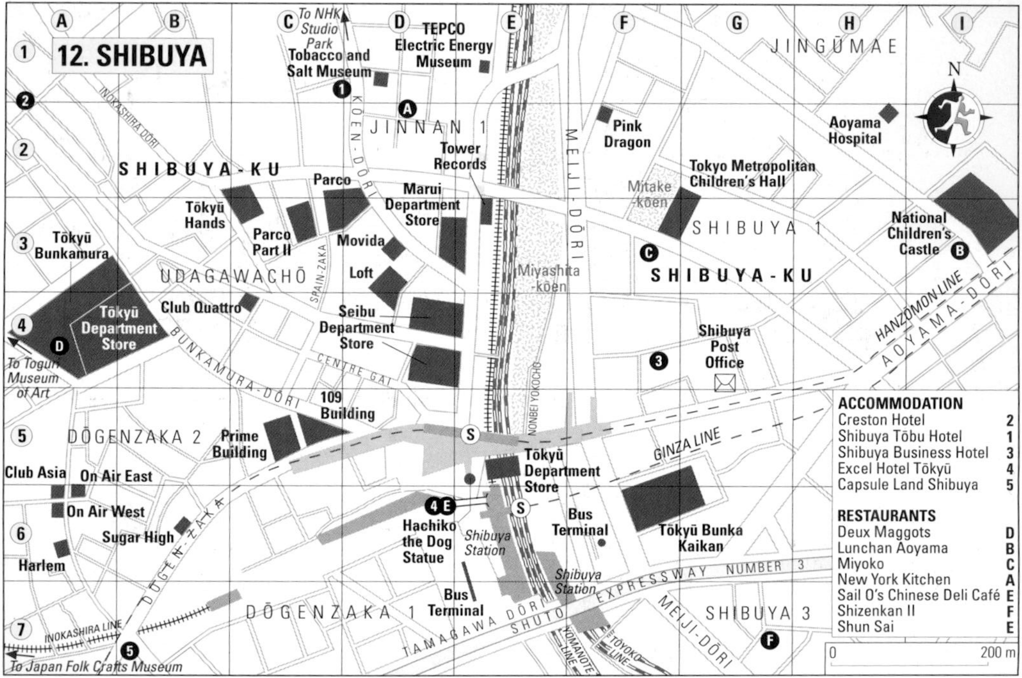
12. SHIBUYA
ACCOMMODATION
Creston Hotel 2
Shibuya Tōbu Hotel 1
Shibuya Business Hotel 3
Excel Hotel Tōkyū 4
Capsule Land Shibuya 5
RESTAURANTS
Deux Maggots D
Lunchan Aoyama B
Miyoko C
New York Kitchen A
Sail O's Chinese Deli Café E
Shizenkan II F
Shun Sai E
0 200 m
To NHK Studio Park
Tobacco and Salt Museum
TEPCO Electric Energy Museum
JINGŪMAE
JINNAN 1
Tower Records
Pink Dragon
Aoyama Hospital
Tokyo Metropolitan Children's Hall
Mitake-kōen
National Children's Castle
SHIBUYA 1
SHIBUYA-KU
Parco
Marui Department Store
Tōkyū Hands
Parco Part II
Movida
Loft
Tōkyū Bunkamura
UDAGAWACHŌ
SPAIN-ZAKA
Club Quattro
Seibu Department Store
Tōkyū Department Store
To Togun Museum of Art
BUNKAMURA-DŌRI
CENTRE GAI
109 Building
INOKASHIRA DŌRI
KŌEN-DŌRI
MEIJI-DŌRI
Miyashita-kōen
NONBEI YOKOCHO
Shibuya Post Office
HANZŌMON LINE
AOYAMA-DŌRI
GINZA LINE
DŌGENZAKA 2
Prime Building
Club Asia
On Air East
On Air West
Sugar High
Harlem
DŌGEN-ZAKA
Tōkyū Department Store
Hachiko the Dog Statue
Shibuya Station
Bus Terminal
Tōkyū Bunka Kaikan
EXPRESSWAY NUMBER 3
DŌGENZAKA 1
TAMAGAWA DŌRI
SHUTO
YOMANOTE LINE
TOYOKO LINE
SHIBUYA 3
INOKASHIRA LINE
To Japan Folk Crafts Museum
N

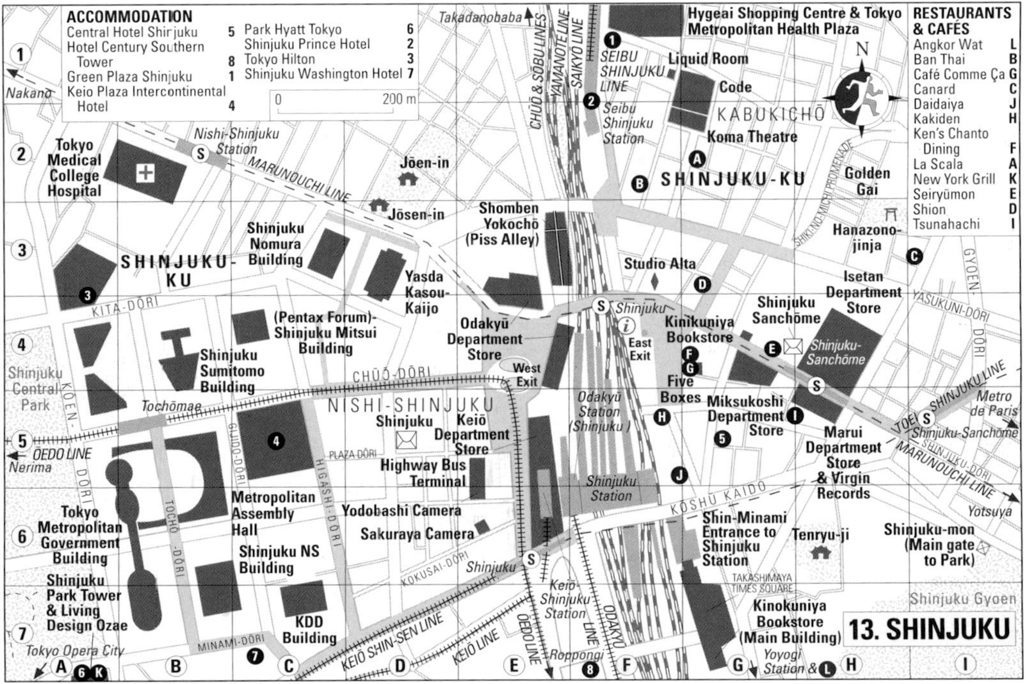
13. SHINJUKU
ACCOMMODATION
Central Hotel Shirjuku 5
Hotel Century Southern Tower 8
Green Plaza Shinjuku 1
Keio Plaza Intercontinental Hotel 4
Park Hyatt Tokyo 6
Shinjuku Prince Hotel 2
Tokyo Hilton 3
Shinjuku Washington Hotel 7
0 200 m
RESTAURANTS & CAFÉS
Angkor Wat L
Ban Thai B
Café Comme Ça G
Canard C
Daidaiya J
Kakiden H
Ken's Chanto Dining F
La Scala A
New York Grill K
Seiryūmon E
Shion D
Tsunahachi I
N
Takadanobaba
Nakano
Nerima
Yotsuya
Roppongi
Yoyogi Station &
Tokyo Opera City
Metro de Paris
CHŪŌ & SŌBU LINES
YAMANOTE LINE
SAIKYŌ LINE
SEIBU SHINJUKU LINE
Seibu Shinjuku Station
Hygeai Shopping Centre & Tokyo Metropolitan Health Plaza
Liquid Room
Code
KABUKICHŌ
Koma Theatre
SHINJUKU-KU
Golden Gai
SHIKI-NO-MICHI PROMENADE
Hanazono-jinja
Tokyo Medical College Hospital
Nishi-Shinjuku Station
MARUNOUCHI LINE
Jōen-in
Jōsen-in
Shomben Yokochō (Piss Alley)
Studio Alta
Isetan Department Store
GYOEN-DŌRI
YASUKUNI-DŌRI
Shinjuku Nomura Building
Yasda Kasou-Kaijo
Shinjuku Sanchōme
Shinjuku-Sanchōme
Kinikuniya Bookstore
Shinjuku
East Exit
West Exit
Odakyū Department Store
(Pentax Forum)-Shinjuku Mitsui Building
Shinjuku Sumitomo Building
KITA-DŌRI
CHŪŌ-DŌRI
NISHI-SHINJUKU
Shinjuku Central Park
KŌEN-DŌRI
Tochōmae
ŌEDO LINE
Five Boxes
Miksukoshi Department Store
Marui Department Store & Virgin Records
SHINJUKU LINE
TOEI
Shinjuku-Sanchōme
SHINJUKU-DŌRI
MARUNOUCHI LINE
Odakyū Station (Shinjuku)
Shinjuku Keiō Department Store
PLAZA DŌRI
GIJIDO-DŌRI
HIGASHI-DŌRI
Highway Bus Terminal
Shinjuku Station
KOSHU KAIDO
Metropolitan Assembly Hall
Yodobashi Camera
Sakuraya Camera
Shin-Minami Entrance to Shinjuku Station
Tenryu-ji
Shinjuku-mon (Main gate to Park)
Tokyo Metropolitan Government Building
TOCHŌ-DŌRI
Shinjuku NS Building
KOKUSAI-DŌRI
Shinjuku
Keiō Shinjuku Station
TAKASHIMAYA TIMES SQUARE
Shinjuku Gyoen
Shinjuku Park Tower & Living Design Ozae
MINAMI-DŌRI
KDD Building
KEIŌ SHIN-SEN LINE
KEIŌ LINE
ŌEDO LINE
ODAKYŪ LINE
Kinokuniya Bookstore (Main Building)

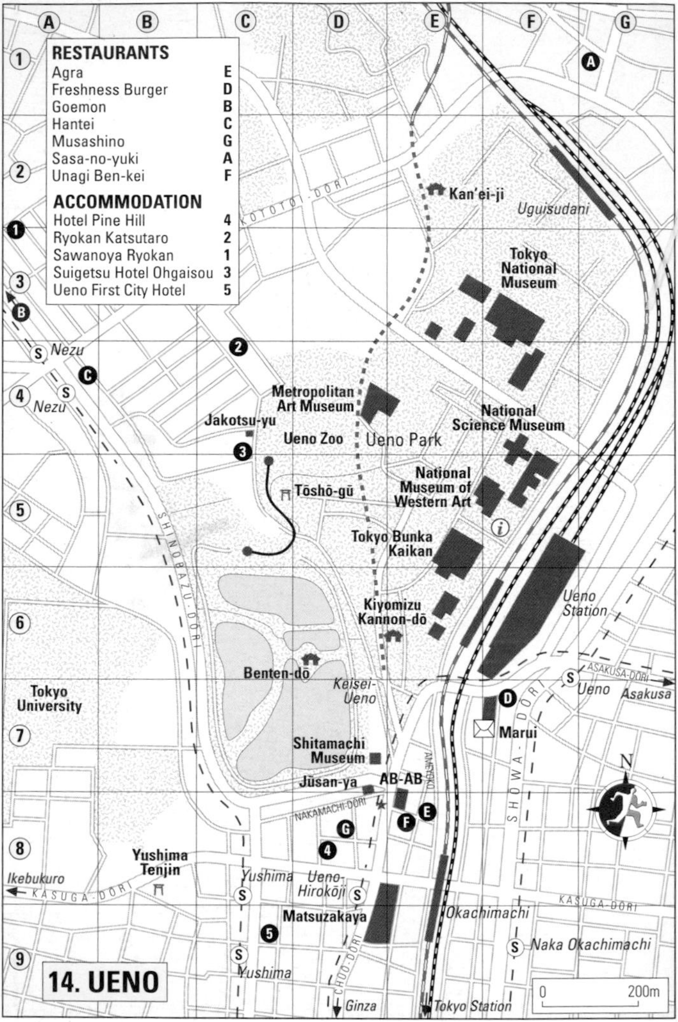
RESTAURANTS
Agra E
Freshness Burger D
Goemon B
Hantei C
Musashino G
Sasa-no-yuki A
Unagi Ben-kei F
ACCOMMODATION
Hotel Pine Hill 4
Ryokan Katsutaro 2
Sawanoya Ryokan 1
Suigetsu Hotel Ohgaisou 3
Ueno First City Hotel 5
Kan'ei-ji
Uguisudani
Tokyo National Museum
Kototoi-dori
Nezu
Nezu
Metropolitan Art Museum
Jakotsu-yu
Ueno Zoo
Ueno Park
National Science Museum
Tōshō-gū
National Museum of Western Art
Tokyo Bunka Kaikan
Shinobazu-dori
Kiyomizu Kannon-dō
Ueno Station
Benten-dō
Keisei-Ueno
Asakusa-dori
Ueno
Asakusa
Tokyo University
Marui
Shitamachi Museum
Ameyoko
Showa-dori
Jūsan-ya
AB-AB
Nakamachi-dori
N
Yushima Tenjin
Ikebukuro
Kasuga-dori
Yushima
Ueno-Hirokōji
Matsuzakaya
Kasuga-dori
Okachimachi
Naka Okachimachi
Yushima
Chūō-dori
14. UENO
Ginza
Tokyo Station
0 200m